Grand Blue Dreaming 7

PRESENTED BY KENJI INOUE & KIMITAKE YOSHIOKA

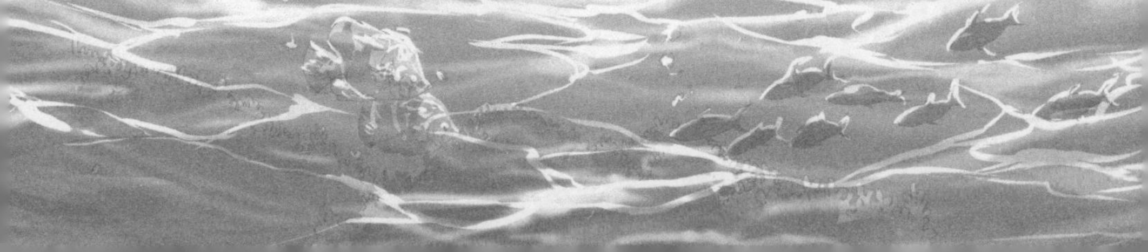

The Colorful Cast of Grand Blue Dreaming

Diving Club Peek-a-Boo (PaB)

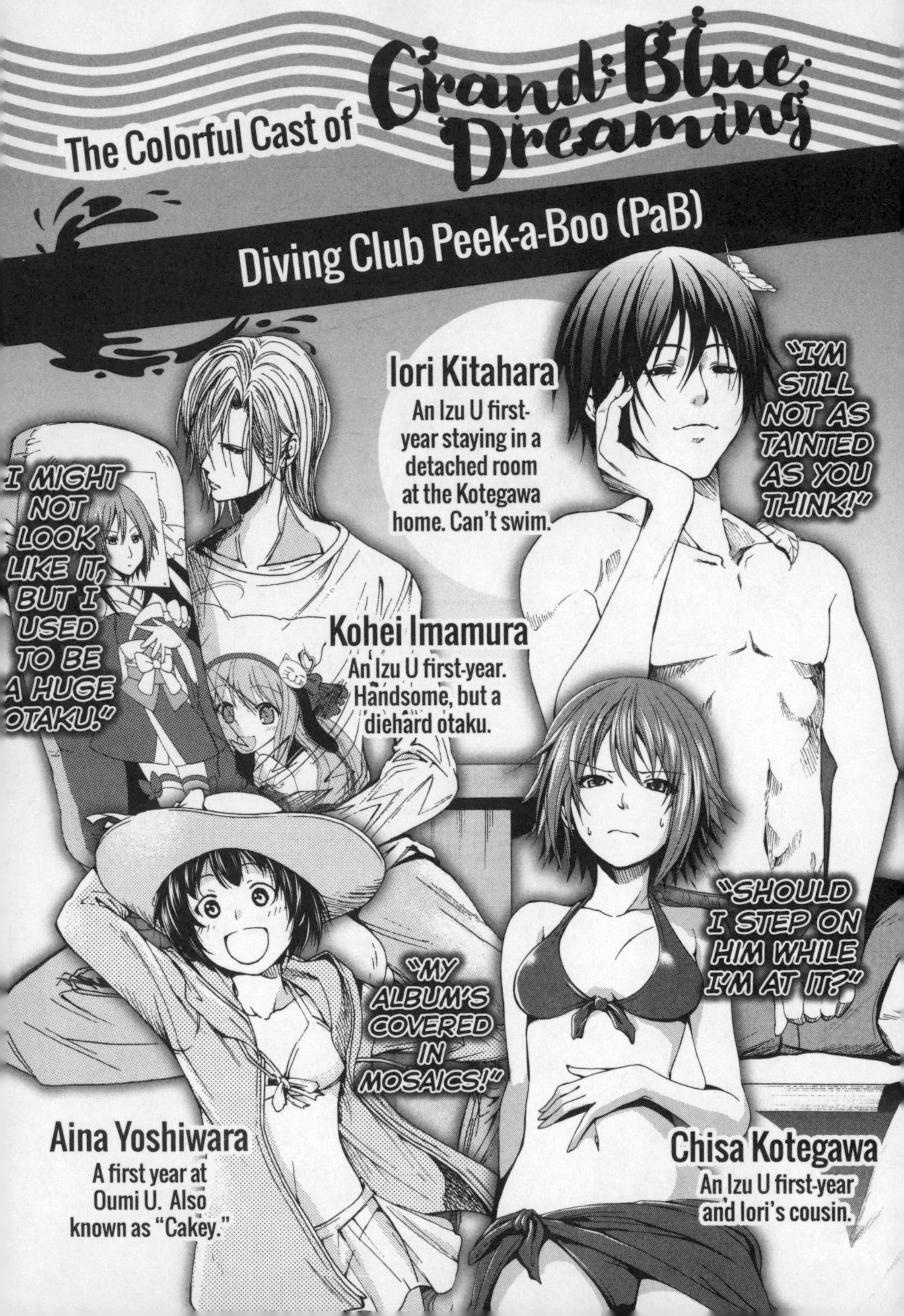
Iori Kitahara
An Izu U first-year staying in a detached room at the Kotegawa home. Can't swim.
"I'M STILL NOT AS TAINTED AS YOU THINK!"
Kohei Imamura
An Izu U first-year. Handsome, but a diehard otaku.
"I MIGHT NOT LOOK LIKE IT, BUT I USED TO BE A HUGE OTAKU."
"SHOULD I STEP ON HIM WHILE I'M AT IT?"
Chisa Kotegawa
An Izu U first-year and Iori's cousin.
"MY ALBUM'S COVERED IN MOSAICS!"
Aina Yoshiwara
A first year at Oumi U. Also known as "Cakey."

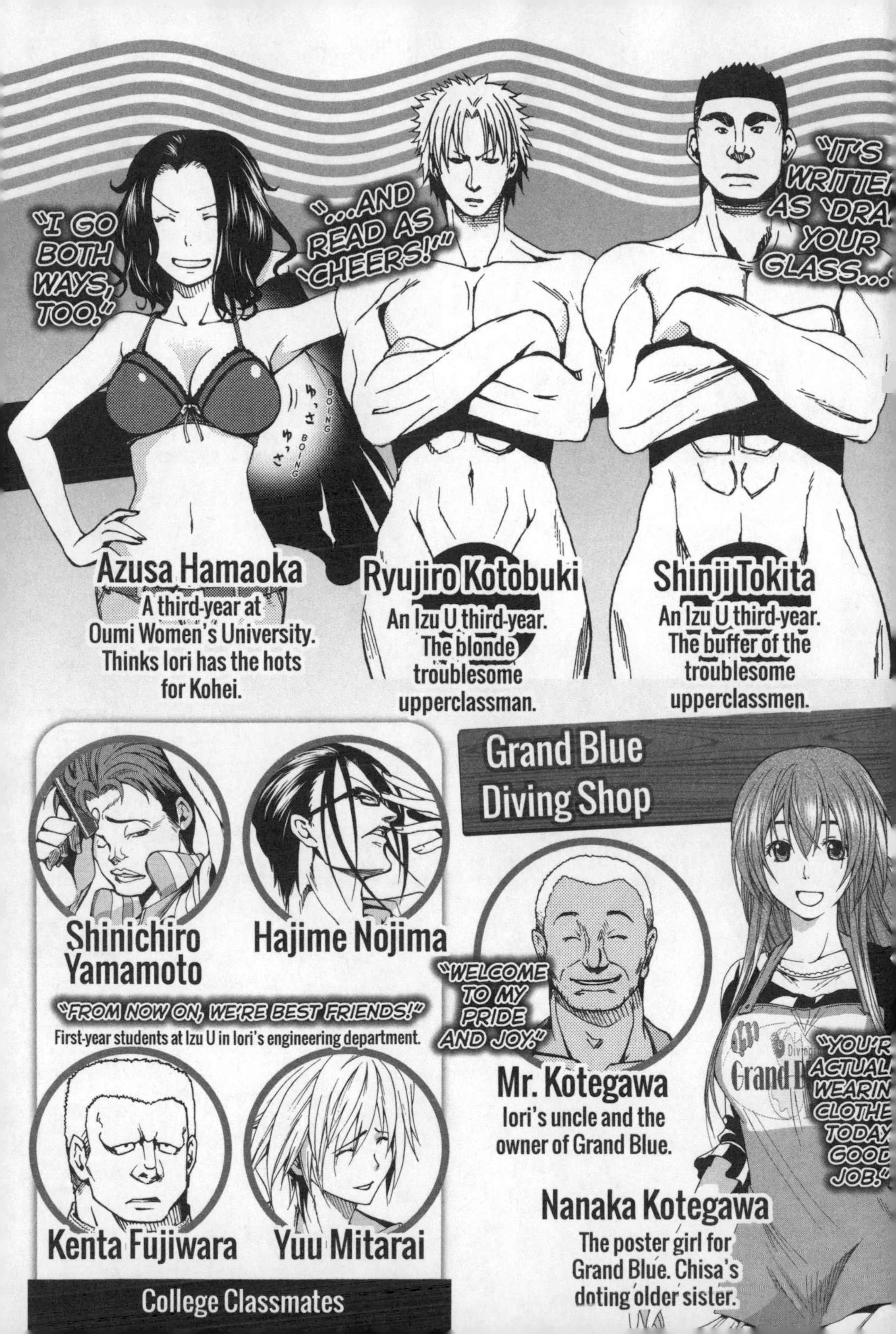
"IT'S WRITTE AS 'DRA YOUR GLASS...'
"...AND READ AS 'CHEERS!'"
"I GO BOTH WAYS, TOO."
ゆっさ ゆっさ
BOING BOING
Shinji Tokita
An Izu U third-year. The buffer of the troublesome upperclassmen.
Ryujiro Kotobuki
An Izu U third-year. The blonde troublesome upperclassman.
Azusa Hamaoka
A third-year at Oumi Women's University. Thinks Iori has the hots for Kohei.
Grand Blue Diving Shop
"YOU'R ACTUAL WEARIN CLOTHE TODAY GOOD JOB."
Grand B
Nanaka Kotegawa
The poster girl for Grand Blue. Chisa's doting older sister.
"WELCOME TO MY PRIDE AND JOY."
Mr. Kotegawa
Iori's uncle and the owner of Grand Blue.
Hajime Nojima
Shinichiro Yamamoto
"FROM NOW ON, WE'RE BEST FRIENDS!"
First-year students at Izu U in Iori's engineering department.
Yuu Mitarai
Kenta Fujiwara
College Classmates

PREVIOUSLY ON GRAND BLUE DREAMING

Iori and the guys manage to infiltrate the Women's University school festival, but...

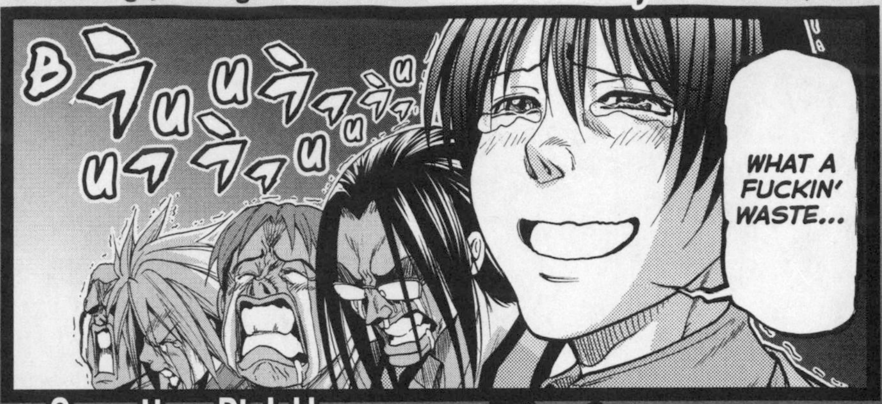
WHAT A FUCKIN' WASTE...

...Operation: Pick-Up goes awry! Then for some reason...

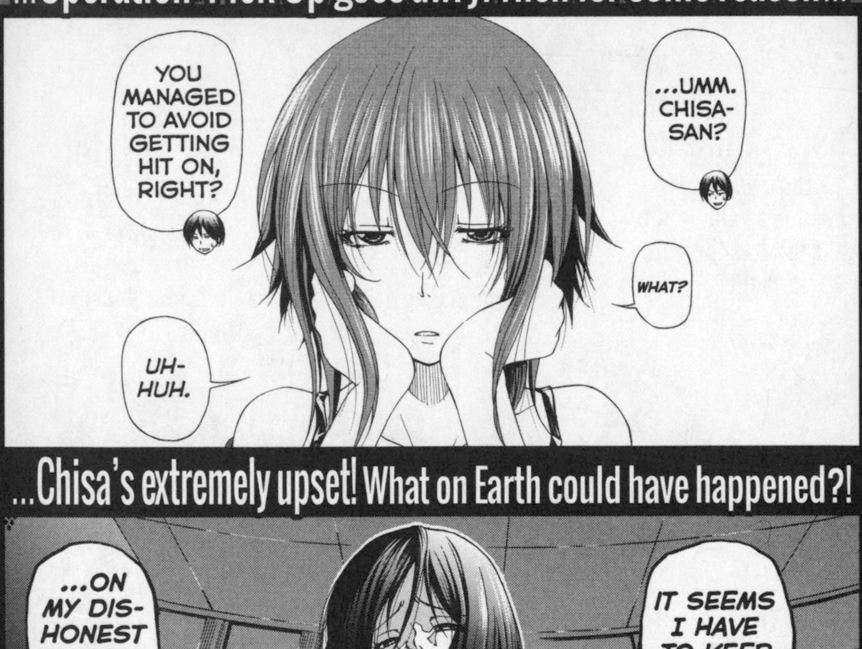
...UMM. CHISA-SAN?
YOU MANAGED TO AVOID GETTING HIT ON, RIGHT?
WHAT?
UH-HUH.

...Chisa's extremely upset! What on Earth could have happened?!

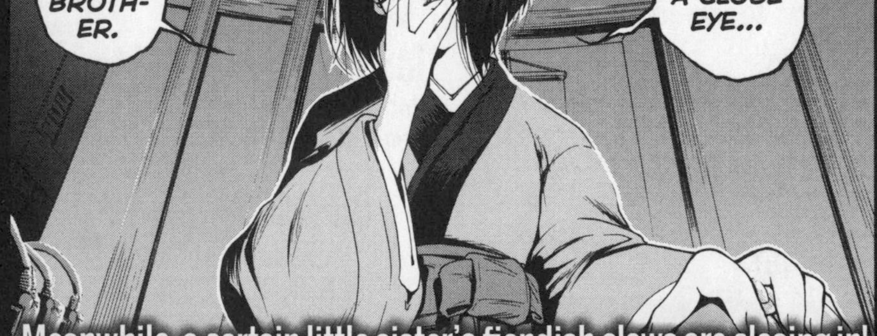
IT SEEMS I HAVE TO KEEP A CLOSE EYE...
...ON MY DIS-HONEST OLDER BROTH-ER.

Meanwhile, a certain little sister's fiendish claws are closing in!

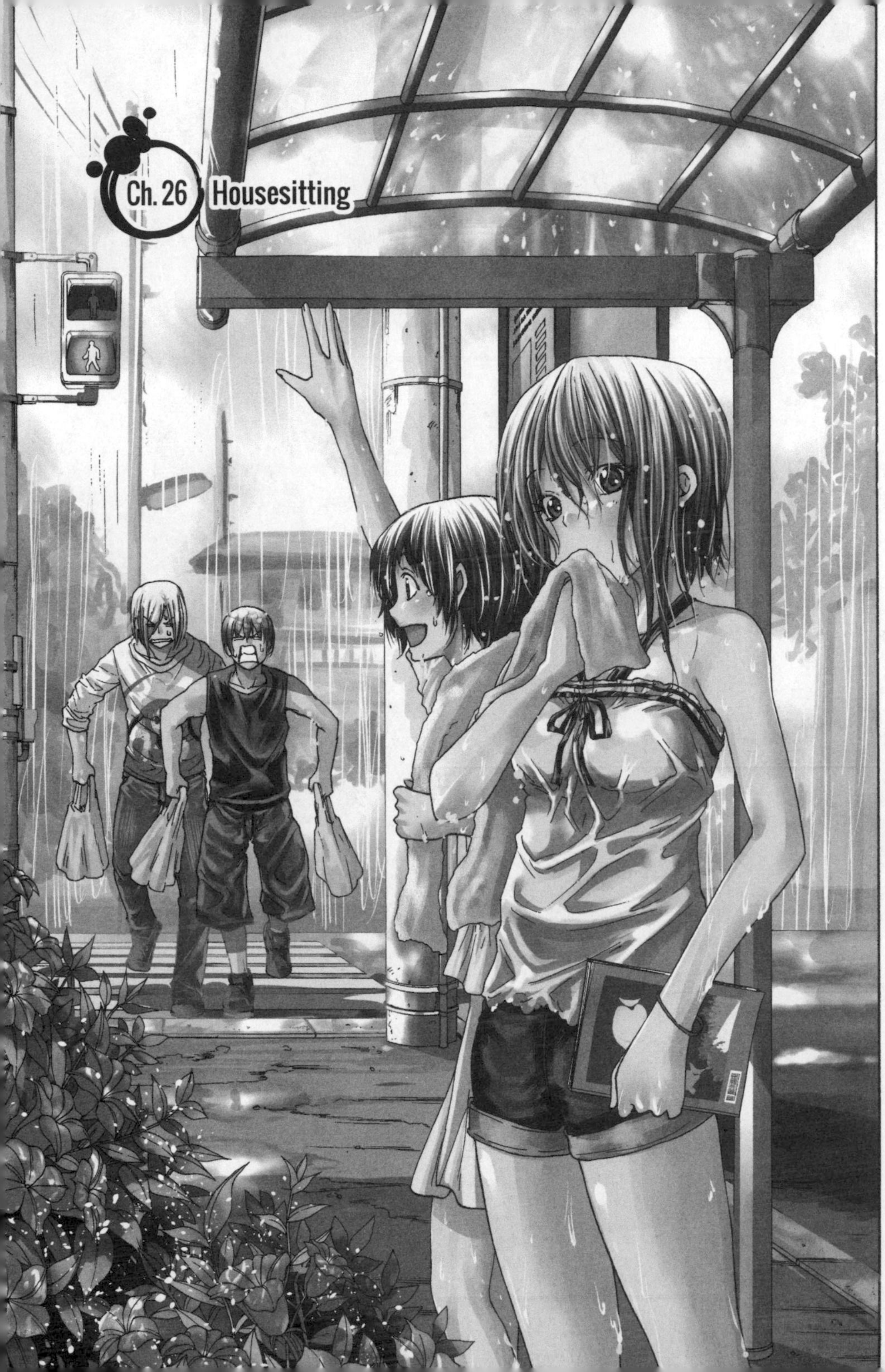
Ch. 26 Housesitting

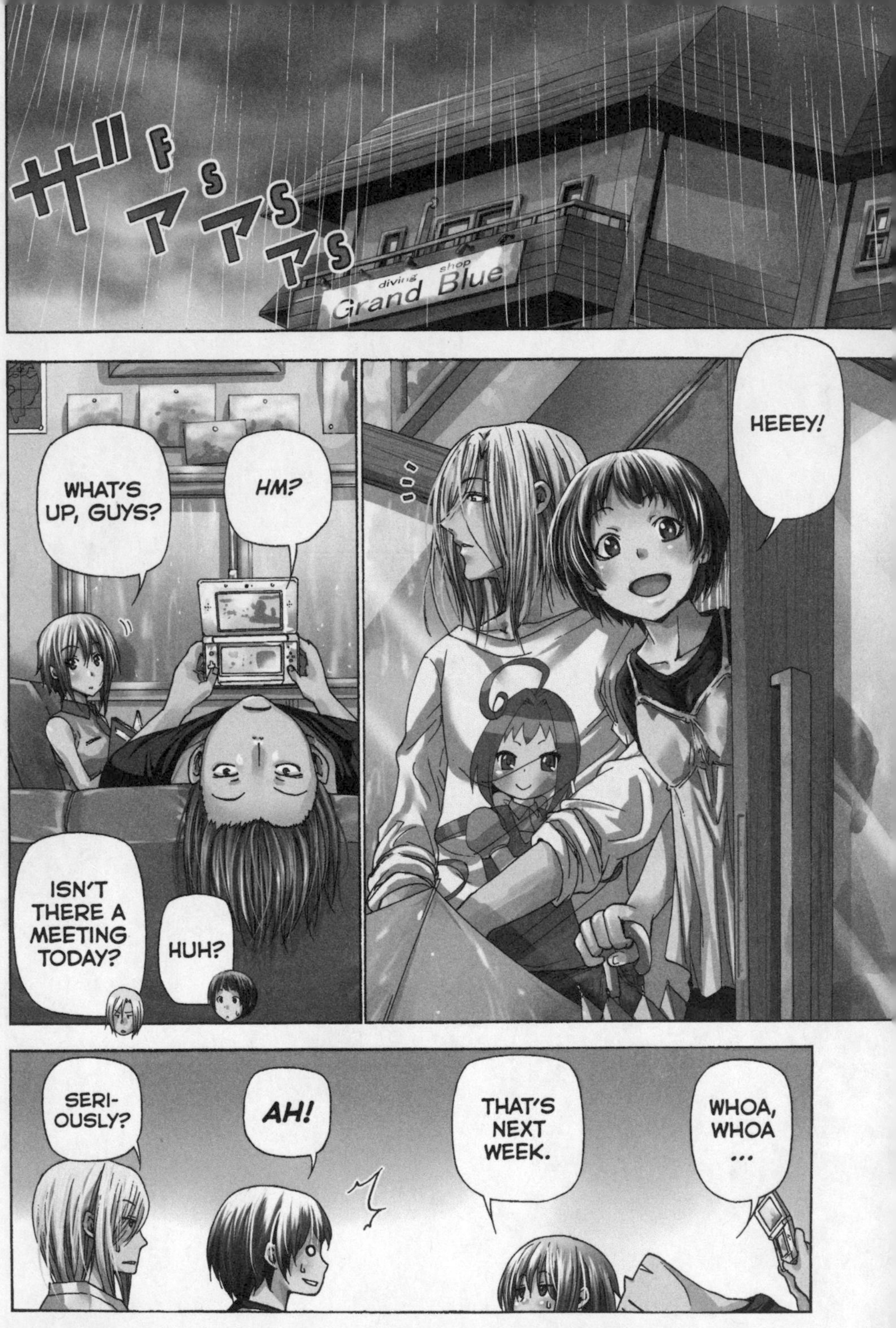
ザァァァ
FSSSS
diving shop
Grand Blue
HEEEY!
HM?
WHAT'S UP, GUYS?
ISN'T THERE A MEETING TODAY?
HUH?
WHOA, WHOA ...
THAT'S NEXT WEEK.
AH!
SERI-OUSLY?

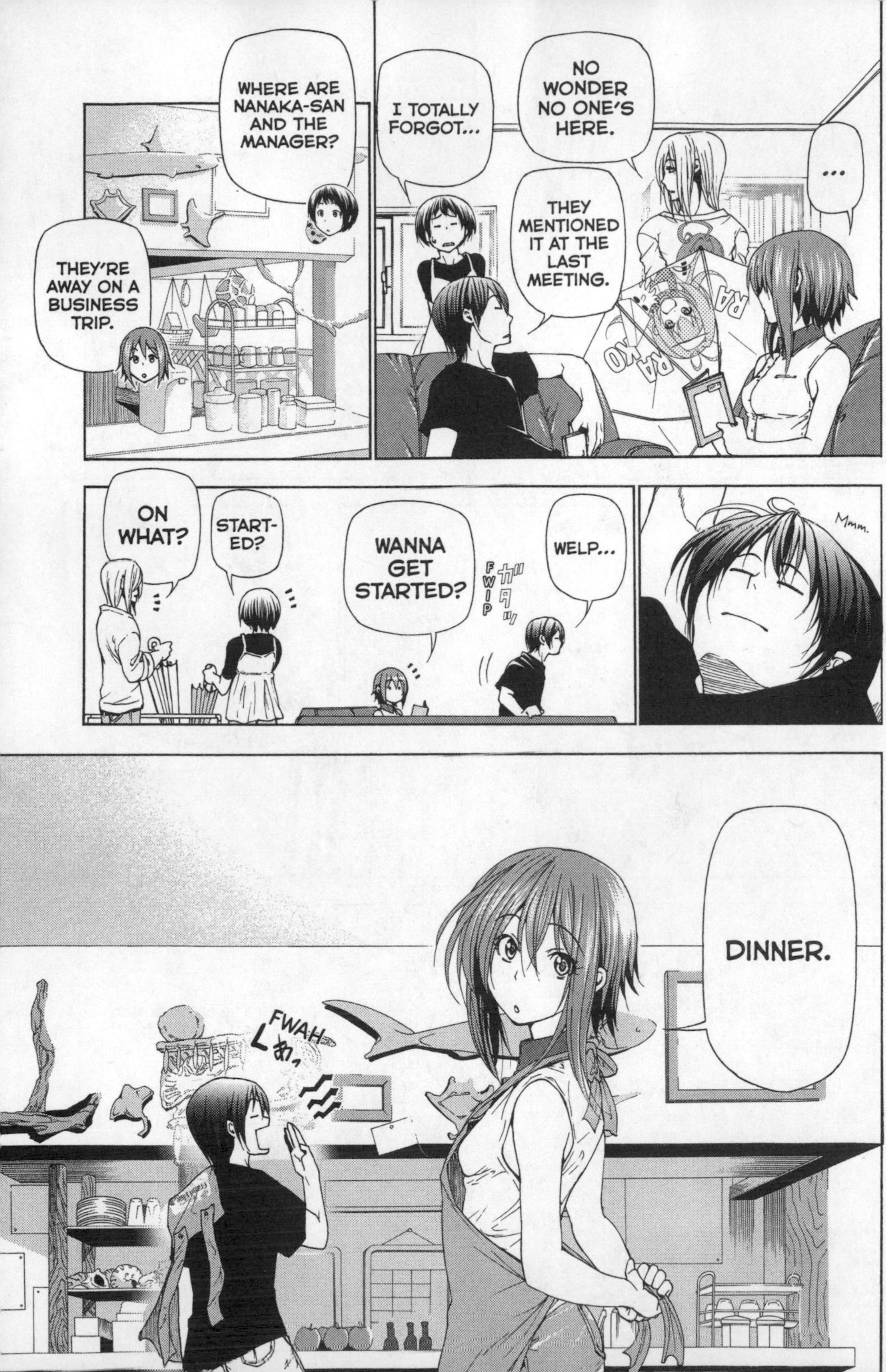
...
NO WONDER NO ONE'S HERE.
THEY MENTIONED IT AT THE LAST MEETING.
I TOTALLY FORGOT...
WHERE ARE NANAKA-SAN AND THE MANAGER?
THEY'RE AWAY ON A BUSINESS TRIP.
Mmm.
WELP...
FWIP
WANNA GET STARTED?
START-ED?
ON WHAT?
DINNER.
FWAH

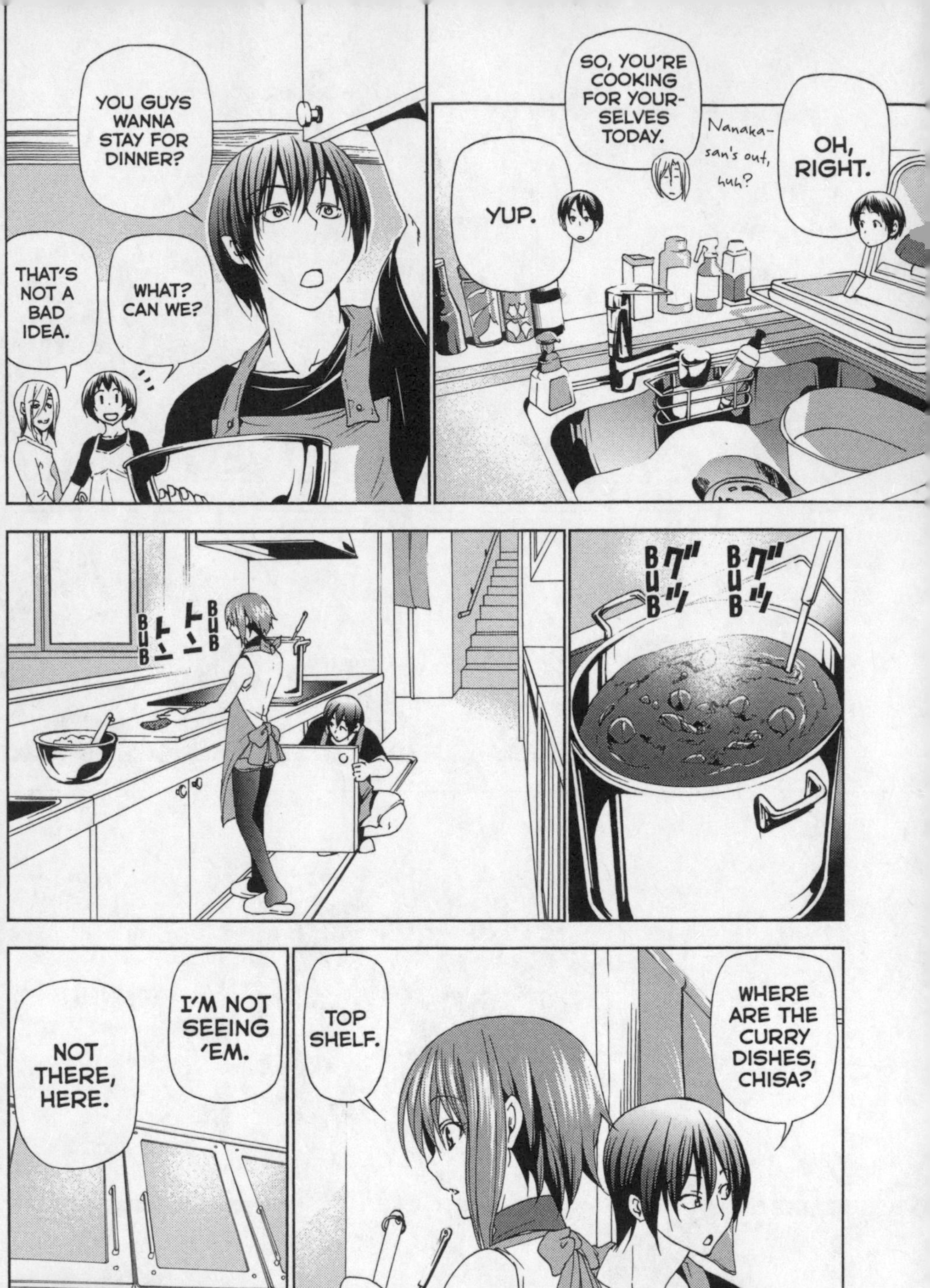
SO, YOU'RE COOKING FOR YOUR-SELVES TODAY.
Nanaka-san's out, huh?
OH, RIGHT.
YUP.
YOU GUYS WANNA STAY FOR DINNER?
WHAT? CAN WE?
THAT'S NOT A BAD IDEA.
BUB BUB
BUB BUB
WHERE ARE THE CURRY DISHES, CHISA?
TOP SHELF.
I'M NOT SEEING 'EM.
NOT THERE, HERE.

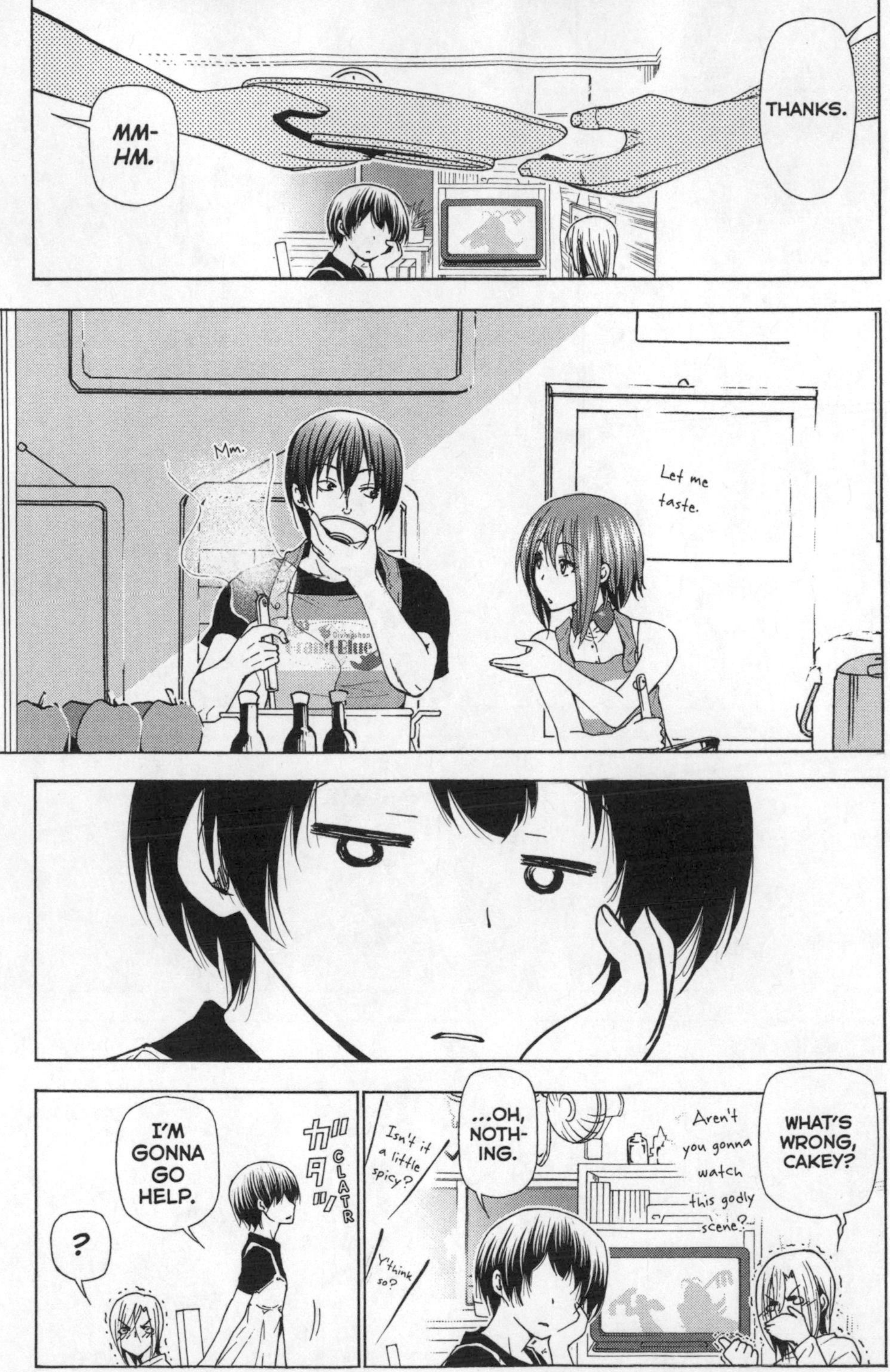
THANKS.
MM-HM.
Let me taste.
Mm.
WHAT'S WRONG, CAKEY?
Aren't you gonna watch this godly scene?...
...OH, NOTHING.
Isn't it a little spicy?
Y'think so?
ガタッ
CLATR
I'M GONNA GO HELP.
?

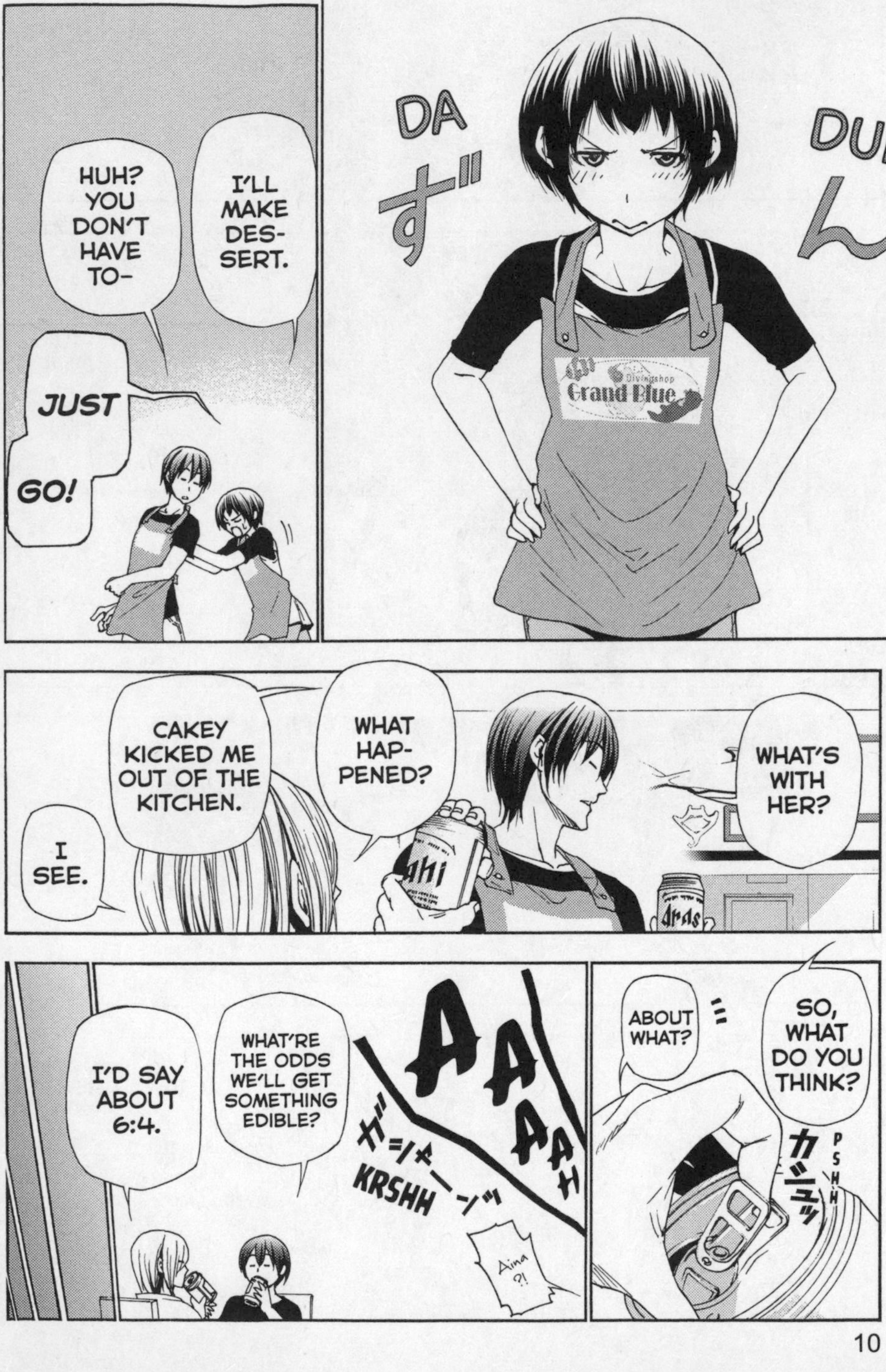
DA
ず
DUM
ん
Divingshop
Grand Blue
I'LL MAKE DES-SERT.
HUH? YOU DON'T HAVE TO-
JUST GO!
WHAT'S WITH HER?
WHAT HAP-PENED?
CAKEY KICKED ME OUT OF THE KITCHEN.
I SEE.
SO, WHAT DO YOU THINK?
ABOUT WHAT?
カシュッ
PSHH
WHAT'RE THE ODDS WE'LL GET SOMETHING EDIBLE?
I'D SAY ABOUT 6:4.
AAAAH
ガシャーン
KRSHH
Aina ?!

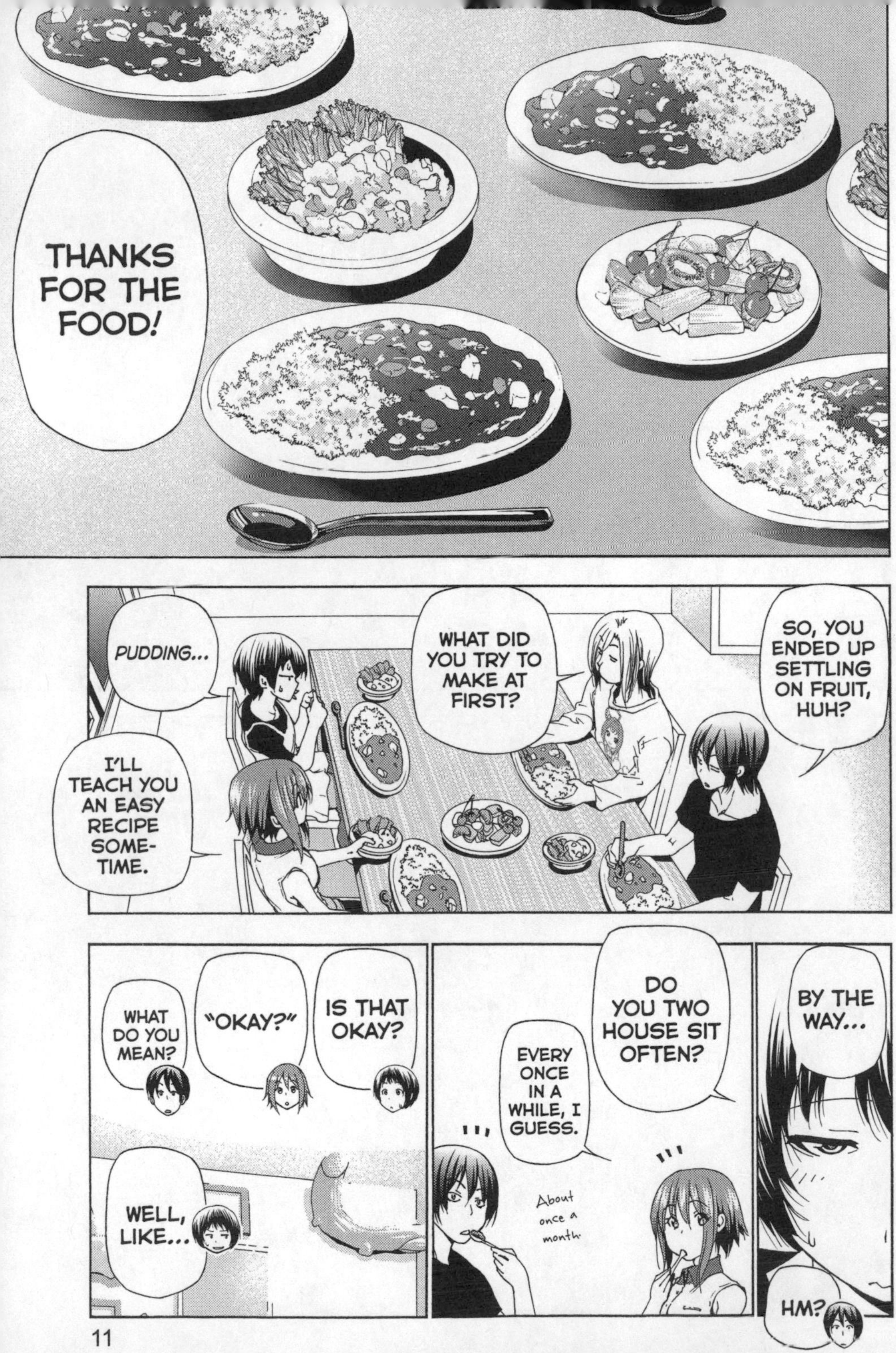
THANKS FOR THE FOOD!
SO, YOU ENDED UP SETTLING ON FRUIT, HUH?
WHAT DID YOU TRY TO MAKE AT FIRST?
PUDDING...
I'LL TEACH YOU AN EASY RECIPE SOME-TIME.
BY THE WAY...
HM?
DO YOU TWO HOUSE SIT OFTEN?
EVERY ONCE IN A WHILE, I GUESS.
About once a month.
IS THAT OKAY?
"OKAY?"
WHAT DO YOU MEAN?
WELL, LIKE...

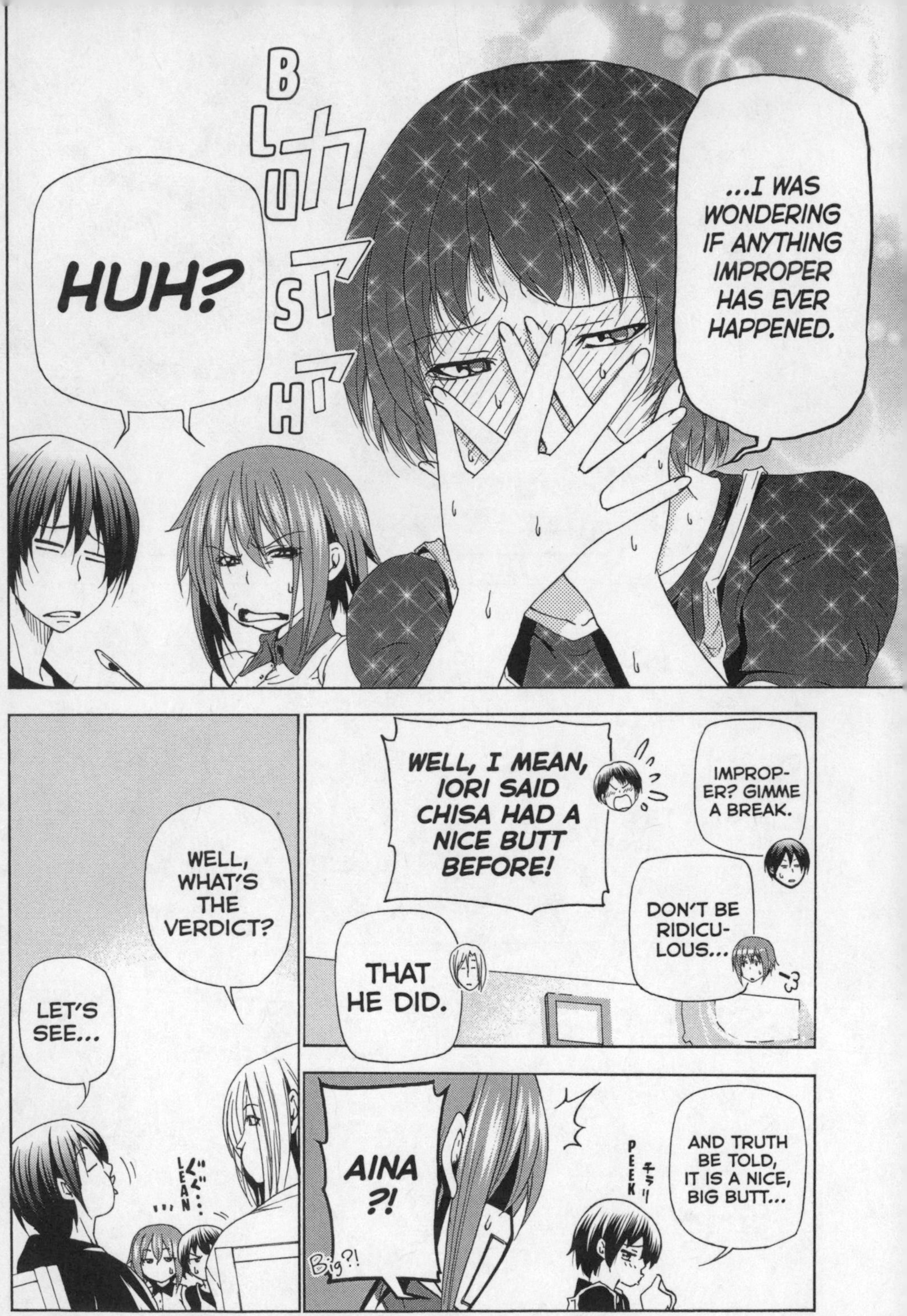
...I WAS WONDERING IF ANYTHING IMPROPER HAS EVER HAPPENED.
BLUSH
HUH?
IMPROP-ER? GIMME A BREAK.
WELL, I MEAN, IORI SAID CHISA HAD A NICE BUTT BEFORE!
DON'T BE RIDICU-LOUS...
THAT HE DID.
AND TRUTH BE TOLD, IT IS A NICE, BIG BUTT...
PEEK
AINA ?!
Big?!
WELL, WHAT'S THE VERDICT?
LET'S SEE...
LEAN

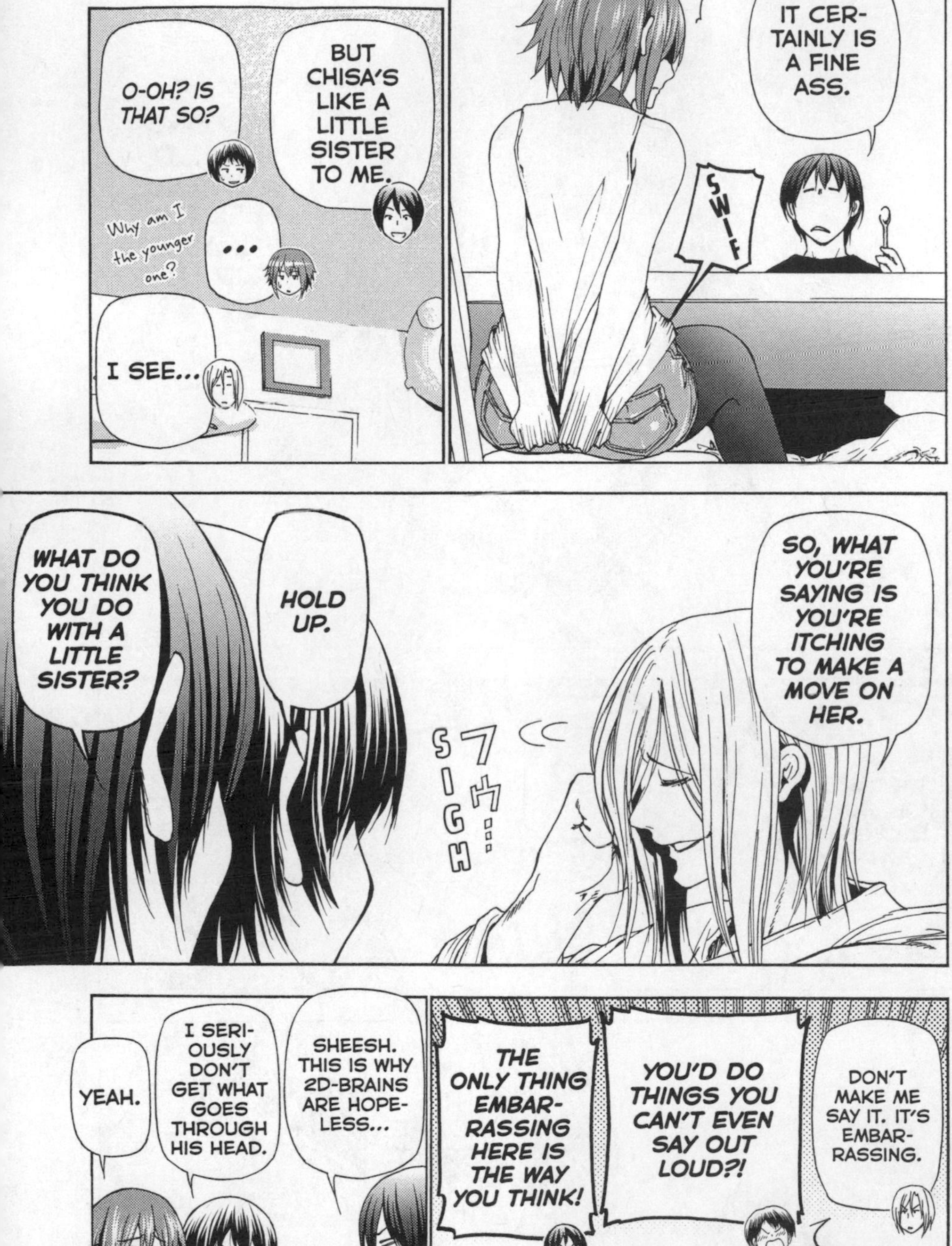
IT CERTAINLY IS A FINE ASS.
SWIF
BUT CHISA'S LIKE A LITTLE SISTER TO ME.
O-OH? IS THAT SO?
...
Why am I the younger one?
I SEE...
SO, WHAT YOU'RE SAYING IS YOU'RE ITCHING TO MAKE A MOVE ON HER.
SIGH
HOLD UP.
WHAT DO YOU THINK YOU DO WITH A LITTLE SISTER?
DON'T MAKE ME SAY IT. IT'S EMBARRASSING.
YOU'D DO THINGS YOU CAN'T EVEN SAY OUT LOUD?!
THE ONLY THING EMBARRASSING HERE IS THE WAY YOU THINK!
SHEESH. THIS IS WHY 2D-BRAINS ARE HOPELESS...
I SERIOUSLY DON'T GET WHAT GOES THROUGH HIS HEAD.
YEAH.

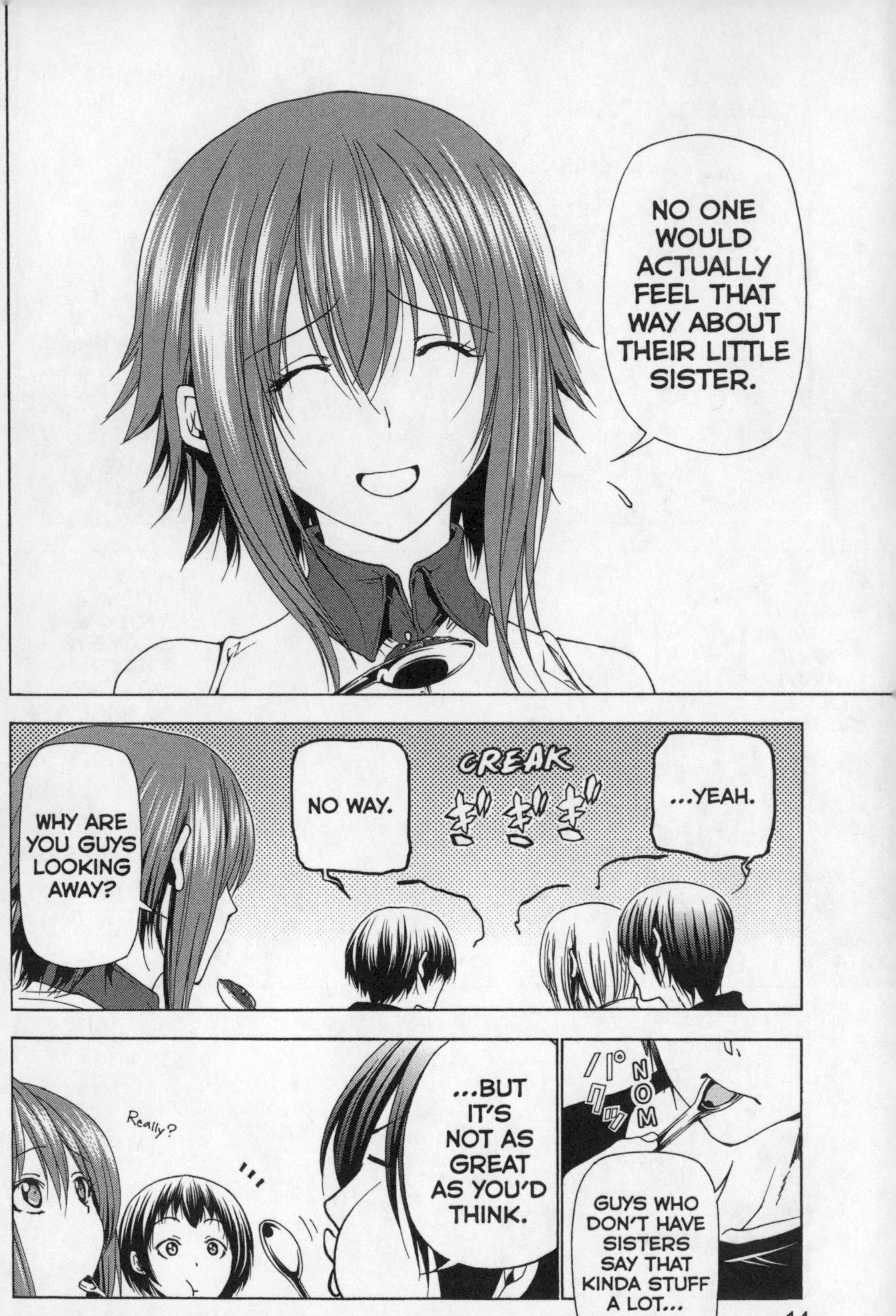
NO ONE WOULD ACTUALLY FEEL THAT WAY ABOUT THEIR LITTLE SISTER.
...YEAH.
CREAK
NO WAY.
WHY ARE YOU GUYS LOOKING AWAY?
NOM
GUYS WHO DON'T HAVE SISTERS SAY THAT KINDA STUFF A LOT...
...BUT IT'S NOT AS GREAT AS YOU'D THINK.
Really?

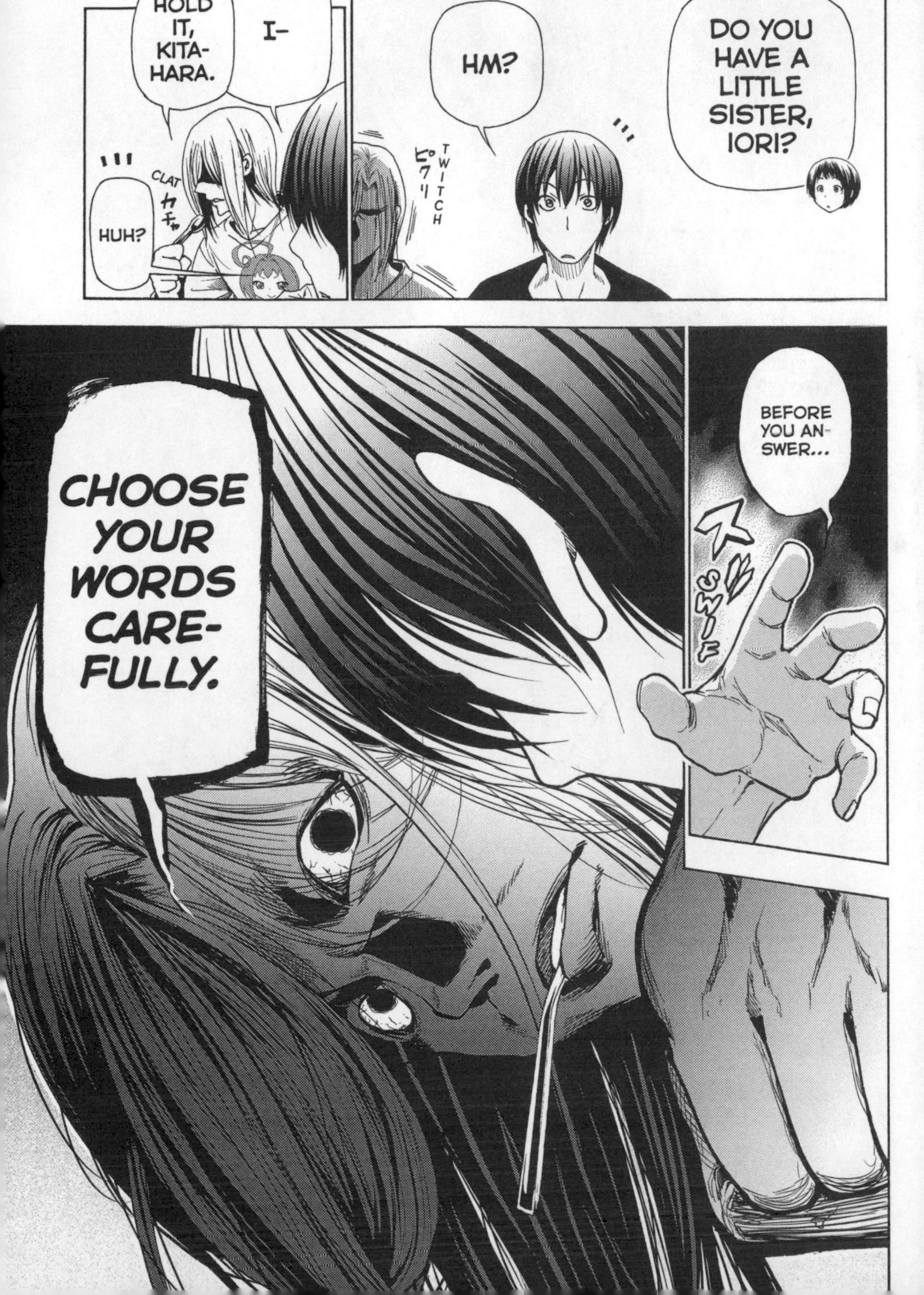
DO YOU HAVE A LITTLE SISTER, IORI?
HM?
ピクリ
TWITCH
I-
HOLD IT, KITA-HARA.
カチャ
CLAT
HUH?
BEFORE YOU AN-SWER...
ス
SWIF
CHOOSE YOUR WORDS CARE-FULLY.

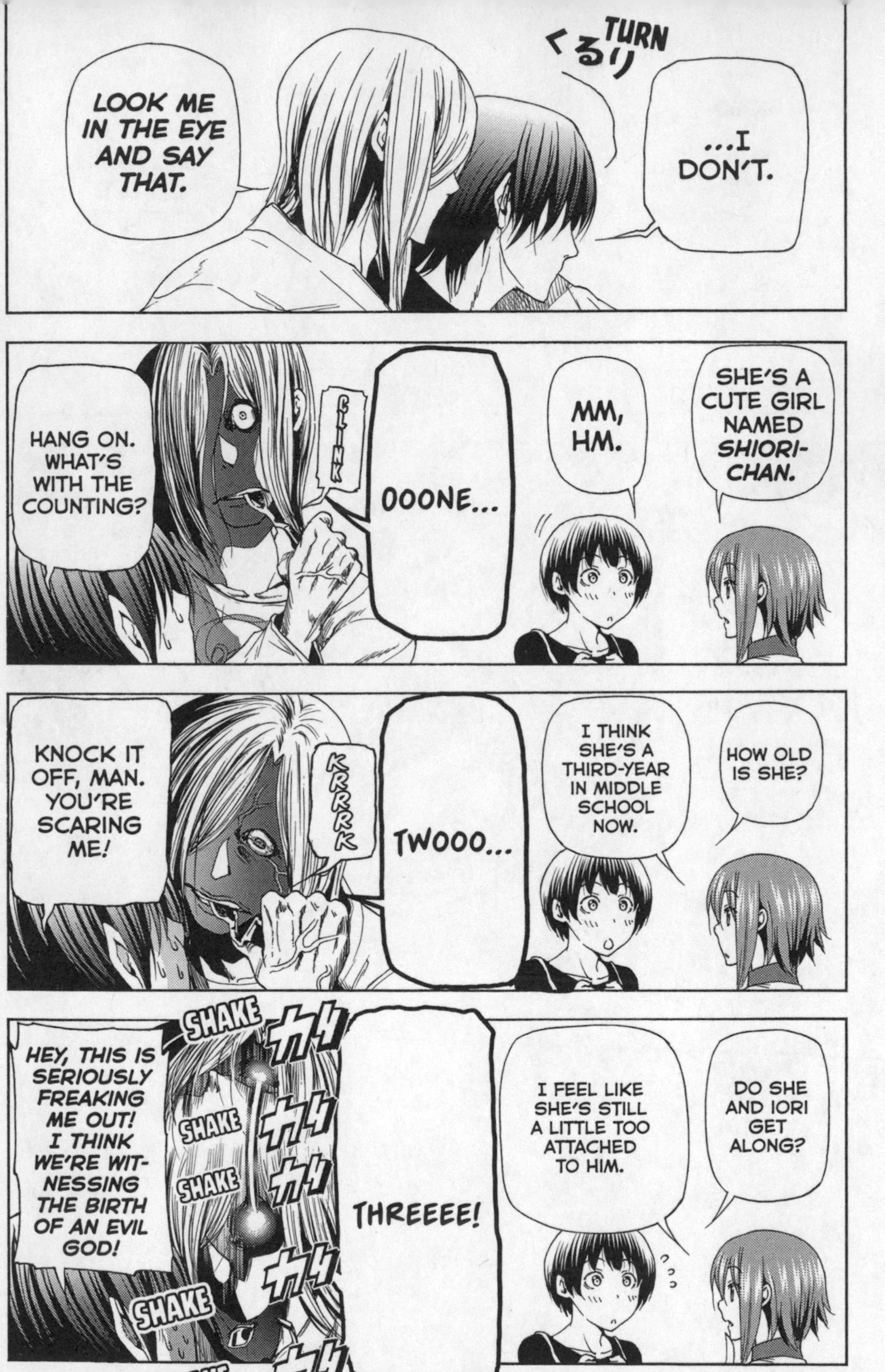
TURN くるり
...I DON'T.
LOOK ME IN THE EYE AND SAY THAT.
SHE'S A CUTE GIRL NAMED SHIORI-CHAN.
MM, HM.
OOONE...
CLINK
HANG ON. WHAT'S WITH THE COUNTING?
HOW OLD IS SHE?
I THINK SHE'S A THIRD-YEAR IN MIDDLE SCHOOL NOW.
TWOOO...
KRRRK
KNOCK IT OFF, MAN. YOU'RE SCARING ME!
DO SHE AND IORI GET ALONG?
I FEEL LIKE SHE'S STILL A LITTLE TOO ATTACHED TO HIM.
THREEEE!
SHAKE
SHAKE
SHAKE
SHAKE
SHAKE
HEY, THIS IS SERIOUSLY FREAKING ME OUT! I THINK WE'RE WITNESSING THE BIRTH OF AN EVIL GOD!

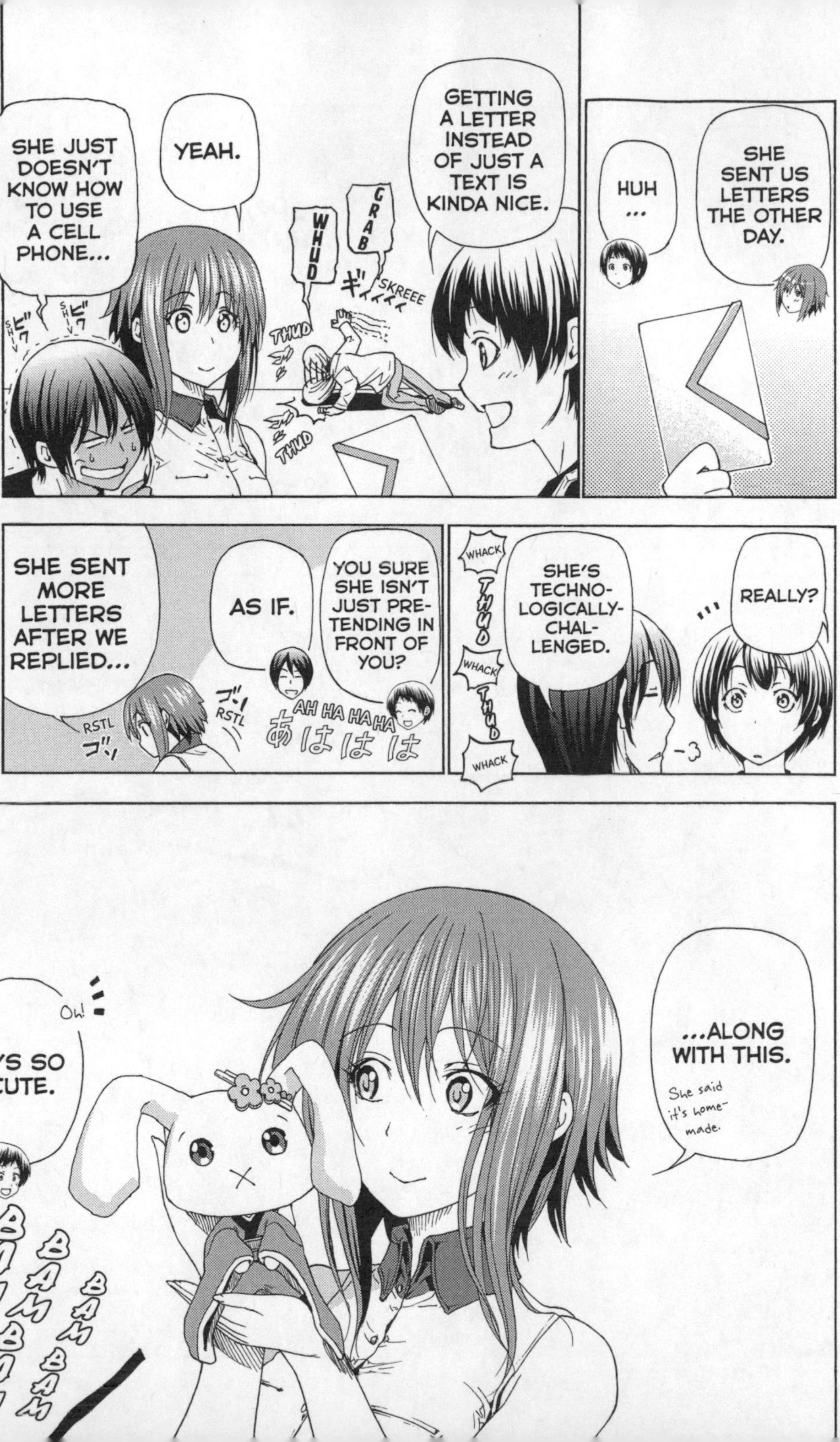
SHE SENT US LETTERS THE OTHER DAY.
HUH ...
GETTING A LETTER INSTEAD OF JUST A TEXT IS KINDA NICE.
GRAB
SKREEE
ギィィィィ
WHUD
THUD
THUD
YEAH.
SHE JUST DOESN'T KNOW HOW TO USE A CELL PHONE...
SHIV
SHIV
ビク
ビク
REALLY?
...
SHE'S TECHNOLOGICALLY-CHALLENGED.
WHACK
THUD
WHACK
THUD
WHACK
YOU SURE SHE ISN'T JUST PRETENDING IN FRONT OF YOU?
AH HA HAHA
あははは
AS IF.
SHE SENT MORE LETTERS AFTER WE REPLIED...
RSTL
RSTL
...ALONG WITH THIS.
She said it's home-made.
Oh!
IT'S SO CUTE.
BAM BAM BAM BAM
BAM BAM BAM BAM
BAM BAM

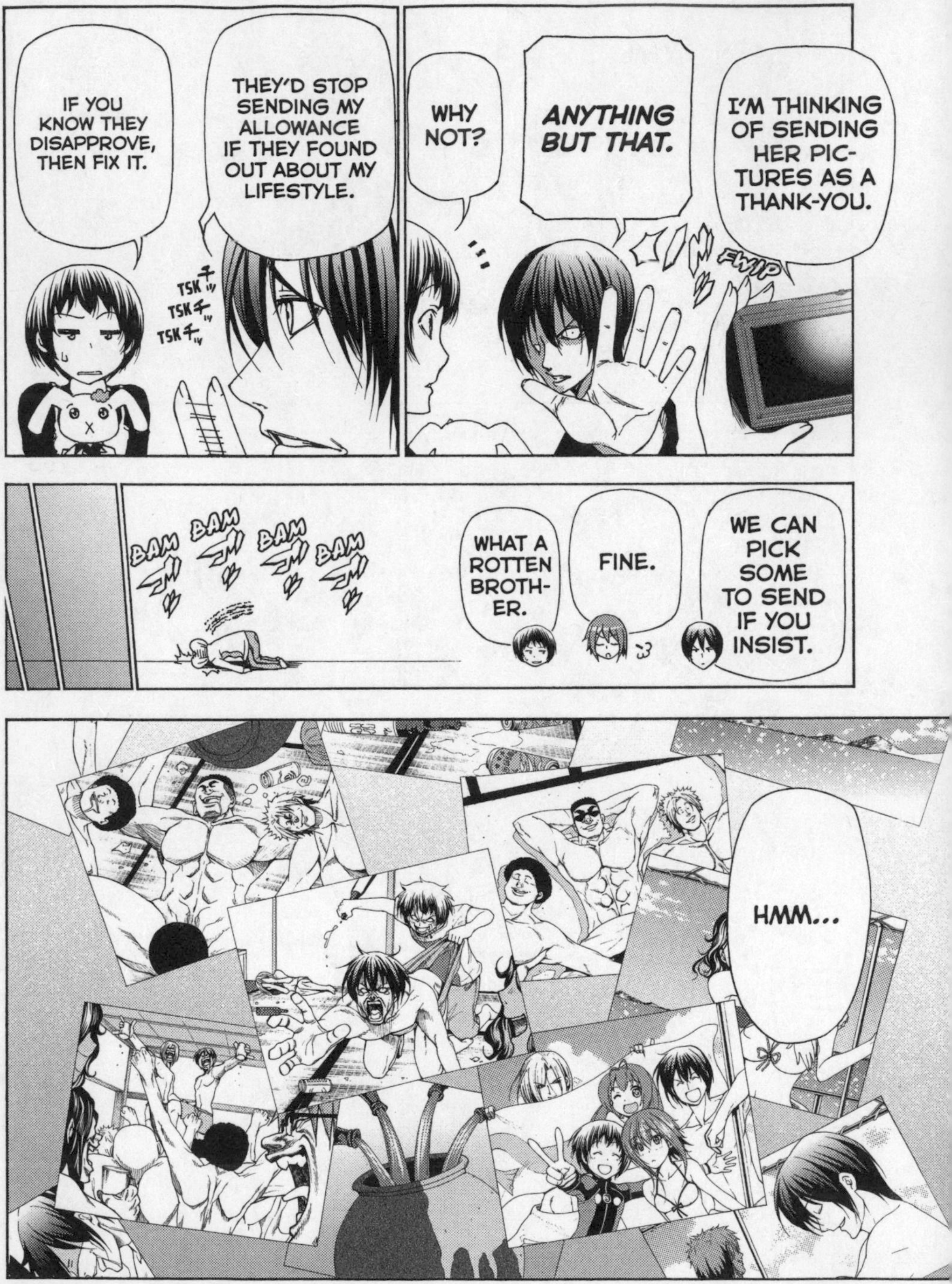
I'M THINKING OF SENDING HER PICTURES AS A THANK-YOU.
FWIP
ANYTHING BUT THAT.
WHY NOT?
THEY'D STOP SENDING MY ALLOWANCE IF THEY FOUND OUT ABOUT MY LIFESTYLE.
IF YOU KNOW THEY DISAPPROVE, THEN FIX IT.
TSK
TSK
TSK
WE CAN PICK SOME TO SEND IF YOU INSIST.
FINE.
WHAT A ROTTEN BROTHER.
BAM
BAM
BAM
BAM
HMM...

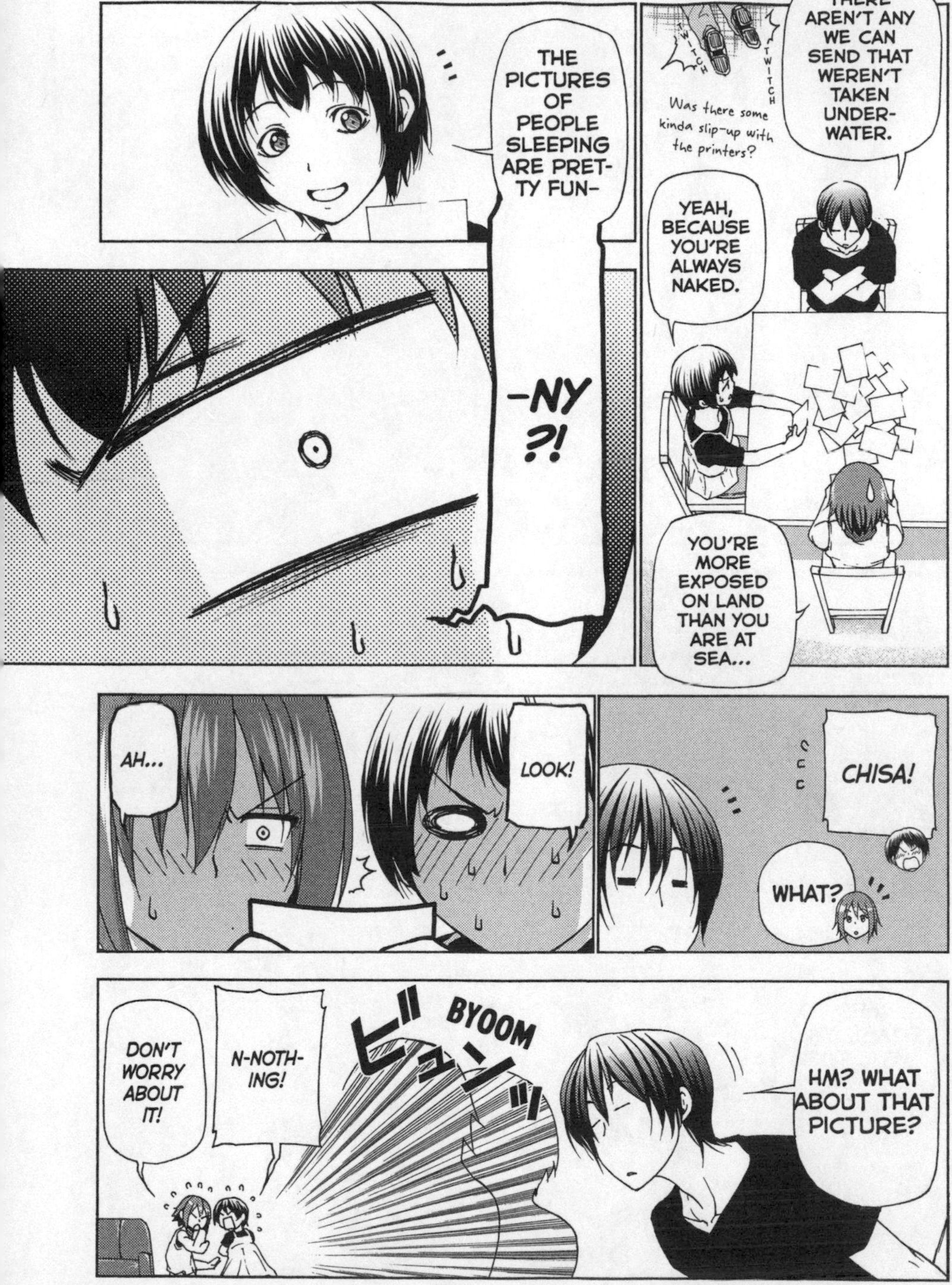
THERE AREN'T ANY WE CAN SEND THAT WEREN'T TAKEN UNDER-WATER.
TWITCH
TWITCH
Was there some kinda slip-up with the printers?
YEAH, BECAUSE YOU'RE ALWAYS NAKED.
YOU'RE MORE EXPOSED ON LAND THAN YOU ARE AT SEA...
THE PICTURES OF PEOPLE SLEEPING ARE PRETTY FUN-
-NY ?!
CHISA!
WHAT?
LOOK!
AH...
HM? WHAT ABOUT THAT PICTURE?
BYOOM
N-NOTHING!
DON'T WORRY ABOUT IT!

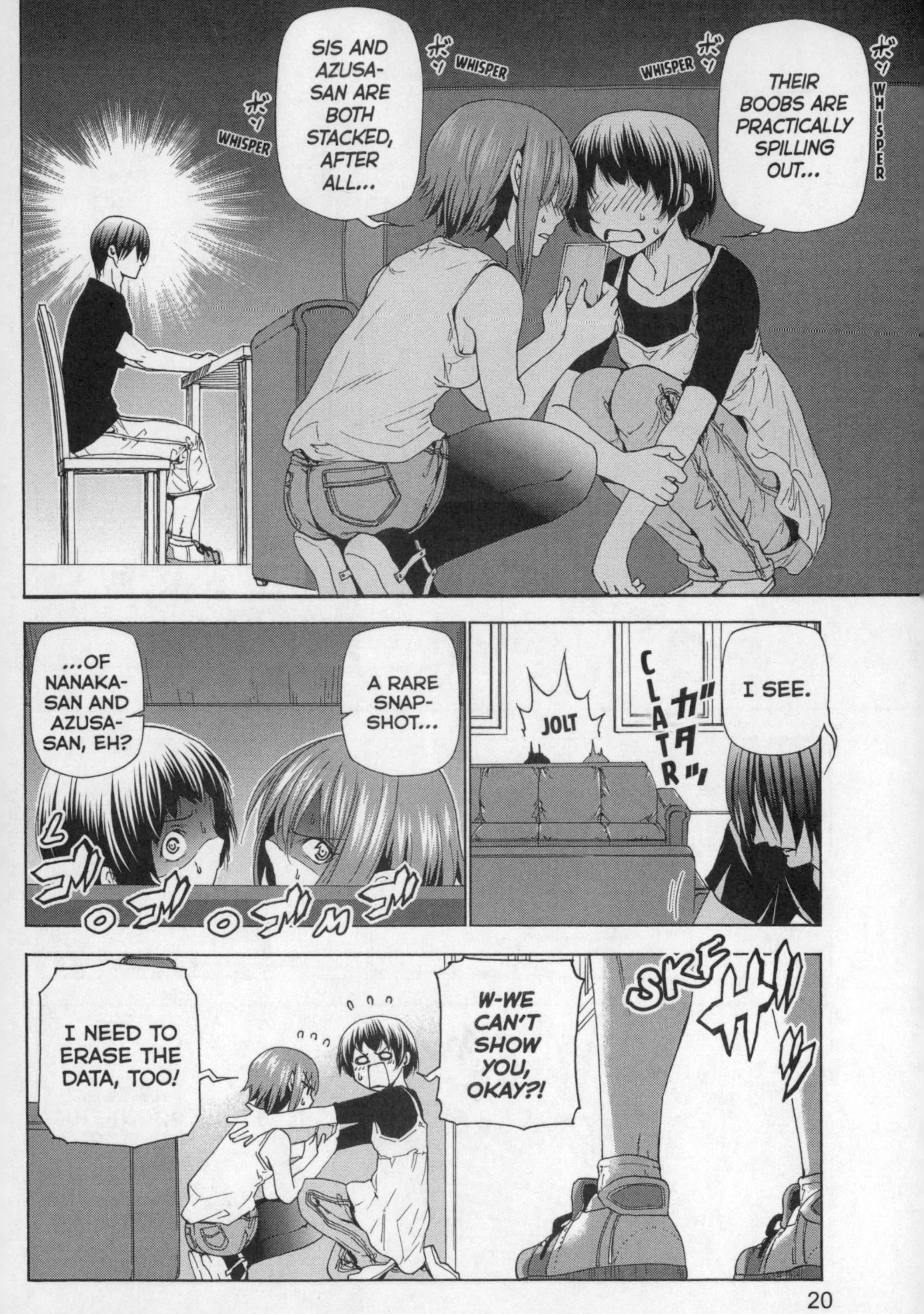
ボソ WHISPER
THEIR BOOBS ARE PRACTICALLY SPILLING OUT...
ボソ WHISPER
ボソ WHISPER
SIS AND AZUSA-SAN ARE BOTH STACKED, AFTER ALL...
ボソ WHISPER
I SEE.
CLATTER ガタッ
JOLT
A RARE SNAPSHOT...
...OF NANAKA-SAN AND AZUSA-SAN, EH?
SKF ザッ
W-WE CAN'T SHOW YOU, OKAY?!
I NEED TO ERASE THE DATA, TOO!

I WON'T ASK YOU TO SHOW ME.

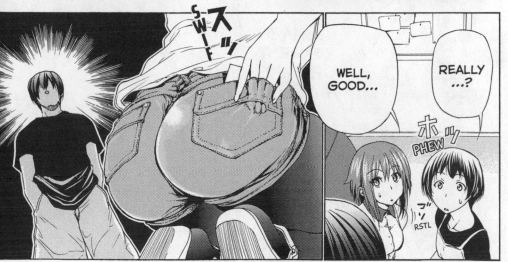

S-W-I-F

WELL, GOOD...

REALLY ...?

PHEW

RSTL

UH, OKAY.

I GOTTA USE THE BATH-ROOM.

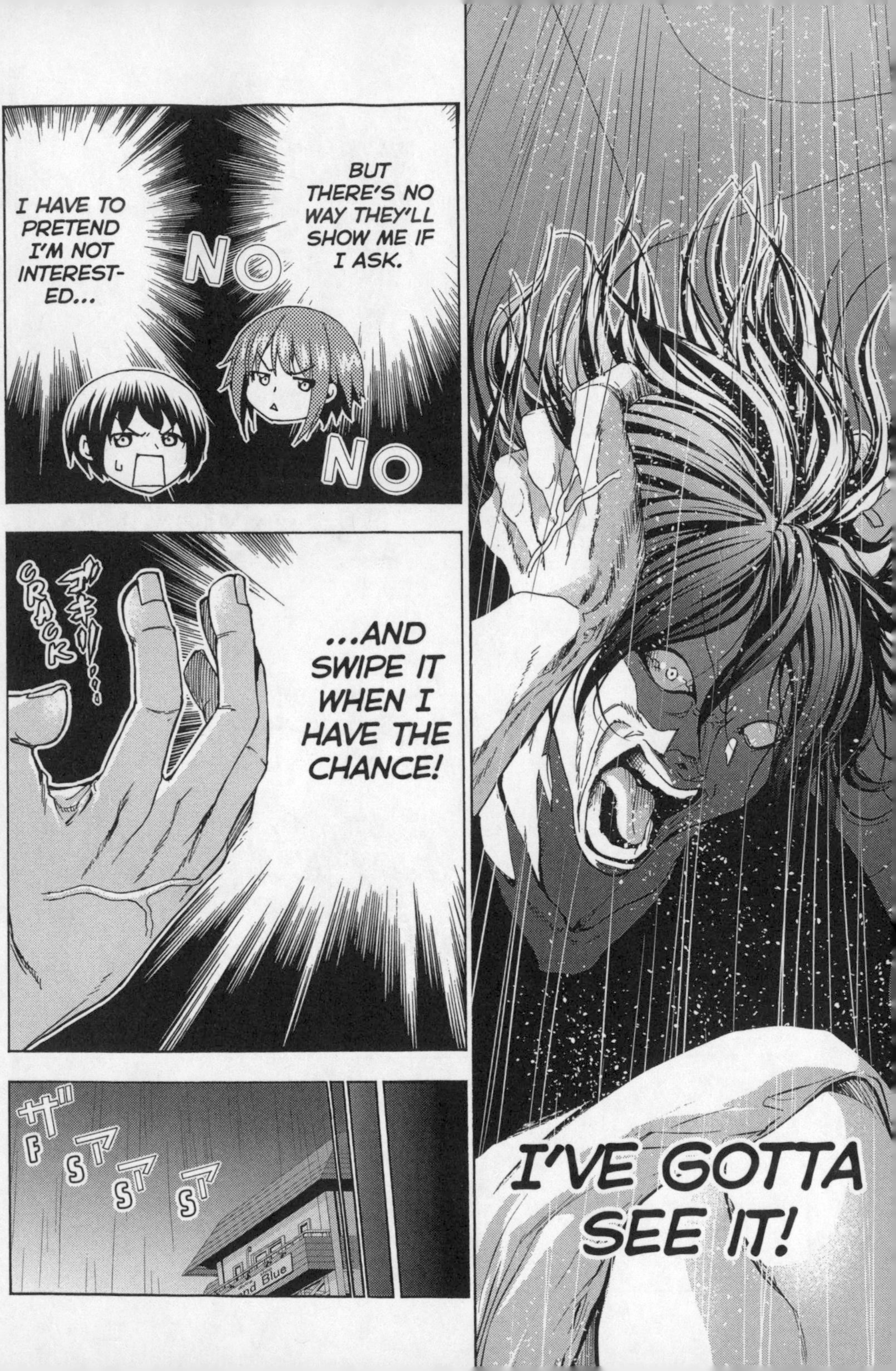
I'VE GOTTA SEE IT!
I HAVE TO PRETEND I'M NOT INTEREST-ED...
BUT THERE'S NO WAY THEY'LL SHOW ME IF I ASK.
NO
NO
CRACK
...AND SWIPE IT WHEN I HAVE THE CHANCE!
FSSS

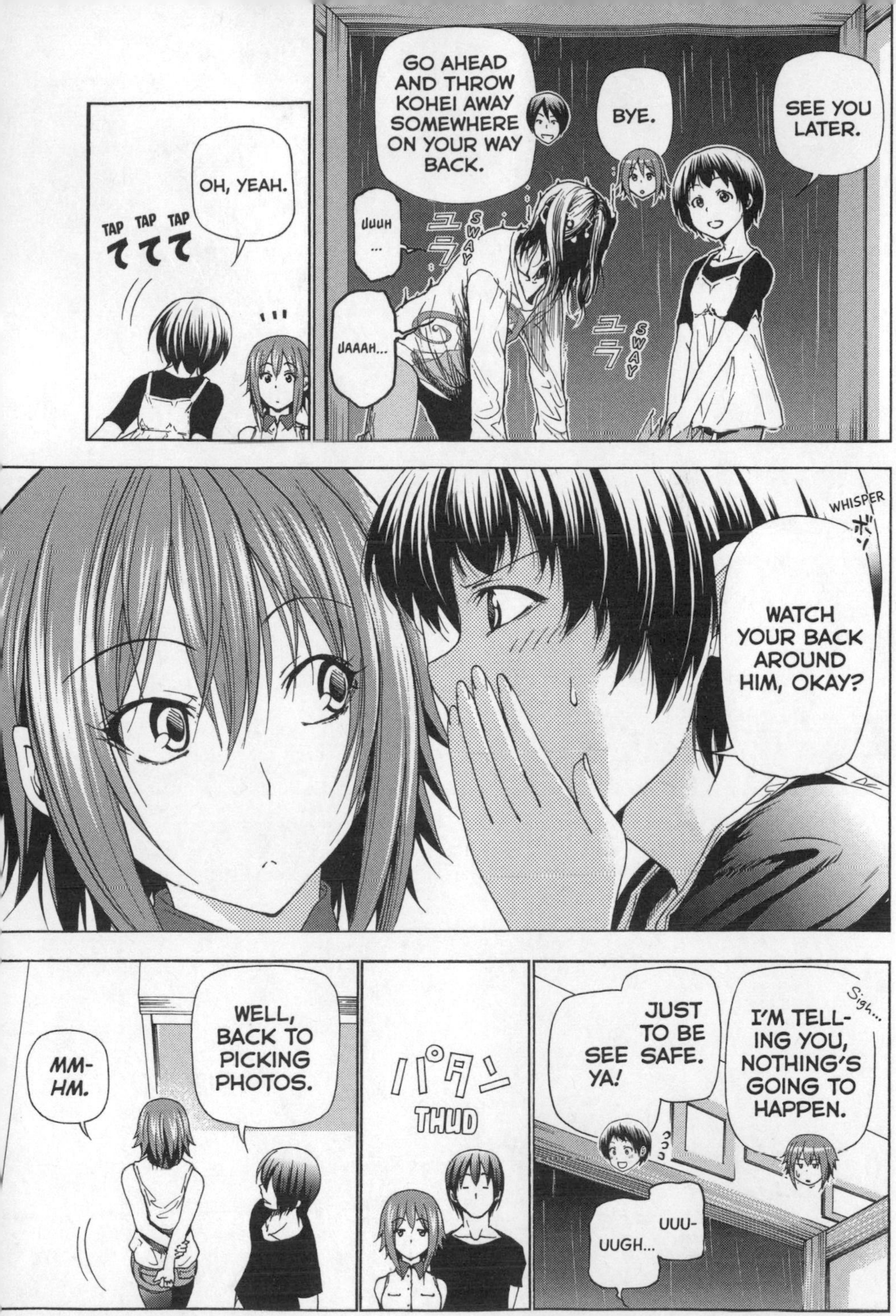
SEE YOU LATER.
BYE.
GO AHEAD AND THROW KOHEI AWAY SOMEWHERE ON YOUR WAY BACK.
SWAY ユラ
UUUH ...
SWAY ユラ
UAAAH...
OH, YEAH.
TAP TAP TAP てててて
WHISPER ボソ
WATCH YOUR BACK AROUND HIM, OKAY?
Sigh...
I'M TELL-ING YOU, NOTHING'S GOING TO HAPPEN.
JUST TO BE SAFE.
SEE YA!
UUU-UUGH...
パタン THUD
WELL, BACK TO PICKING PHOTOS.
MM-HM.

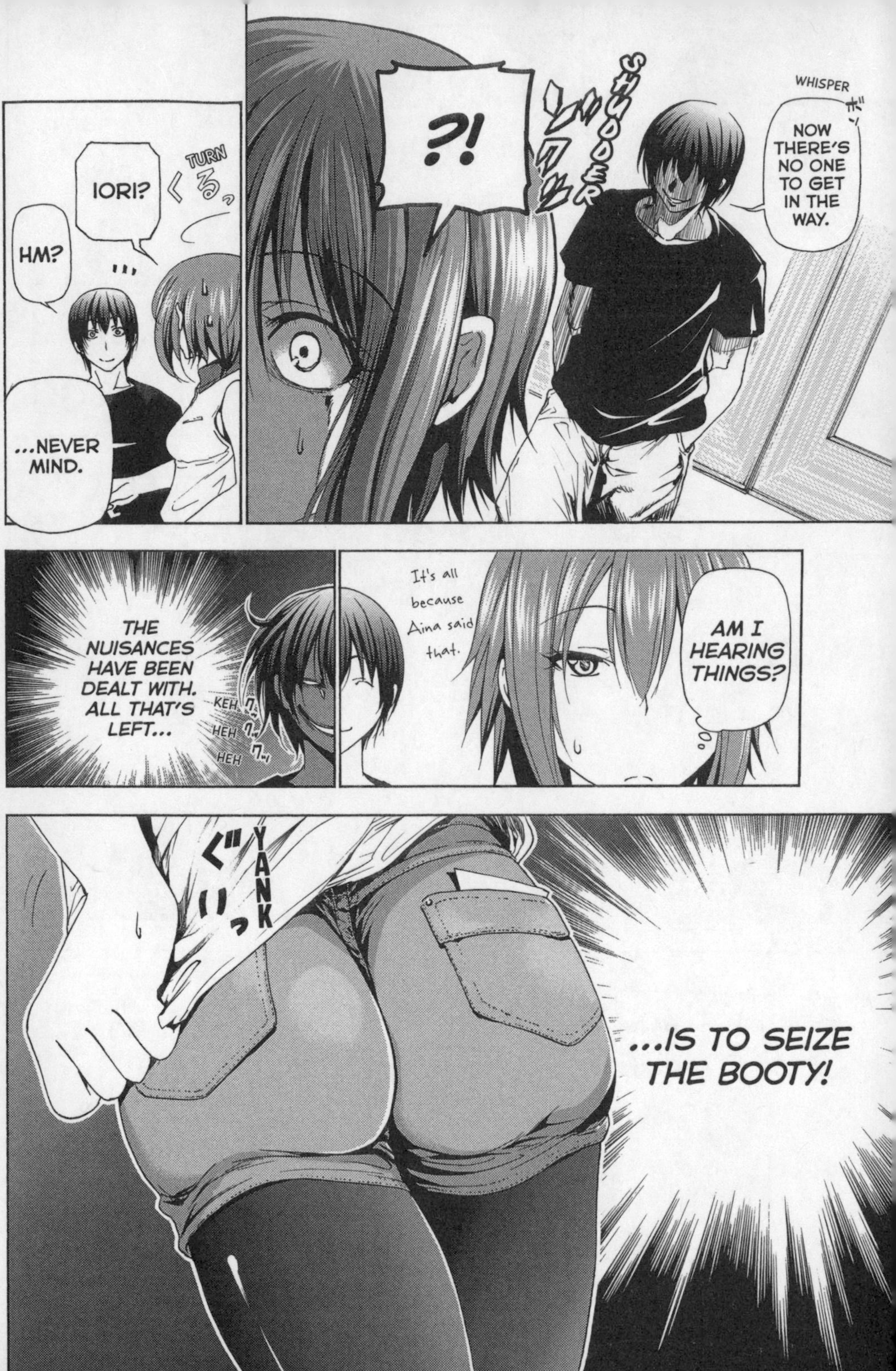
WHISPER
NOW THERE'S NO ONE TO GET IN THE WAY.
SHUDDER
?!
TURN
くるっ
IORI?
HM?
...
...NEVER MIND.
It's all because Aina said that.
AM I HEARING THINGS?
THE NUISANCES HAVE BEEN DEALT WITH. ALL THAT'S LEFT...
KEH
HEH
HEH
YANK
ぐいっ
...IS TO SEIZE THE BOOTY!

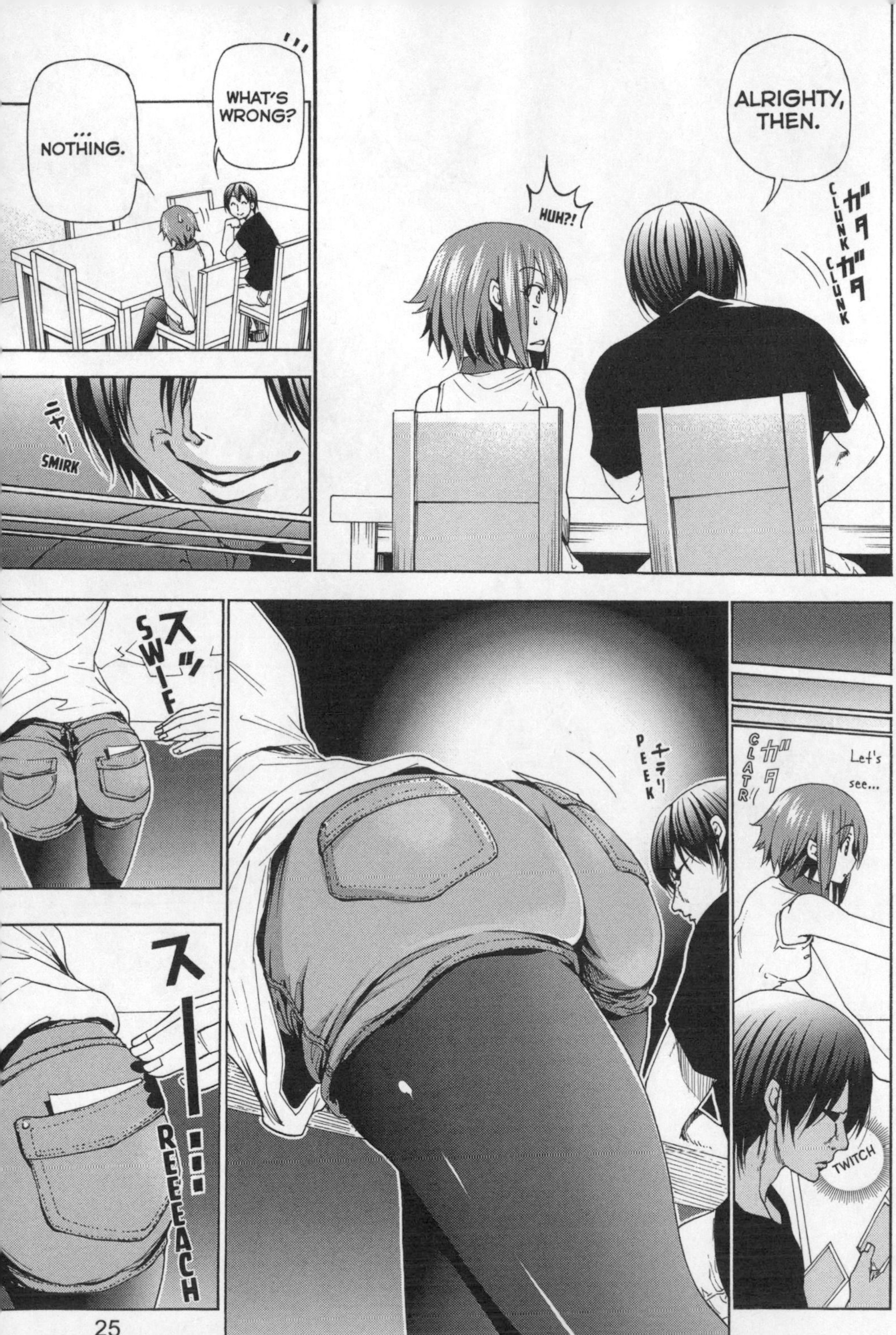
ALRIGHTY, THEN.
ガタ CLUNK ガタ CLUNK
HUH?!
WHAT'S WRONG?
... NOTHING.
ニヤ〜 SMIRK
ガタ CLATR
Let's see...
TWITCH
チラリ PEEK
スッ SWIF
スー... REEEACH

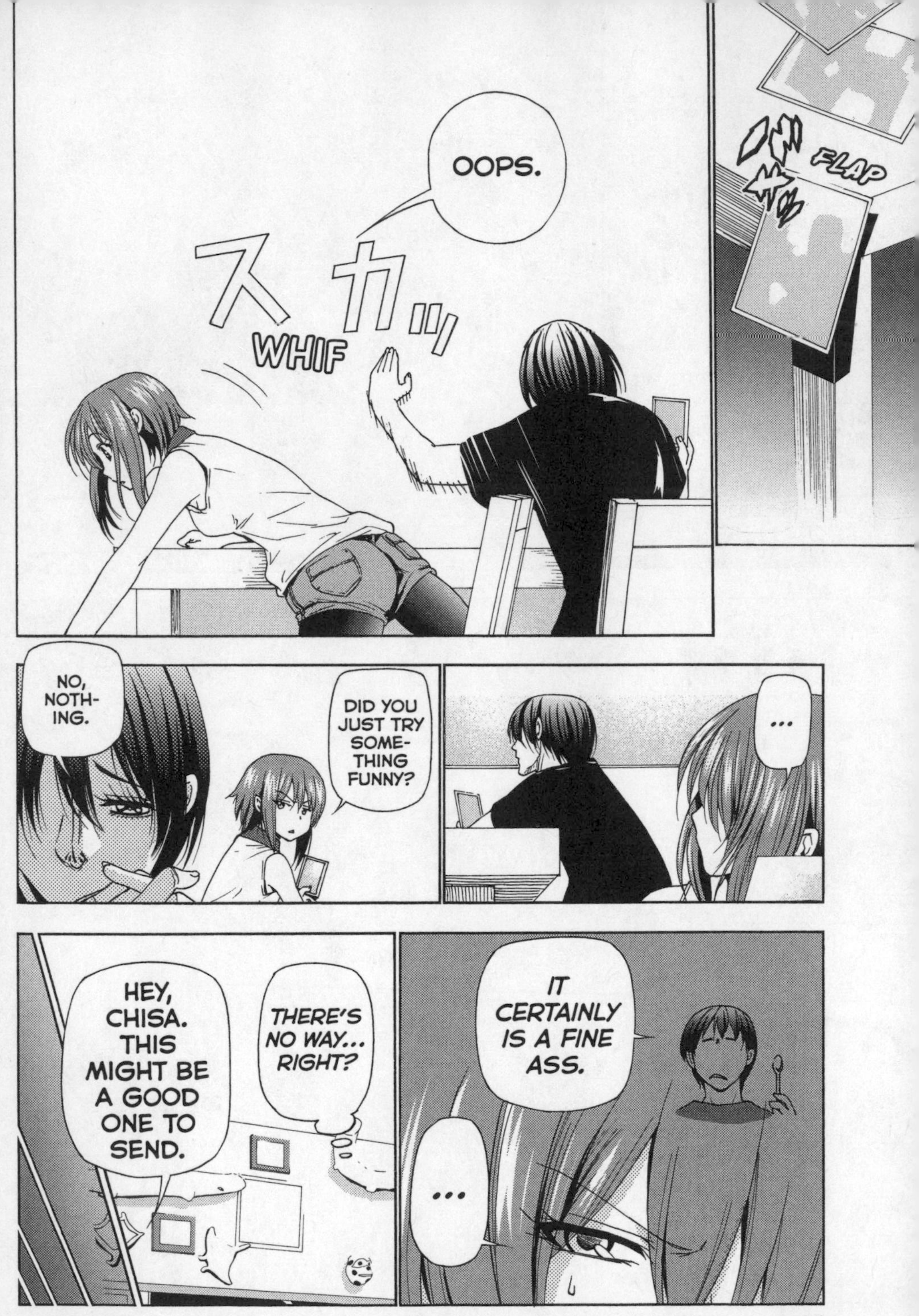
FLAP
OOPS.
スカッ
WHIF
...
DID YOU JUST TRY SOME-THING FUNNY?
NO, NOTH-ING.
IT CERTAINLY IS A FINE ASS.
...
THERE'S NO WAY... RIGHT?
HEY, CHISA. THIS MIGHT BE A GOOD ONE TO SEND.

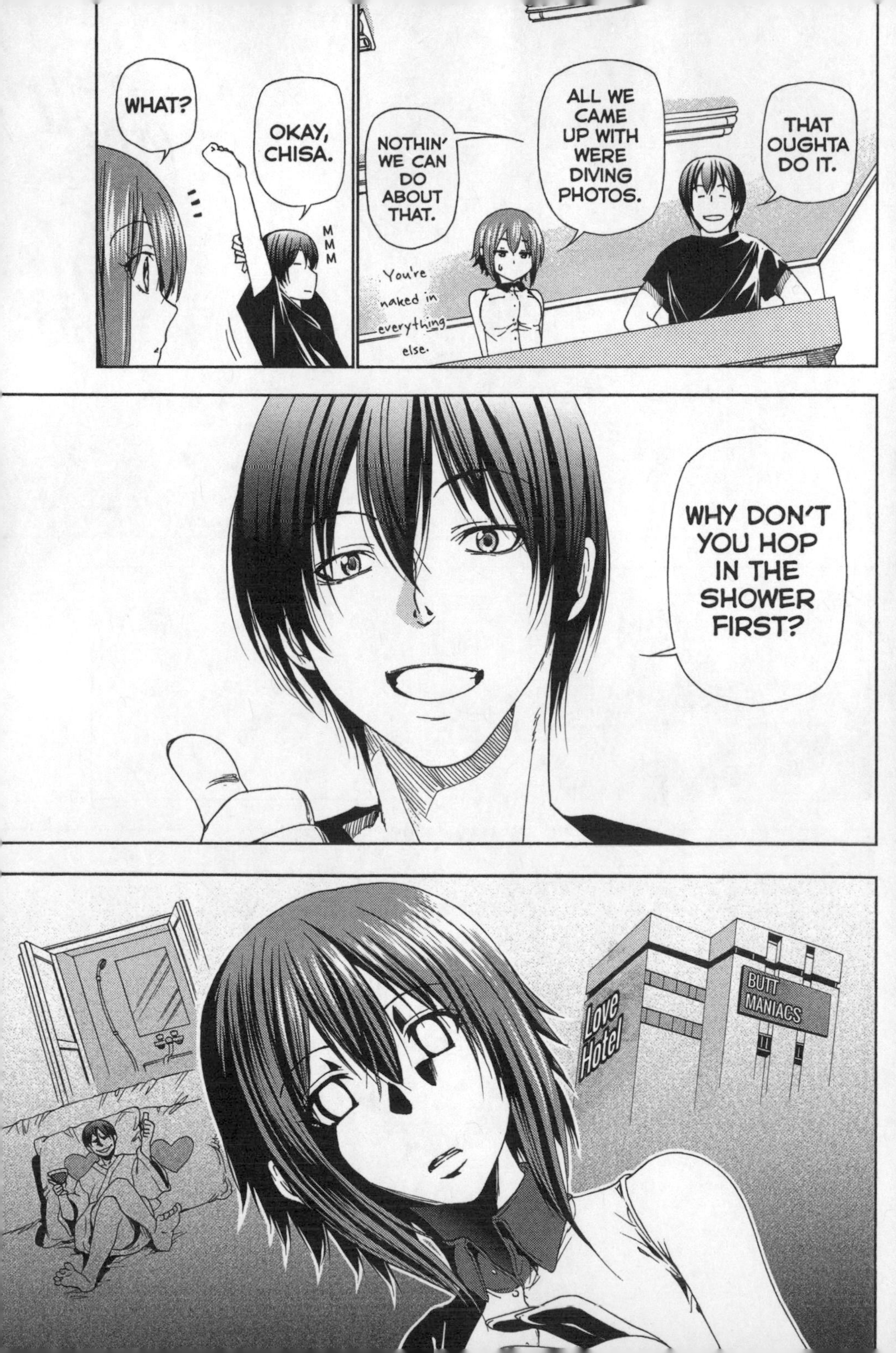
THAT OUGHTA DO IT.
ALL WE CAME UP WITH WERE DIVING PHOTOS.
NOTHIN' WE CAN DO ABOUT THAT.
You're naked in everything else.
OKAY, CHISA.
MMM
WHAT?
WHY DON'T YOU HOP IN THE SHOWER FIRST?
BUTT MANIACS
Love Hotel

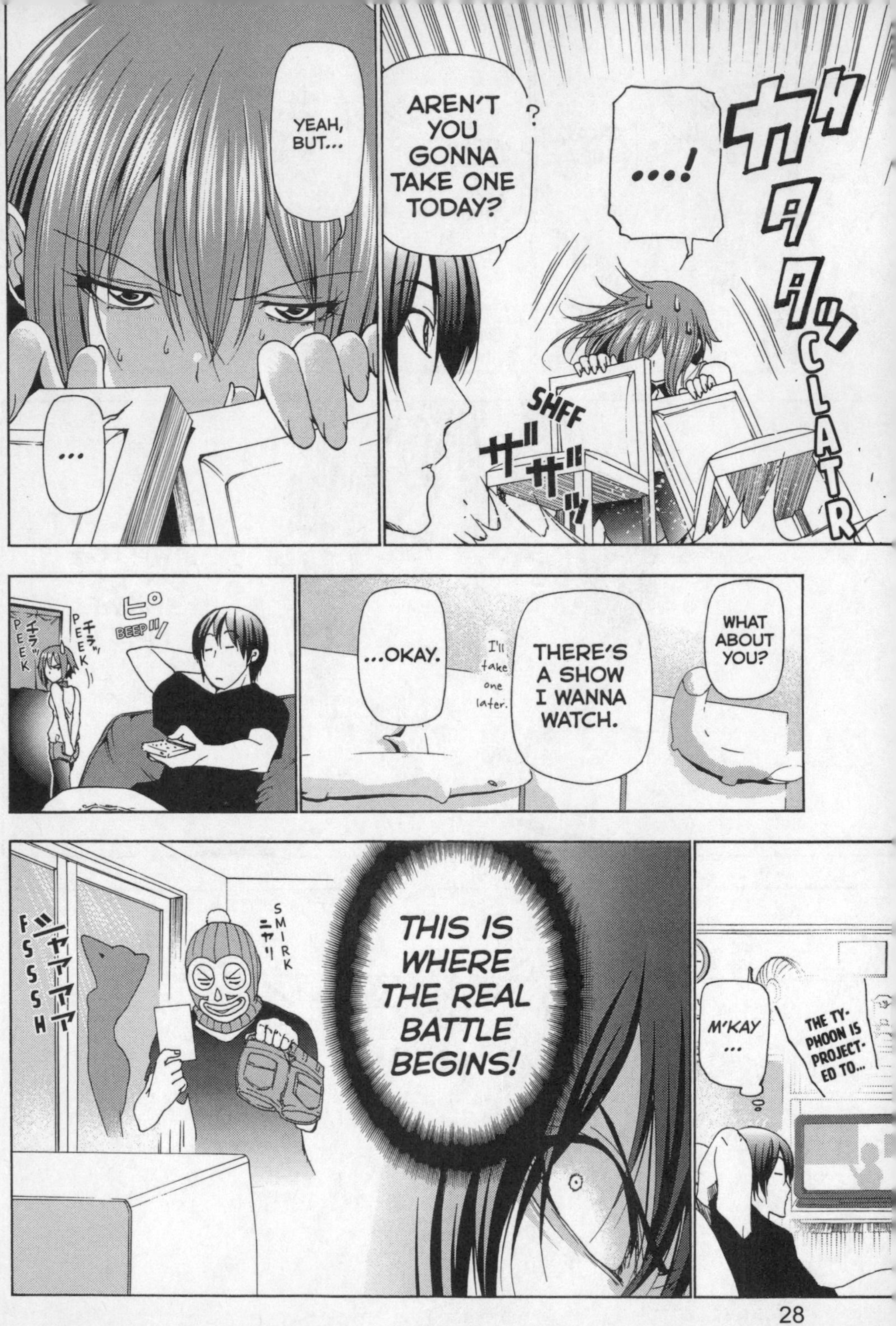
カタタッ
CLATR
...!
AREN'T YOU GONNA TAKE ONE TODAY?
SHFF
ザザッ
YEAH, BUT...
...
WHAT ABOUT YOU?
THERE'S A SHOW I WANNA WATCH.
I'll take one later.
...OKAY.
ピ
BEEP
チラッ
PEEK
PEEK
THE TY-PHOON IS PROJECT-ED TO...
M'KAY...
THIS IS WHERE THE REAL BATTLE BEGINS!
ニヤリ
SMIRK
ジャアアア
FSSSH

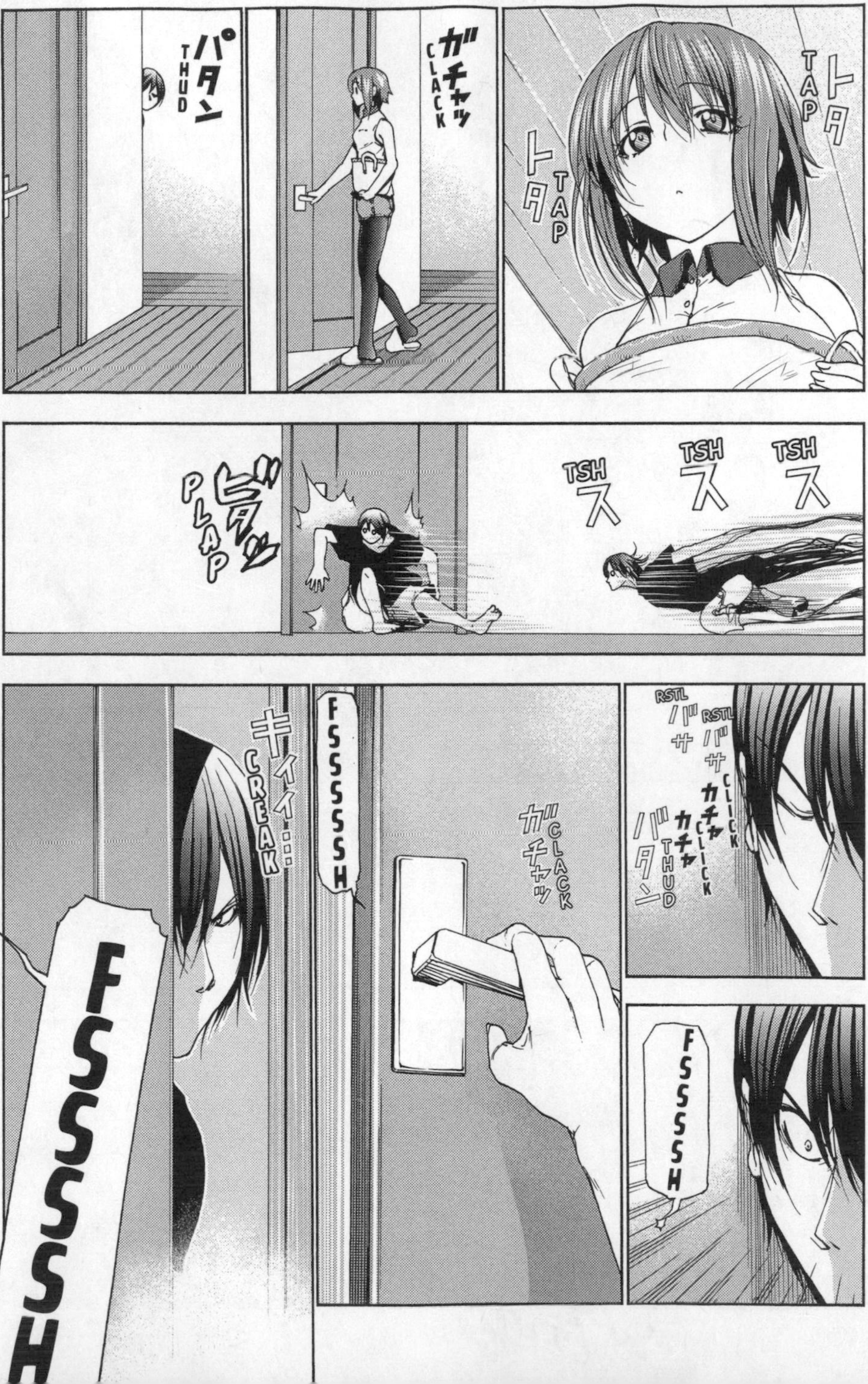
トタ
TAP
トタ
TAP
ガチャッ
CLACK
パタン
THUD
ス
TSH
ス
TSH
ス
TSH
ビダッ
PLAP
バサ
RSTL
バサ
RSTL
カチャ
CLICK
カチャ
CLICK
バタン
THUD
FSSSSH
ガチャッ
CLACK
FSSSSSH
キィイ…
CREAK
FSSSSSH

FSSSH

AH
T

MP
‼

FN FN
DASH

DASH
FN FN

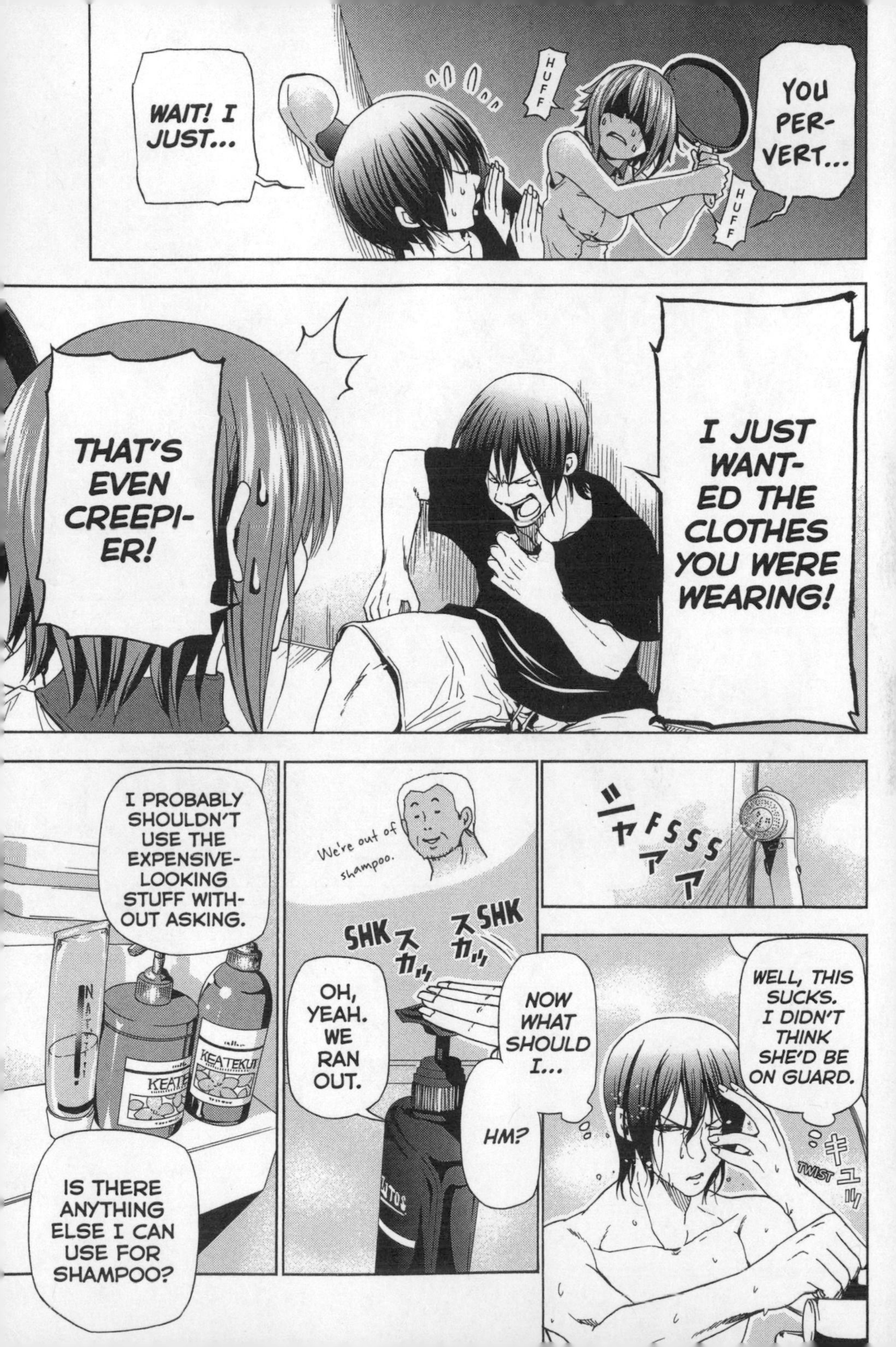
YOU PER-VERT...
HUFF
HUFF
WAIT! I JUST...
I JUST WANT-ED THE CLOTHES YOU WERE WEARING!
THAT'S EVEN CREEPI-ER!
FSSSS
WELL, THIS SUCKS. I DIDN'T THINK SHE'D BE ON GUARD.
TWIST
NOW WHAT SHOULD I...
HM?
We're out of shampoo.
SHK
SHK
OH, YEAH. WE RAN OUT.
I PROBABLY SHOULDN'T USE THE EXPENSIVE-LOOKING STUFF WITH-OUT ASKING.
KEATEKUT
IS THERE ANYTHING ELSE I CAN USE FOR SHAMPOO?

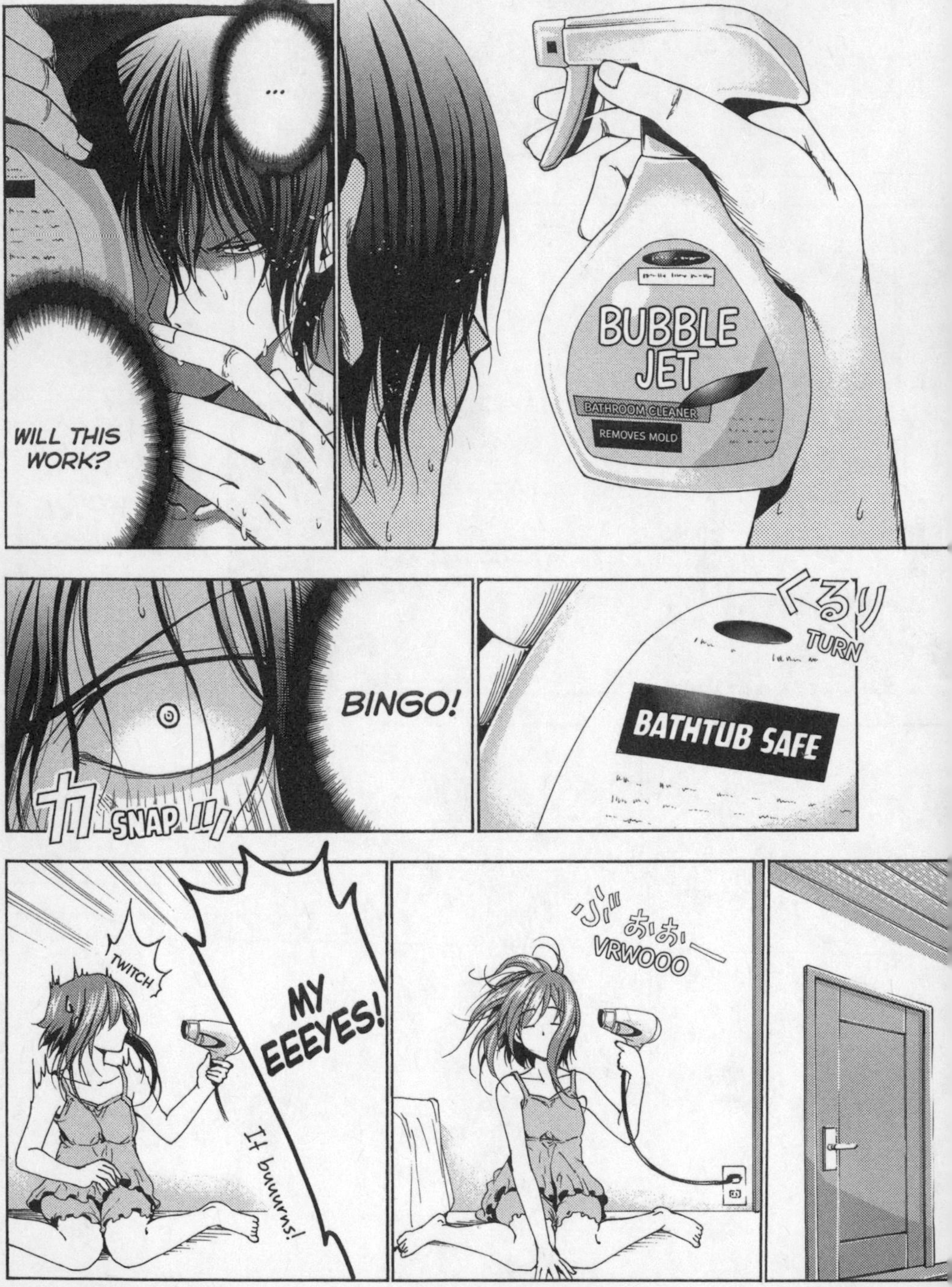
BUBBLE JET
BATHROOM CLEANER
REMOVES MOLD
...
WILL THIS WORK?
くるり
TURN
BATHTUB SAFE
BINGO!
カッ
SNAP
ぶおぉー
VRWOOO
TWITCH
MY EEEYES!
It buuurns!

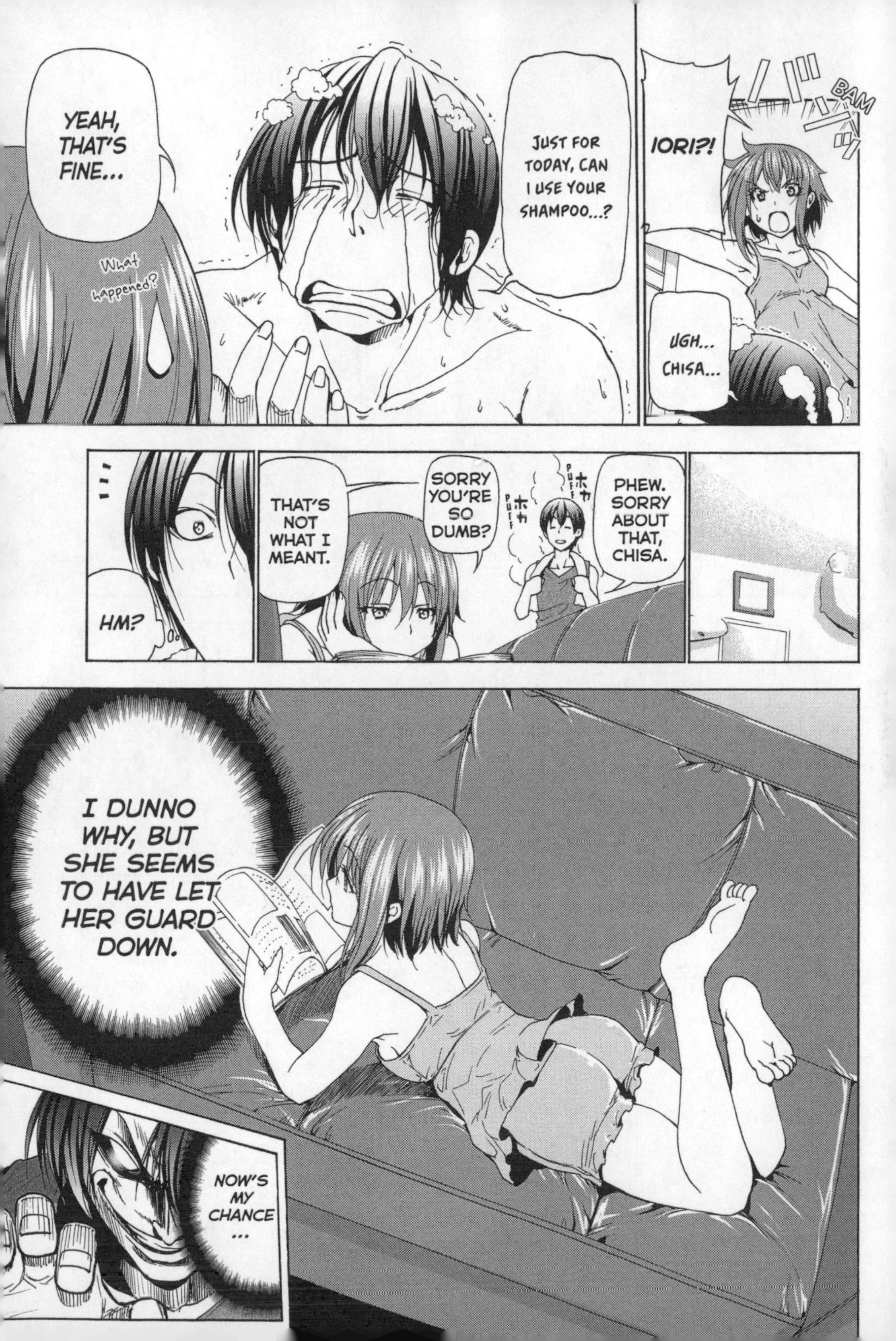
BAM
IORI?!
UGH... CHISA...
JUST FOR TODAY, CAN I USE YOUR SHAMPOO...?
YEAH, THAT'S FINE...
What happened?
PUFF
PUFF
PHEW. SORRY ABOUT THAT, CHISA.
SORRY YOU'RE SO DUMB?
THAT'S NOT WHAT I MEANT.
HM?
I DUNNO WHY, BUT SHE SEEMS TO HAVE LET HER GUARD DOWN.
NOW'S MY CHANCE ...

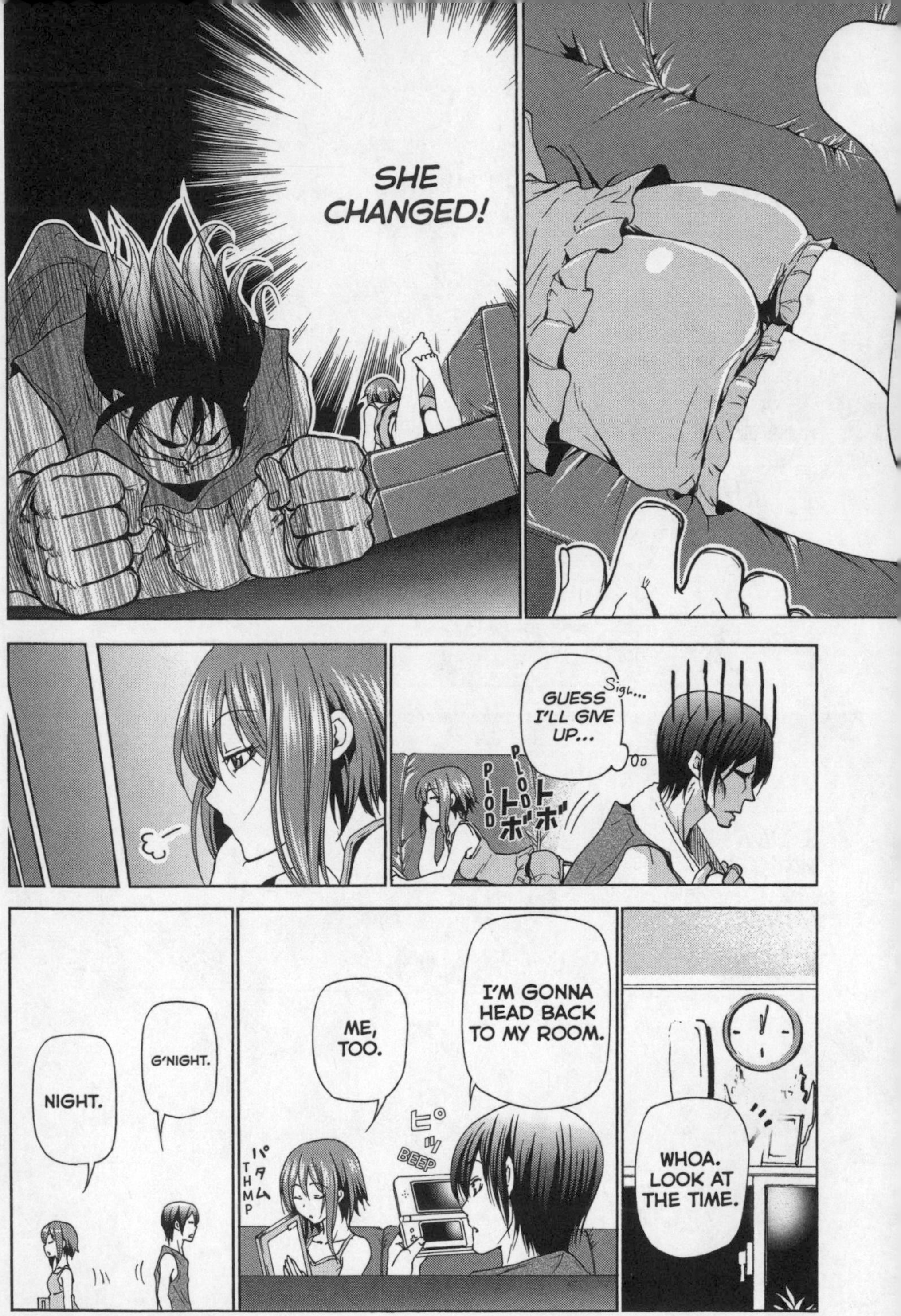
SHE CHANGED!
Sigh...
GUESS I'LL GIVE UP...
PLOD PLOD
トボトボ
WHOA. LOOK AT THE TIME.
I'M GONNA HEAD BACK TO MY ROOM.
ピッ
BEEP
ME, TOO.
パタム
THMP
G'NIGHT.
NIGHT.

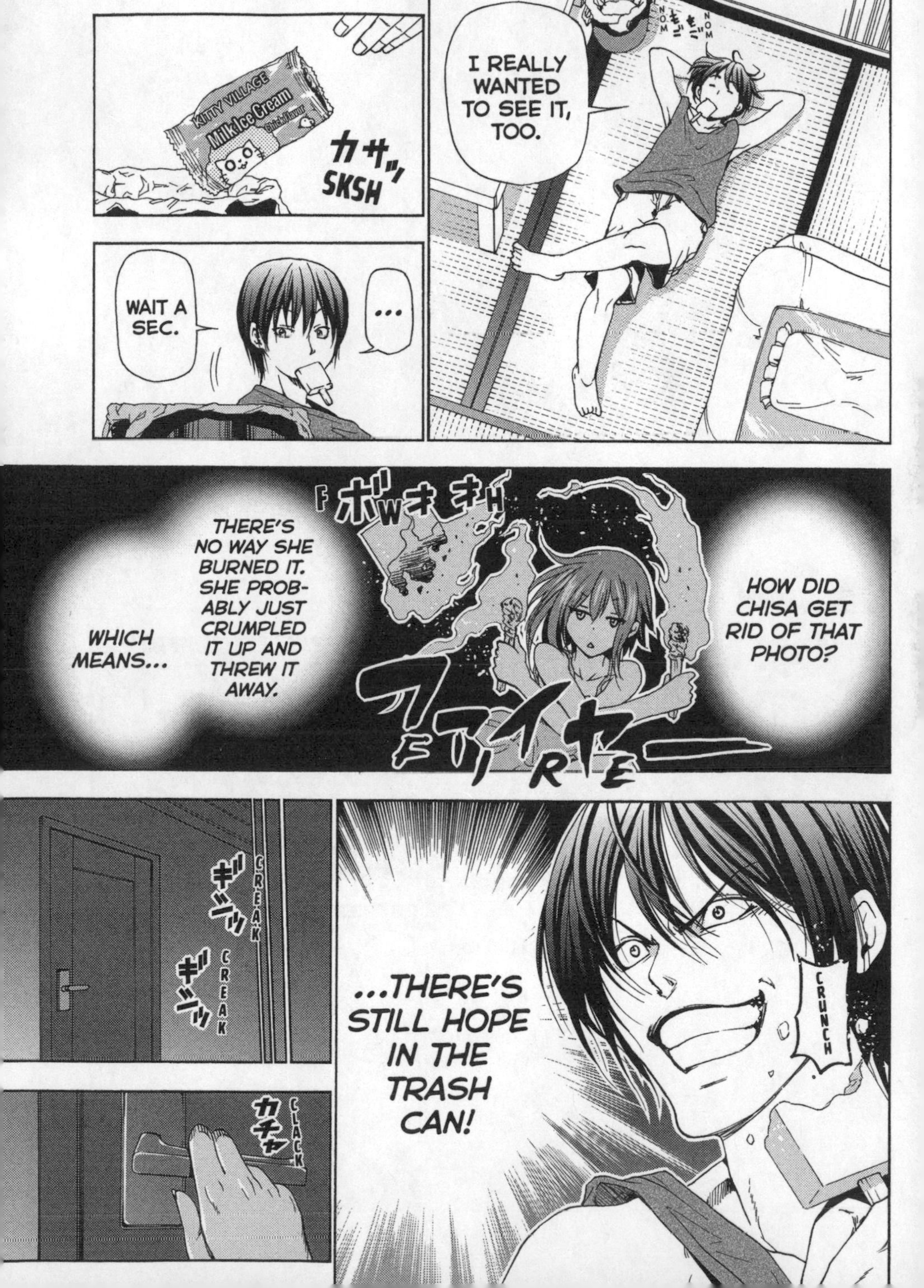
NOM NOM
I REALLY WANTED TO SEE IT, TOO.
KITTY VILLAGE
Milk Ice Cream
カサッ
SKSH
...
WAIT A SEC.
FWOOSH
HOW DID CHISA GET RID OF THAT PHOTO?
THERE'S NO WAY SHE BURNED IT. SHE PROBABLY JUST CRUMPLED IT UP AND THREW IT AWAY.
WHICH MEANS...
ファイヤー
FIRE
...THERE'S STILL HOPE IN THE TRASH CAN!
CRUNCH
CREAK
CREAK
CLACK

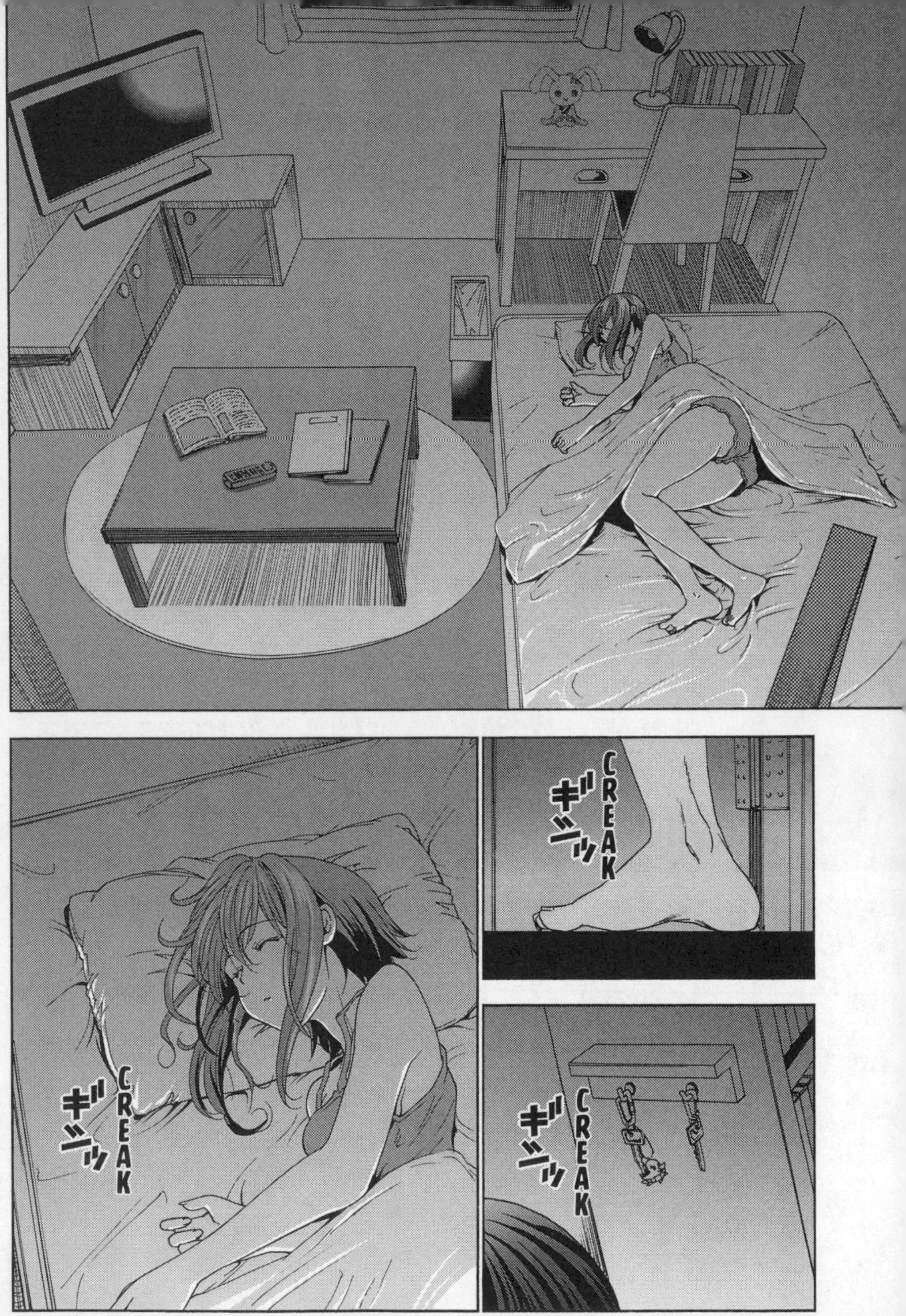
CREAK
ギシッ
CREAK
ギシッ
CREAK
ギシッ

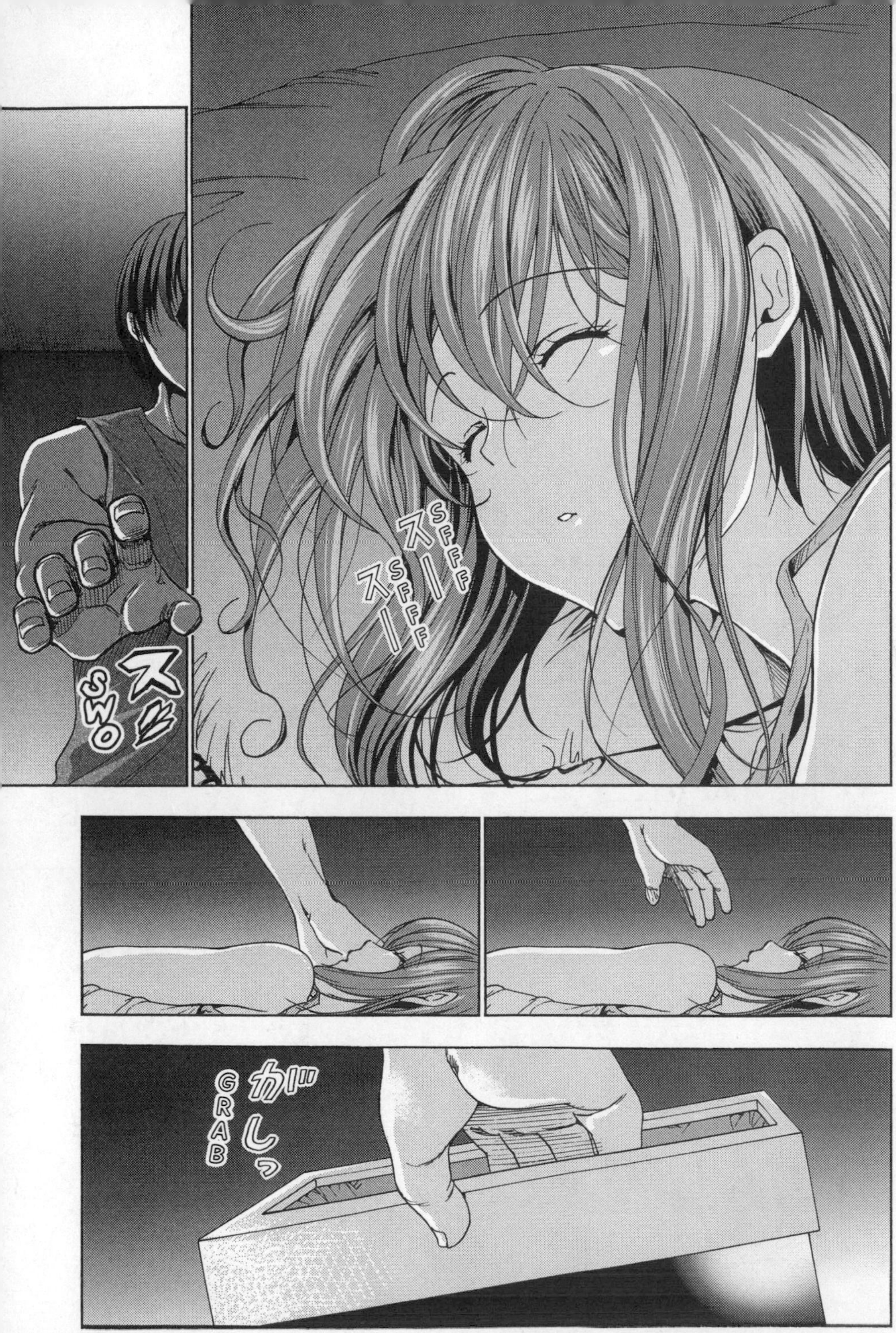
スー SFFF
スー SFFF
ス SWO
がしっ GRAB

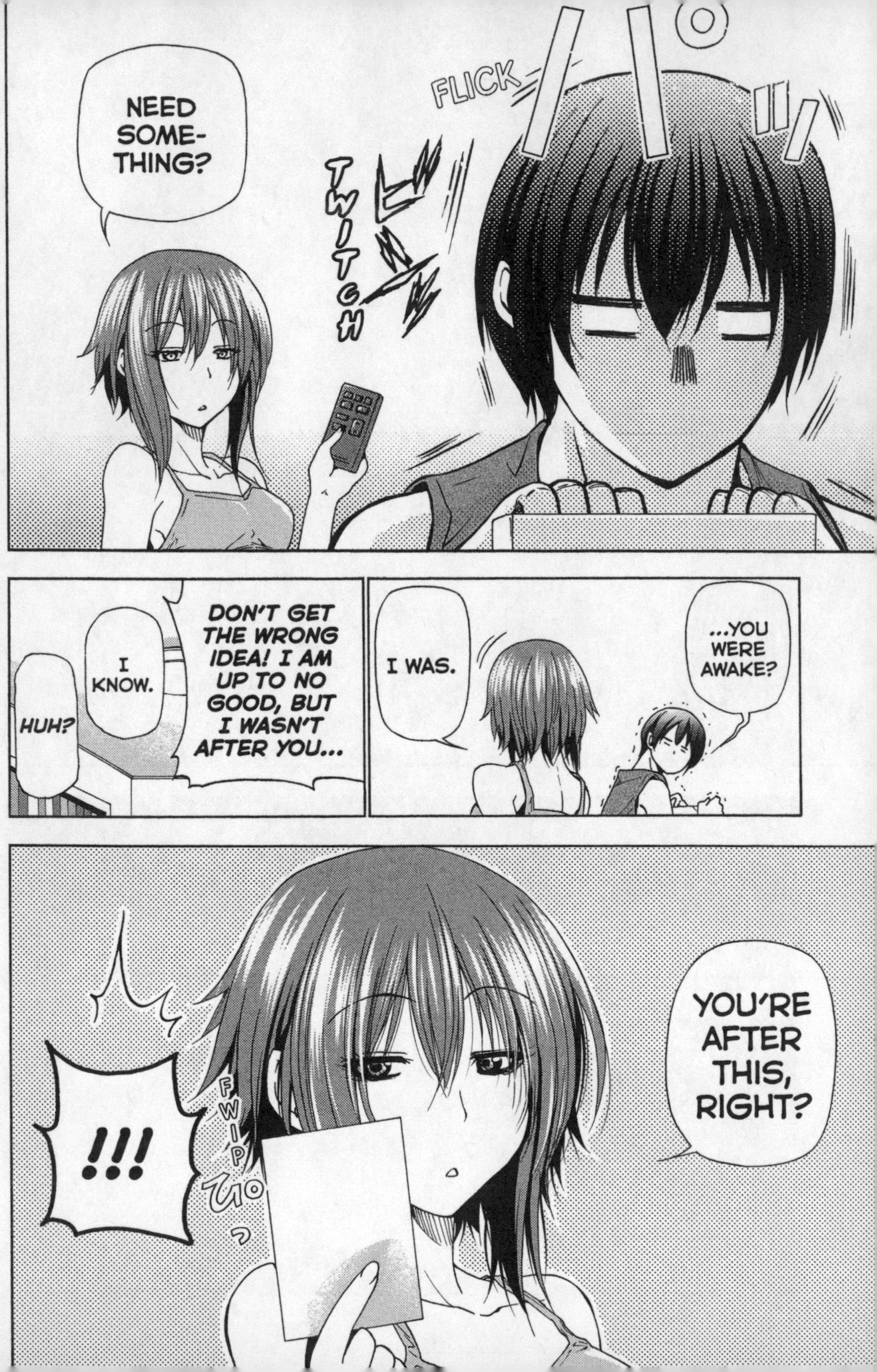
FLICK
TWITCH
NEED SOME-THING?
...YOU WERE AWAKE?
I WAS.
DON'T GET THE WRONG IDEA! I AM UP TO NO GOOD, BUT I WASN'T AFTER YOU...
I KNOW.
HUH?
YOU'RE AFTER THIS, RIGHT?
FWIP
!!!

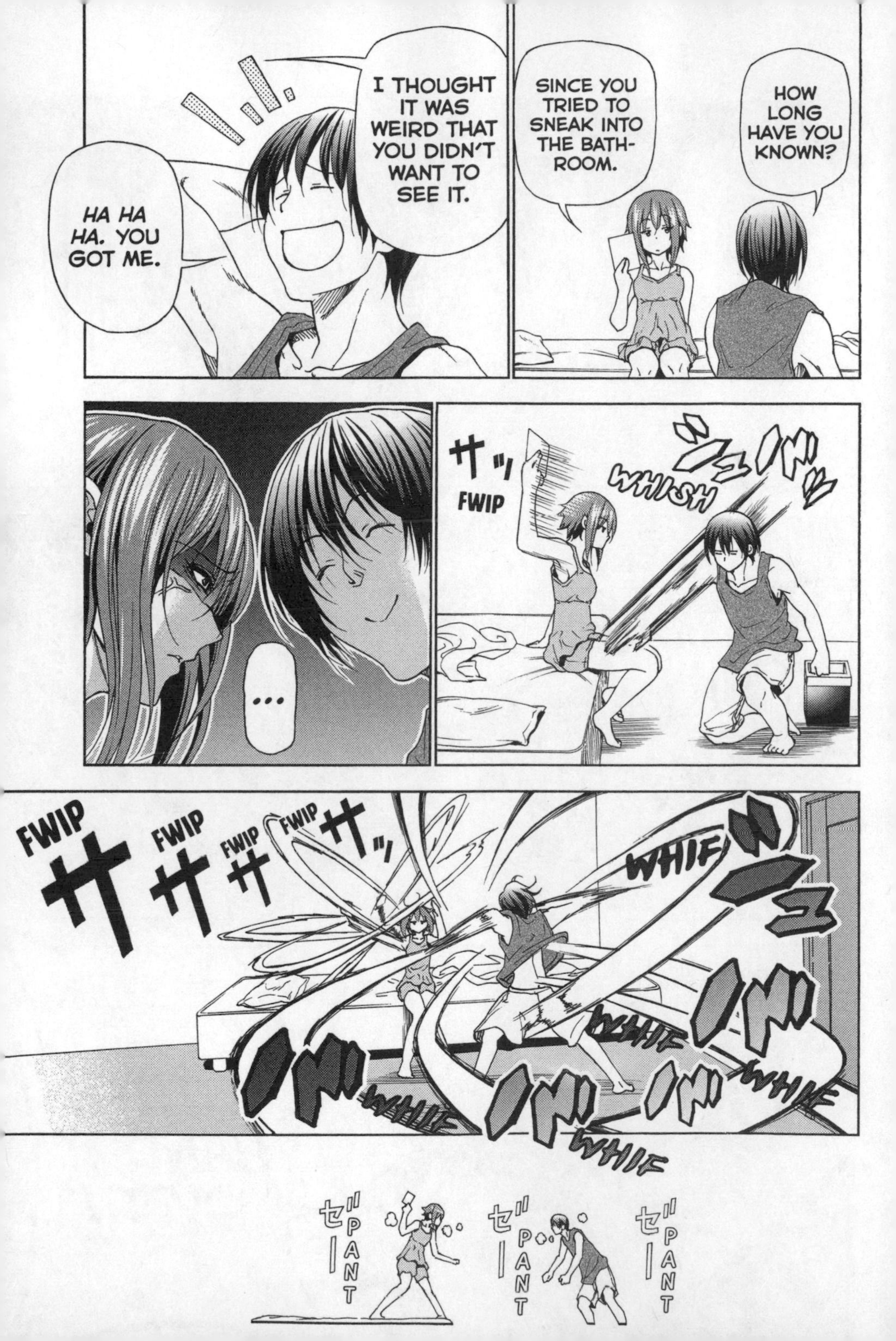
HOW LONG HAVE YOU KNOWN?
SINCE YOU TRIED TO SNEAK INTO THE BATH-ROOM.
I THOUGHT IT WAS WEIRD THAT YOU DIDN'T WANT TO SEE IT.
HA HA HA. YOU GOT ME.
シュバッ
WHISH
サッ
FWIP
...
サッ
FWIP
サ
FWIP
サ
FWIP
サ
FWIP
WHIF
WHIF
WHIF
WHIF
WHIF
ゼー
PANT
ゼー
PANT
ゼー
PANT

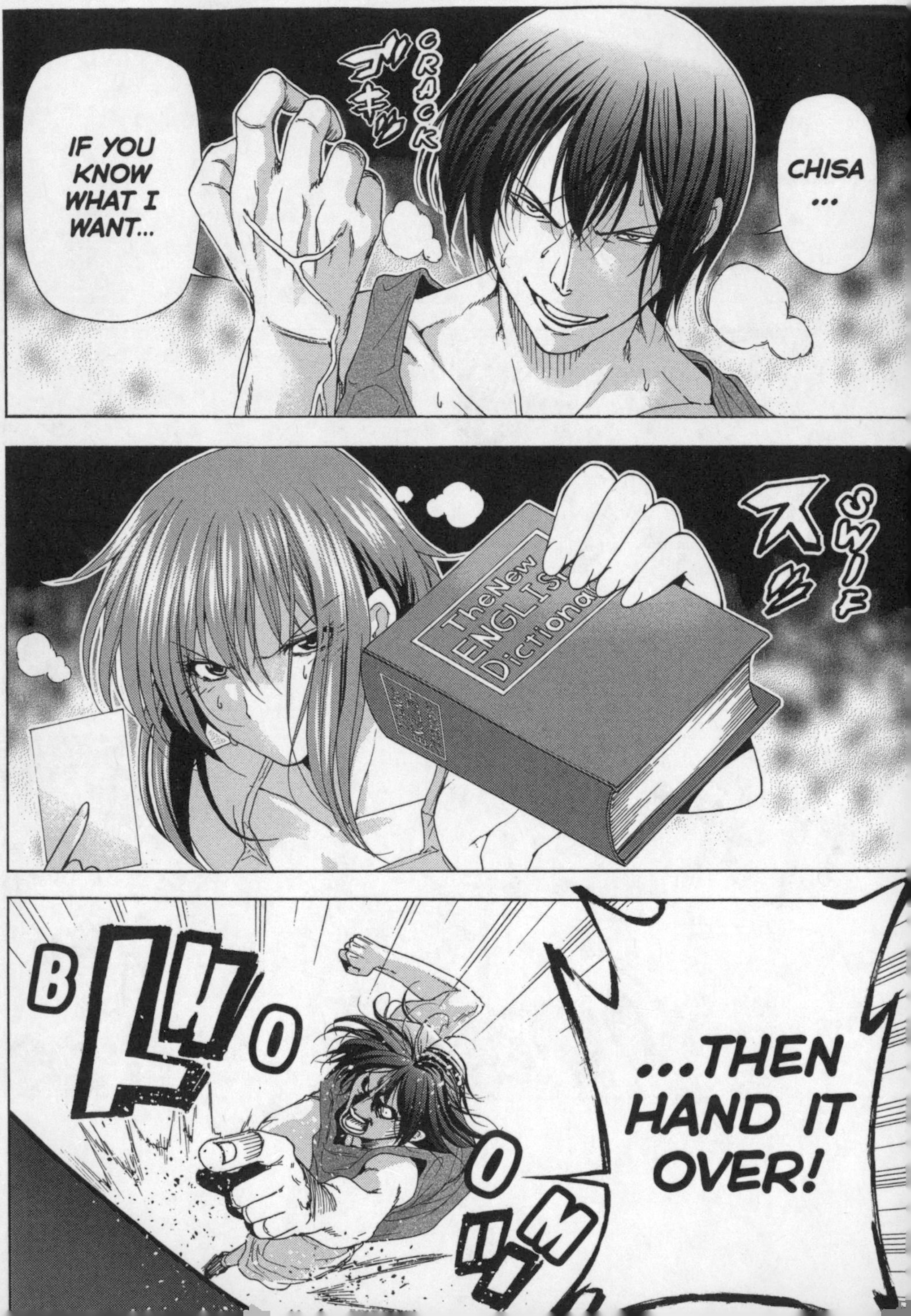
CHISA ...
CRACK
ゴキッ
IF YOU KNOW WHAT I WANT...
SWIF
スッ
...THEN HAND IT OVER!
BWHOOM

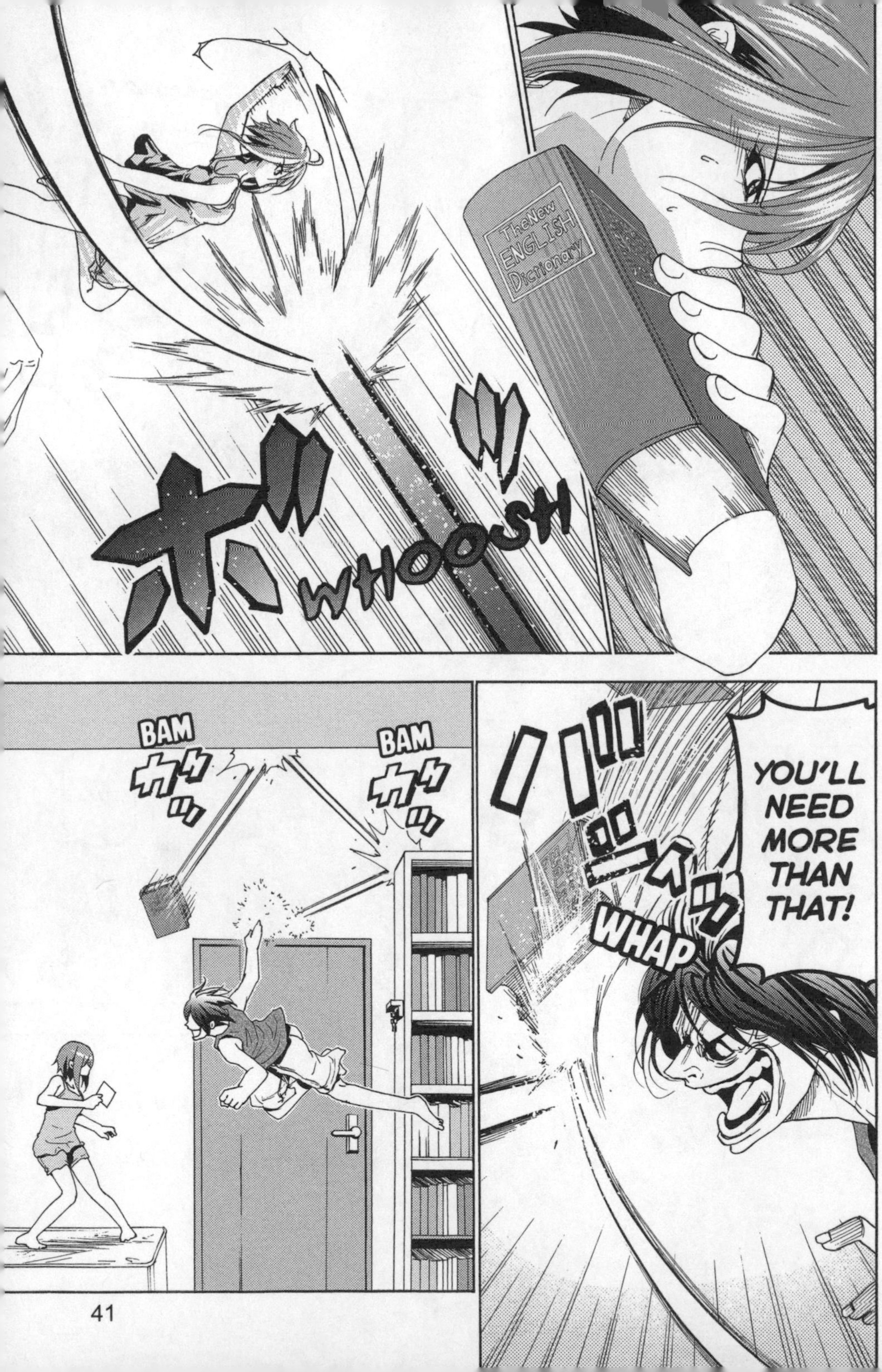
The New ENGLISH Dictionary
WHOOSH
YOU'LL NEED MORE THAN THAT!
WHAP
BAM
BAM

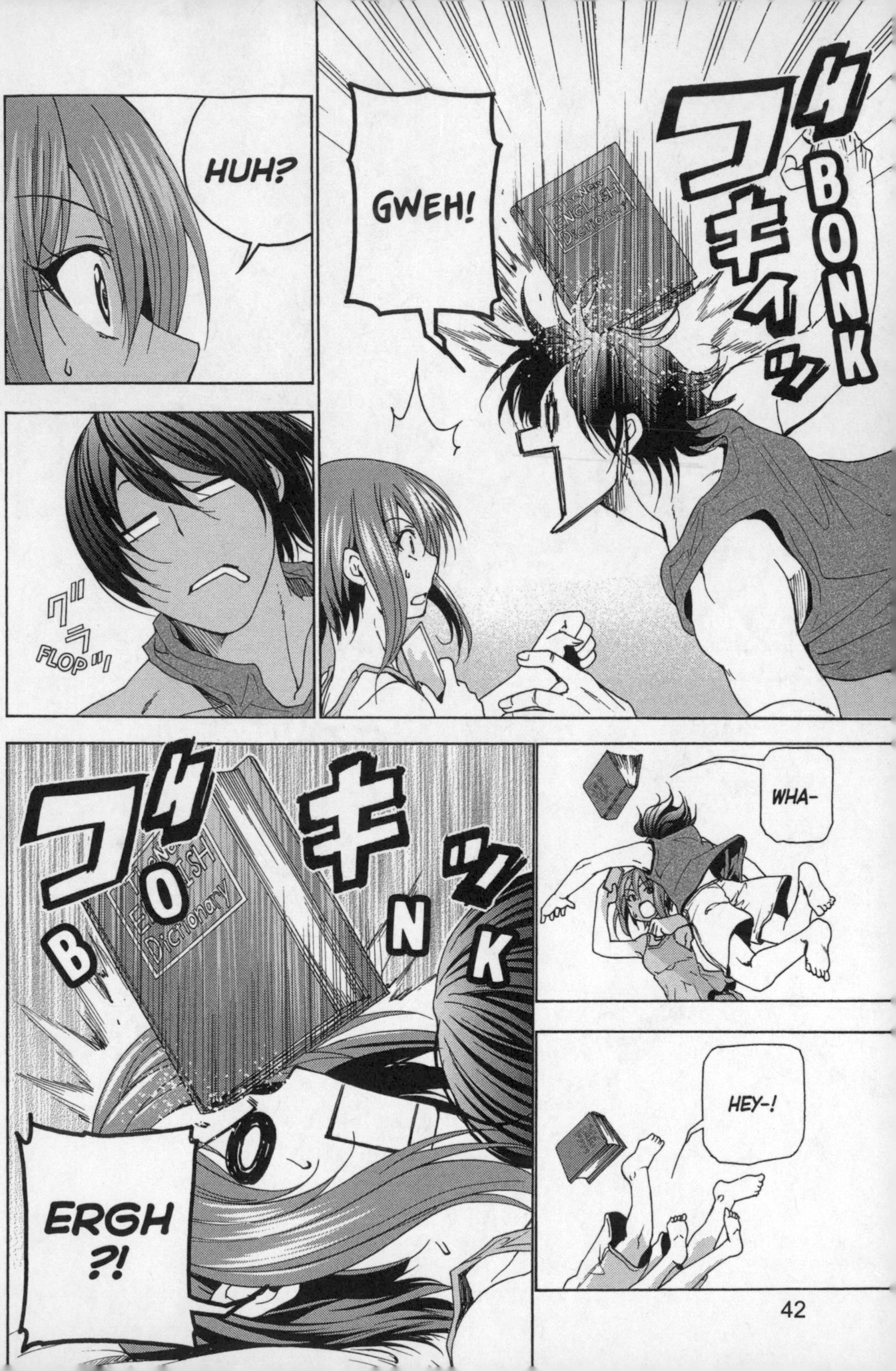
GWEH!
コキッ BONK
HUH?
グラッ FLOP
WHA-
HEY-!
コキッ BONK
ERGH ?!

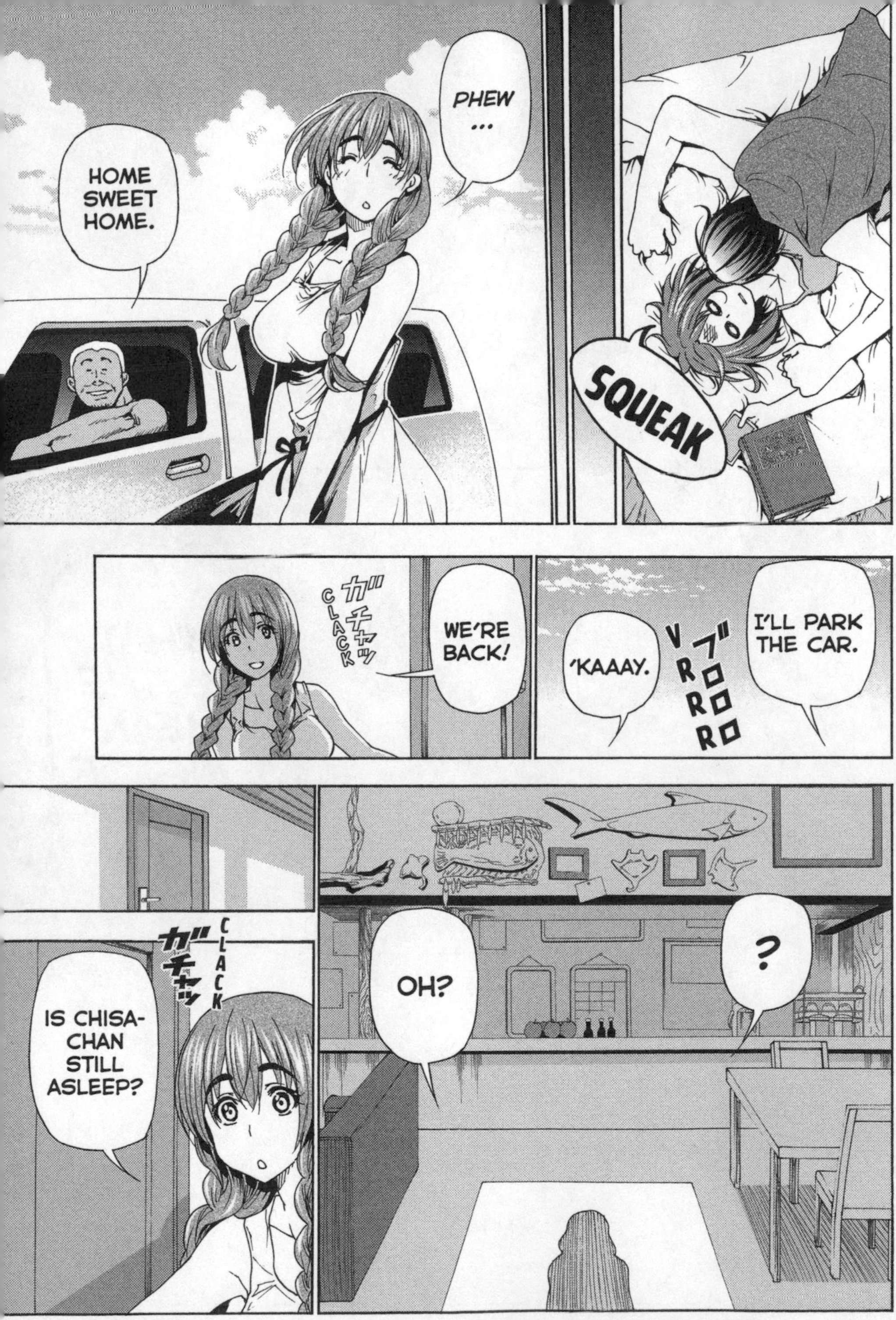
SQUEAK
PHEW ...
HOME SWEET HOME.
I'LL PARK THE CAR.
VRRRR
ブロロロ
'KAAAY.
WE'RE BACK!
ガチャッ
CLACK
?
OH?
ガチャッ
CLACK
IS CHISA-CHAN STILL ASLEEP?

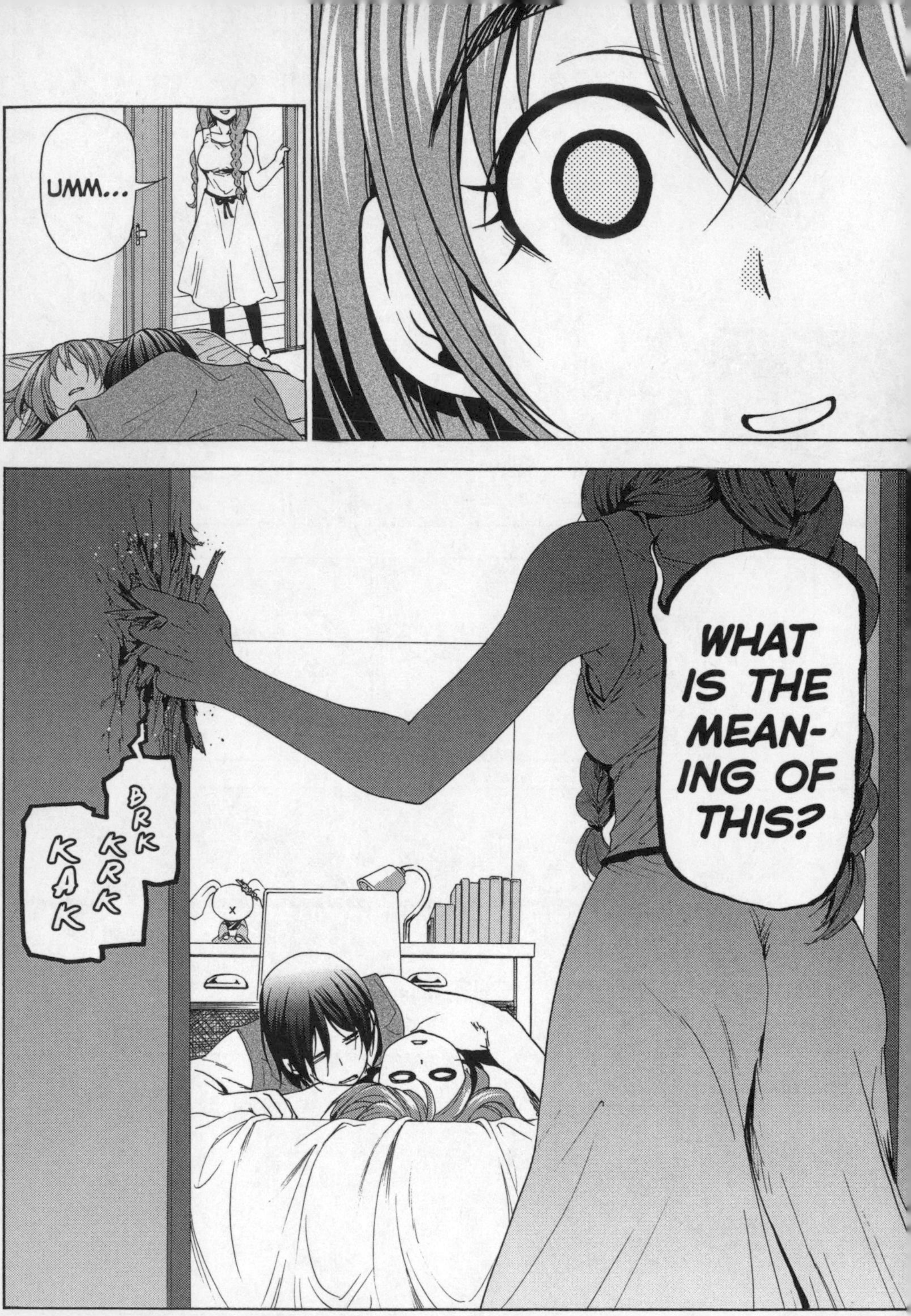
UMM...
WHAT IS THE MEANING OF THIS?
BRK KRK KAK

CH.26 / End

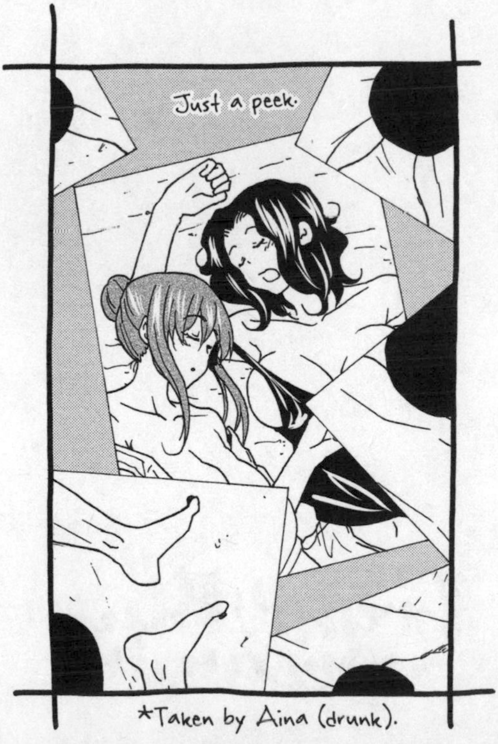
Just a peek.
*Taken by Aina (drunk).

Grand Blue
Dreaming

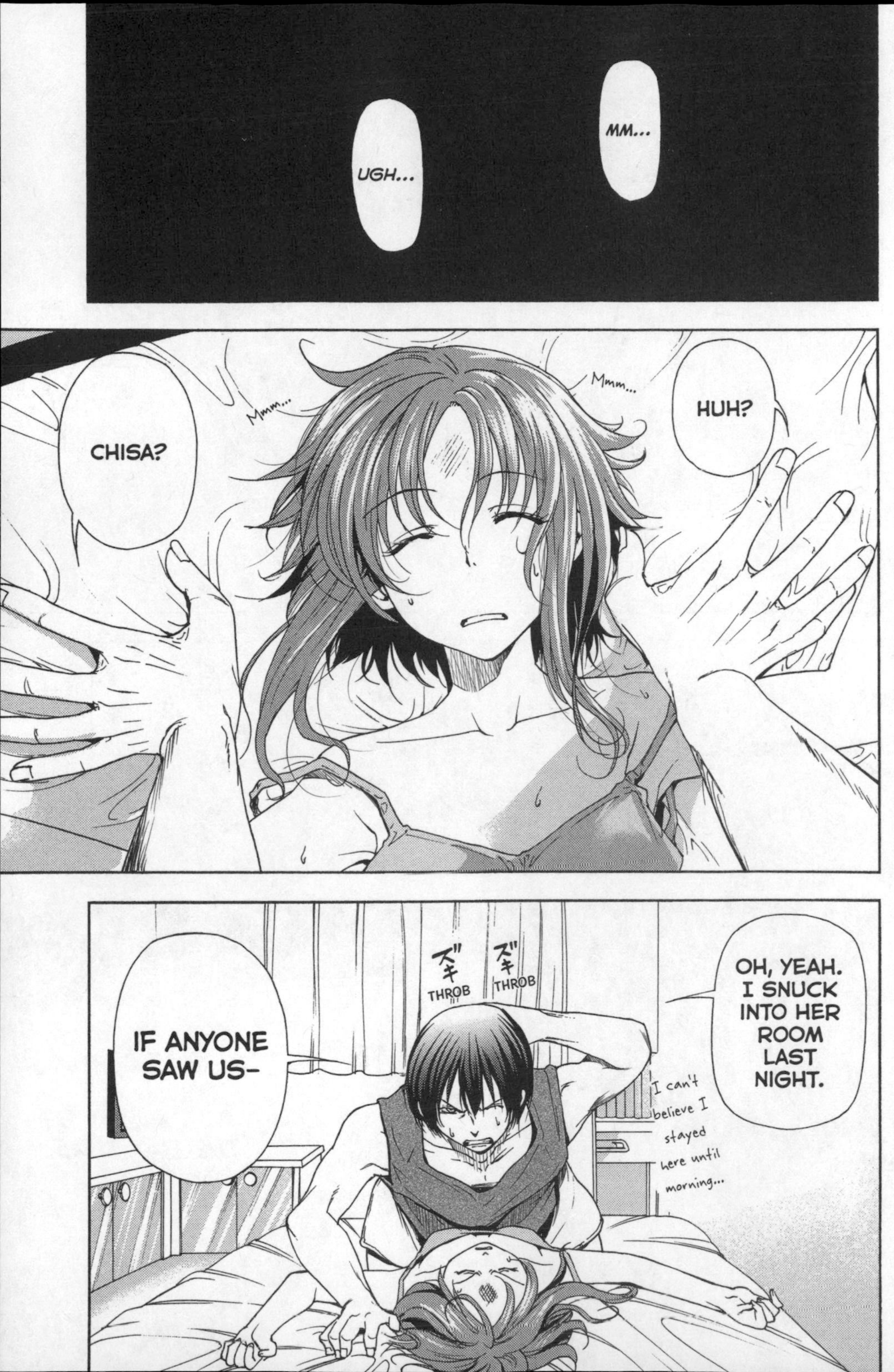
MM...
UGH...
HUH?
Mmm...
Mmm...
CHISA?
OH, YEAH. I SNUCK INTO HER ROOM LAST NIGHT.
I can't believe I stayed here until morning...
ズキ THROB
ズキ THROB
IF ANYONE SAW US-

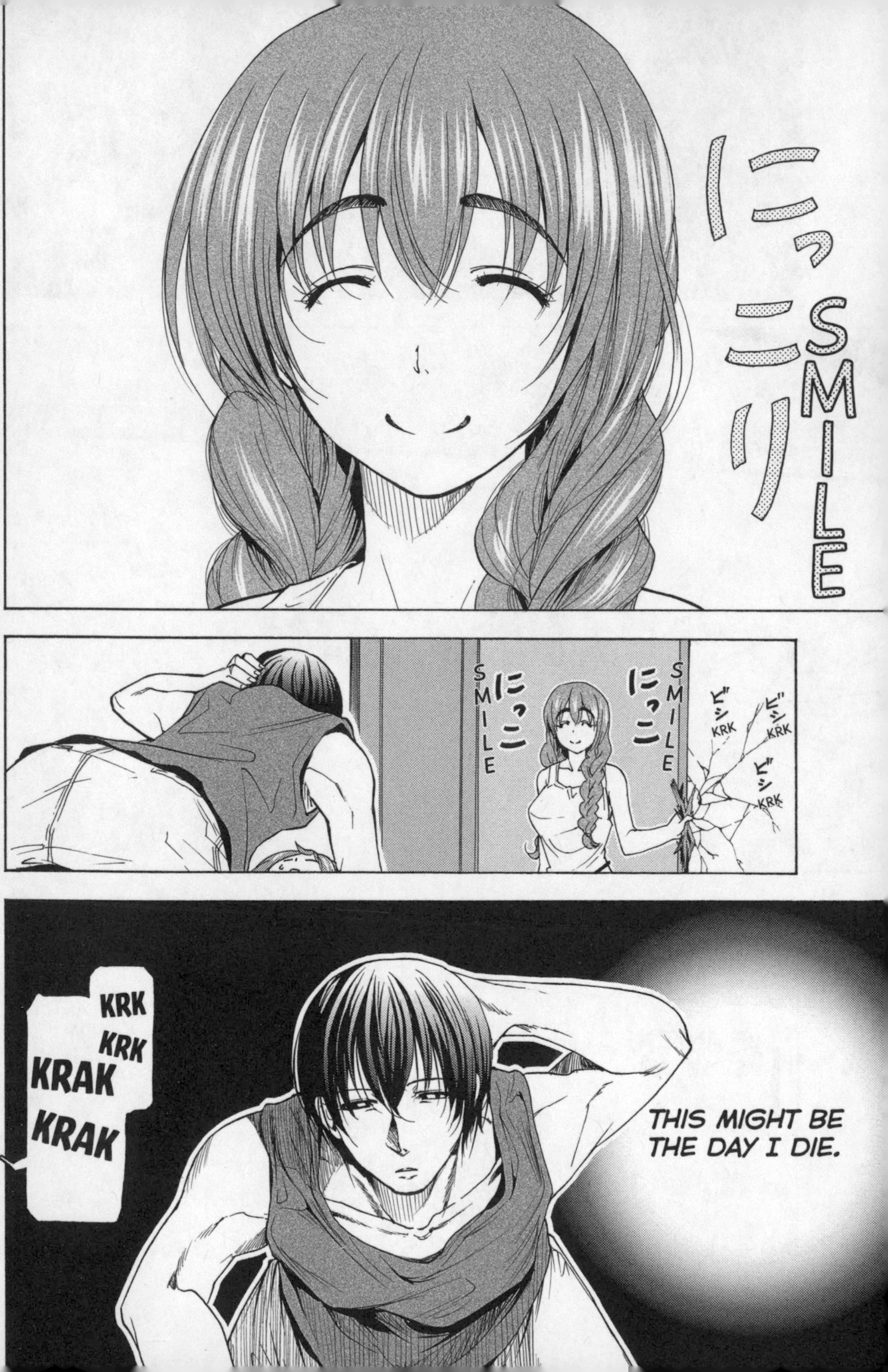
にっこり
SMILE
ビシ KRK
ビシ KRK
ビシ KRK
にっこ
SMILE
にっこ
SMILE
THIS MIGHT BE THE DAY I DIE.
KRK KRK KRAK KRAK

Ch. 27 Little Sister

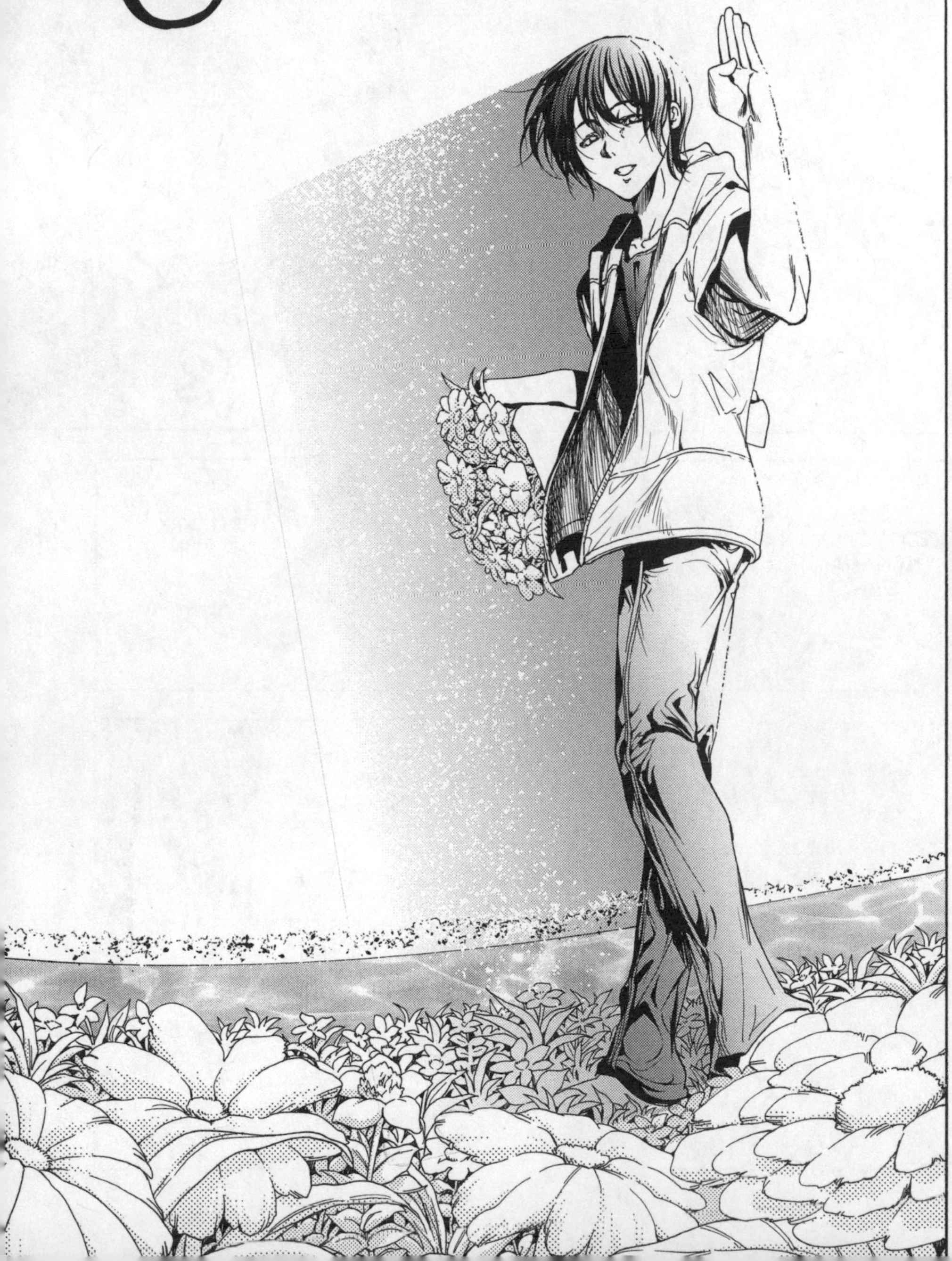

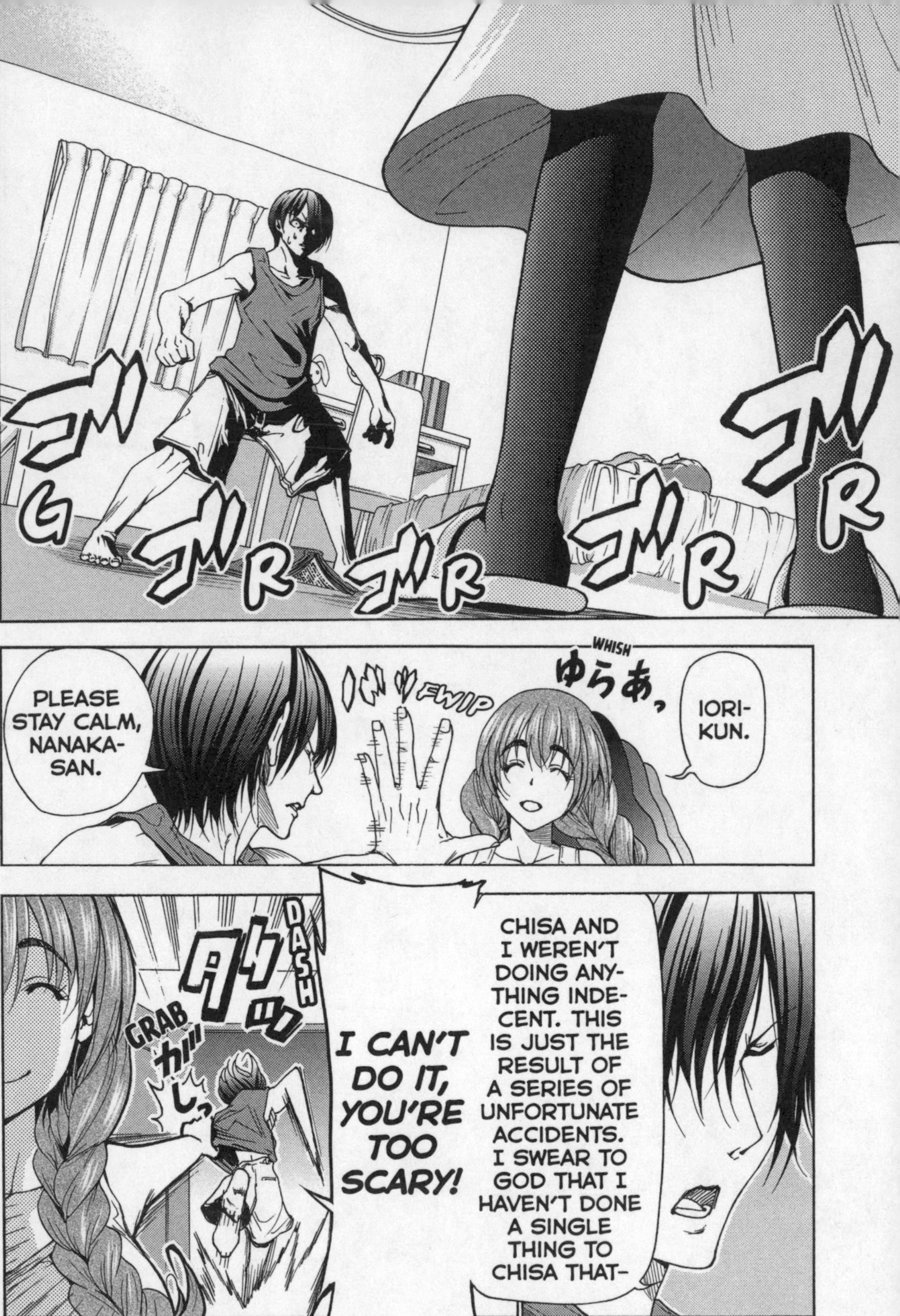
R
R
R
R
G
WHISH
ゆらあっ
IORI-KUN.
FWIP
PLEASE STAY CALM, NANAKA-SAN.
CHISA AND I WEREN'T DOING ANY-THING INDE-CENT. THIS IS JUST THE RESULT OF A SERIES OF UNFORTUNATE ACCIDENTS. I SWEAR TO GOD THAT I HAVEN'T DONE A SINGLE THING TO CHISA THAT-
I CAN'T DO IT, YOU'RE TOO SCARY!
DASH
GRAB

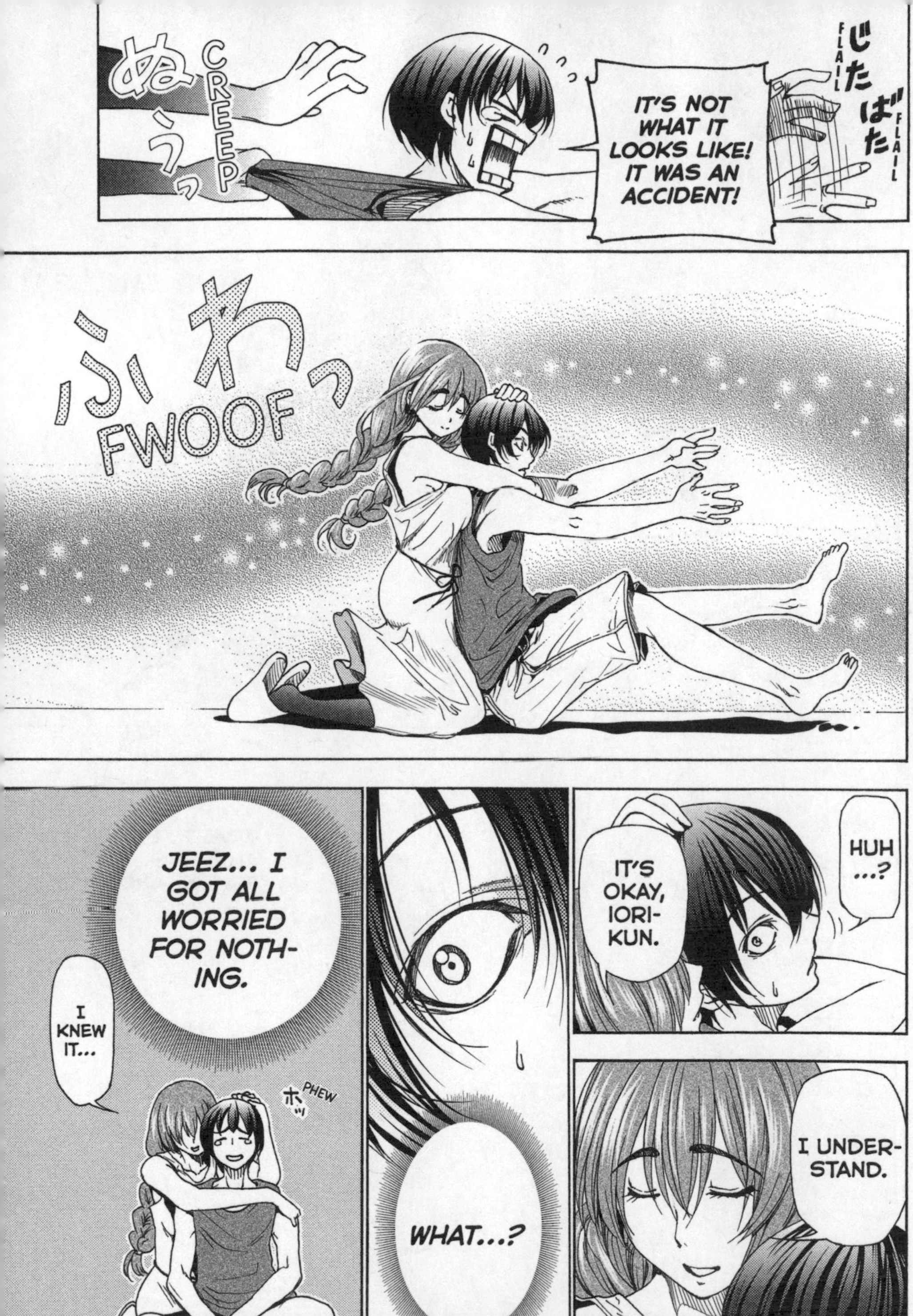
じたばた
FLAIL FLAIL
IT'S NOT WHAT IT LOOKS LIKE! IT WAS AN ACCIDENT!
ぬうっ
CREEP
ふわっ
FWOOF
HUH ...?
IT'S OKAY, IORI-KUN.
I UNDER-STAND.
WHAT...?
JEEZ... I GOT ALL WORRIED FOR NOTH-ING.
I KNEW IT...
ホッ
PHEW

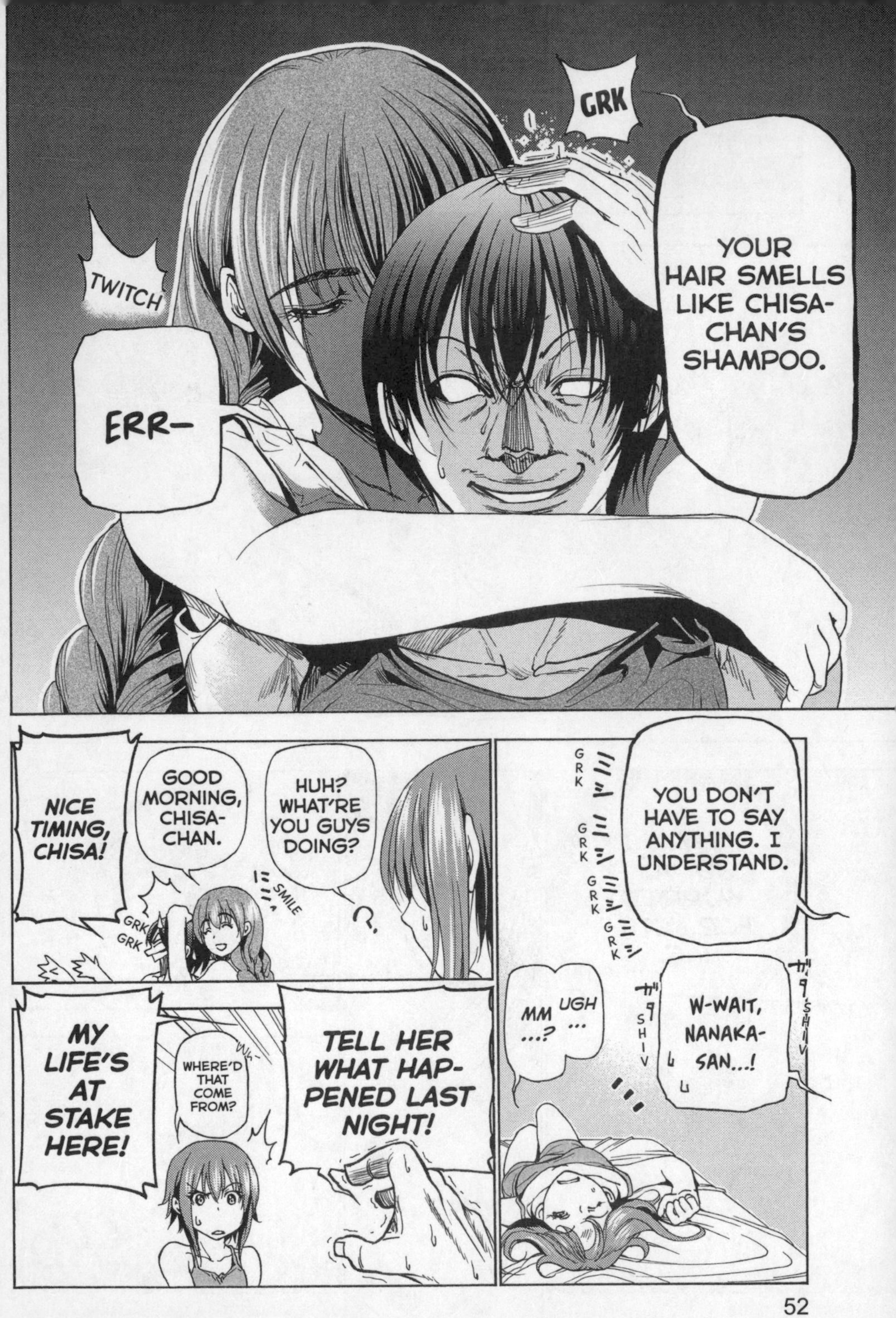
GRK
YOUR HAIR SMELLS LIKE CHISA-CHAN'S SHAMPOO.
TWITCH
ERR–
YOU DON'T HAVE TO SAY ANYTHING. I UNDERSTAND.
GRK GRK GRK GRK GRK
W-WAIT, NANAKA-SAN...!
SHIV
SHIV
UGH...
MM...?
HUH? WHAT'RE YOU GUYS DOING?
GOOD MORNING, CHISA-CHAN.
SMILE
NICE TIMING, CHISA!
GRK GRK
TELL HER WHAT HAPPENED LAST NIGHT!
WHERE'D THAT COME FROM?
MY LIFE'S AT STAKE HERE!

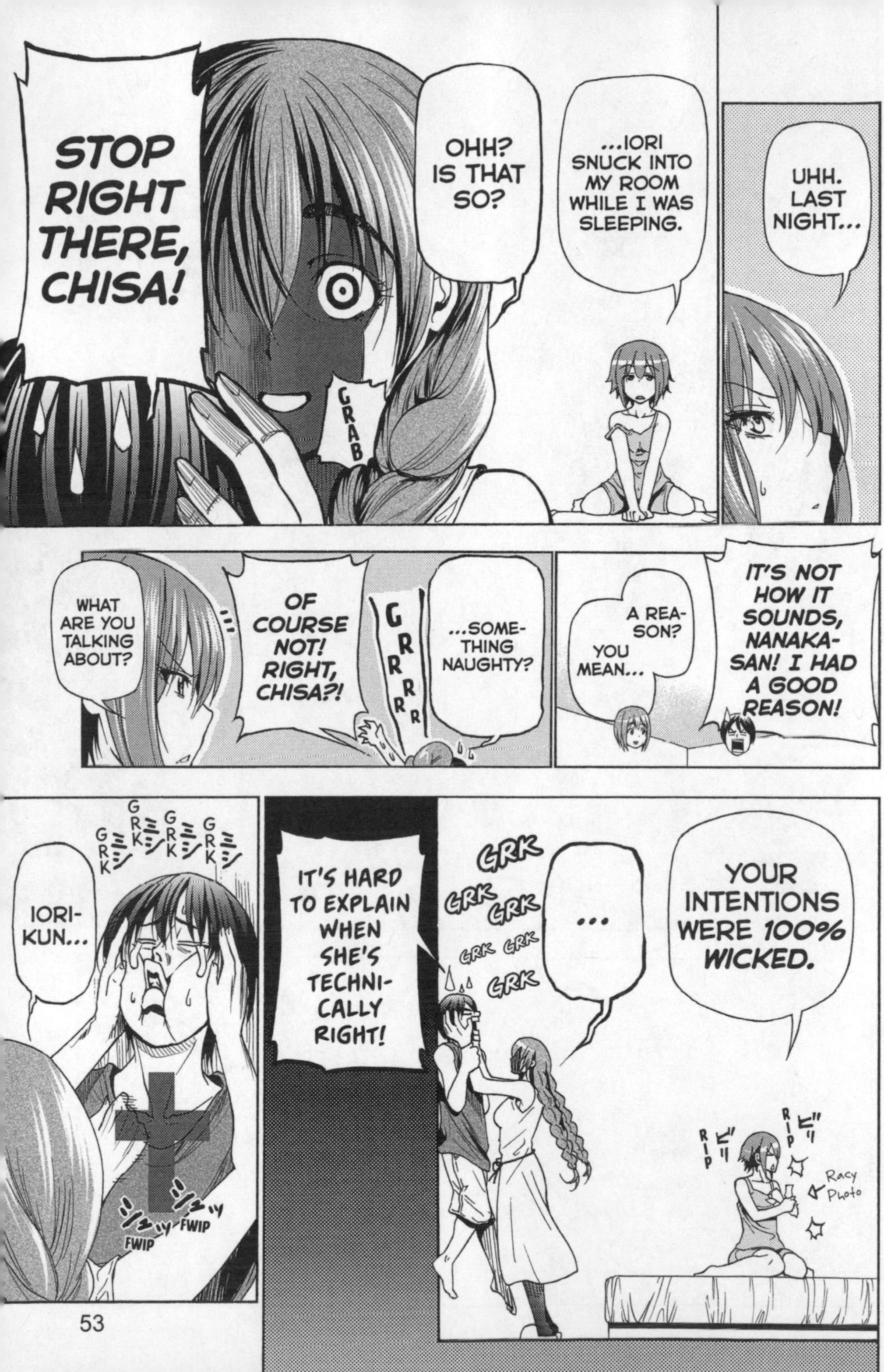
UHH. LAST NIGHT...
...IORI SNUCK INTO MY ROOM WHILE I WAS SLEEPING.
OHH? IS THAT SO?
STOP RIGHT THERE, CHISA!
GRAB
IT'S NOT HOW IT SOUNDS, NANAKA-SAN! I HAD A GOOD REASON!
A REA-SON? YOU MEAN...
...SOME-THING NAUGHTY?
GRRRRR
OF COURSE NOT! RIGHT, CHISA?!
WHAT ARE YOU TALKING ABOUT?
YOUR INTENTIONS WERE 100% WICKED.
RIP
RIP
Racy Photo
...
GRK
GRK GRK
GRK GRK
GRK
IT'S HARD TO EXPLAIN WHEN SHE'S TECHNI-CALLY RIGHT!
GRK GRK GRK
IORI-KUN...
FWIP FWIP

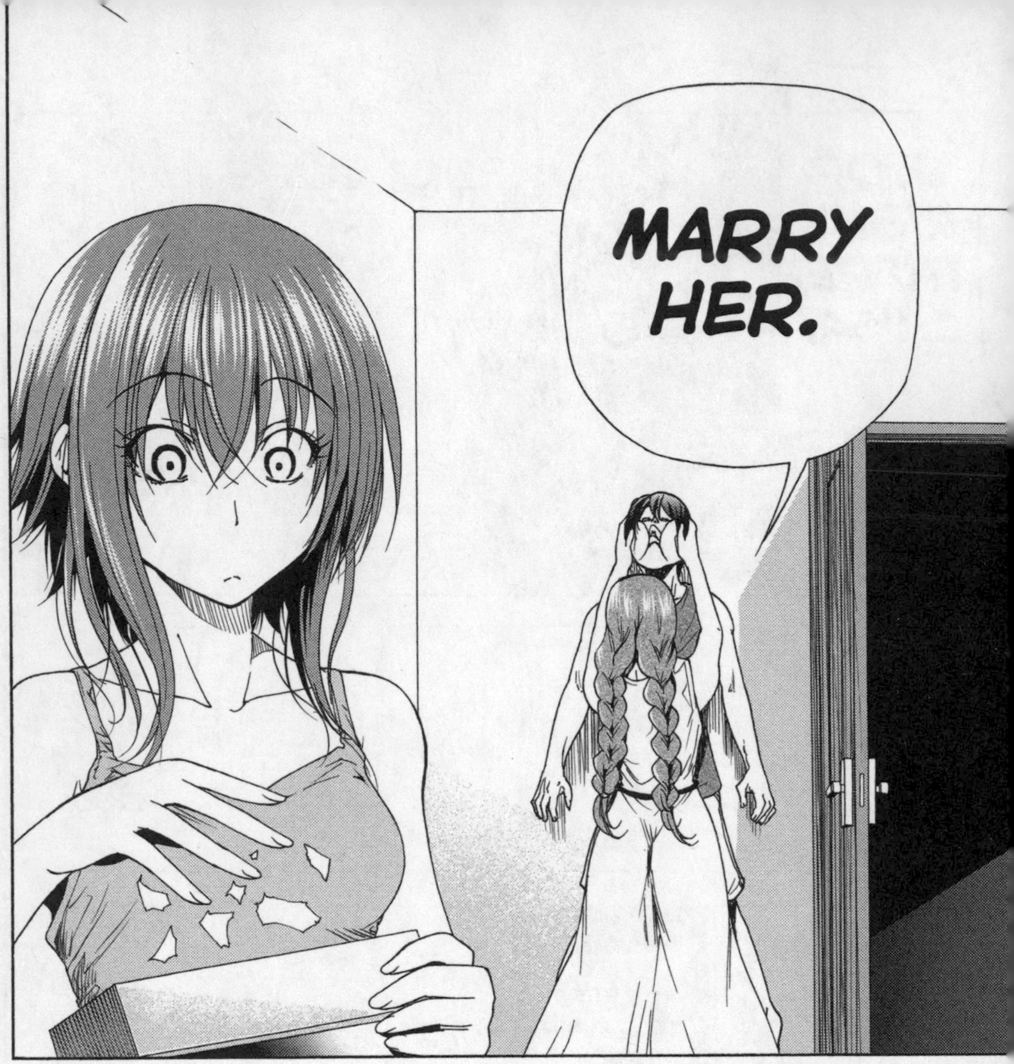
MARRY HER.
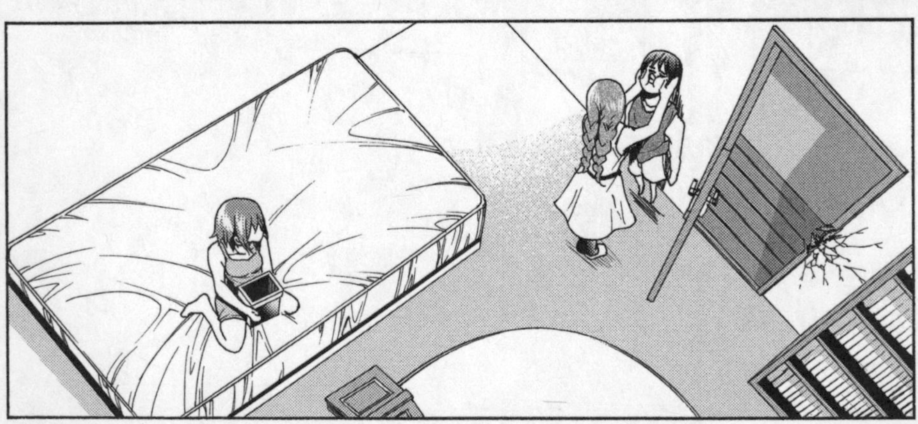

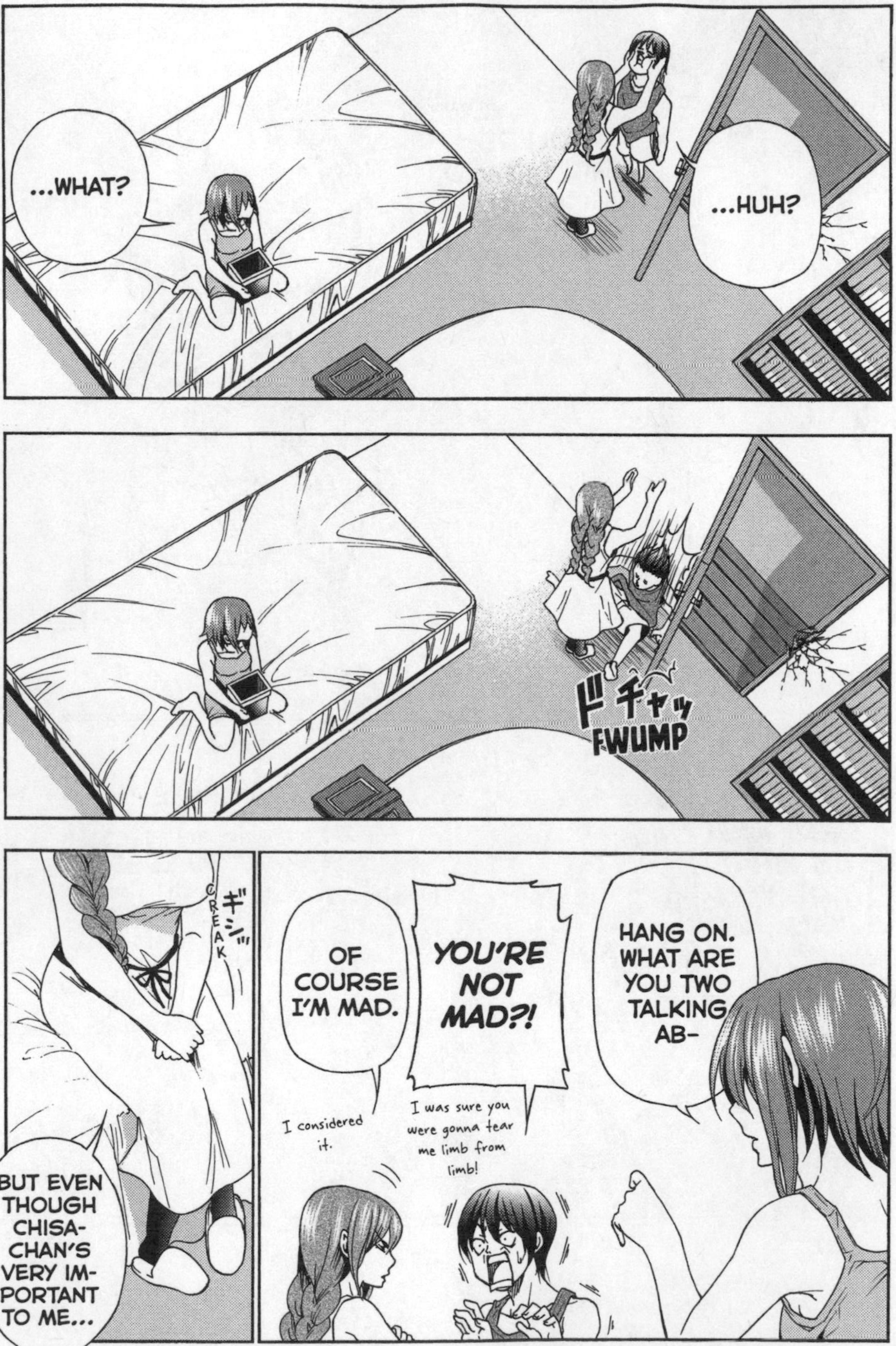
...HUH?
...WHAT?
ドチャッ
FWUMP
HANG ON. WHAT ARE YOU TWO TALKING AB-
YOU'RE NOT MAD?!
I was sure you were gonna tear me limb from limb!
OF COURSE I'M MAD.
I considered it.
ギシッ
CREAK
BUT EVEN THOUGH CHISA-CHAN'S VERY IMPORTANT TO ME...

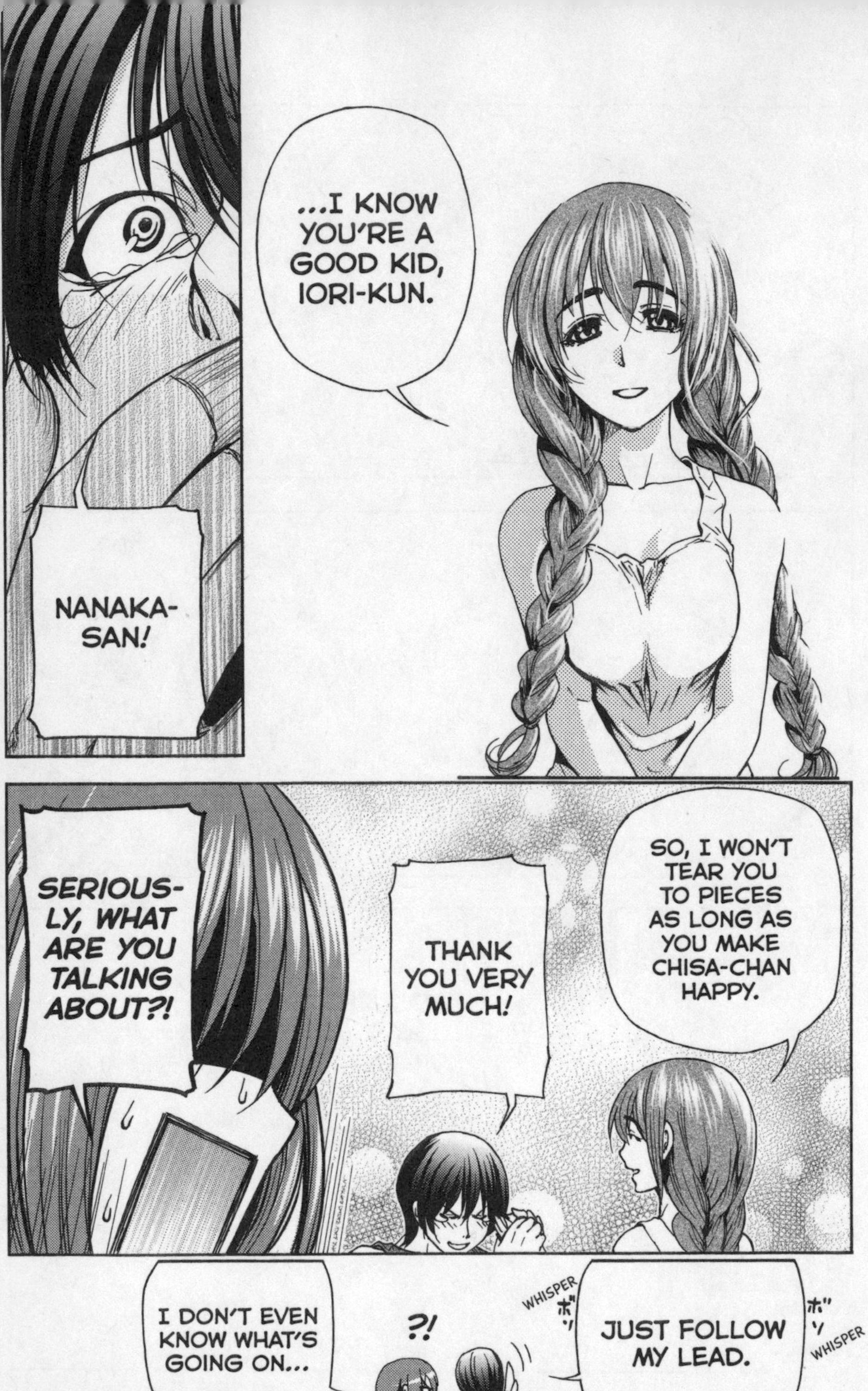
...I KNOW YOU'RE A GOOD KID, IORI-KUN.
NANAKA-SAN!
SO, I WON'T TEAR YOU TO PIECES AS LONG AS YOU MAKE CHISA-CHAN HAPPY.
THANK YOU VERY MUCH!
SERIOUSLY, WHAT ARE YOU TALKING ABOUT?!
ボソ
WHISPER
JUST FOLLOW MY LEAD.
ボソ
WHISPER
?!
I DON'T EVEN KNOW WHAT'S GOING ON...

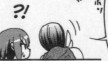

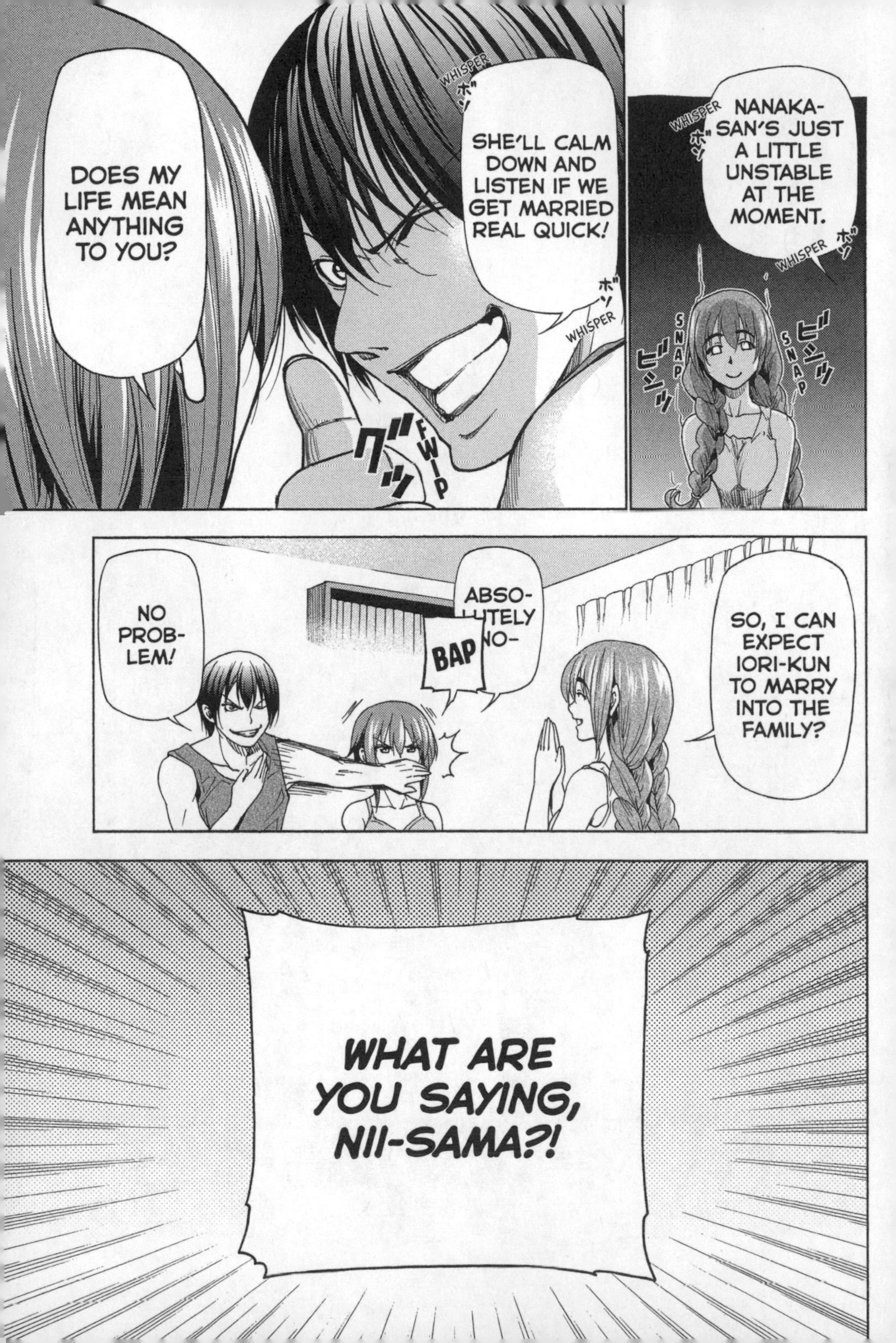
WHISPER ボソ
NANAKA-SAN'S JUST A LITTLE UNSTABLE AT THE MOMENT.
WHISPER ボソ
SNAP ビシッ
SNAP ビシッ
WHISPER ボソ
SHE'LL CALM DOWN AND LISTEN IF WE GET MARRIED REAL QUICK!
ボソ WHISPER
DOES MY LIFE MEAN ANYTHING TO YOU?
グッ FWIP
SO, I CAN EXPECT IORI-KUN TO MARRY INTO THE FAMILY?
ABSO-LUTELY NO-
BAP
NO PROB-LEM!
WHAT ARE YOU SAYING, NII-SAMA?!

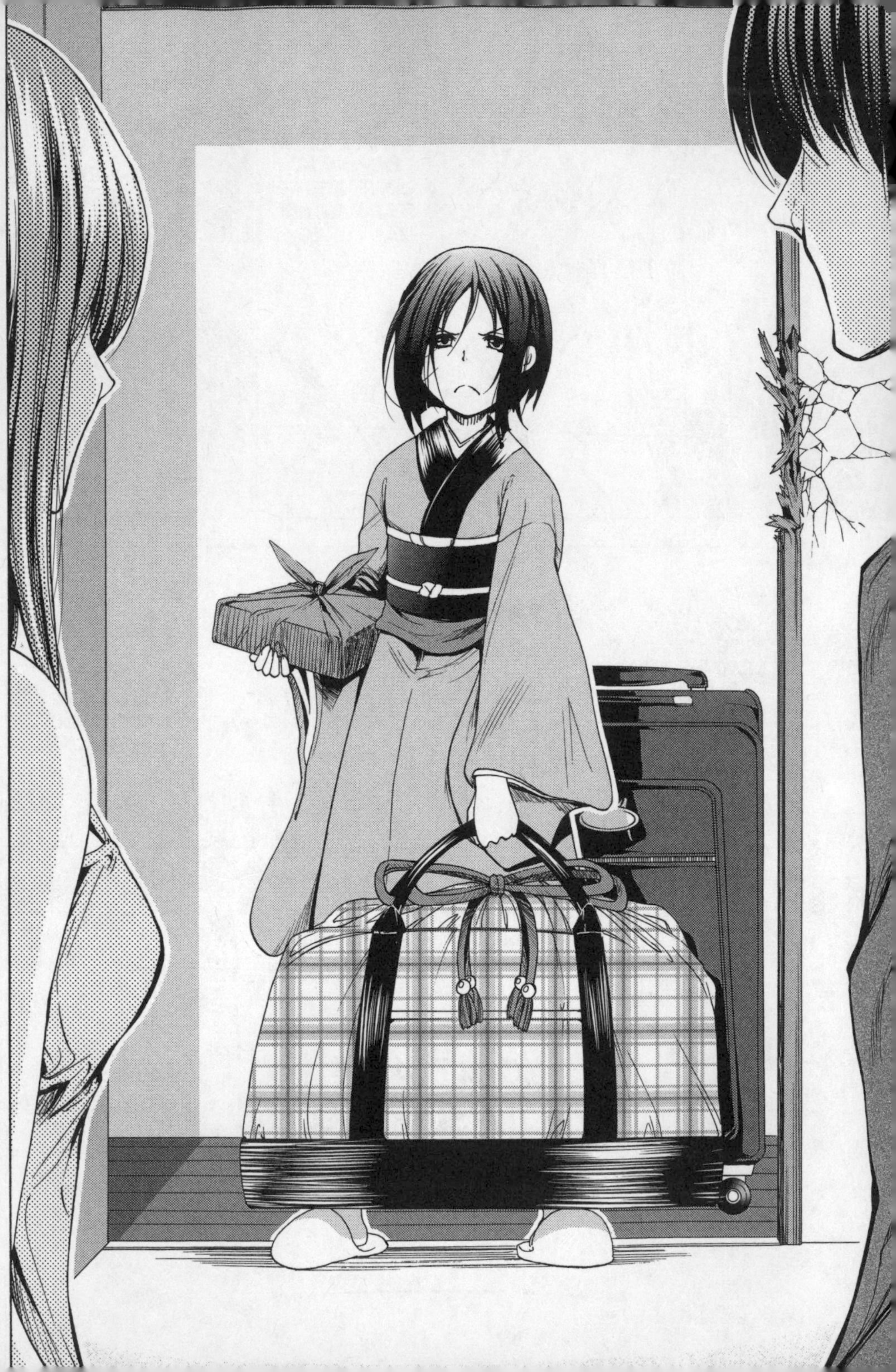

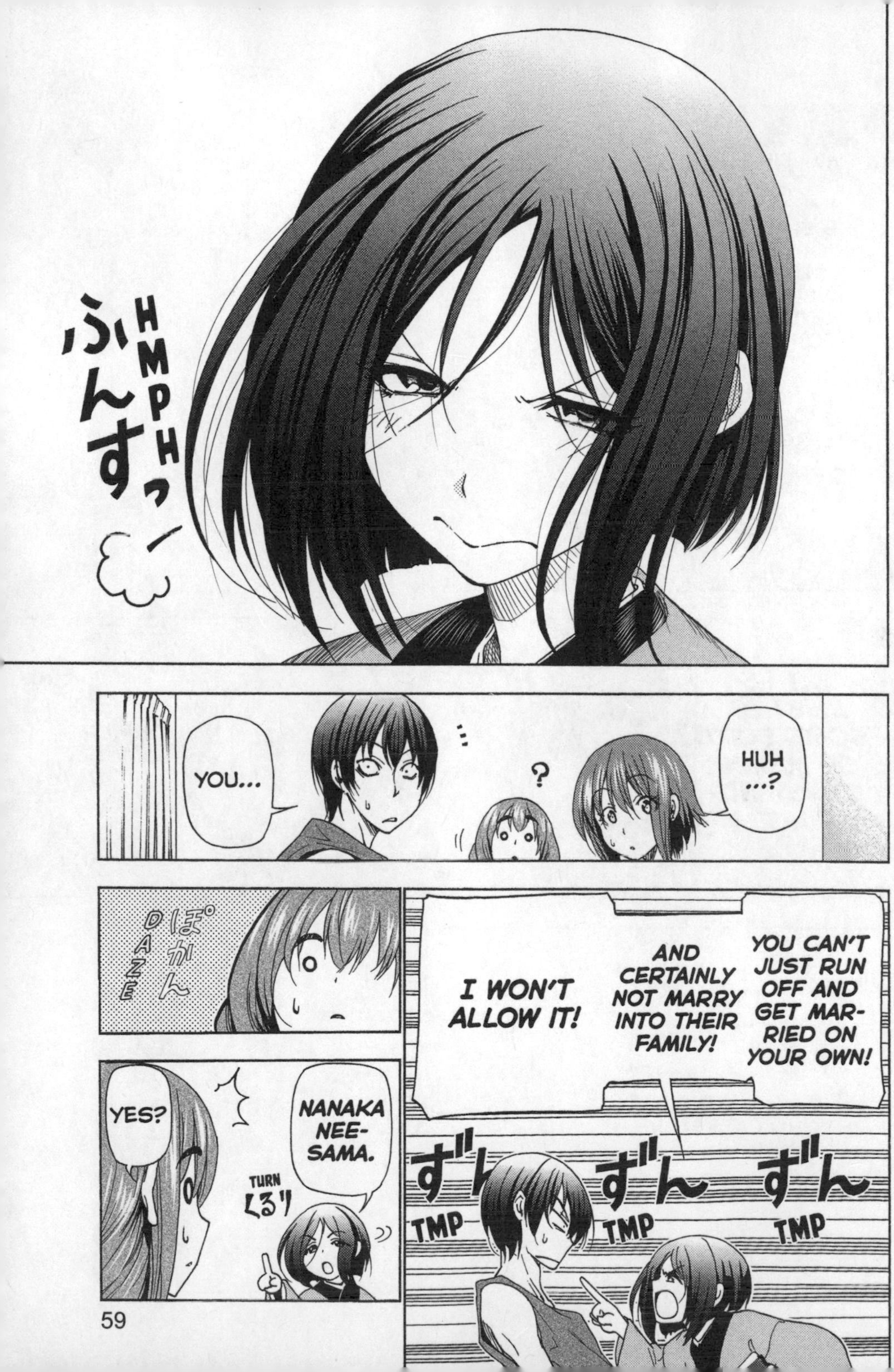
HMPH
ふんすっ
HUH ...?
?
YOU...
YOU CAN'T JUST RUN OFF AND GET MAR-RIED ON YOUR OWN!
AND CERTAINLY NOT MARRY INTO THEIR FAMILY!
I WON'T ALLOW IT!
ずん
TMP
ずん
TMP
ずん
TMP
DAZE
ぽかん
NANAKA NEE-SAMA.
TURN
くるり
YES?

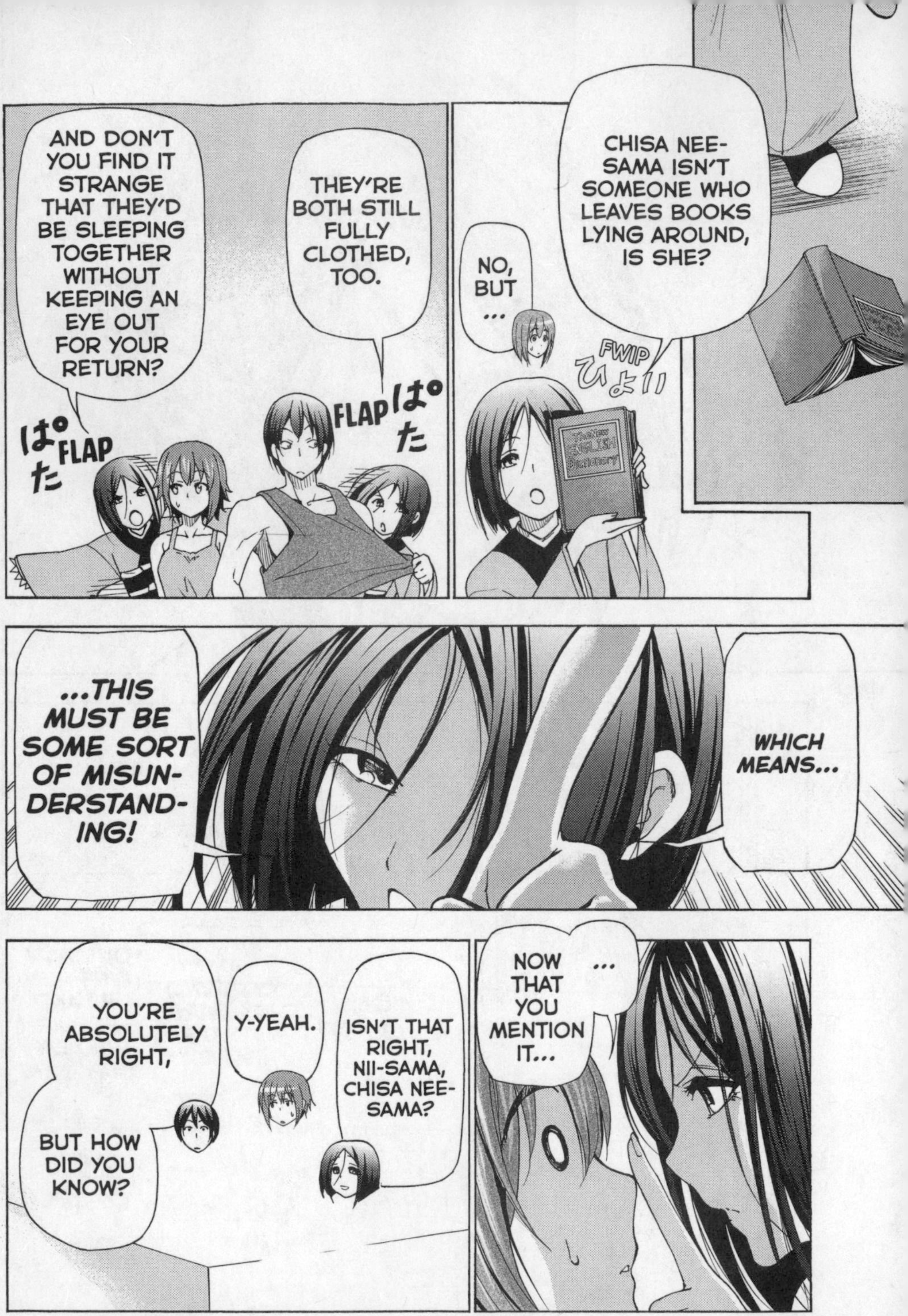
CHISA NEE-SAMA ISN'T SOMEONE WHO LEAVES BOOKS LYING AROUND, IS SHE?
NO, BUT...
FWIP ひょい
The New ENGLISH Dictionary
THEY'RE BOTH STILL FULLY CLOTHED, TOO.
FLAP ぱた
AND DON'T YOU FIND IT STRANGE THAT THEY'D BE SLEEPING TOGETHER WITHOUT KEEPING AN EYE OUT FOR YOUR RETURN?
ぱた FLAP
WHICH MEANS...
...THIS MUST BE SOME SORT OF MISUNDERSTANDING!
...
NOW THAT YOU MENTION IT...
ISN'T THAT RIGHT, NII-SAMA, CHISA NEE-SAMA?
Y-YEAH.
YOU'RE ABSOLUTELY RIGHT,
BUT HOW DID YOU KNOW?

JUST AN EDUCATED GUESS.

SMILE

IT'S ALMOST LIKE YOU SAW THE WHOLE THING.

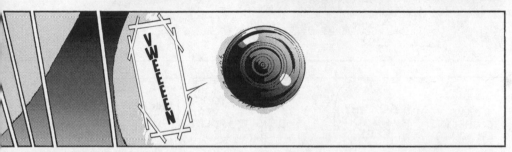

VWEEEEEN

AAH

IORI'S SISTER, HUH?

OOH

HUH...

Grand Blue

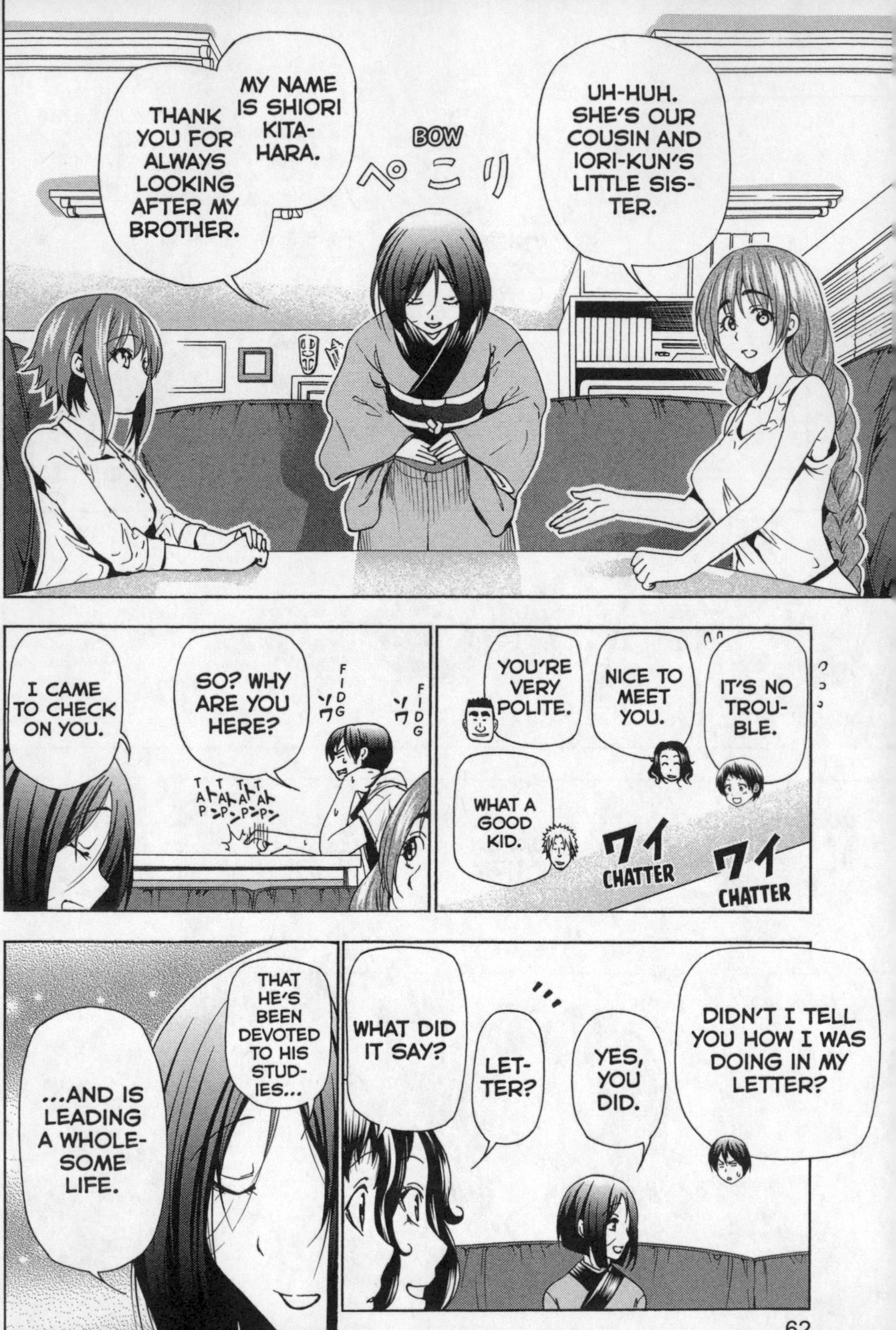
UH-HUH. SHE'S OUR COUSIN AND IORI-KUN'S LITTLE SIS-TER.
BOW
ぺこり
MY NAME IS SHIORI KITA-HARA.
THANK YOU FOR ALWAYS LOOKING AFTER MY BROTHER.
IT'S NO TROU-BLE.
NICE TO MEET YOU.
YOU'RE VERY POLITE.
WHAT A GOOD KID.
ワイ CHATTER
ワイ CHATTER
FIDG ソワ
FIDG ソワ
SO? WHY ARE YOU HERE?
TAP TAP TAP TAP
I CAME TO CHECK ON YOU.
DIDN'T I TELL YOU HOW I WAS DOING IN MY LETTER?
YES, YOU DID.
...
LET-TER?
WHAT DID IT SAY?
THAT HE'S BEEN DEVOTED TO HIS STUD-IES...
...AND IS LEADING A WHOLE-SOME LIFE.

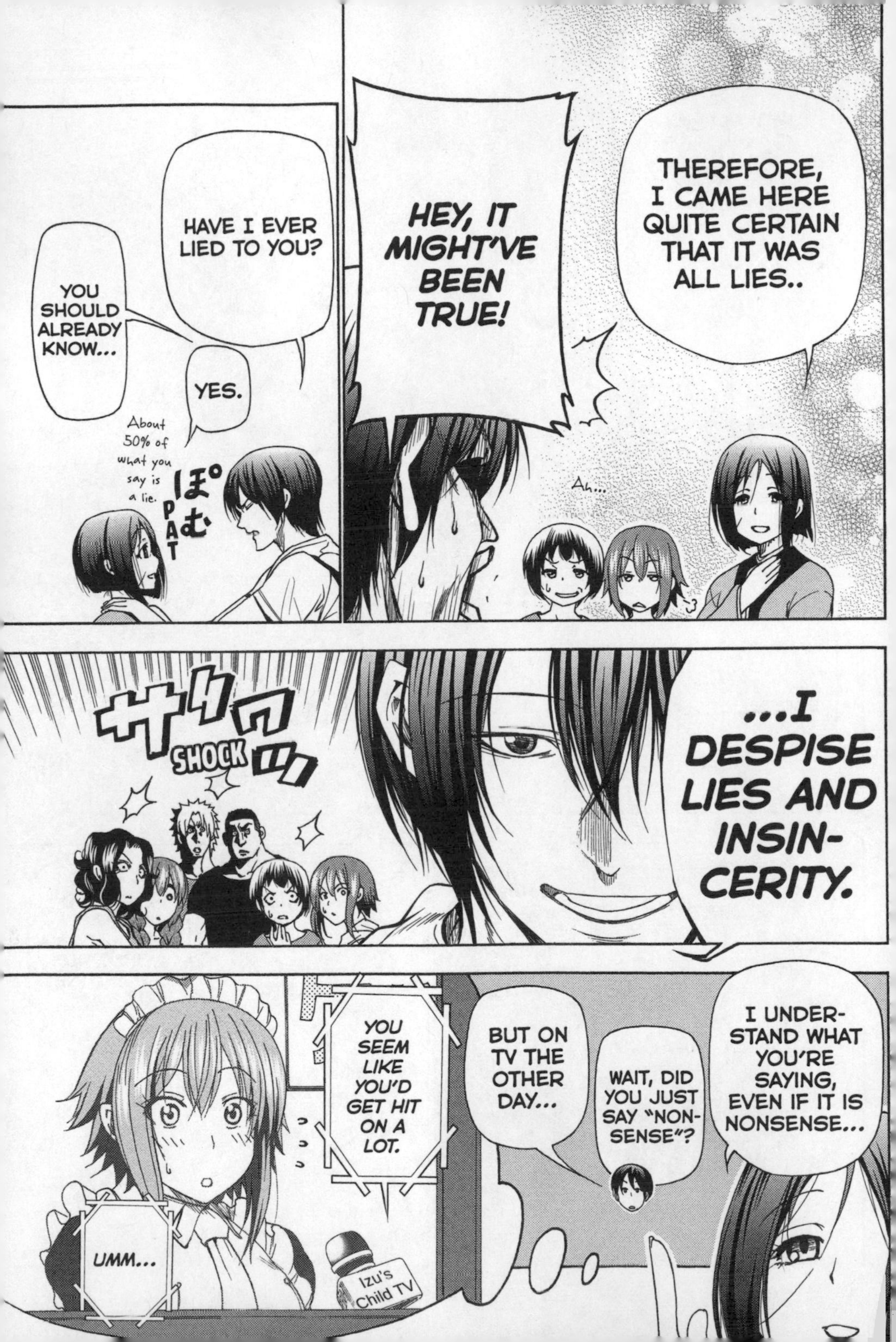
THEREFORE, I CAME HERE QUITE CERTAIN THAT IT WAS ALL LIES..
HEY, IT MIGHT'VE BEEN TRUE!
Ah...
HAVE I EVER LIED TO YOU?
YES.
YOU SHOULD ALREADY KNOW...
About 50% of what you say is a lie.
ぽむ
PAT
...I DESPISE LIES AND INSIN-CERITY.
SHOCK
I UNDER-STAND WHAT YOU'RE SAYING, EVEN IF IT IS NONSENSE...
WAIT, DID YOU JUST SAY "NON-SENSE"?
BUT ON TV THE OTHER DAY...
YOU SEEM LIKE YOU'D GET HIT ON A LOT.
UMM...
Izu's Child TV

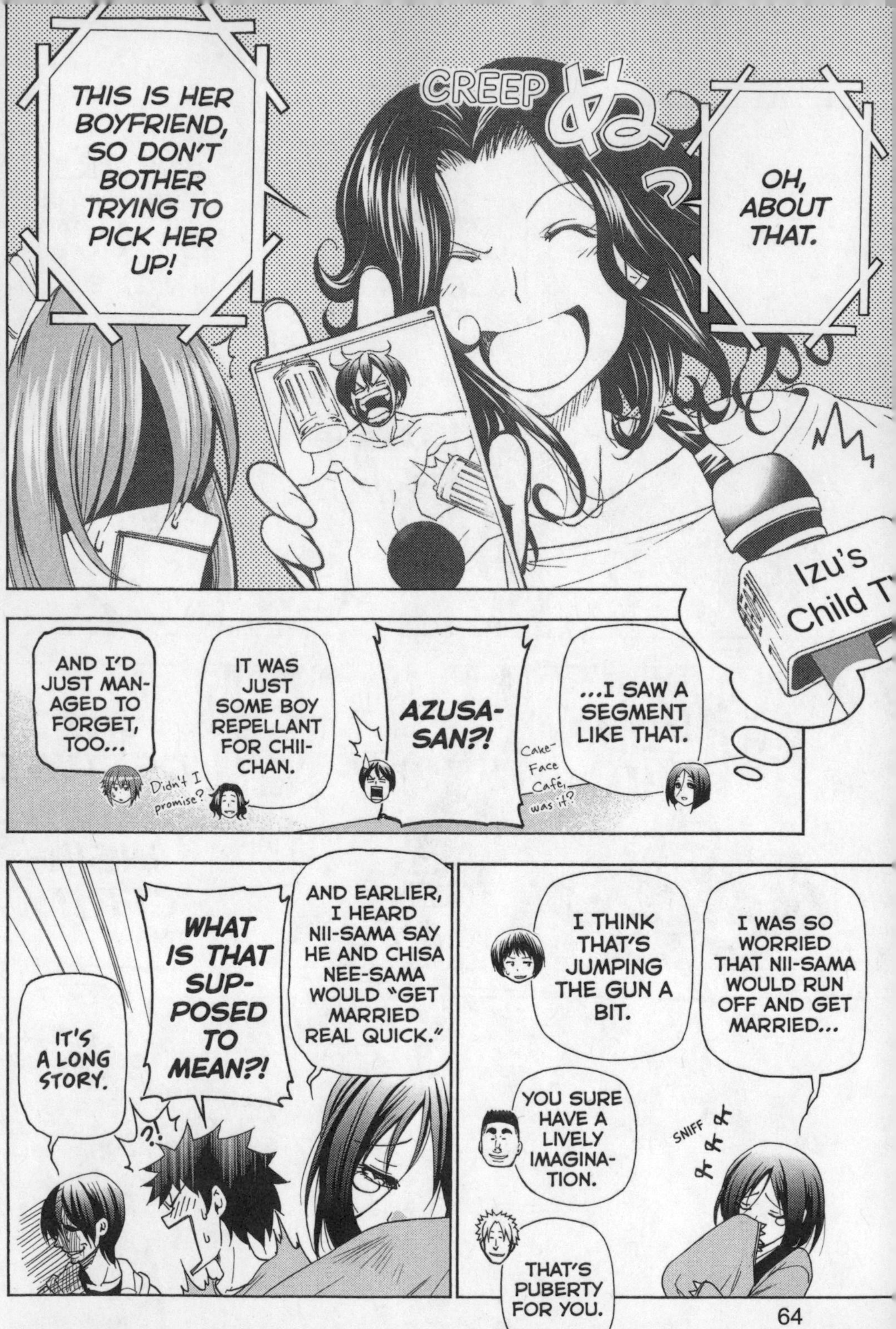
OH, ABOUT THAT.
CREEP
ぬっ
THIS IS HER BOYFRIEND, SO DON'T BOTHER TRYING TO PICK HER UP!
Izu's Child T
...I SAW A SEGMENT LIKE THAT.
Cake-Face Café, was it?
AZUSA-SAN?!
IT WAS JUST SOME BOY REPELLANT FOR CHII-CHAN.
Didn't I promise?
AND I'D JUST MAN-AGED TO FORGET, TOO...
I WAS SO WORRIED THAT NII-SAMA WOULD RUN OFF AND GET MARRIED...
I THINK THAT'S JUMPING THE GUN A BIT.
YOU SURE HAVE A LIVELY IMAGINA-TION.
SNIFF
THAT'S PUBERTY FOR YOU.
AND EARLIER, I HEARD NII-SAMA SAY HE AND CHISA NEE-SAMA WOULD "GET MARRIED REAL QUICK."
WHAT IS THAT SUP-POSED TO MEAN?!
?!
IT'S A LONG STORY.

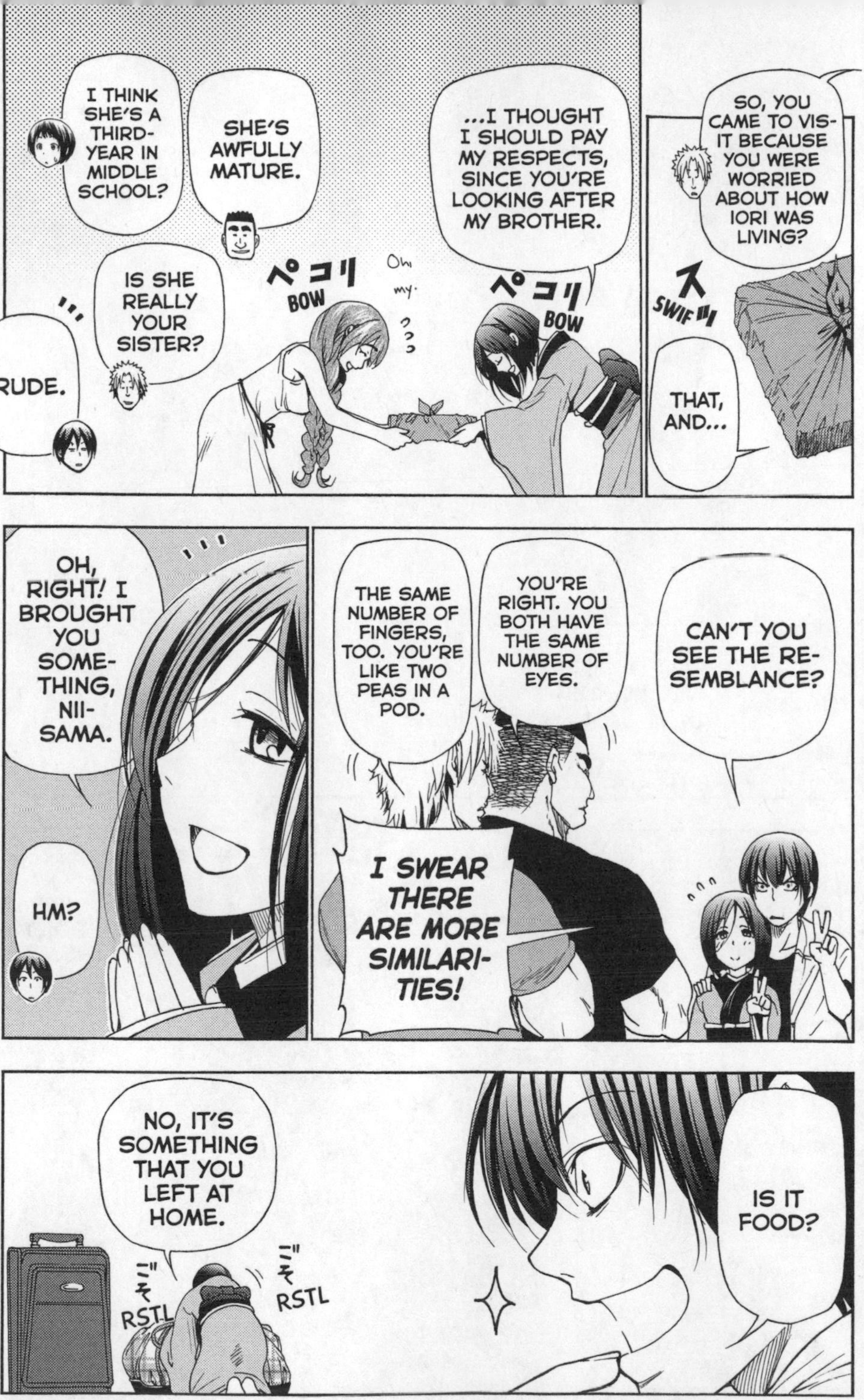
SO, YOU CAME TO VIS-IT BECAUSE YOU WERE WORRIED ABOUT HOW IORI WAS LIVING?
SWIF
THAT, AND...
...I THOUGHT I SHOULD PAY MY RESPECTS, SINCE YOU'RE LOOKING AFTER MY BROTHER.
ペコリ BOW
Oh my.
ペコリ BOW
SHE'S AWFULLY MATURE.
I THINK SHE'S A THIRD-YEAR IN MIDDLE SCHOOL?
IS SHE REALLY YOUR SISTER?
RUDE.
CAN'T YOU SEE THE RE-SEMBLANCE?
YOU'RE RIGHT. YOU BOTH HAVE THE SAME NUMBER OF EYES.
THE SAME NUMBER OF FINGERS, TOO. YOU'RE LIKE TWO PEAS IN A POD.
I SWEAR THERE ARE MORE SIMILARI-TIES!
OH, RIGHT! I BROUGHT YOU SOME-THING, NII-SAMA.
HM?
IS IT FOOD?
ごそ RSTL
NO, IT'S SOMETHING THAT YOU LEFT AT HOME.
ごそ RSTL

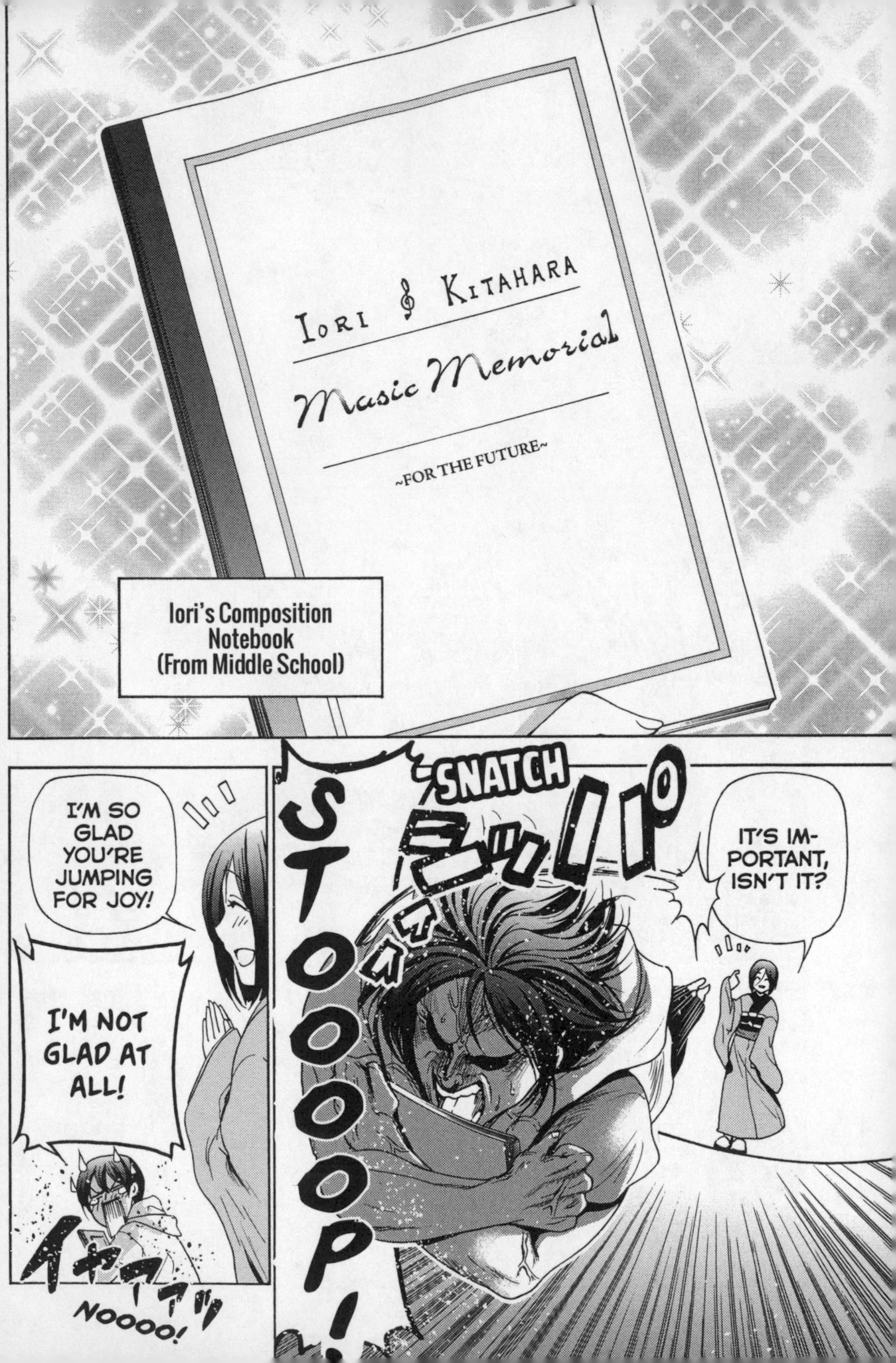
Iori 𝄞 Kitahara
Music Memorial
~FOR THE FUTURE~
Iori's Composition Notebook (From Middle School)
IT'S IM-PORTANT, ISN'T IT?
SNATCH
STOOOOP!
I'M SO GLAD YOU'RE JUMPING FOR JOY!
I'M NOT GLAD AT ALL!
NOOOO!

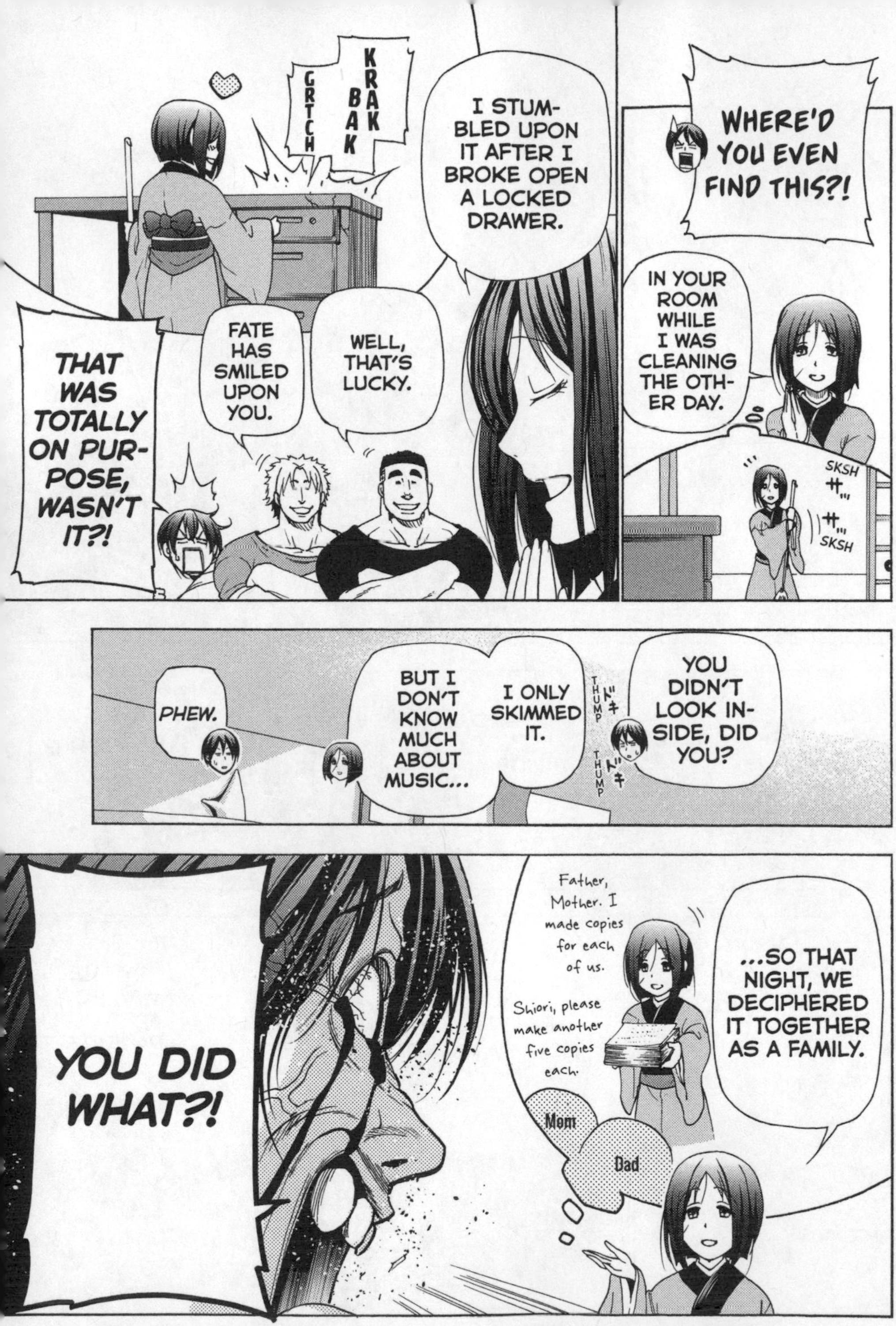

WHERE'D YOU EVEN FIND THIS?!
IN YOUR ROOM WHILE I WAS CLEANING THE OTHER DAY.
SKSH
SKSH
I STUMBLED UPON IT AFTER I BROKE OPEN A LOCKED DRAWER.
KRAK
BAK
GRTCH
WELL, THAT'S LUCKY.
FATE HAS SMILED UPON YOU.
THAT WAS TOTALLY ON PURPOSE, WASN'T IT?!
YOU DIDN'T LOOK INSIDE, DID YOU?
THUMP
THUMP
I ONLY SKIMMED IT.
BUT I DON'T KNOW MUCH ABOUT MUSIC...
PHEW.
...SO THAT NIGHT, WE DECIPHERED IT TOGETHER AS A FAMILY.
Father, Mother. I made copies for each of us.
Shiori, please make another five copies each.
Mom
Dad
YOU DID WHAT?!

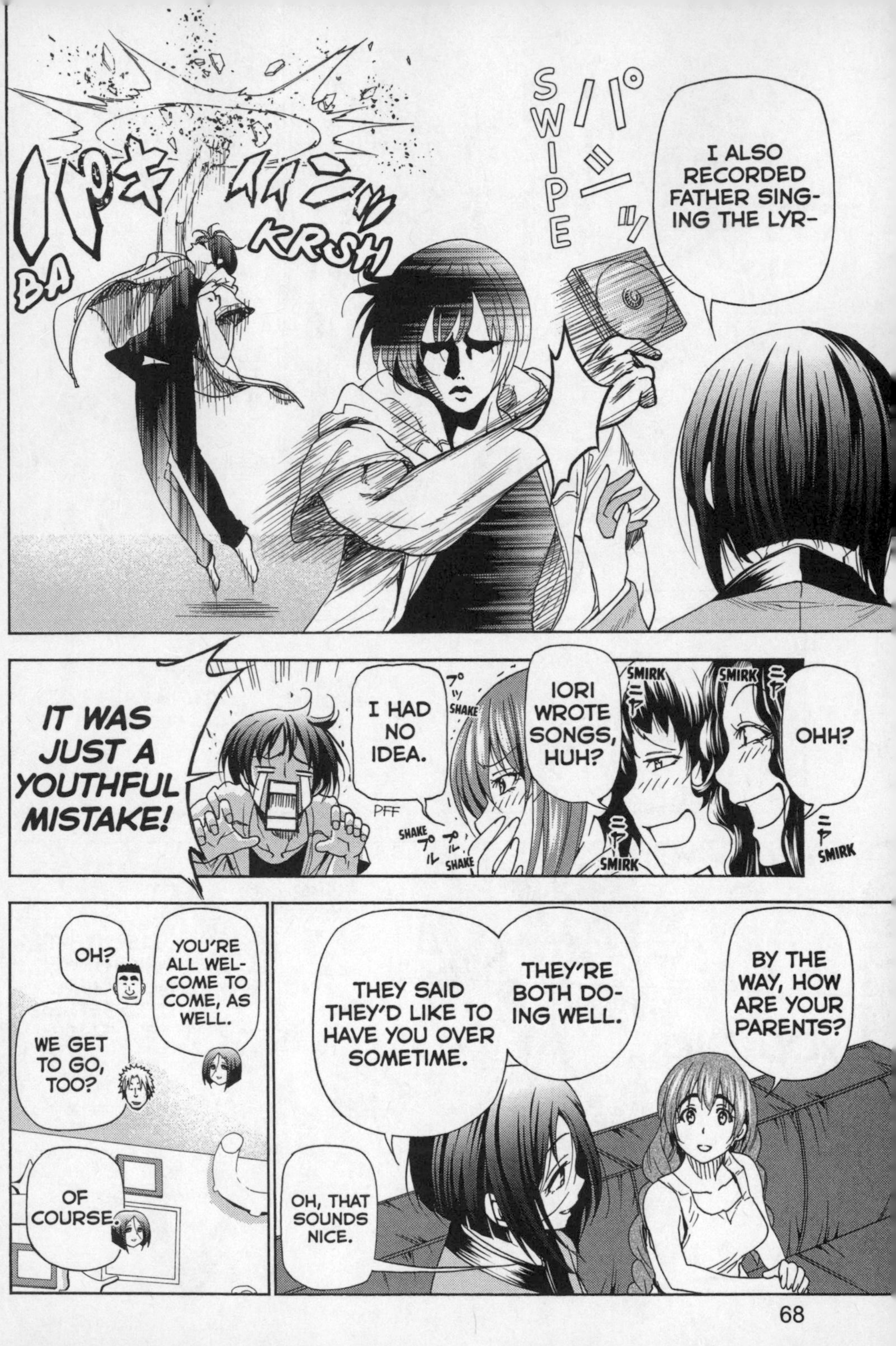
I ALSO RECORDED FATHER SINGING THE LYR-
SWIPE
KRSH
BA
OHH?
SMIRK
SMIRK
IORI WROTE SONGS, HUH?
SMIRK
SMIRK
SHAKE
I HAD NO IDEA.
SHAKE
SHAKE
PFF
IT WAS JUST A YOUTHFUL MISTAKE!
BY THE WAY, HOW ARE YOUR PARENTS?
THEY'RE BOTH DO-ING WELL.
THEY SAID THEY'D LIKE TO HAVE YOU OVER SOMETIME.
OH, THAT SOUNDS NICE.
YOU'RE ALL WEL-COME TO COME, AS WELL.
OH?
WE GET TO GO, TOO?
OF COURSE.

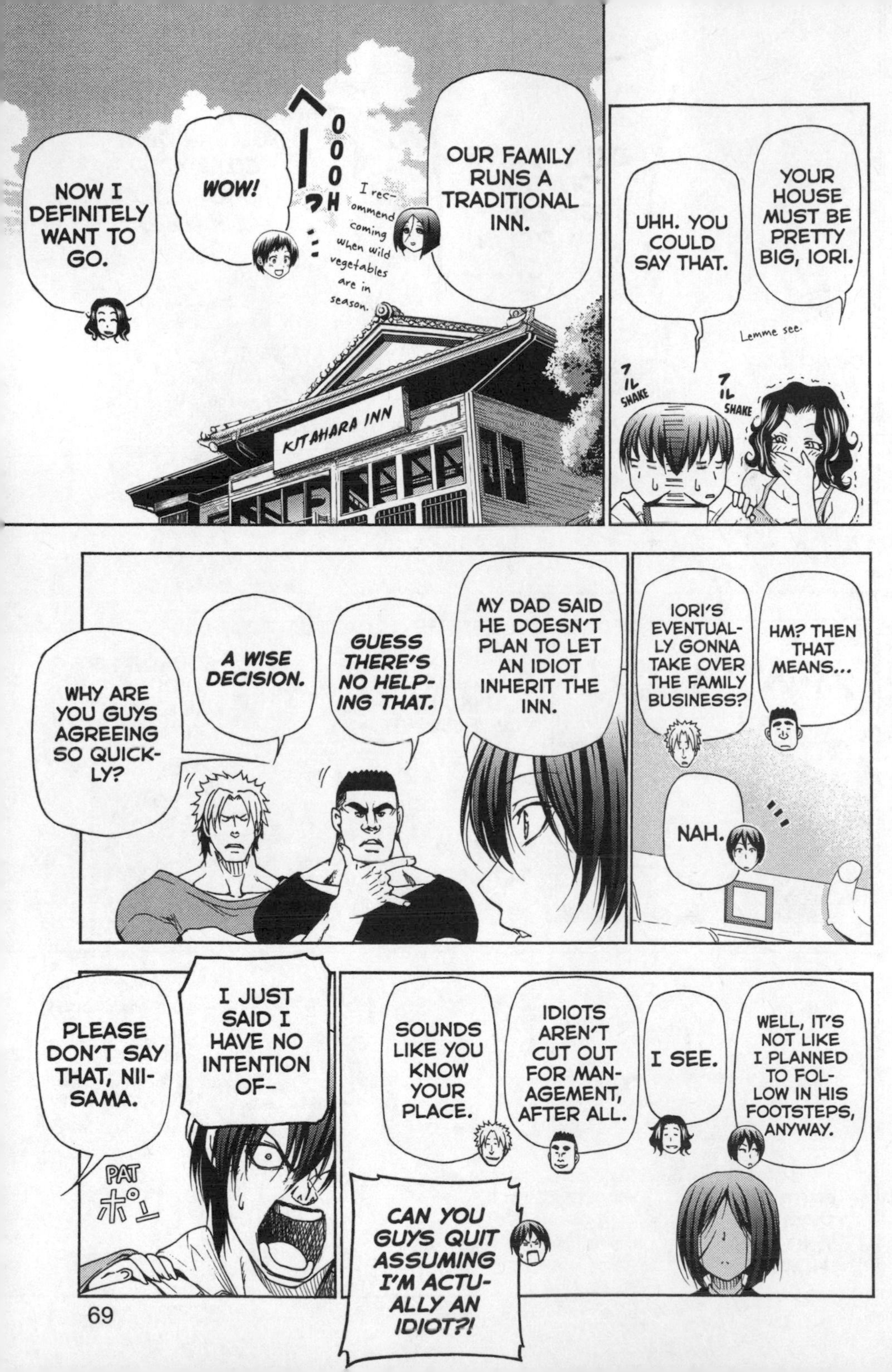
YOUR HOUSE MUST BE PRETTY BIG, IORI.
UHH. YOU COULD SAY THAT.
Lemme see.
フル SHAKE
フル SHAKE
OUR FAMILY RUNS A TRADITIONAL INN.
I recommend coming when wild vegetables are in season.
OOOH
WOW!
NOW I DEFINITELY WANT TO GO.
KITAHARA INN
HM? THEN THAT MEANS...
IORI'S EVENTUALLY GONNA TAKE OVER THE FAMILY BUSINESS?
NAH.
MY DAD SAID HE DOESN'T PLAN TO LET AN IDIOT INHERIT THE INN.
GUESS THERE'S NO HELPING THAT.
A WISE DECISION.
WHY ARE YOU GUYS AGREEING SO QUICKLY?
WELL, IT'S NOT LIKE I PLANNED TO FOLLOW IN HIS FOOTSTEPS, ANYWAY.
I SEE.
IDIOTS AREN'T CUT OUT FOR MANAGEMENT, AFTER ALL.
SOUNDS LIKE YOU KNOW YOUR PLACE.
CAN YOU GUYS QUIT ASSUMING I'M ACTUALLY AN IDIOT?!
I JUST SAID I HAVE NO INTENTION OF-
PLEASE DON'T SAY THAT, NII-SAMA.
PAT ポン

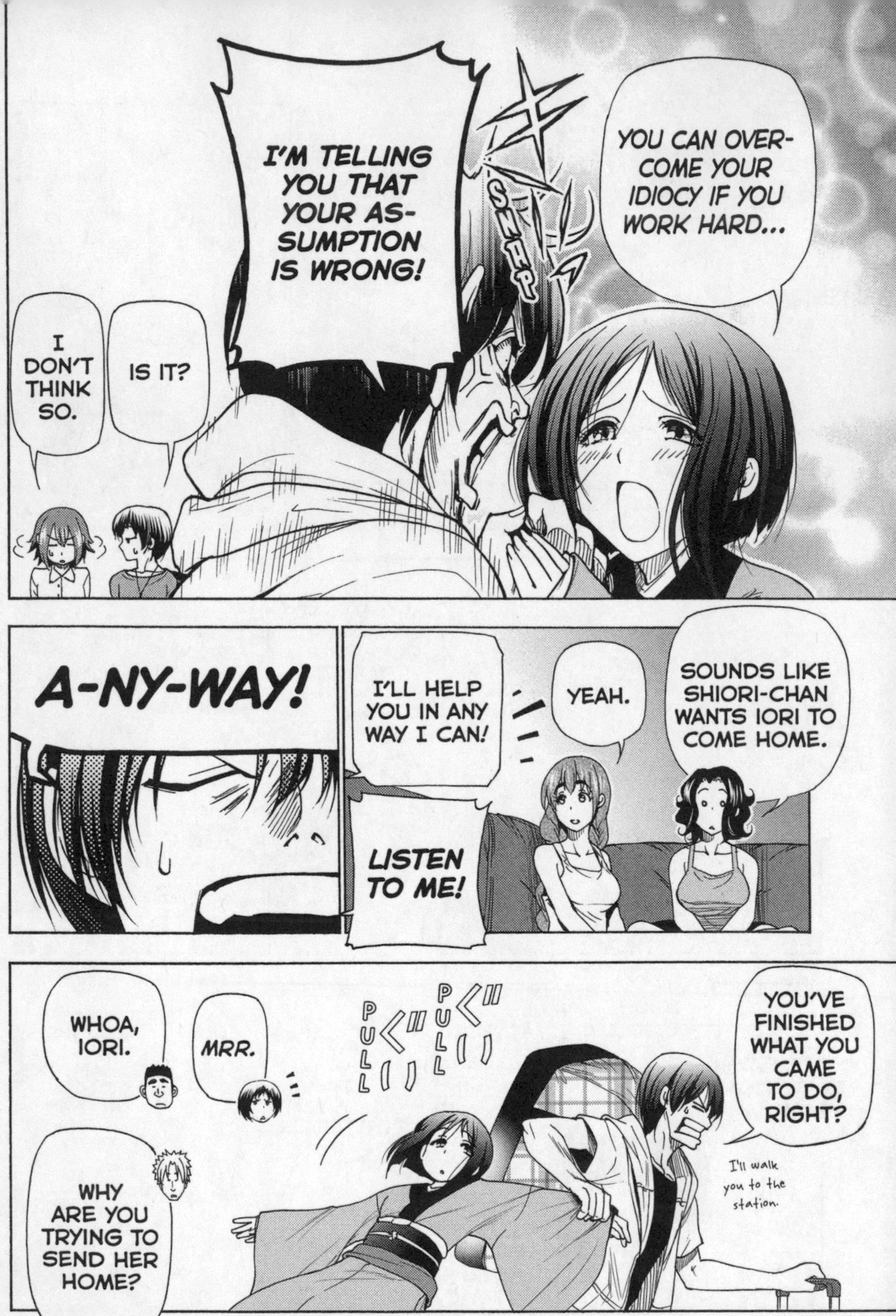
YOU CAN OVER-COME YOUR IDIOCY IF YOU WORK HARD...
SNAP
I'M TELLING YOU THAT YOUR AS-SUMPTION IS WRONG!
IS IT?
I DON'T THINK SO.
SOUNDS LIKE SHIORI-CHAN WANTS IORI TO COME HOME.
YEAH.
I'LL HELP YOU IN ANY WAY I CAN!
LISTEN TO ME!
A-NY-WAY!
YOU'VE FINISHED WHAT YOU CAME TO DO, RIGHT?
I'll walk you to the station.
PULL
PULL
MRR.
WHOA, IORI.
WHY ARE YOU TRYING TO SEND HER HOME?

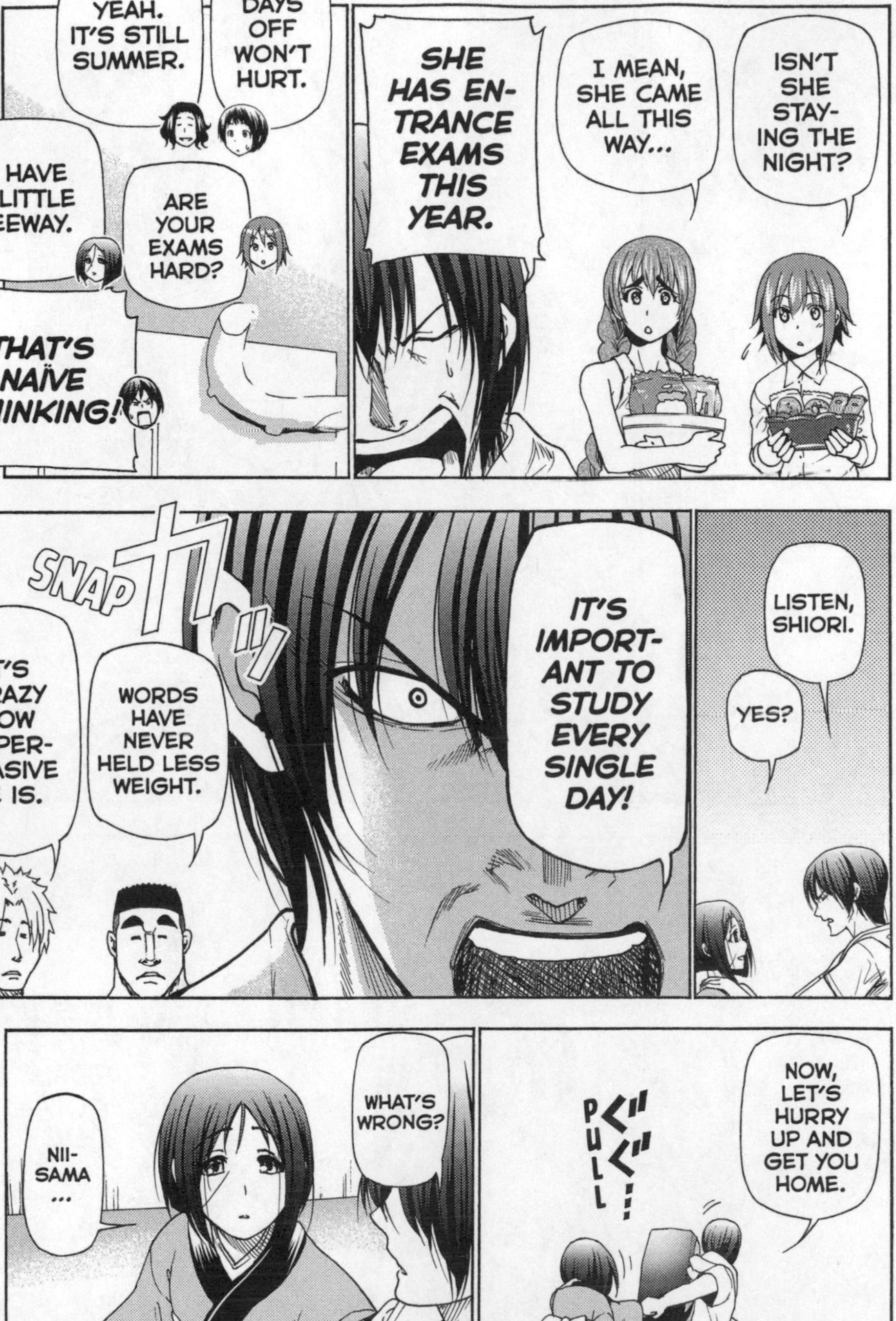
ISN'T SHE STAYING THE NIGHT?
I MEAN, SHE CAME ALL THIS WAY...
SHE HAS ENTRANCE EXAMS THIS YEAR.
A FEW DAYS OFF WON'T HURT.
YEAH. IT'S STILL SUMMER.
ARE YOUR EXAMS HARD?
I HAVE A LITTLE LEEWAY.
THAT'S NAÏVE THINKING!
LISTEN, SHIORI.
YES?
IT'S IMPORTANT TO STUDY EVERY SINGLE DAY!
SNAP
WORDS HAVE NEVER HELD LESS WEIGHT.
IT'S CRAZY HOW UNPERSUASIVE HE IS.
NOW, LET'S HURRY UP AND GET YOU HOME.
PULL
WHAT'S WRONG?
NII-SAMA...

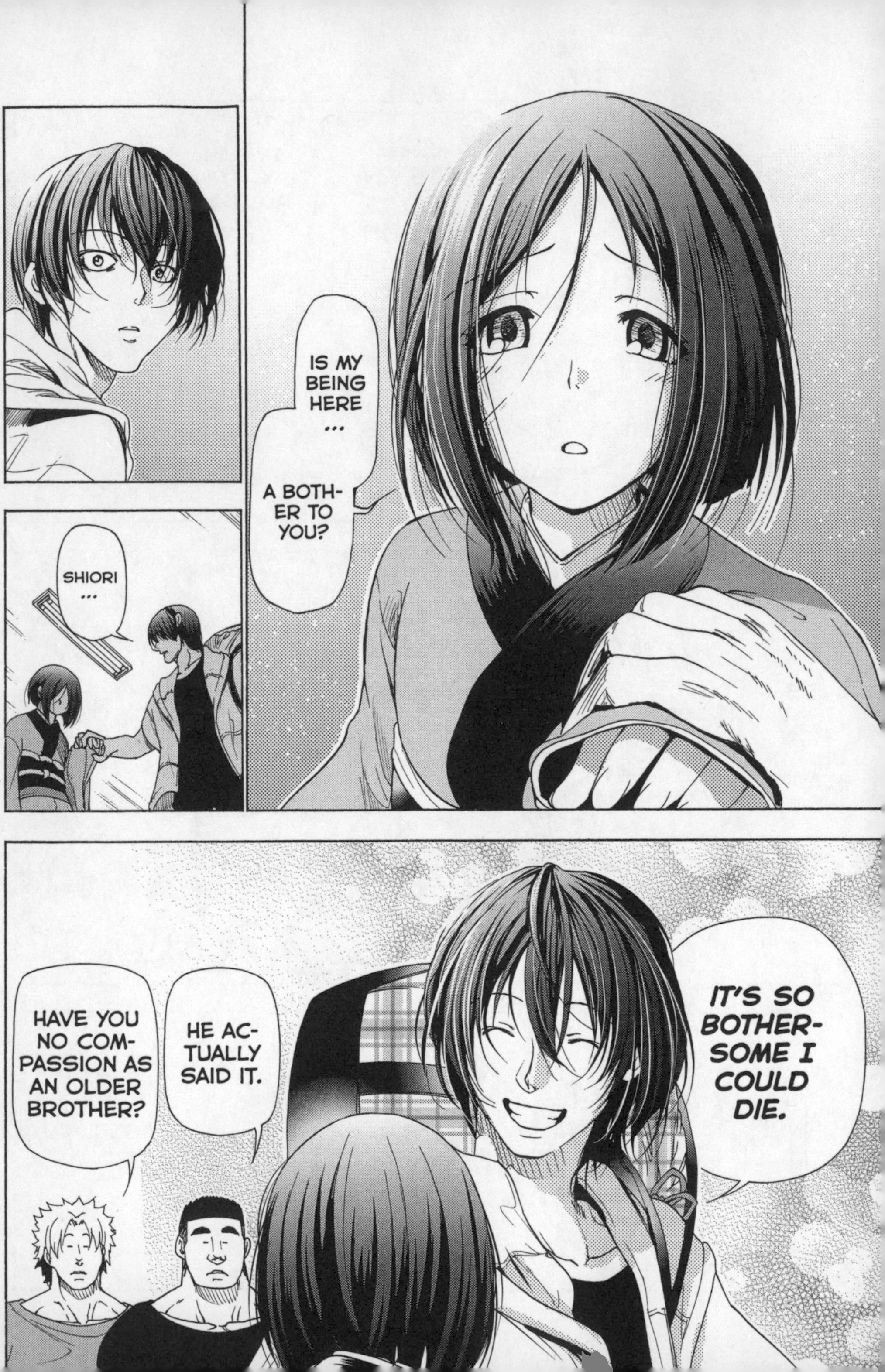
IS MY BEING HERE ...
A BOTH-ER TO YOU?
SHIORI ...
IT'S SO BOTHER-SOME I COULD DIE.
HE AC-TUALLY SAID IT.
HAVE YOU NO COM-PASSION AS AN OLDER BROTHER?

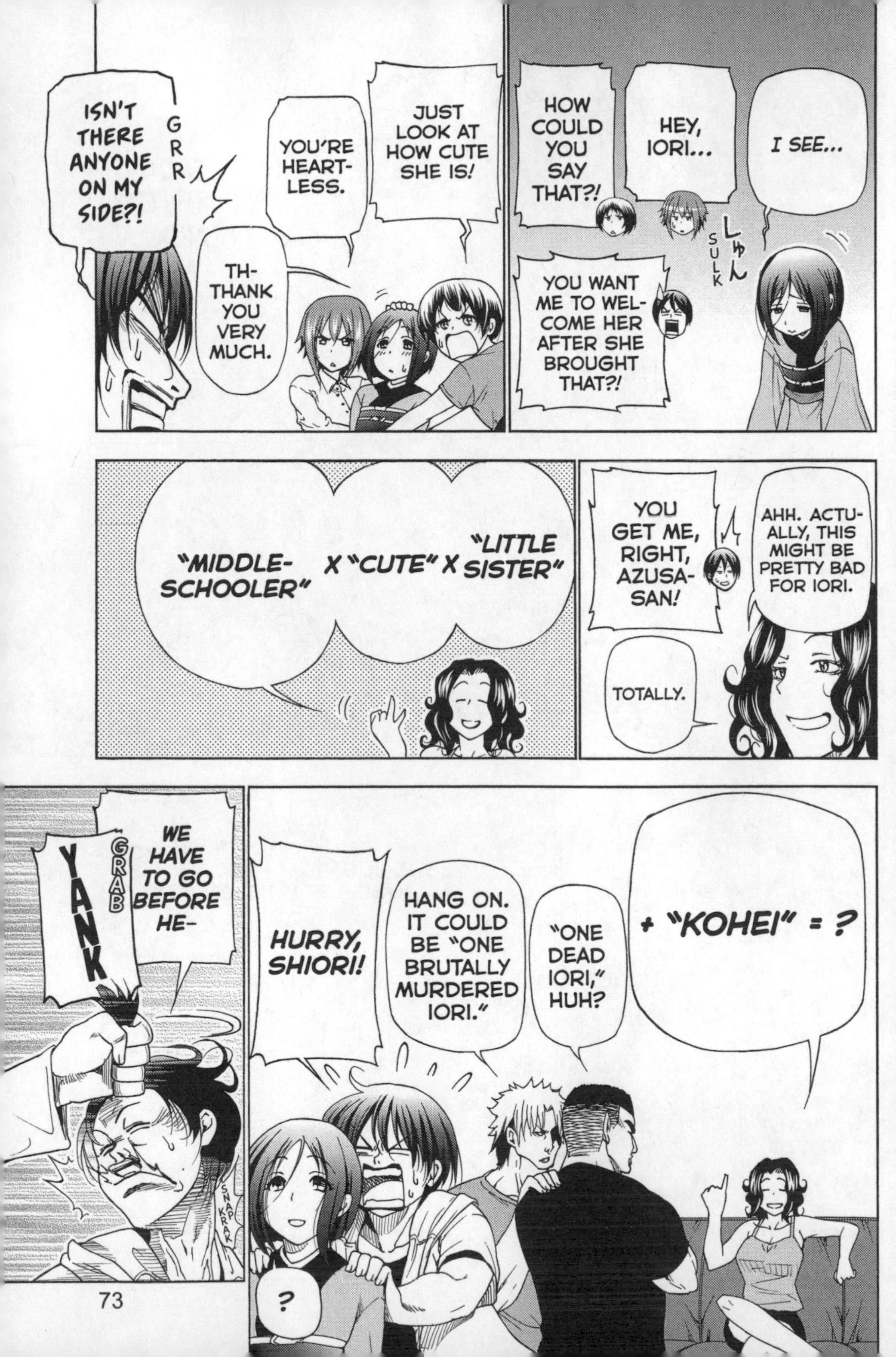
I SEE...
しゅん
SULK
HEY, IORI...
HOW COULD YOU SAY THAT?!
YOU WANT ME TO WEL-COME HER AFTER SHE BROUGHT THAT?!
JUST LOOK AT HOW CUTE SHE IS!
YOU'RE HEART-LESS.
TH-THANK YOU VERY MUCH.
GRR
ISN'T THERE ANYONE ON MY SIDE?!
AHH. ACTU-ALLY, THIS MIGHT BE PRETTY BAD FOR IORI.
YOU GET ME, RIGHT, AZUSA-SAN!
TOTALLY.
"MIDDLE-SCHOOLER" X "CUTE" X "LITTLE SISTER"
+ "KOHEI" = ?
"ONE DEAD IORI," HUH?
HANG ON. IT COULD BE "ONE BRUTALLY MURDERED IORI."
HURRY, SHIORI!
?
WE HAVE TO GO BEFORE HE-
GRAB
YANK
SNAP
KRAK

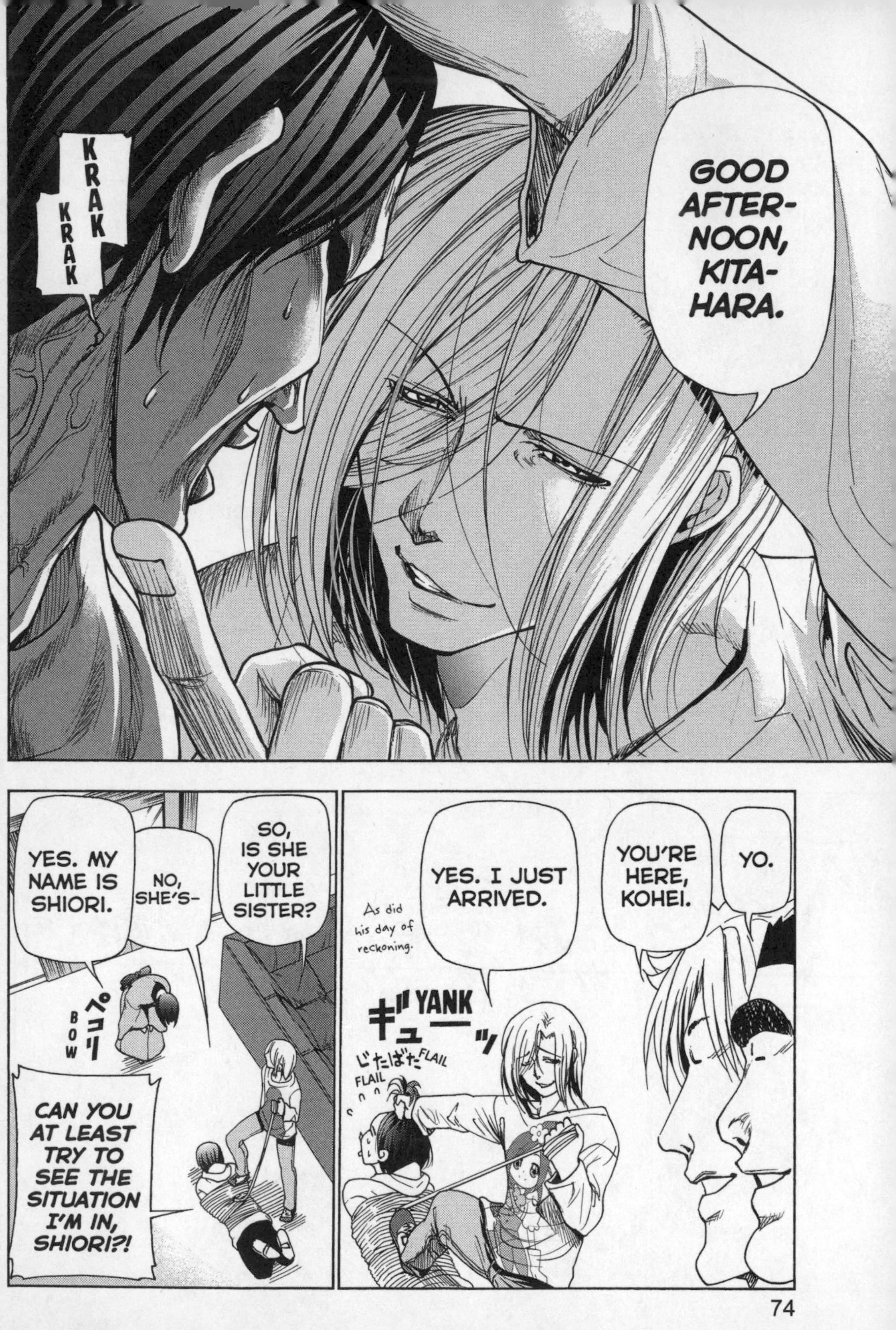
GOOD AFTER-NOON, KITA-HARA.
KRAK KRAK
YO.
YOU'RE HERE, KOHEI.
YES. I JUST ARRIVED.
As did his day of reckoning.
ギューッ YANK
じたばた FLAIL FLAIL
SO, IS SHE YOUR LITTLE SISTER?
NO, SHE'S-
YES. MY NAME IS SHIORI.
ペコリ BOW
CAN YOU AT LEAST TRY TO SEE THE SITUATION I'M IN, SHIORI?!

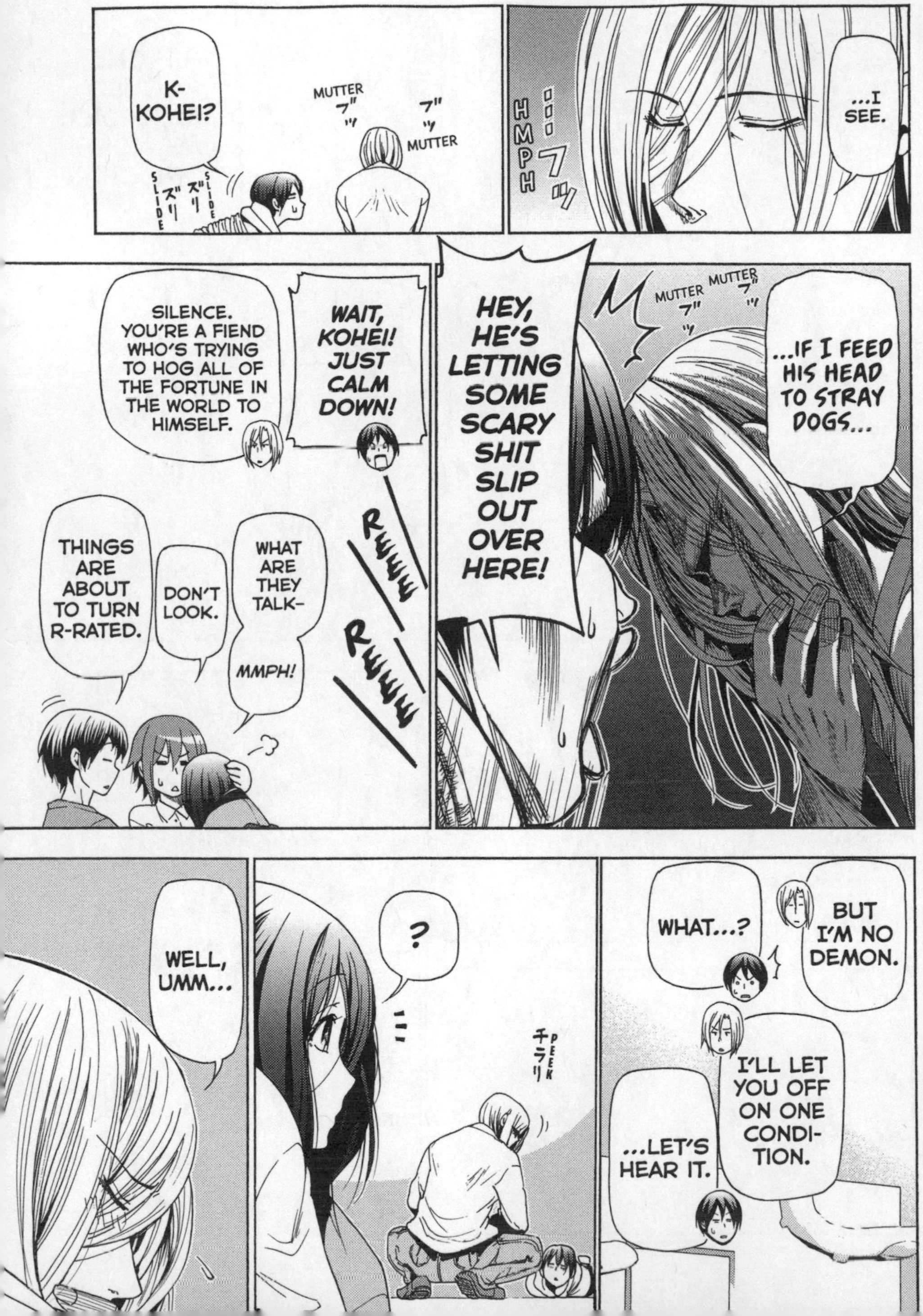
...I SEE.
HMPH
フッ
MUTTER
ブツ
ブツ
MUTTER
K-KOHEI?
SLIDE ズリ ズリ SLIDE
MUTTER
MUTTER
ブツ
ブツ
...IF I FEED HIS HEAD TO STRAY DOGS...
HEY, HE'S LETTING SOME SCARY SHIT SLIP OUT OVER HERE!
WAIT, KOHEI! JUST CALM DOWN!
SILENCE. YOU'RE A FIEND WHO'S TRYING TO HOG ALL OF THE FORTUNE IN THE WORLD TO HIMSELF.
REEEE
REEEE
WHAT ARE THEY TALK-
MMPH!
DON'T LOOK.
THINGS ARE ABOUT TO TURN R-RATED.
BUT I'M NO DEMON.
WHAT...?
I'LL LET YOU OFF ON ONE CONDITION.
...LET'S HEAR IT.
?
PEEK
チラリ
WELL, UMM...

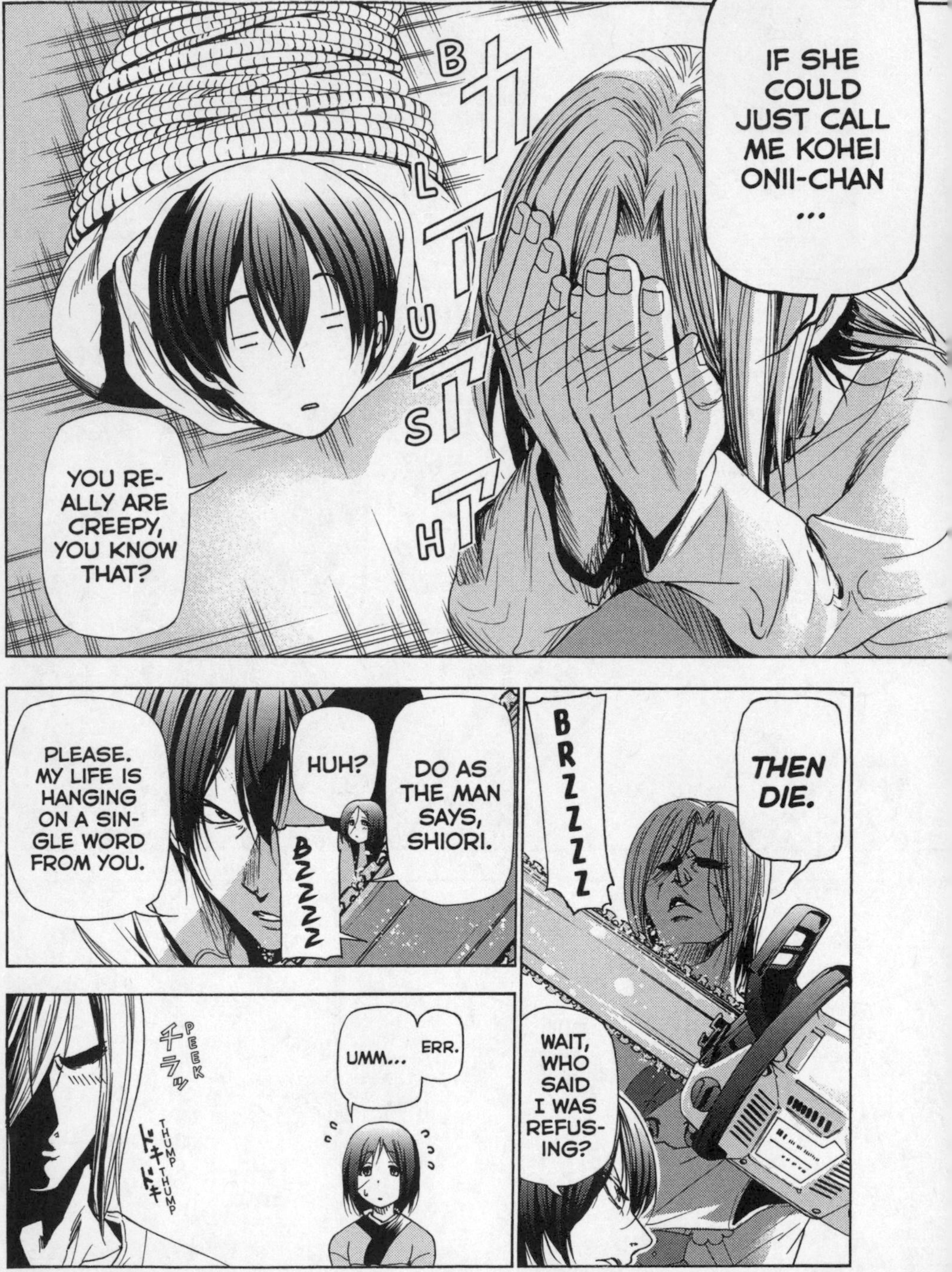
IF SHE COULD JUST CALL ME KOHEI ONII-CHAN ...
BLUSH
YOU REALLY ARE CREEPY, YOU KNOW THAT?
THEN DIE.
BRZZZZZ
WAIT, WHO SAID I WAS REFUSING?
DO AS THE MAN SAYS, SHIORI.
HUH?
PLEASE. MY LIFE IS HANGING ON A SINGLE WORD FROM YOU.
BZZZZZ
ERR.
UMM...
PEEK
THUMP THUMP

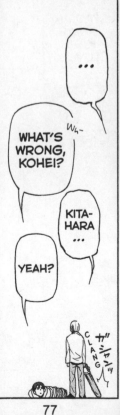

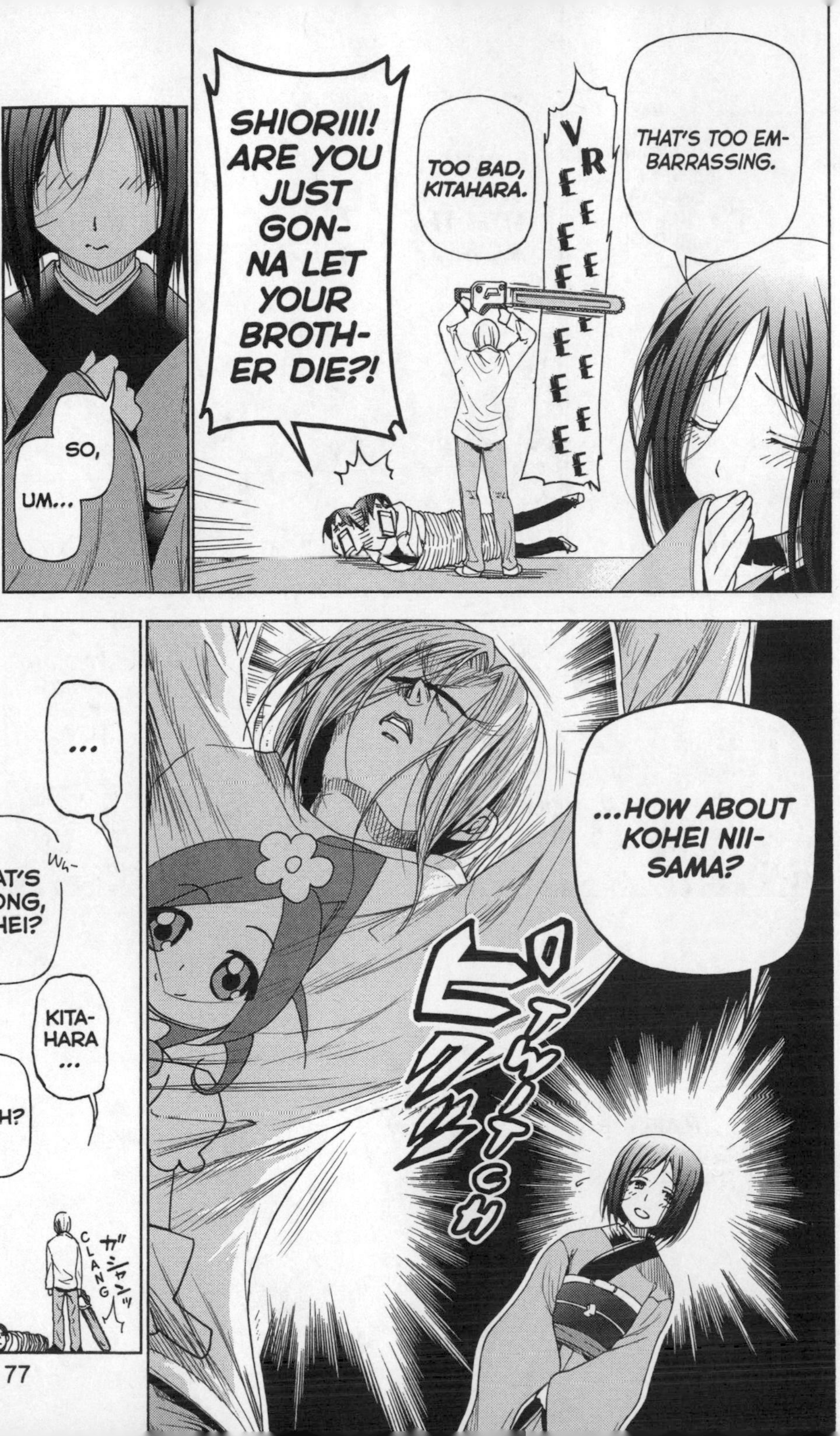
THAT'S TOO EM-BARRASSING.
TOO BAD, KITAHARA.
VREEEEEEEEEEEEE
SHIORIII! ARE YOU JUST GON-NA LET YOUR BROTH-ER DIE?!
SO, UM...
...HOW ABOUT KOHEI NII-SAMA?
TWITCH
...
WH-
WHAT'S WRONG, KOHEI?
KITA-HARA ...
YEAH?
CLANG

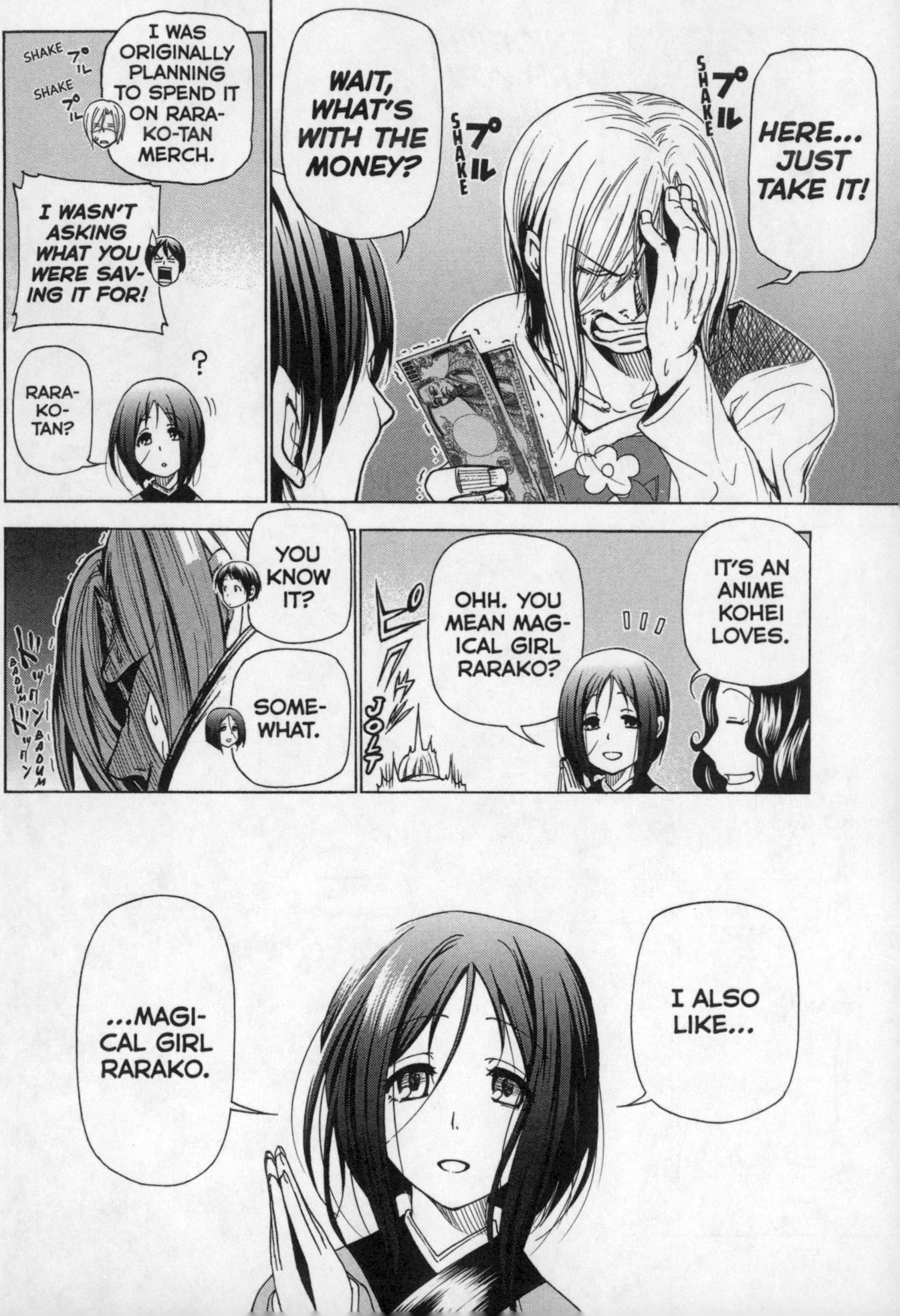
SHAKE
HERE... JUST TAKE IT!
SHAKE
WAIT, WHAT'S WITH THE MONEY?
I WAS ORIGINALLY PLANNING TO SPEND IT ON RARAKO-TAN MERCH.
SHAKE
SHAKE
I WASN'T ASKING WHAT YOU WERE SAVING IT FOR!
?
RARAKO-TAN?
IT'S AN ANIME KOHEI LOVES.
OHH. YOU MEAN MAGICAL GIRL RARAKO?
JOLT
YOU KNOW IT?
SOMEWHAT.
BADUM BADUM
I ALSO LIKE...
...MAGICAL GIRL RARAKO.

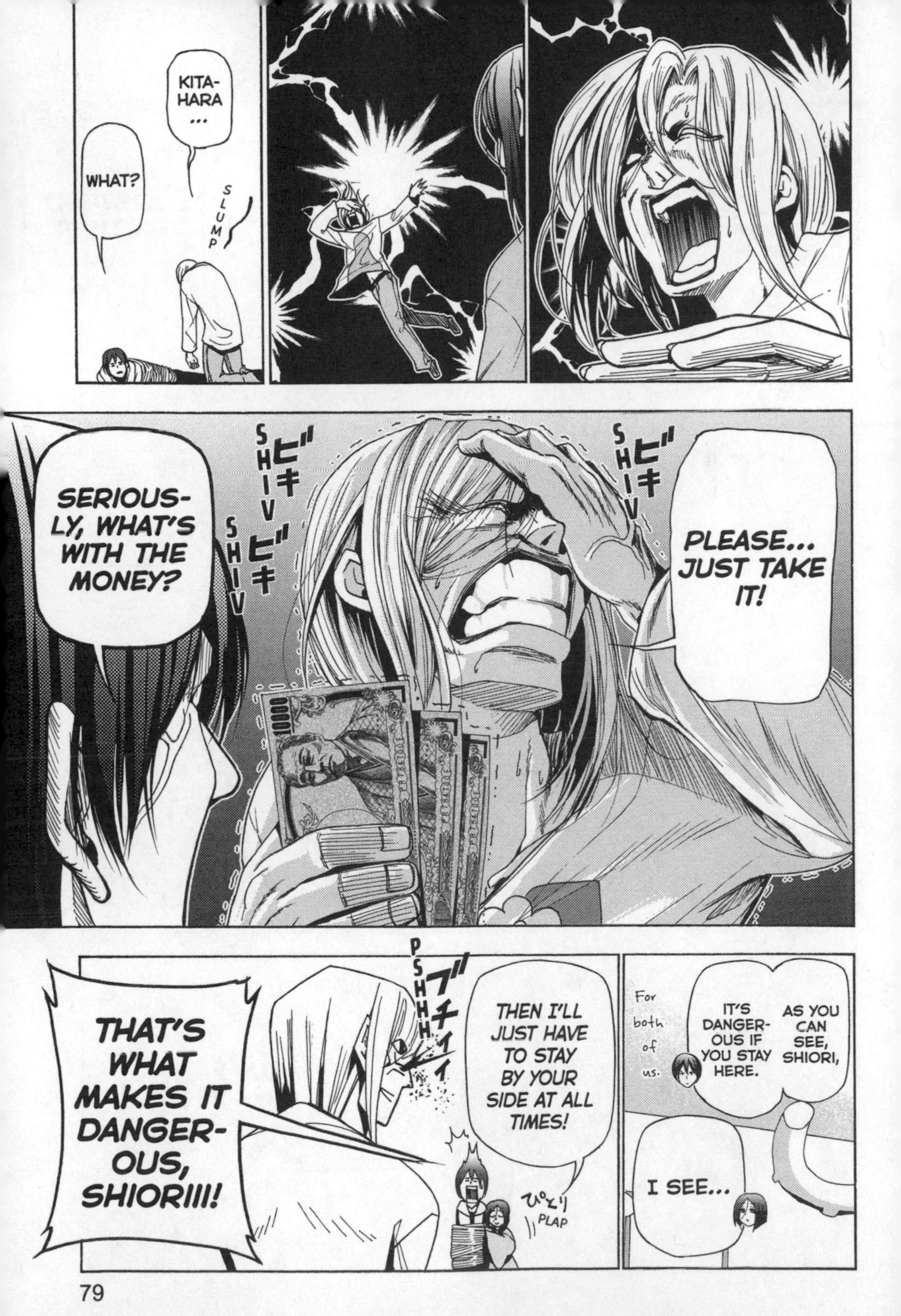
KITA-HARA...
SLUMP
WHAT?
SHIV ビキ
PLEASE... JUST TAKE IT!
SHIV ビキ
SHIV ビキ
SERIOUSLY, WHAT'S WITH THE MONEY?
AS YOU CAN SEE, SHIORI,
IT'S DANGEROUS IF YOU STAY HERE.
For both of us.
I SEE...
PSHHH ブチィィ
THEN I'LL JUST HAVE TO STAY BY YOUR SIDE AT ALL TIMES!
ぴとり PLAP
THAT'S WHAT MAKES IT DANGEROUS, SHIORIII!

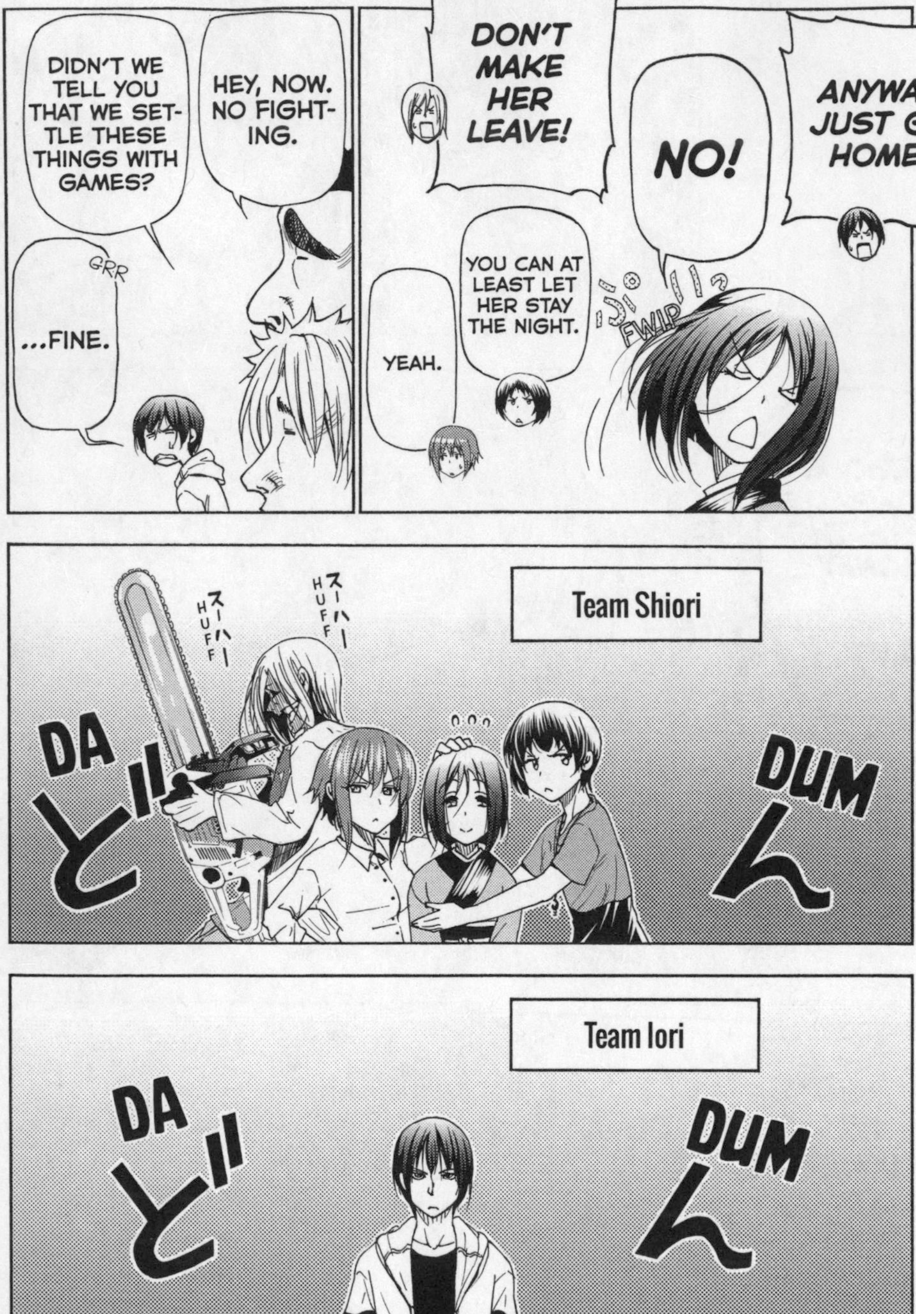
ANYWAY, JUST GO HOME!
NO!
DON'T MAKE HER LEAVE!
FWIP
YOU CAN AT LEAST LET HER STAY THE NIGHT.
YEAH.
HEY, NOW. NO FIGHT-ING.
DIDN'T WE TELL YOU THAT WE SET-TLE THESE THINGS WITH GAMES?
GRR
...FINE.
Team Shiori
HUFF
HUFF
DUM
DA
Team Iori
DUM
DA

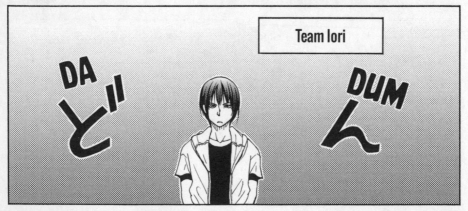

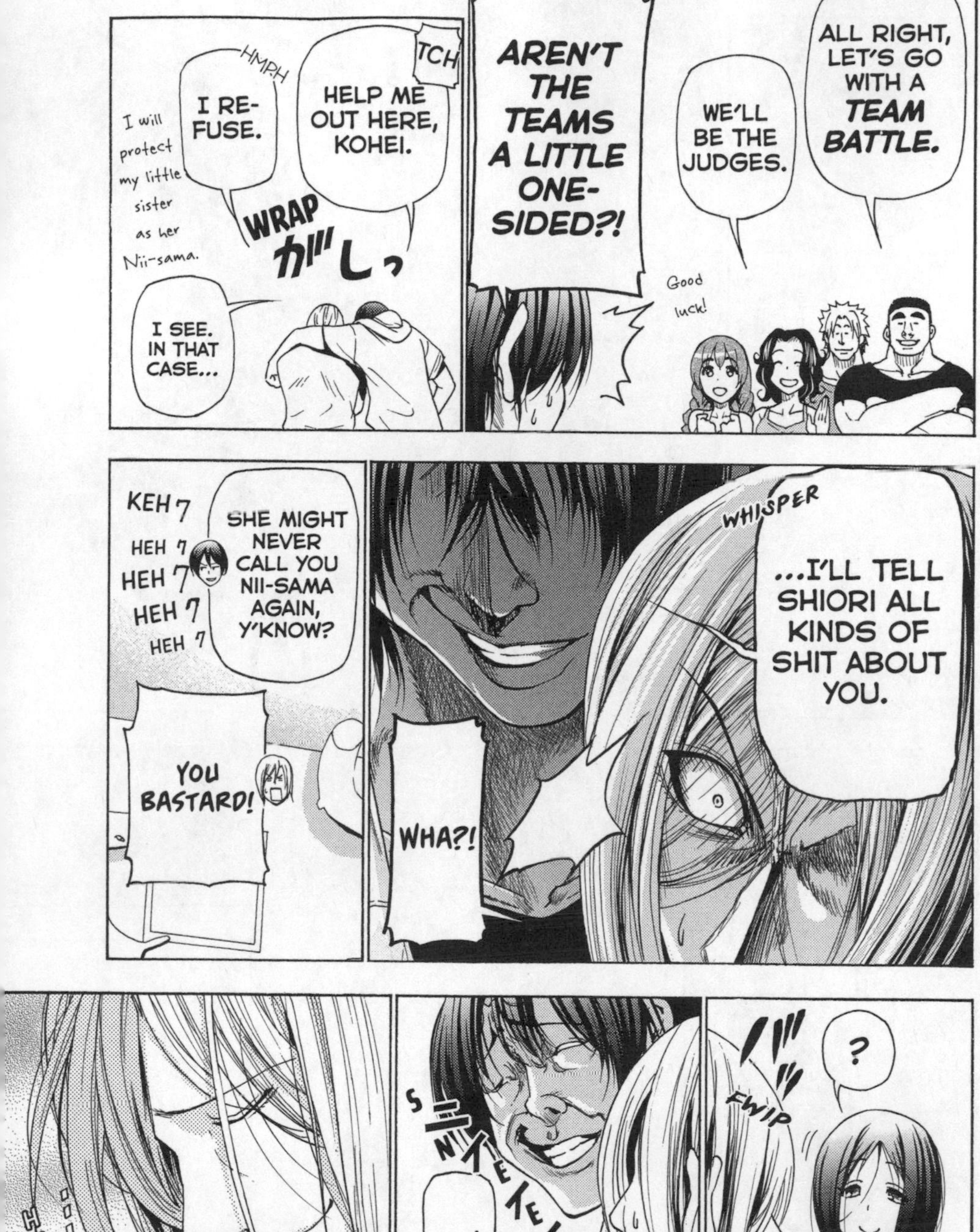
ALL RIGHT, LET'S GO WITH A TEAM BATTLE.
WE'LL BE THE JUDGES.
Good luck!
AREN'T THE TEAMS A LITTLE ONE-SIDED?!
TCH
HELP ME OUT HERE, KOHEI.
HMPH
I RE-FUSE.
I will protect my little sister as her Nii-sama.
WRAP
I SEE. IN THAT CASE...
WHISPER
...I'LL TELL SHIORI ALL KINDS OF SHIT ABOUT YOU.
WHA?!
SHE MIGHT NEVER CALL YOU NII-SAMA AGAIN, Y'KNOW?
KEH HEH HEH HEH HEH
YOU BASTARD!
?
FWIP
SNEEER
...!
HMPH

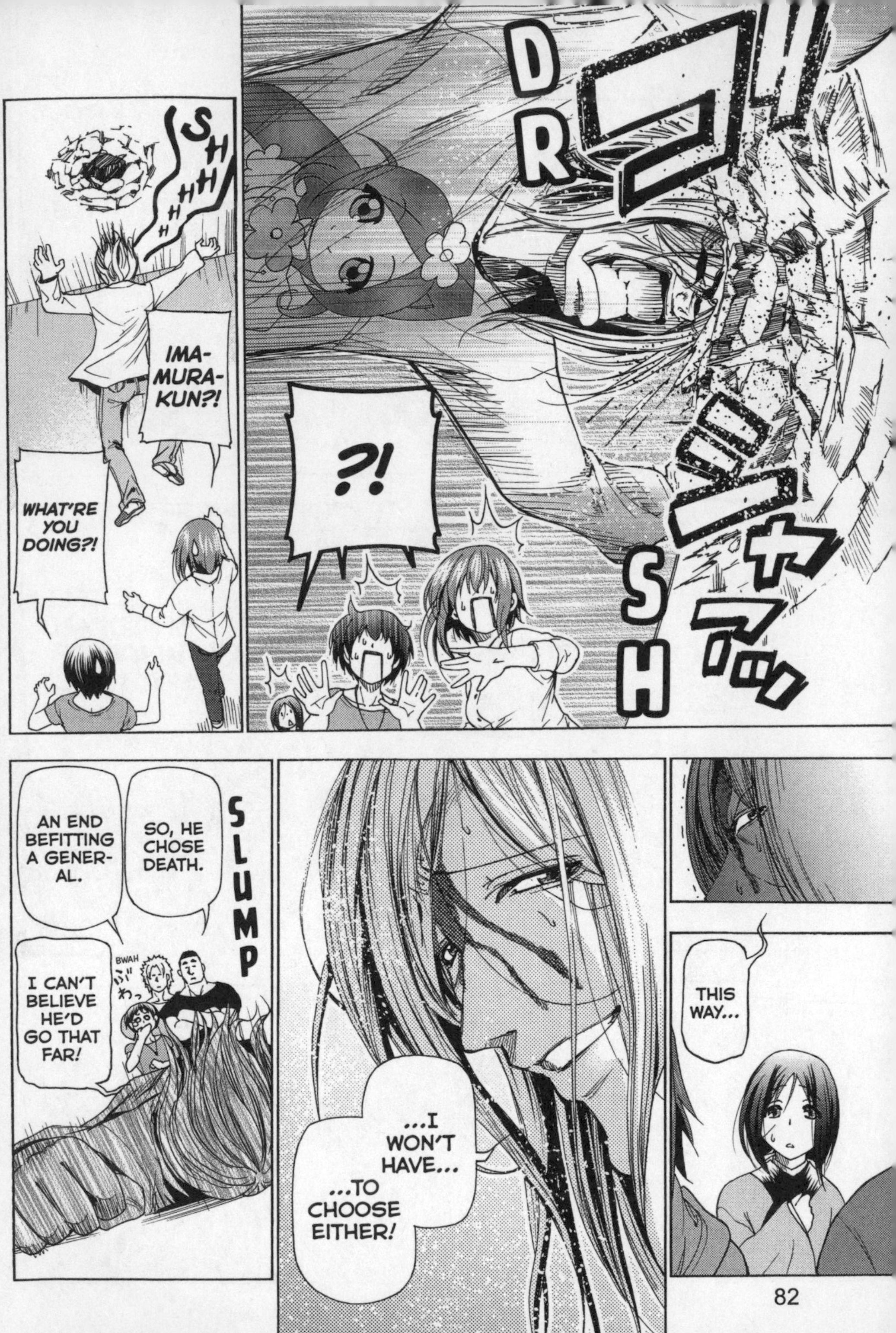
DR
?!
SH
SHHHHHH
IMA-MURA-KUN?!
WHAT'RE YOU DOING?!
THIS WAY...
...I WON'T HAVE...
...TO CHOOSE EITHER!
SLUMP
SO, HE CHOSE DEATH.
AN END BEFITTING A GENER-AL.
BWAH
ぶわっ
I CAN'T BELIEVE HE'D GO THAT FAR!

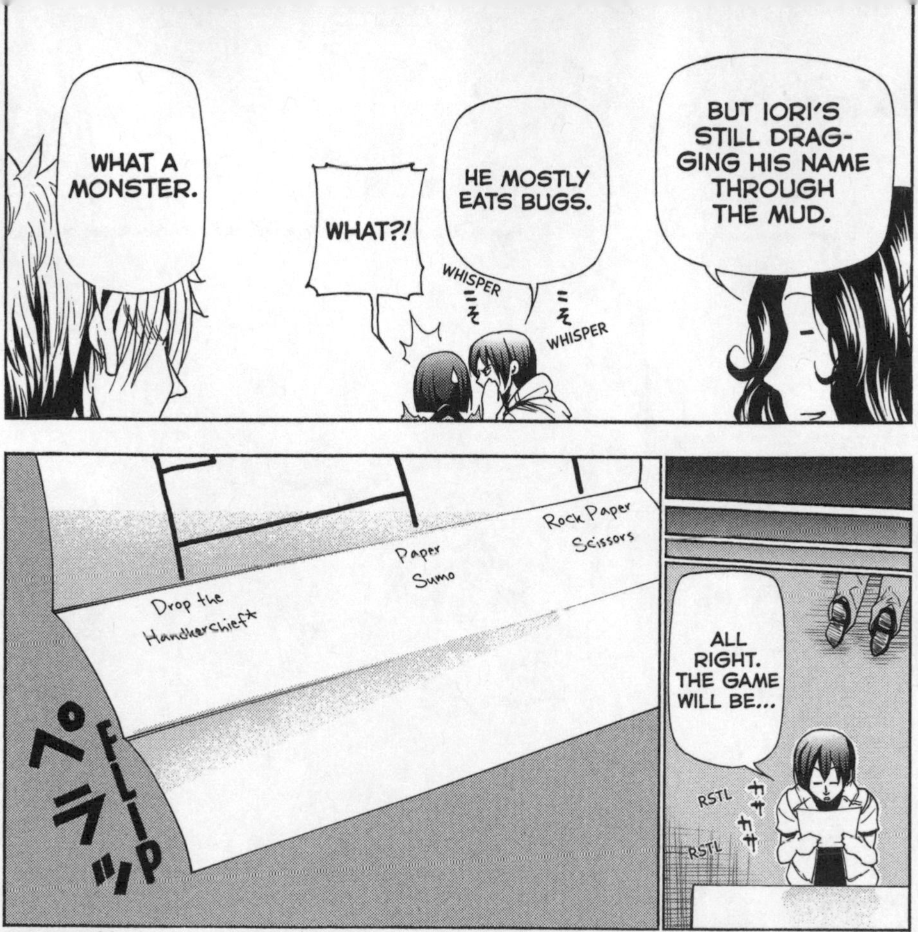
BUT IORI'S STILL DRAG-GING HIS NAME THROUGH THE MUD.
HE MOSTLY EATS BUGS.
WHISPER
WHISPER
WHAT?!
WHAT A MONSTER.
ALL RIGHT. THE GAME WILL BE...
RSTL
RSTL
Rock Paper Scissors
Paper Sumo
Drop the Handkerchief*
FLIP

*A variant of the American game Duck, Duck, Goose. As the name suggests, dropping a handkerchief is involved.

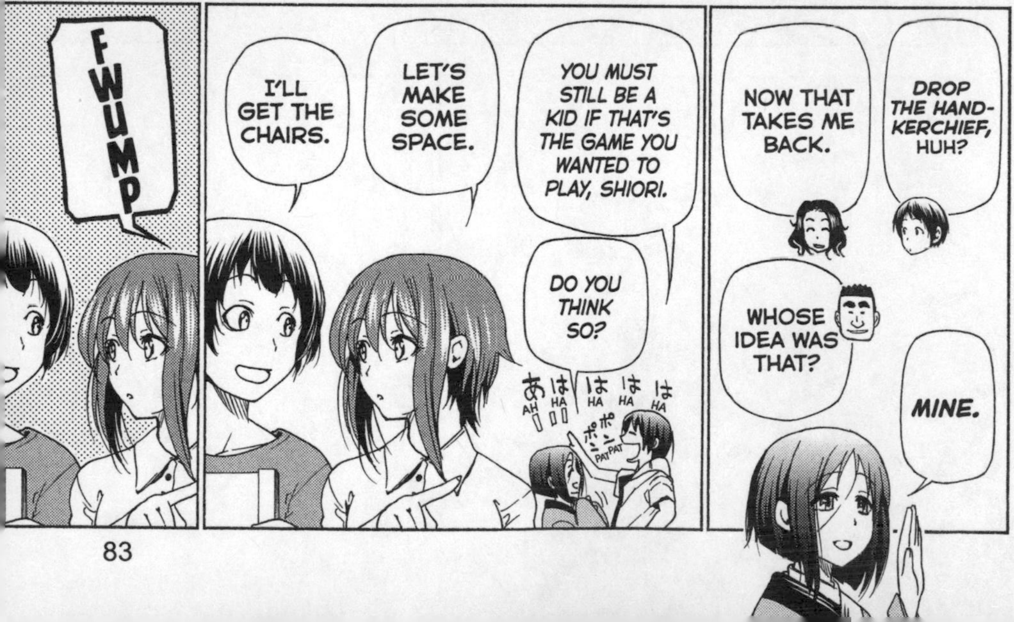
DROP THE HAND-KERCHIEF, HUH?
NOW THAT TAKES ME BACK.
WHOSE IDEA WAS THAT?
MINE.
YOU MUST STILL BE A KID IF THAT'S THE GAME YOU WANTED TO PLAY, SHIORI.
DO YOU THINK SO?
AH HA HA HA HA
PAT PAT
LET'S MAKE SOME SPACE.
I'LL GET THE CHAIRS.
FWUMP

THIS IS WHAT I CALL...

NII-SAMA.

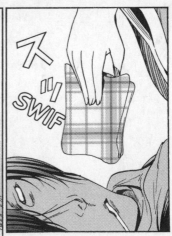

スッ
SWIF

84

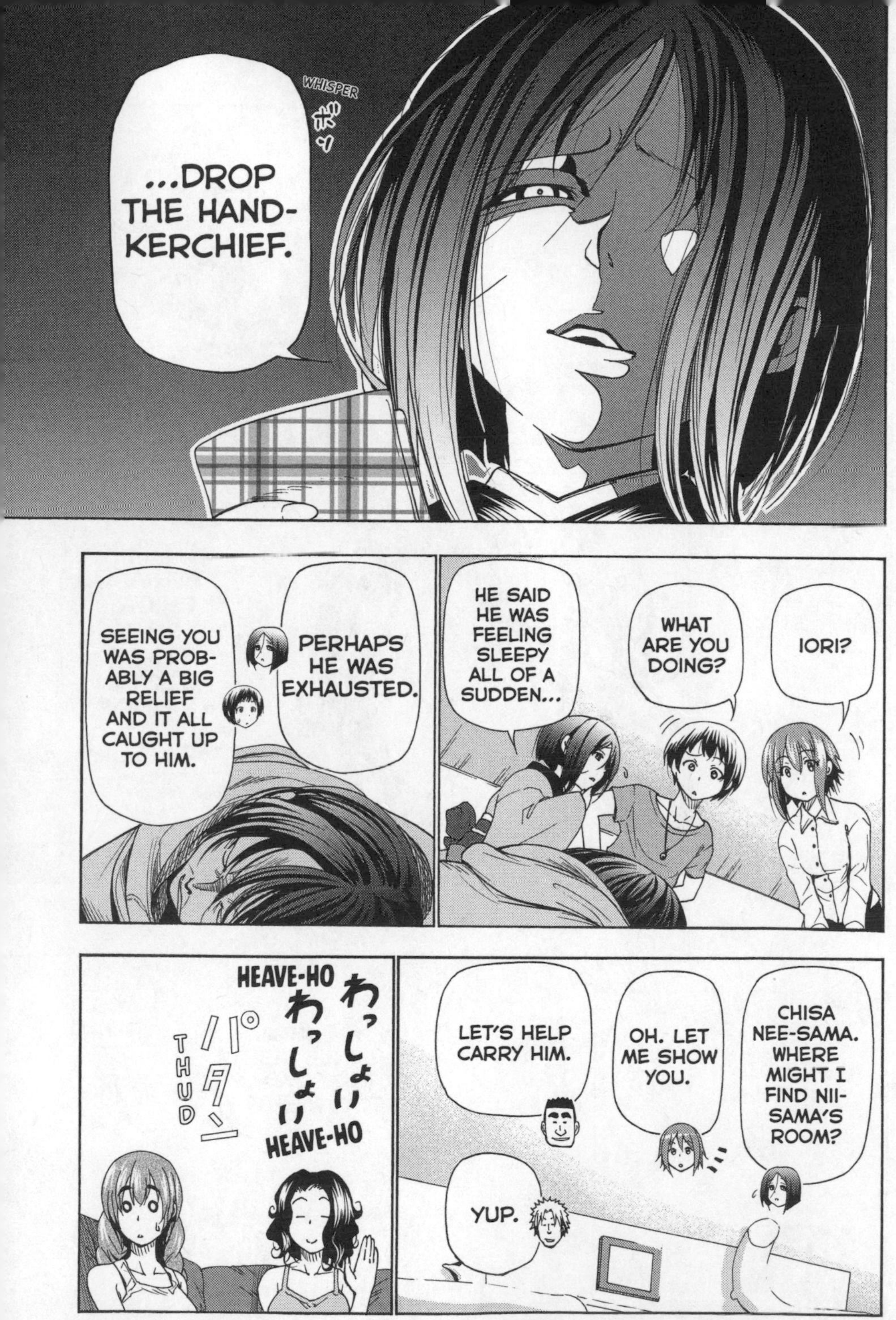
WHISPER
ボソ
...DROP THE HAND-KERCHIEF.
IORI?
WHAT ARE YOU DOING?
HE SAID HE WAS FEELING SLEEPY ALL OF A SUDDEN...
PERHAPS HE WAS EXHAUSTED.
SEEING YOU WAS PROB-ABLY A BIG RELIEF AND IT ALL CAUGHT UP TO HIM.
CHISA NEE-SAMA. WHERE MIGHT I FIND NII-SAMA'S ROOM?
OH. LET ME SHOW YOU.
LET'S HELP CARRY HIM.
YUP.
わっしょい
HEAVE-HO
わっしょい
HEAVE-HO
パタン
THUD

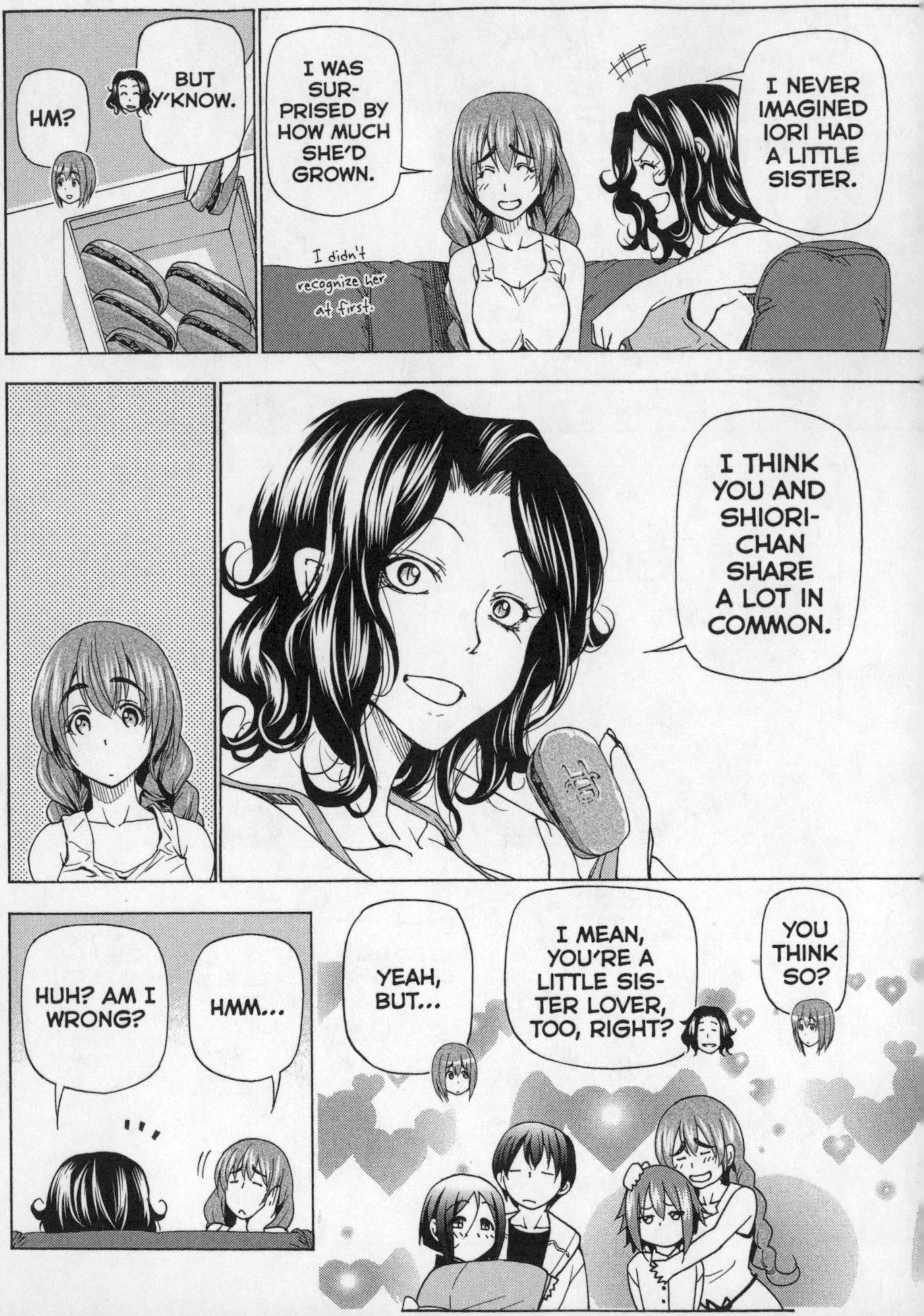
I NEVER IMAGINED IORI HAD A LITTLE SISTER.
I WAS SUR-PRISED BY HOW MUCH SHE'D GROWN.
I didn't recognize her at first.
BUT Y'KNOW.
HM?
I THINK YOU AND SHIORI-CHAN SHARE A LOT IN COMMON.
YOU THINK SO?
I MEAN, YOU'RE A LITTLE SIS-TER LOVER, TOO, RIGHT?
YEAH, BUT...
HMM...
HUH? AM I WRONG?

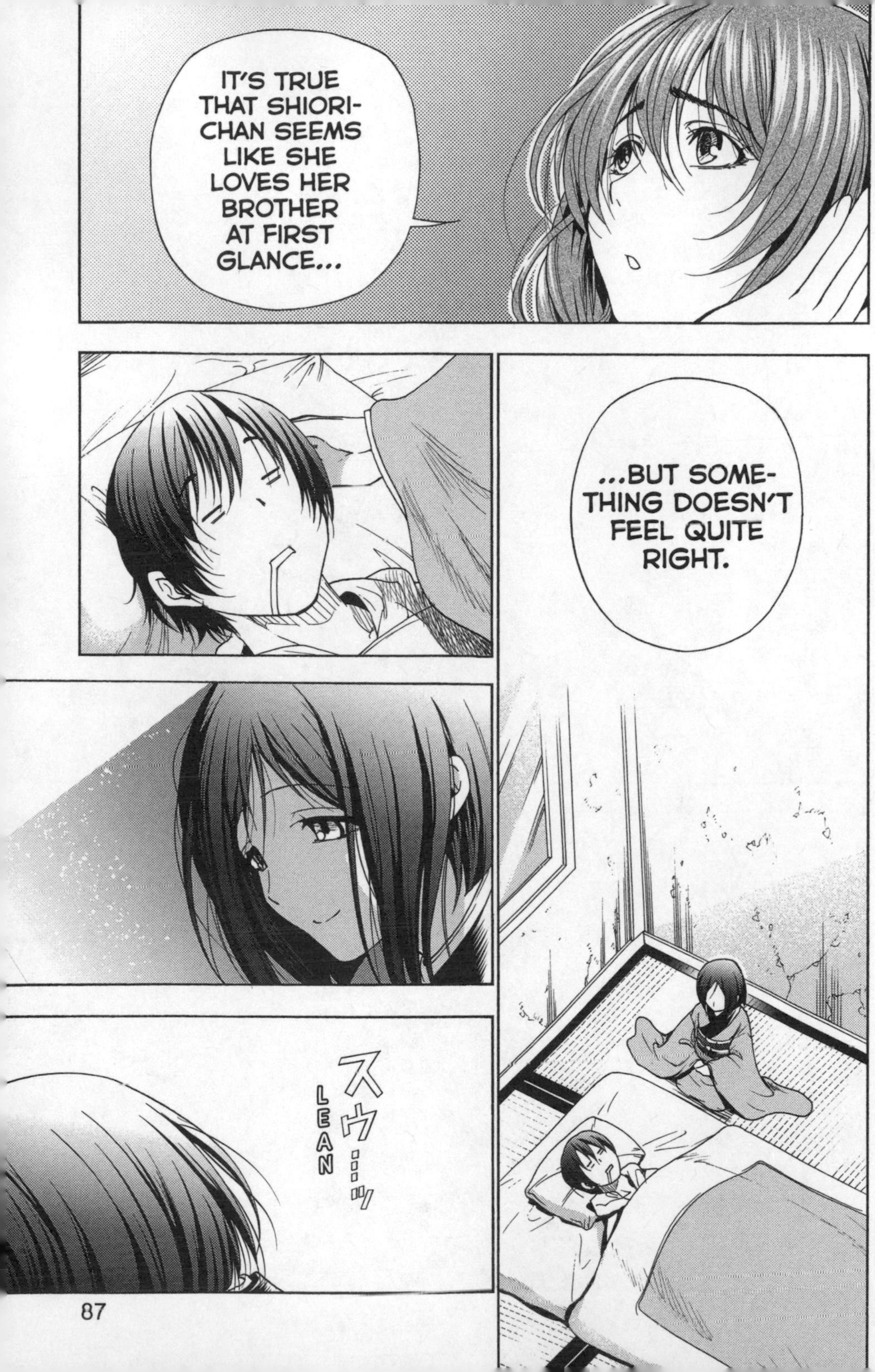
IT'S TRUE THAT SHIORI-CHAN SEEMS LIKE SHE LOVES HER BROTHER AT FIRST GLANCE...
...BUT SOME-THING DOESN'T FEEL QUITE RIGHT.
スウ…ッ
LEAN

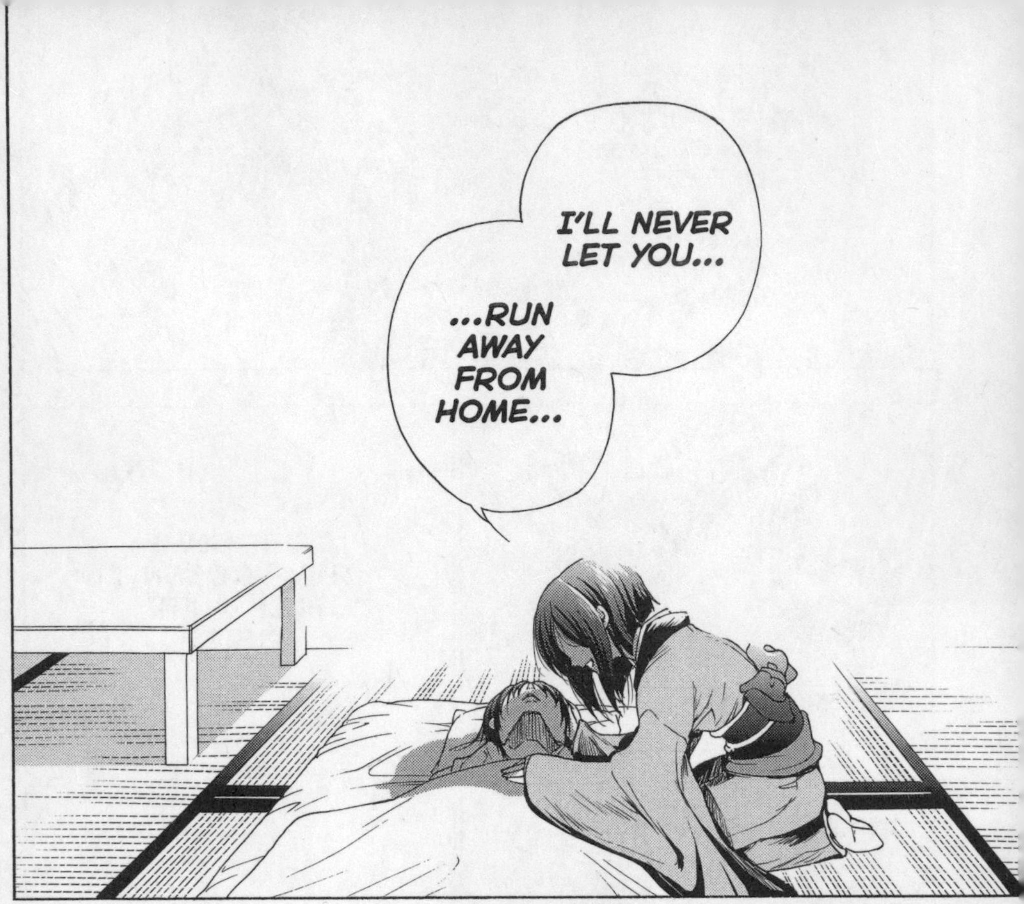
I'LL NEVER LET YOU...
...RUN AWAY FROM HOME...
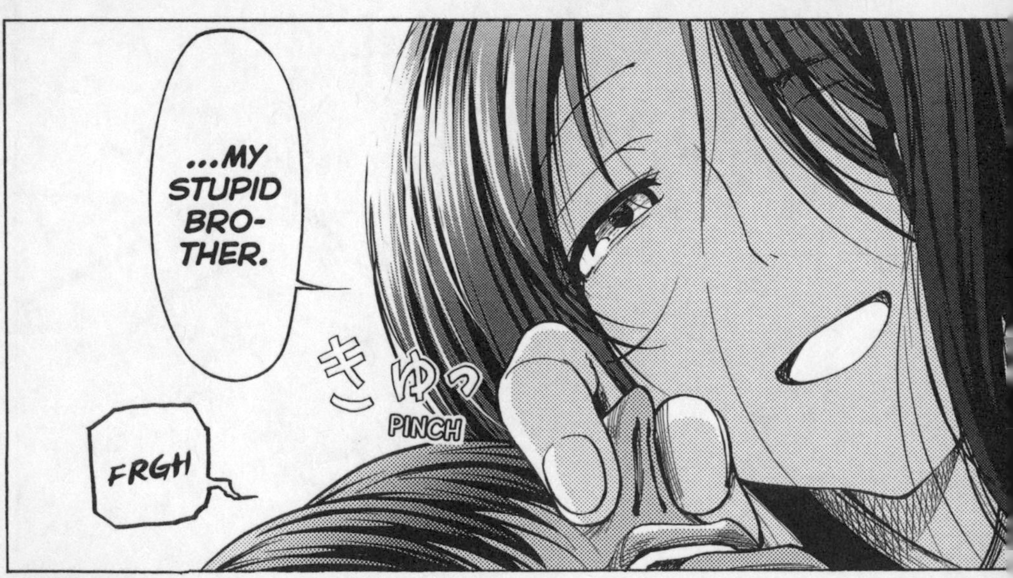
...MY STUPID BRO- THER.
きゅっ
PINCH
FRGH

CH.27 / End

The wall was fixed with familial love.

Grand Blue Dreaming

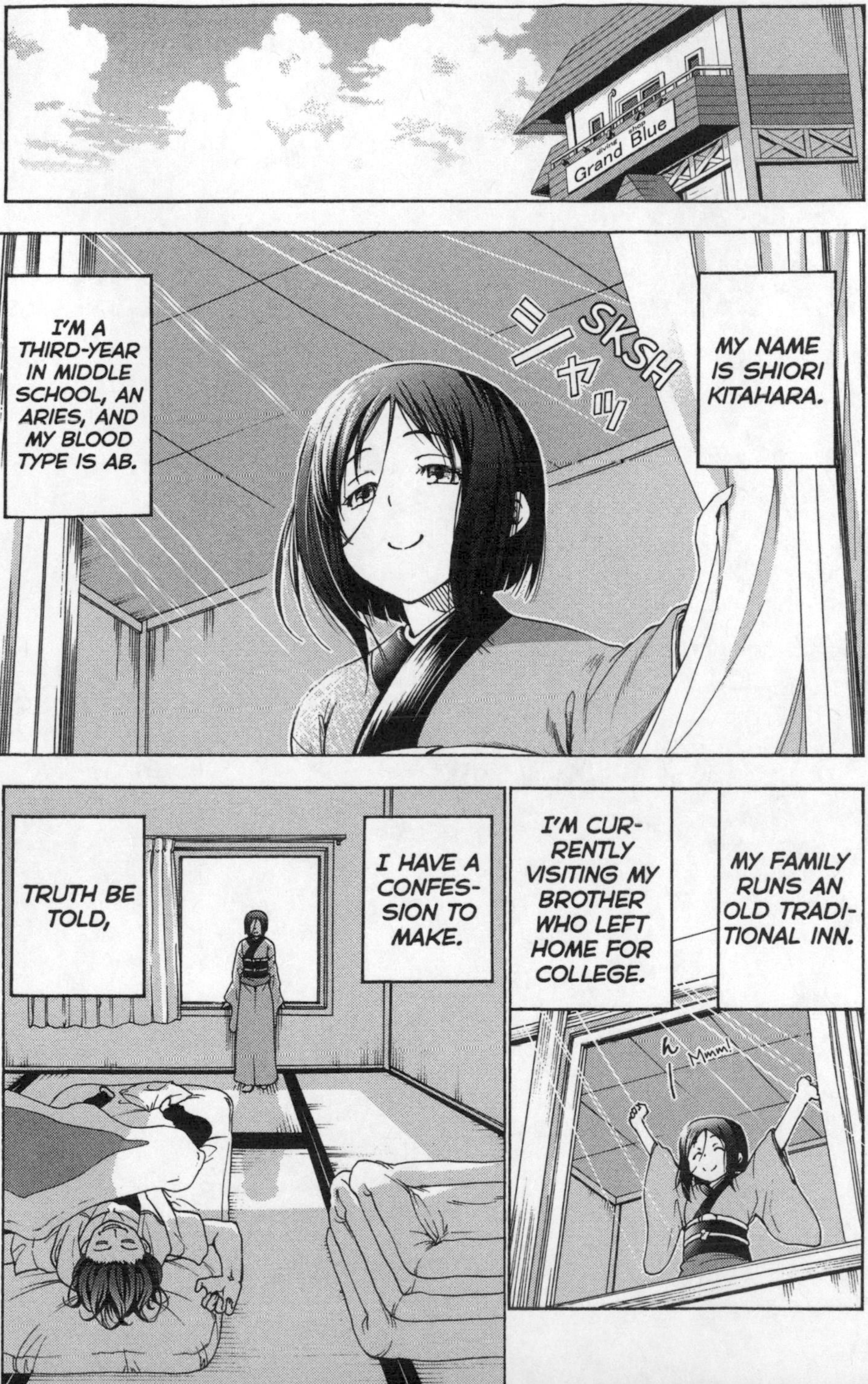
diving shop
Grand Blue
MY NAME IS SHIORI KITAHARA.
SKSH
シャッ
I'M A THIRD-YEAR IN MIDDLE SCHOOL, AN ARIES, AND MY BLOOD TYPE IS AB.
MY FAMILY RUNS AN OLD TRADITIONAL INN.
I'M CURRENTLY VISITING MY BROTHER WHO LEFT HOME FOR COLLEGE.
んー
Mmm!
I HAVE A CONFESSION TO MAKE.
TRUTH BE TOLD,

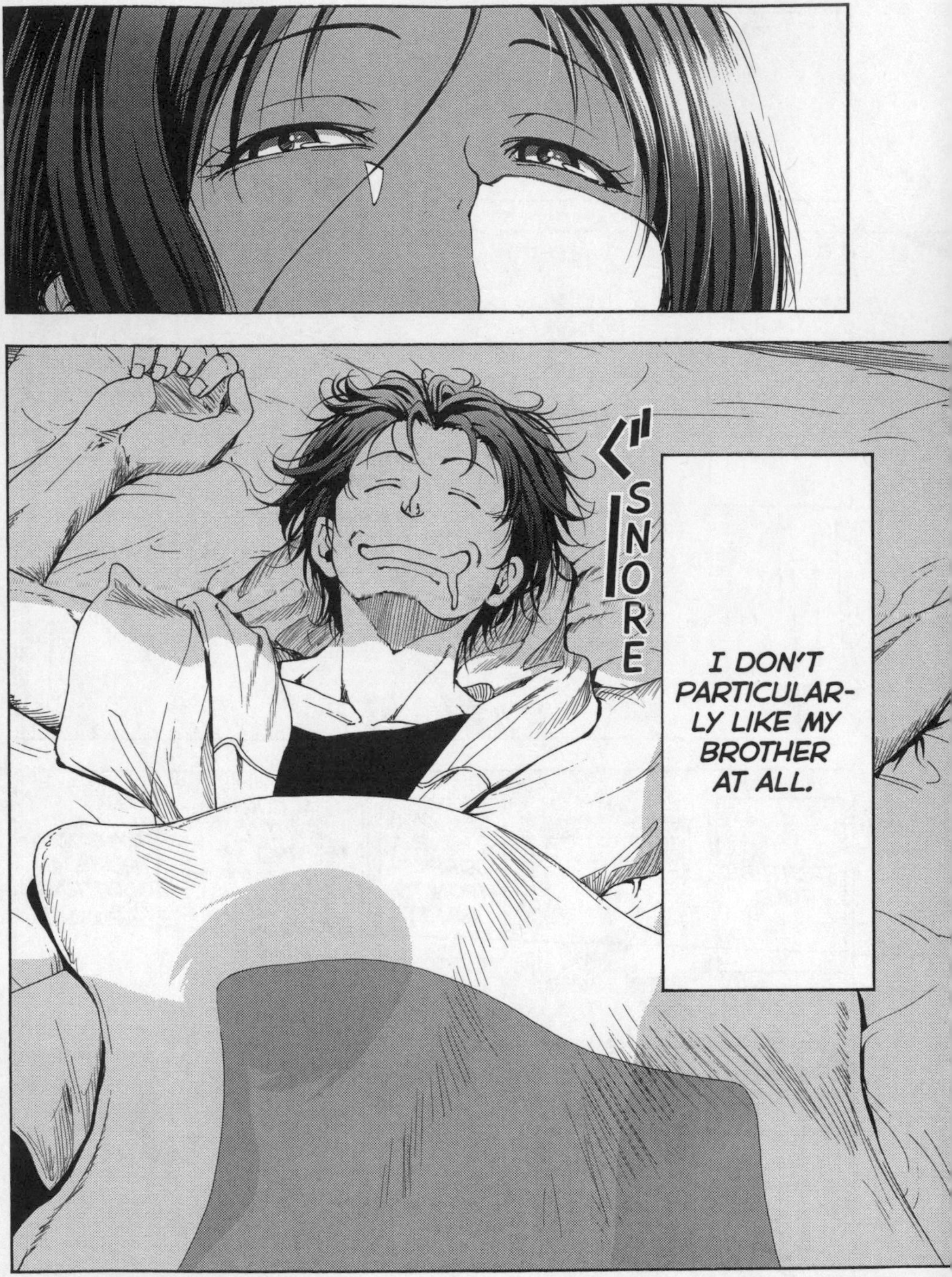
I DON'T PARTICULAR-LY LIKE MY BROTHER AT ALL.
ぐ
SNORE

Ch. 28 Big Brother

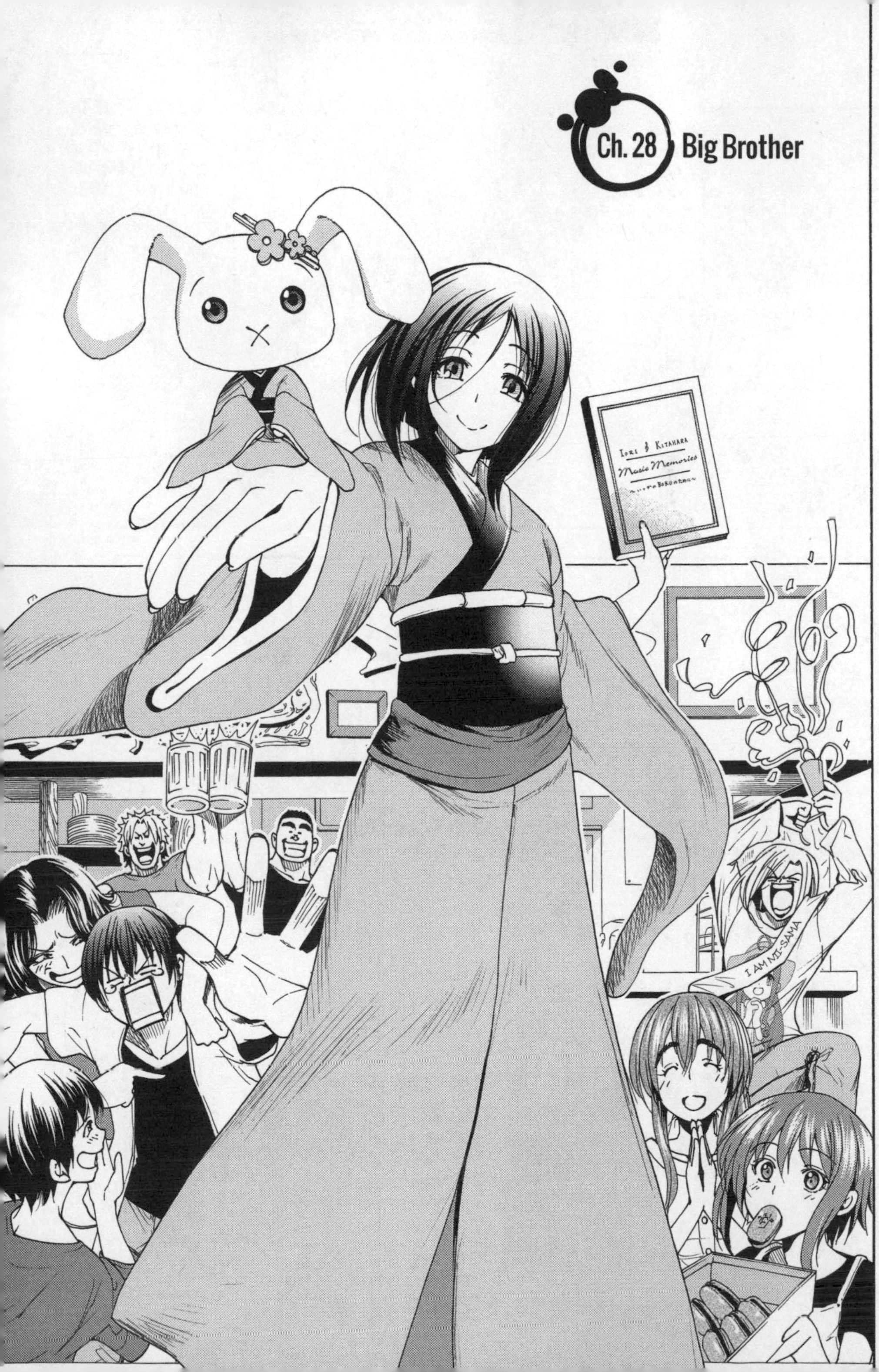
IORI KITAHARA
Music Memories
I AM NII-SAMA

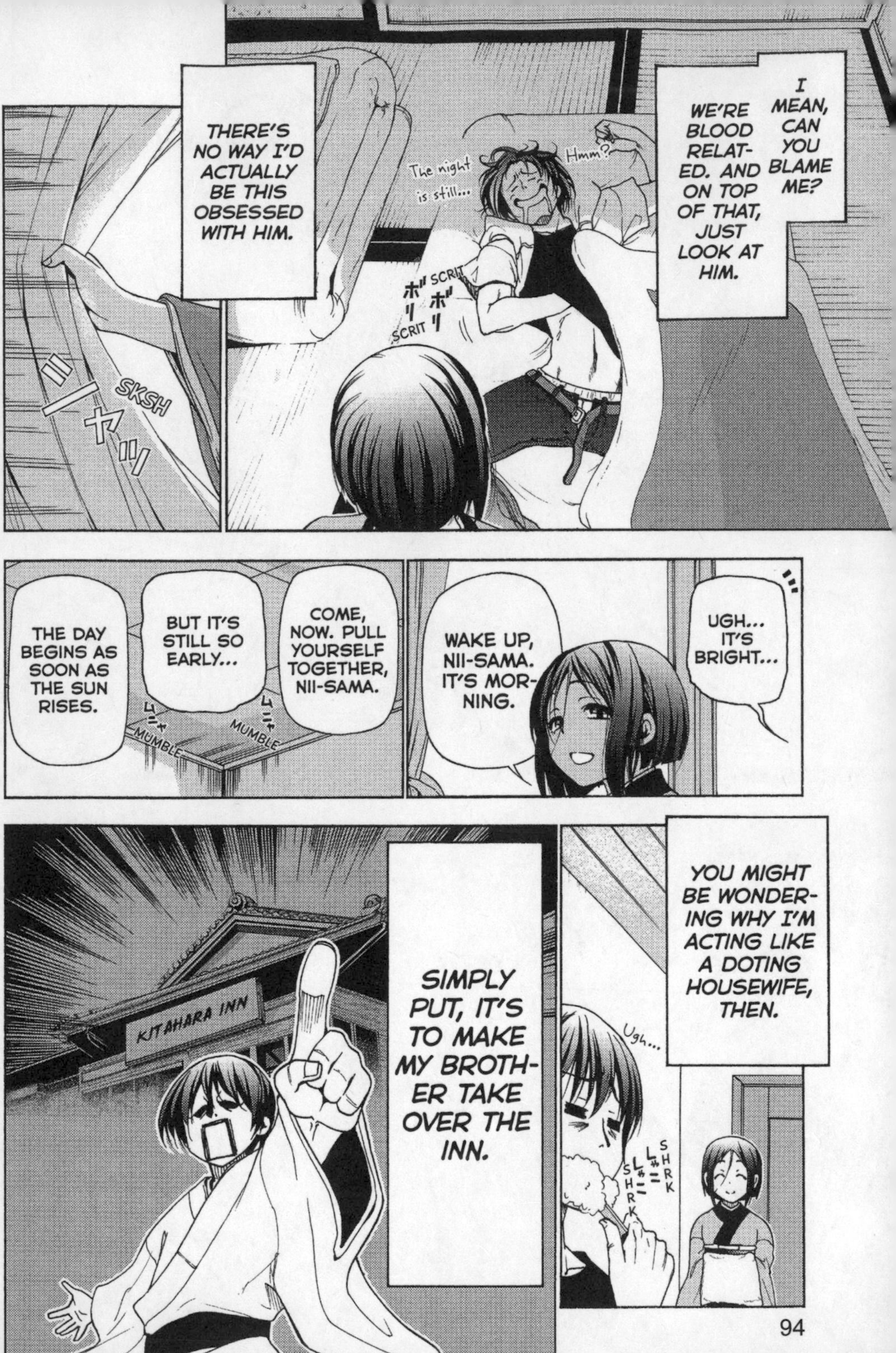
I MEAN, CAN YOU BLAME ME?
WE'RE BLOOD RELAT-ED. AND ON TOP OF THAT, JUST LOOK AT HIM.
Hmm?
The night is still...
THERE'S NO WAY I'D ACTUALLY BE THIS OBSESSED WITH HIM.
SCRIT SCRIT
SKSH
UGH... IT'S BRIGHT...
WAKE UP, NII-SAMA. IT'S MOR-NING.
COME, NOW. PULL YOURSELF TOGETHER, NII-SAMA.
MUMBLE
BUT IT'S STILL SO EARLY...
MUMBLE
THE DAY BEGINS AS SOON AS THE SUN RISES.
YOU MIGHT BE WONDER-ING WHY I'M ACTING LIKE A DOTING HOUSEWIFE, THEN.
Ugh...
SHRK SHRK
SIMPLY PUT, IT'S TO MAKE MY BROTH-ER TAKE OVER THE INN.
KITAHARA INN

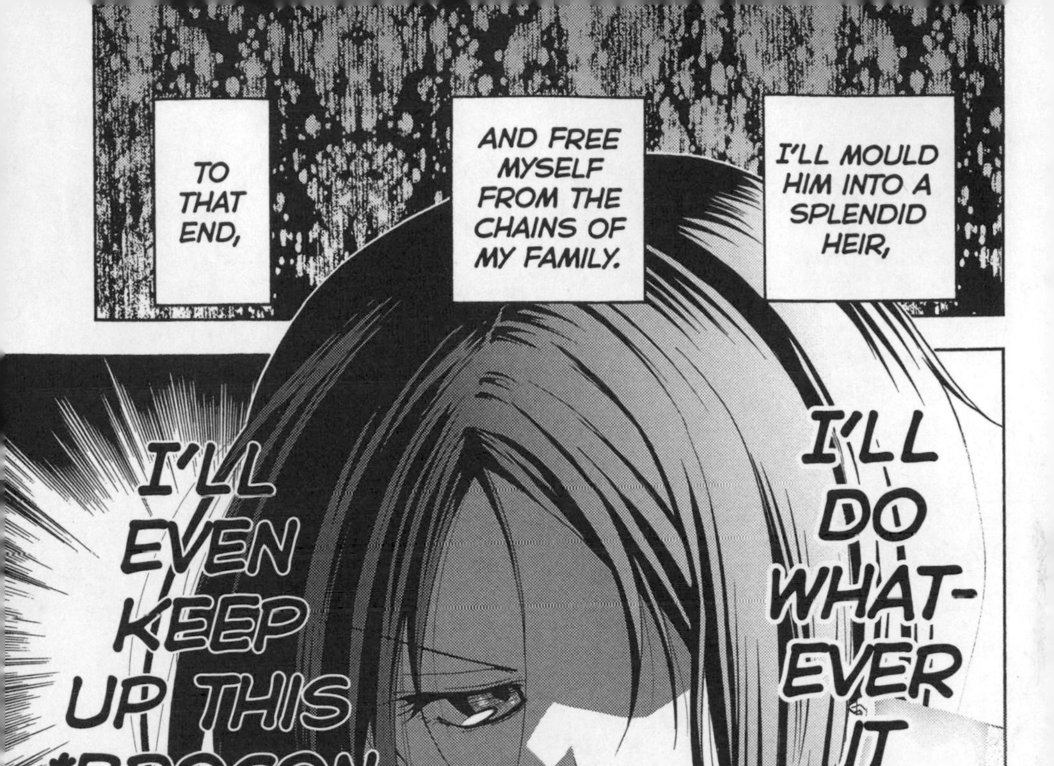
I'LL MOULD HIM INTO A SPLENDID HEIR,
AND FREE MYSELF FROM THE CHAINS OF MY FAMILY.
TO THAT END,
I'LL DO WHAT-EVER IT TAKES ooo
I'LL EVEN KEEP UP THIS *BROCON ACT.

*Brocon: Short for "brother complex." Someone who is way too attached to their brother.

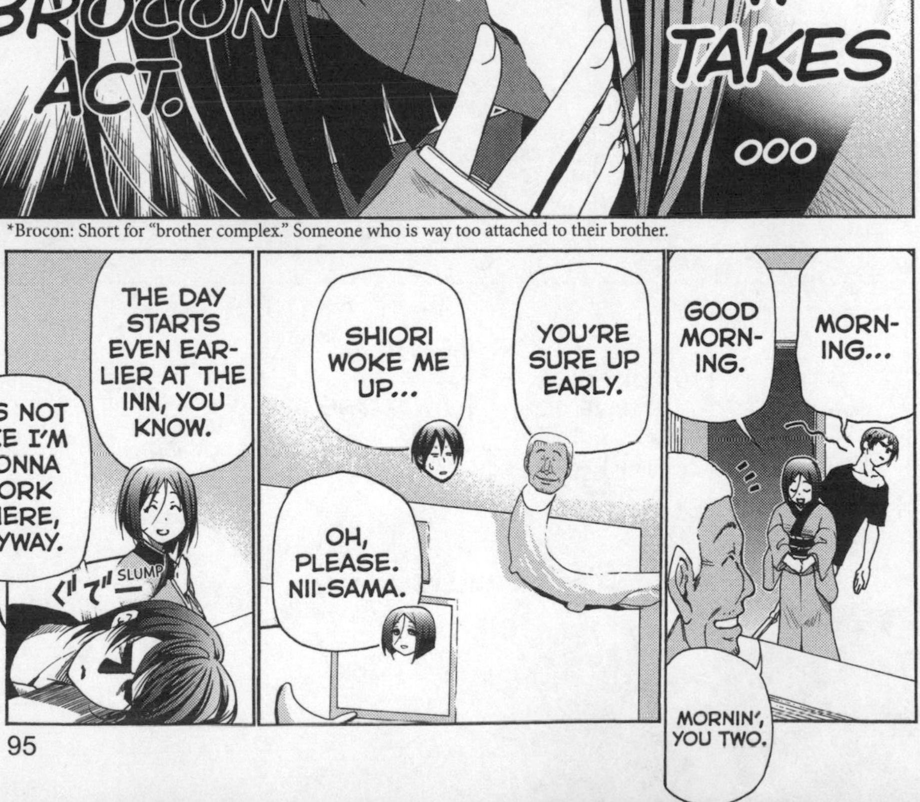
MORN-ING...
GOOD MORN-ING.
MORNIN', YOU TWO.
YOU'RE SURE UP EARLY.
SHIORI WOKE ME UP...
OH, PLEASE. NII-SAMA.
THE DAY STARTS EVEN EAR-LIER AT THE INN, YOU KNOW.
IT'S NOT LIKE I'M GONNA WORK THERE, ANYWAY.
ぐでー
SLUMP

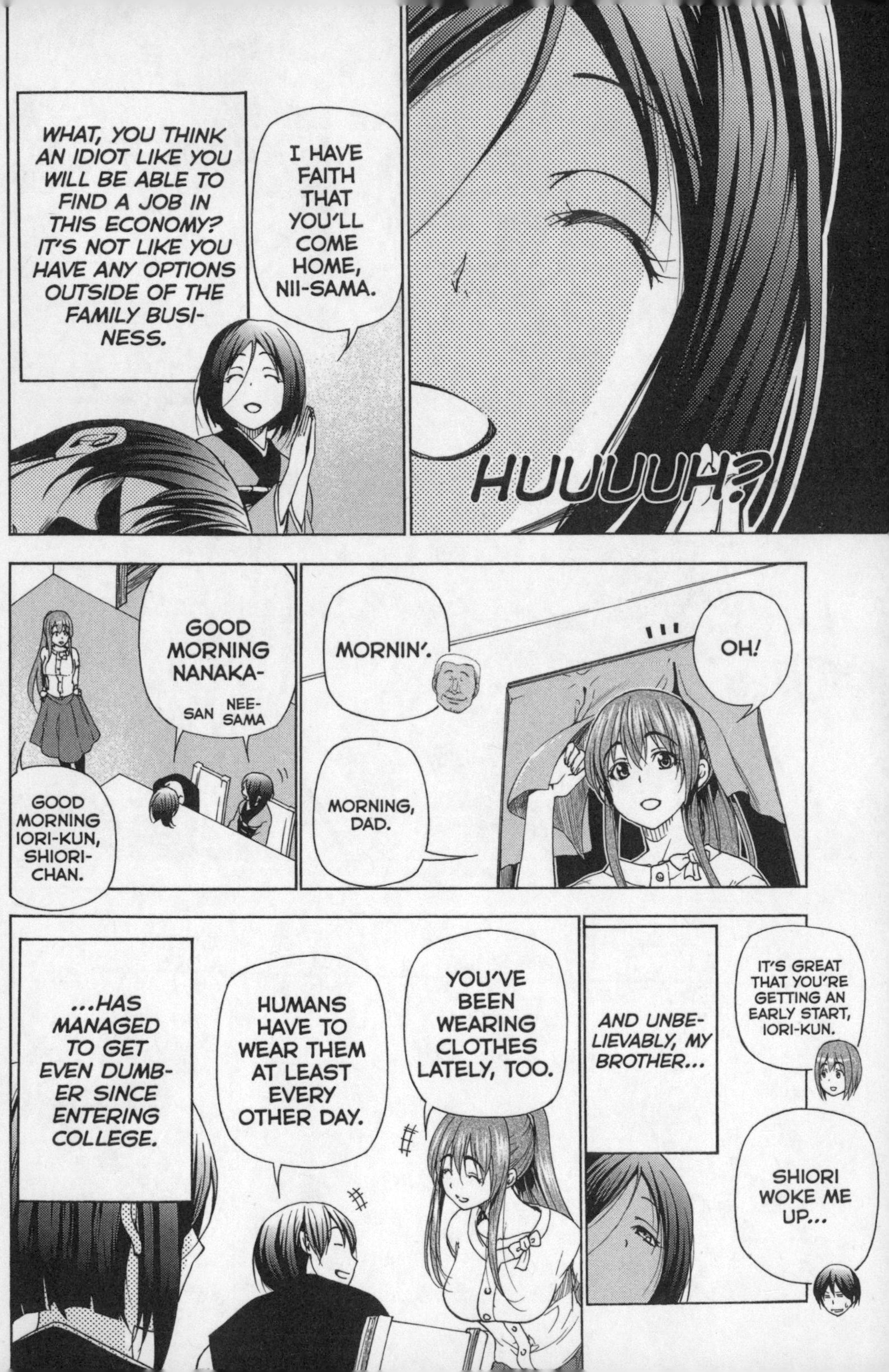
HUUUUH?
I HAVE FAITH THAT YOU'LL COME HOME, NII-SAMA.
WHAT, YOU THINK AN IDIOT LIKE YOU WILL BE ABLE TO FIND A JOB IN THIS ECONOMY? IT'S NOT LIKE YOU HAVE ANY OPTIONS OUTSIDE OF THE FAMILY BUSINESS.
OH!
MORNIN'.
MORNING, DAD.
GOOD MORNING NANAKA- SAN NEE-SAMA
GOOD MORNING IORI-KUN, SHIORI-CHAN.
IT'S GREAT THAT YOU'RE GETTING AN EARLY START, IORI-KUN.
AND UNBELIEVABLY, MY BROTHER...
SHIORI WOKE ME UP...
YOU'VE BEEN WEARING CLOTHES LATELY, TOO.
HUMANS HAVE TO WEAR THEM AT LEAST EVERY OTHER DAY.
...HAS MANAGED TO GET EVEN DUMBER SINCE ENTERING COLLEGE.

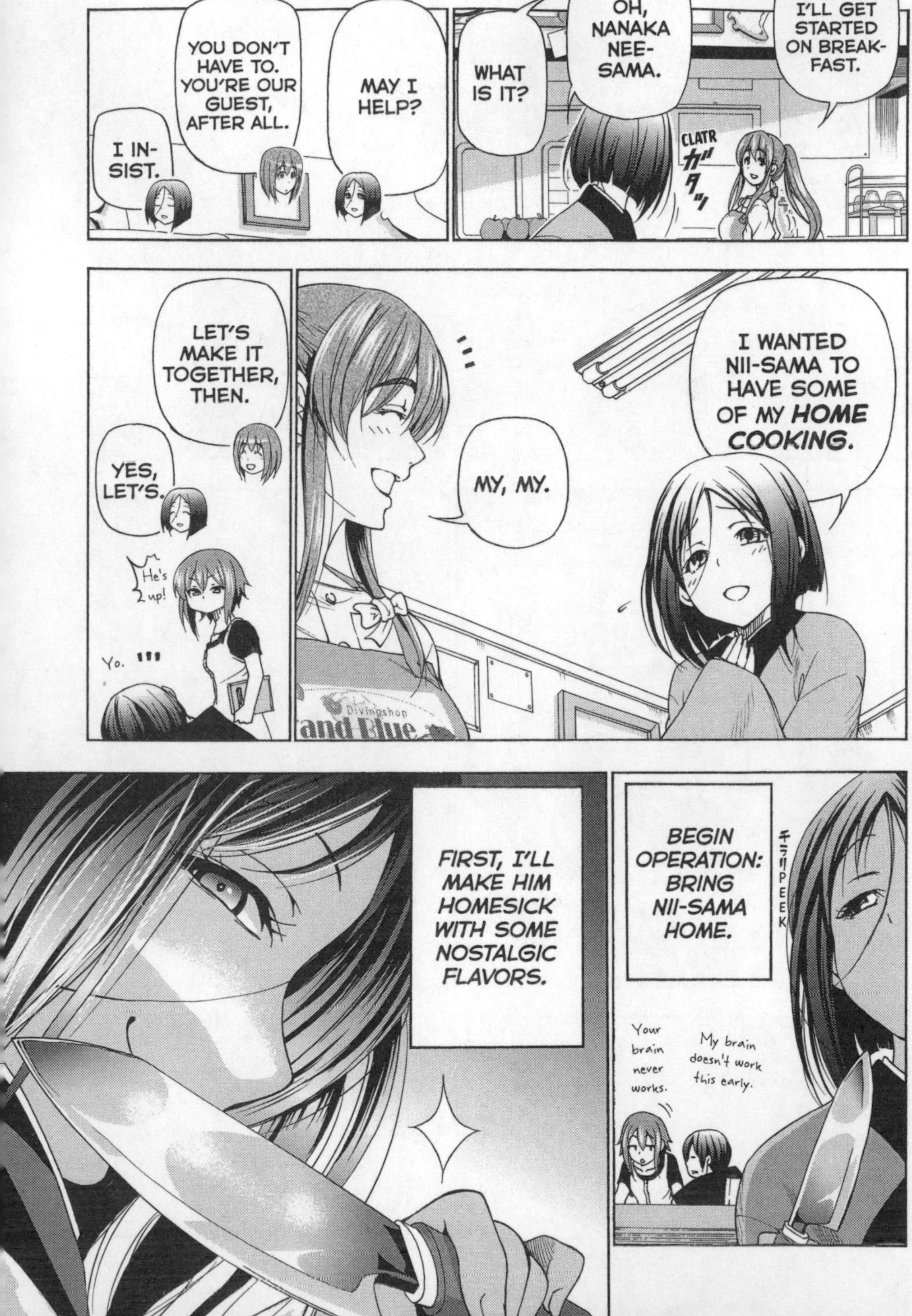
HANG ON. I'LL GET STARTED ON BREAK-FAST.
OH, NANAKA NEE-SAMA.
WHAT IS IT?
CLATR ガタッ
MAY I HELP?
YOU DON'T HAVE TO. YOU'RE OUR GUEST, AFTER ALL.
I IN-SIST.
I WANTED NII-SAMA TO HAVE SOME OF MY HOME COOKING.
MY, MY.
Divingshop
LET'S MAKE IT TOGETHER, THEN.
YES, LET'S.
He's up!
Yo.
BEGIN OPERATION: BRING NII-SAMA HOME.
チラリ PEEK
My brain doesn't work this early.
Your brain never works.
FIRST, I'LL MAKE HIM HOMESICK WITH SOME NOSTALGIC FLAVORS.

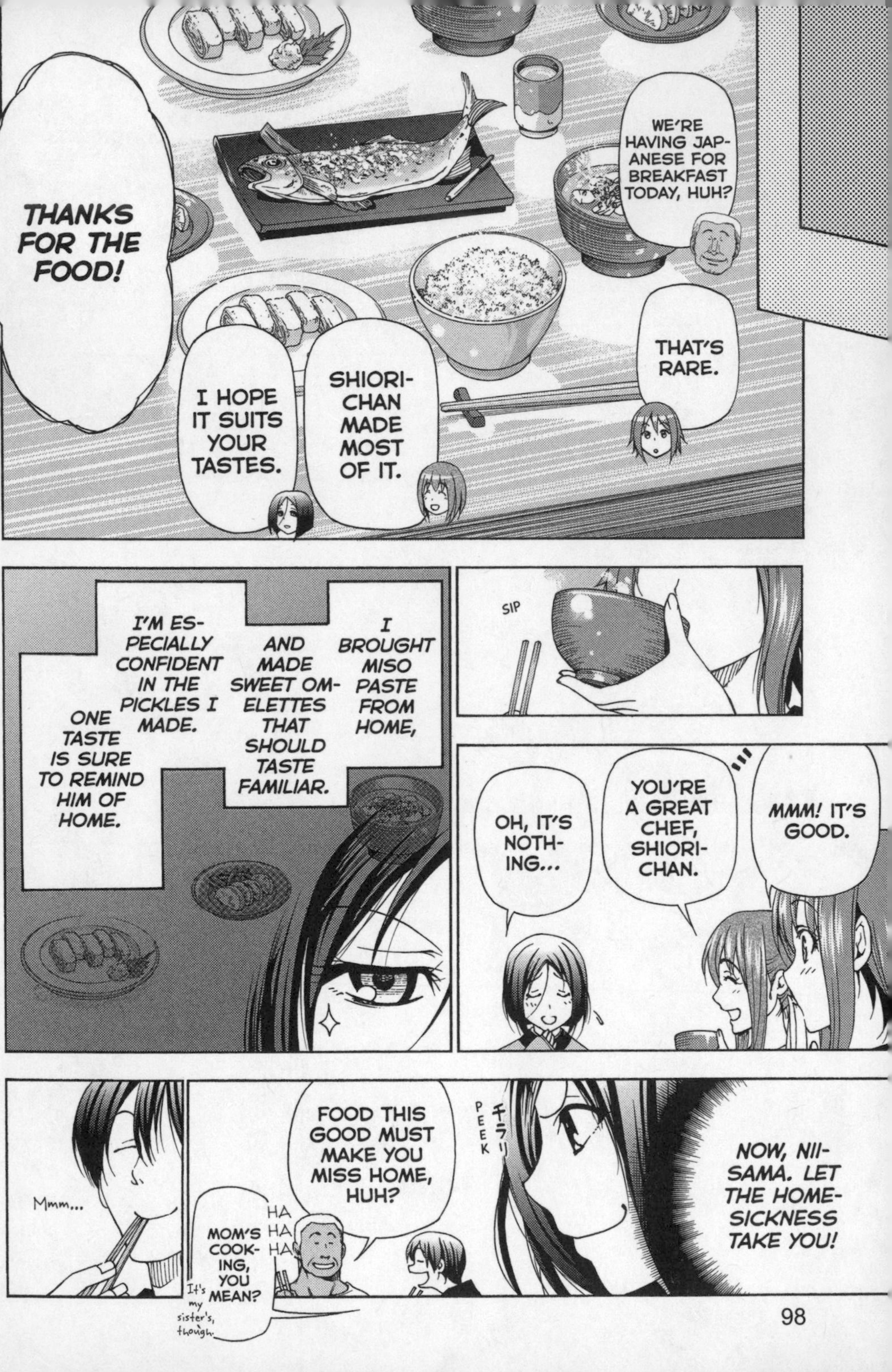
WE'RE HAVING JAPANESE FOR BREAKFAST TODAY, HUH?
THAT'S RARE.
SHIORI-CHAN MADE MOST OF IT.
I HOPE IT SUITS YOUR TASTES.
THANKS FOR THE FOOD!
SIP
MMM! IT'S GOOD.
YOU'RE A GREAT CHEF, SHIORI-CHAN.
OH, IT'S NOTHING...
I BROUGHT MISO PASTE FROM HOME,
AND MADE SWEET OMELETTES THAT SHOULD TASTE FAMILIAR.
I'M ESPECIALLY CONFIDENT IN THE PICKLES I MADE.
ONE TASTE IS SURE TO REMIND HIM OF HOME.
NOW, NII-SAMA. LET THE HOMESICKNESS TAKE YOU!
チラリ
PEEK
FOOD THIS GOOD MUST MAKE YOU MISS HOME, HUH?
HA HA HA
MOM'S COOKING, YOU MEAN?
It's my sister's, though.
Mmm...

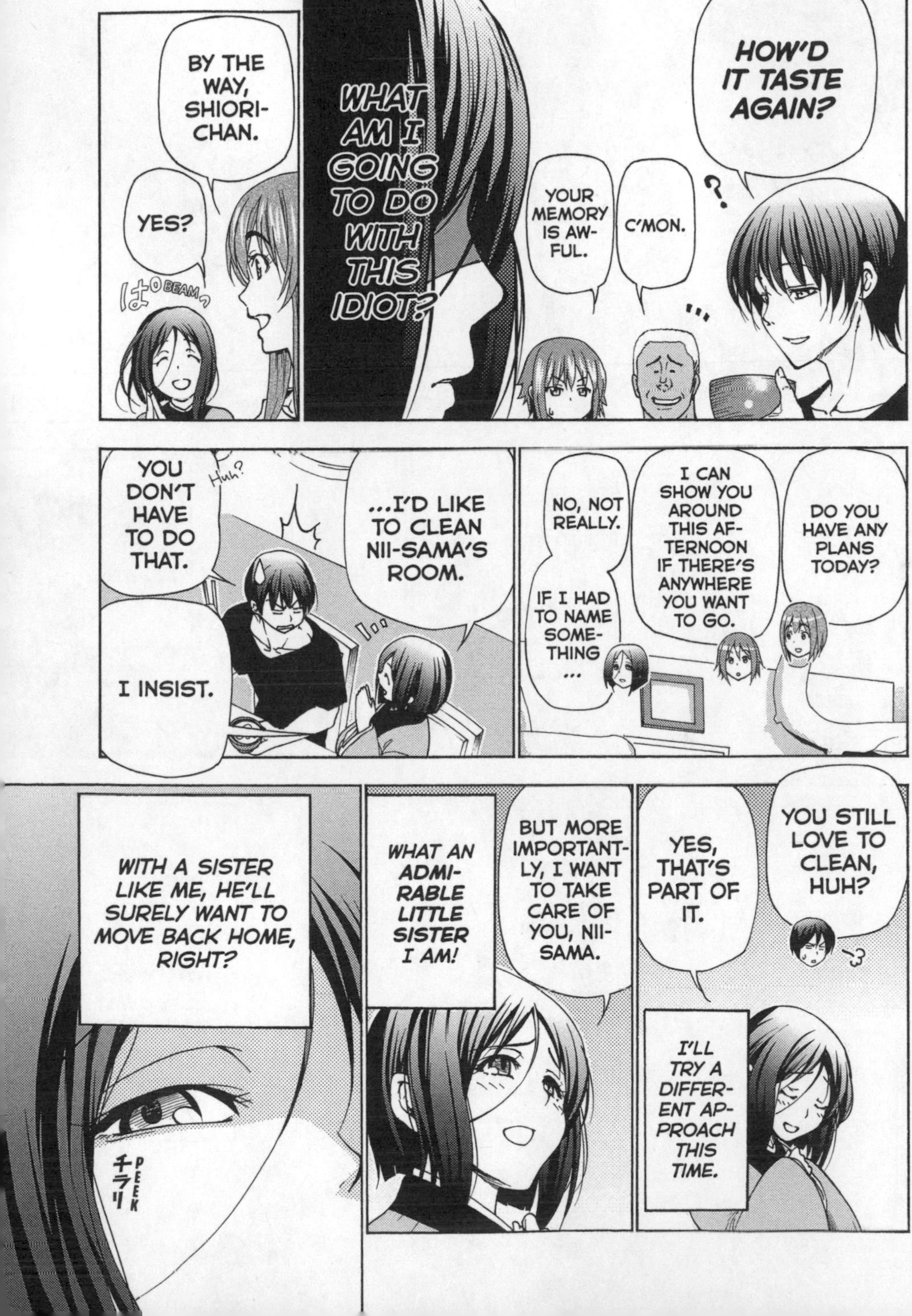
HOW'D IT TASTE AGAIN?
?
C'MON.
YOUR MEMORY IS AW-FUL.
...
WHAT AM I GOING TO DO WITH THIS IDIOT?
BY THE WAY, SHIORI-CHAN.
YES?
は BEAM
DO YOU HAVE ANY PLANS TODAY?
I CAN SHOW YOU AROUND THIS AF-TERNOON IF THERE'S ANYWHERE YOU WANT TO GO.
NO, NOT REALLY.
IF I HAD TO NAME SOME-THING ...
...I'D LIKE TO CLEAN NII-SAMA'S ROOM.
YOU DON'T HAVE TO DO THAT.
Huh?
I INSIST.
YOU STILL LOVE TO CLEAN, HUH?
YES, THAT'S PART OF IT.
I'LL TRY A DIFFER-ENT AP-PROACH THIS TIME.
BUT MORE IMPORTANT-LY, I WANT TO TAKE CARE OF YOU, NII-SAMA.
WHAT AN ADMI-RABLE LITTLE SISTER I AM!
WITH A SISTER LIKE ME, HE'LL SURELY WANT TO MOVE BACK HOME, RIGHT?
チラリ PEEK

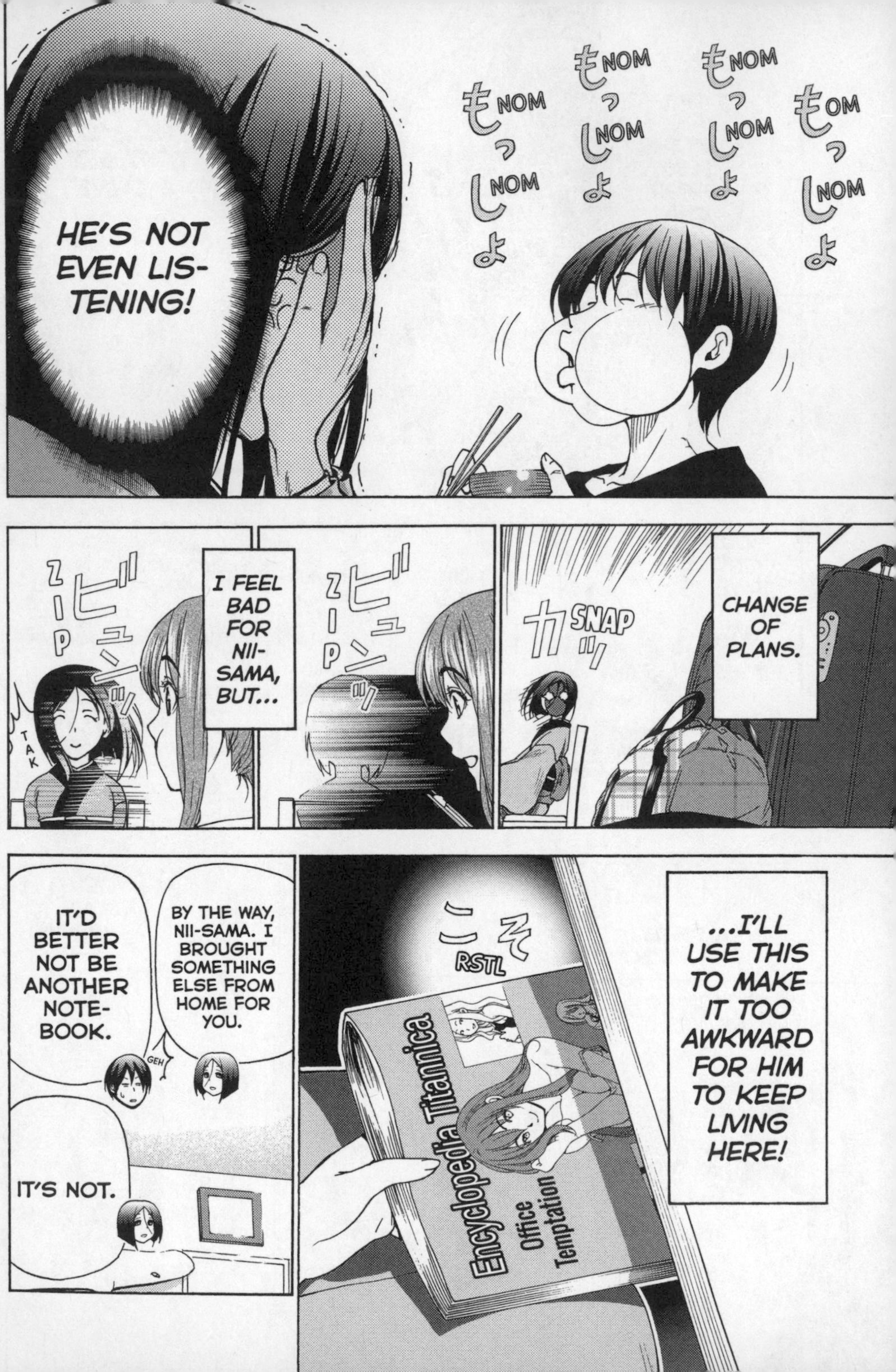
もっしょ NOM NOM
NOM NOM
NOM NOM
OM NOM
HE'S NOT EVEN LIS-TENING!
CHANGE OF PLANS.
カッ SNAP
I FEEL BAD FOR NII-SAMA, BUT...
ビュンッ ZIP
ビュンッ ZIP
TAK
...I'LL USE THIS TO MAKE IT TOO AWKWARD FOR HIM TO KEEP LIVING HERE!
こそ RSTL
Encyclopedia Titannica
Office Temptation
BY THE WAY, NII-SAMA. I BROUGHT SOMETHING ELSE FROM HOME FOR YOU.
IT'D BETTER NOT BE ANOTHER NOTE-BOOK.
GEH
IT'S NOT.

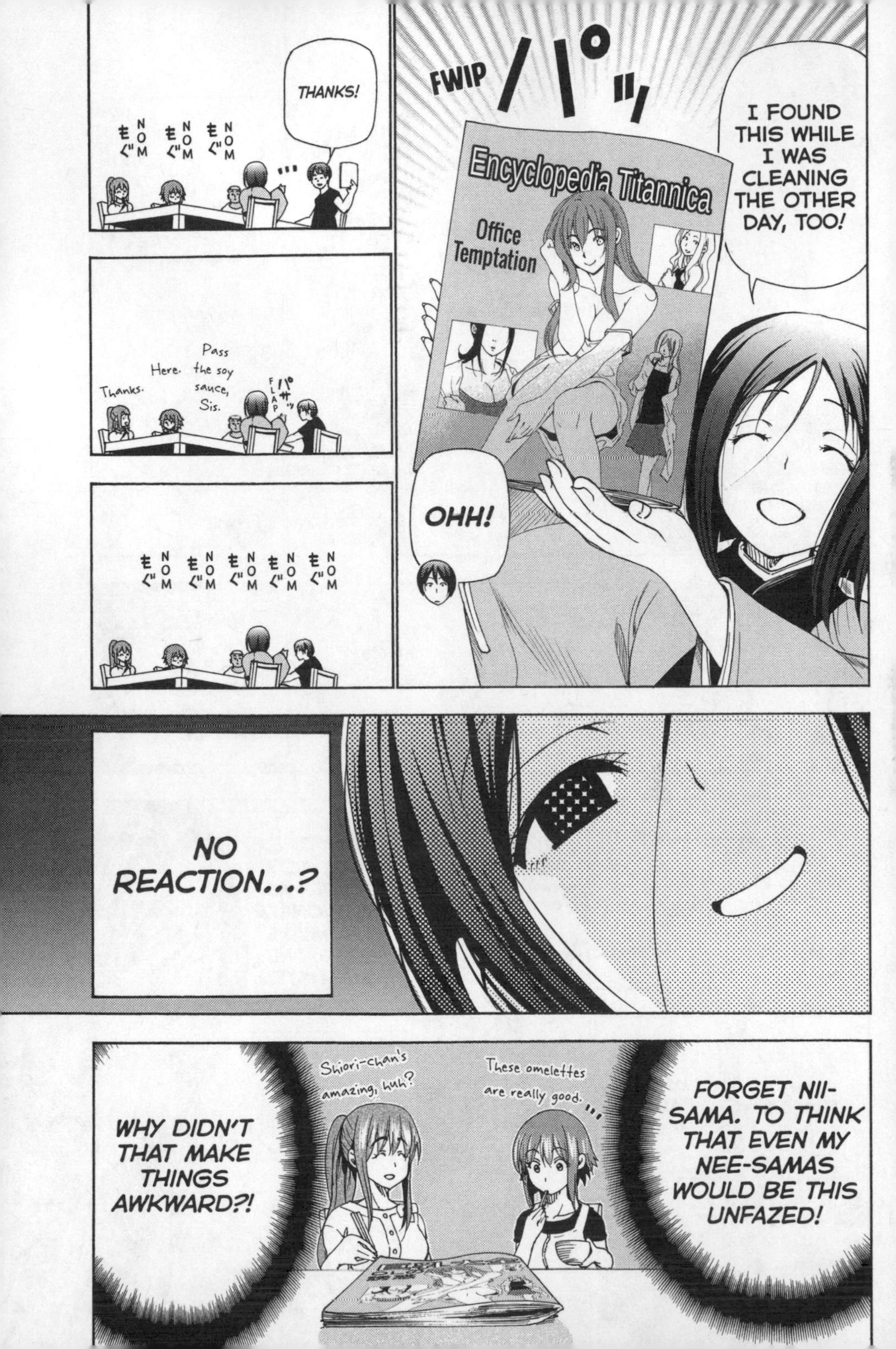

FWIP
パッ
I FOUND THIS WHILE I WAS CLEANING THE OTHER DAY, TOO!
Encyclopedia Titannica
Office Temptation
OHH!
THANKS!
NOM NOM NOM
Pass the soy sauce, Sis.
Here.
Thanks.
FLAP
NOM NOM NOM NOM NOM
NO REACTION...?
FORGET NII-SAMA. TO THINK THAT EVEN MY NEE-SAMAS WOULD BE THIS UNFAZED!
These omelettes are really good.
Shiori-chan's amazing, huh?
WHY DIDN'T THAT MAKE THINGS AWKWARD?!

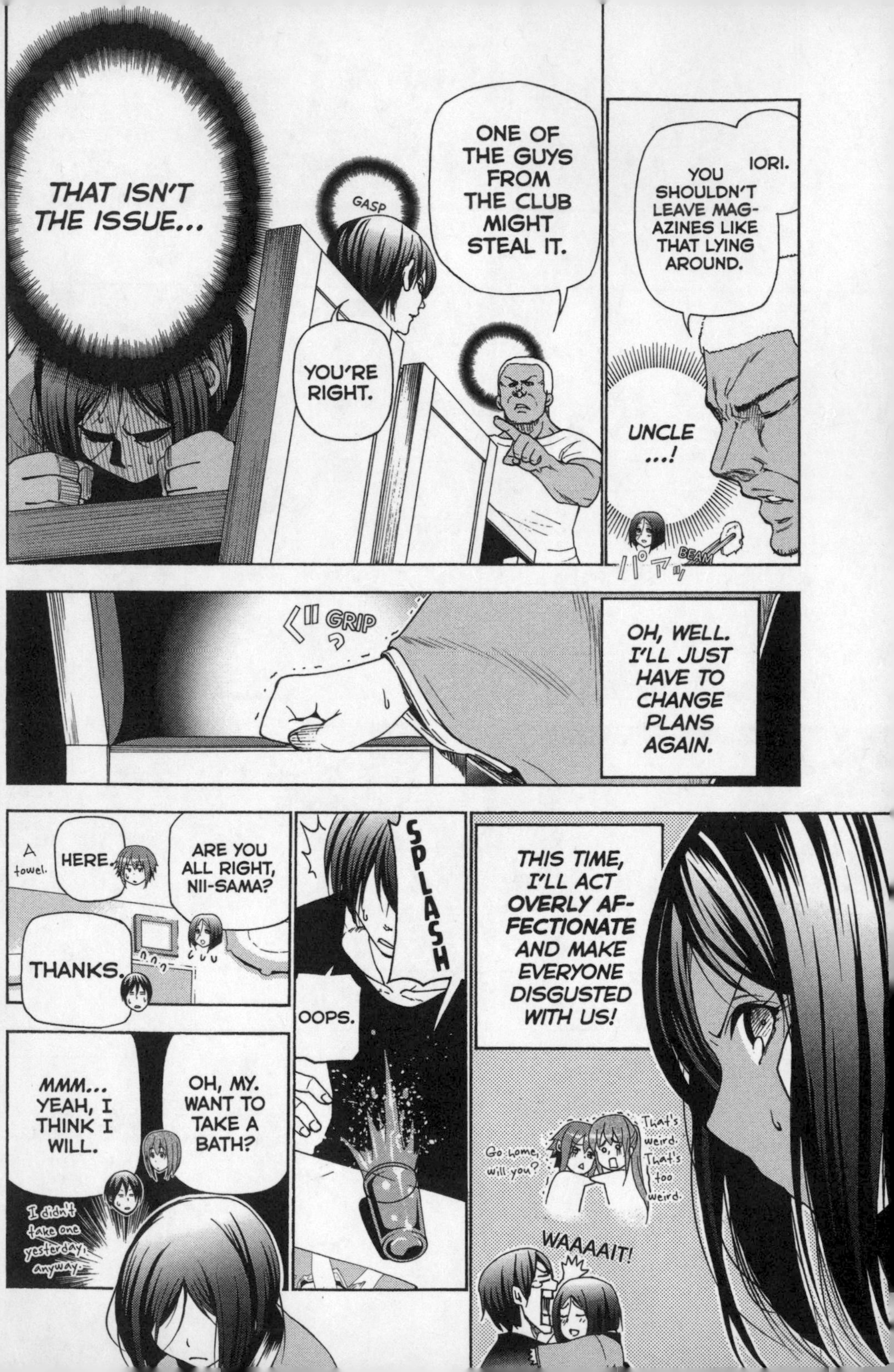
IORI.
YOU SHOULDN'T LEAVE MAG-AZINES LIKE THAT LYING AROUND.
UNCLE ...!
BEAM
ONE OF THE GUYS FROM THE CLUB MIGHT STEAL IT.
GASP
YOU'RE RIGHT.
THAT ISN'T THE ISSUE...
OH, WELL. I'LL JUST HAVE TO CHANGE PLANS AGAIN.
GRIP
THIS TIME, I'LL ACT OVERLY AF-FECTIONATE AND MAKE EVERYONE DISGUSTED WITH US!
That's weird. That's too weird.
Go home, will you?
WAAAAIT!
SPLASH
OOPS.
ARE YOU ALL RIGHT, NII-SAMA?
HERE.
A towel.
THANKS.
OH, MY. WANT TO TAKE A BATH?
MMM... YEAH, I THINK I WILL.
I didn't take one yesterday, anyway.

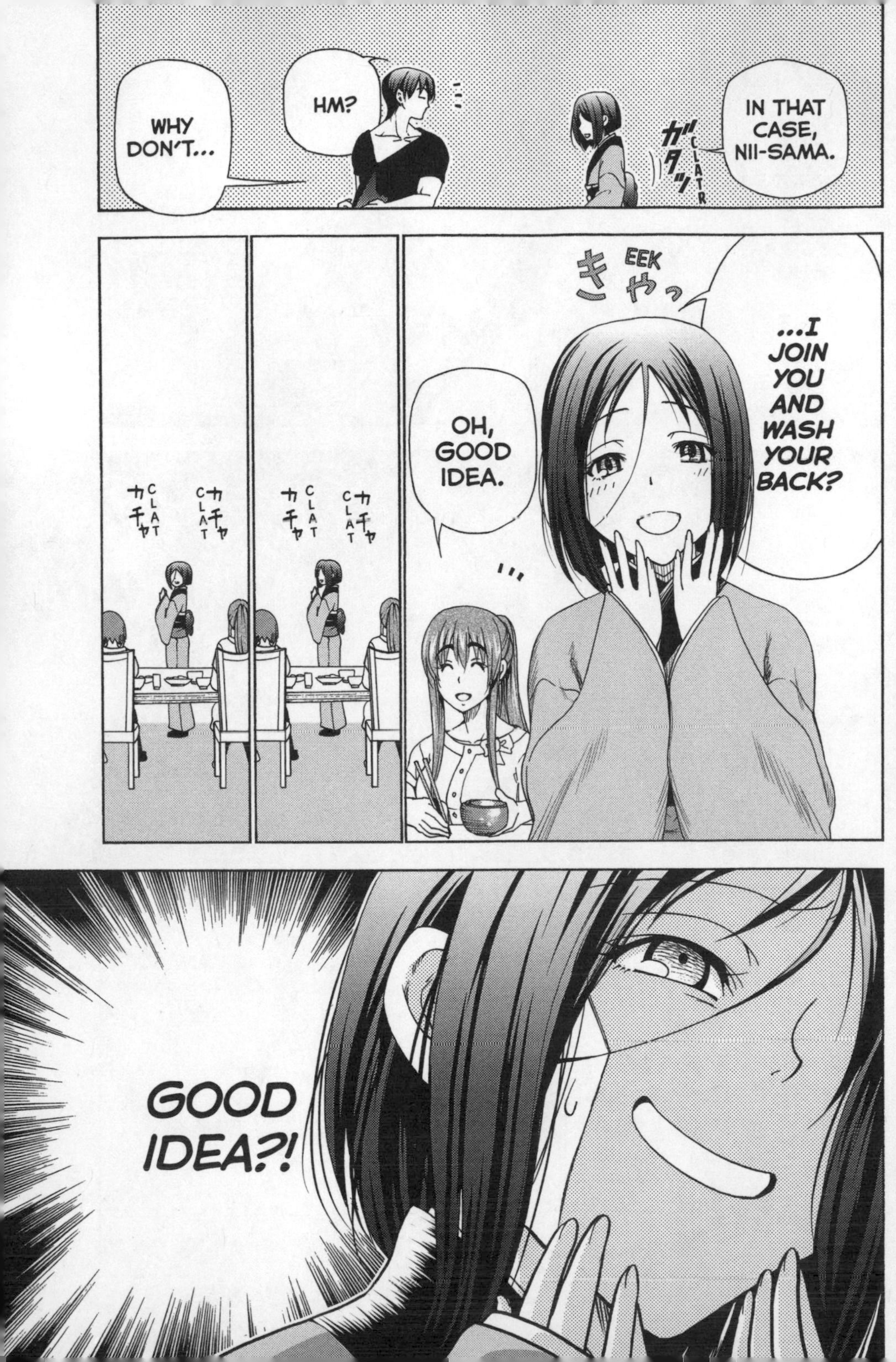
IN THAT CASE, NII-SAMA.
ガタッ CLATR
HM?
WHY DON'T...
きゃっ EEK
...I JOIN YOU AND WASH YOUR BACK?
OH, GOOD IDEA.
カチャ CLAT
カチャ CLAT
カチャ CLAT
カチャ CLAT
GOOD IDEA?!

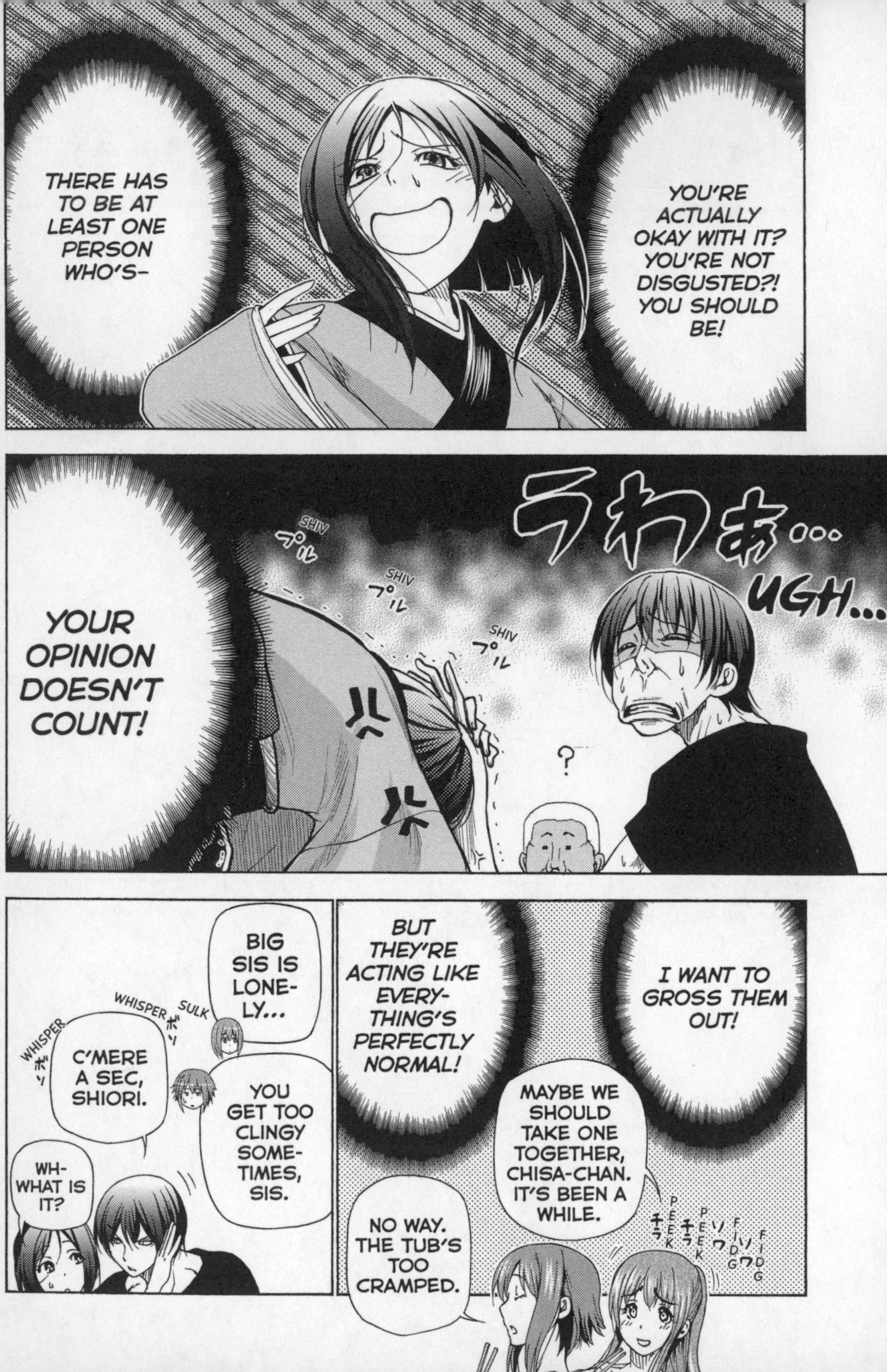
YOU'RE ACTUALLY OKAY WITH IT? YOU'RE NOT DISGUSTED?! YOU SHOULD BE!
THERE HAS TO BE AT LEAST ONE PERSON WHO'S-
うわぁ…
UGH…
SHIV プル
SHIV プル
SHIV プル
YOUR OPINION DOESN'T COUNT!
?
I WANT TO GROSS THEM OUT!
BUT THEY'RE ACTING LIKE EVERY-THING'S PERFECTLY NORMAL!
MAYBE WE SHOULD TAKE ONE TOGETHER, CHISA-CHAN. IT'S BEEN A WHILE.
PEEK チラ
PEEK チラ
FIDG ソワ
FIDG ソワ
NO WAY. THE TUB'S TOO CRAMPED.
BIG SIS IS LONE-LY…
SULK
WHISPER ボソ
YOU GET TOO CLINGY SOME-TIMES, SIS.
WHISPER ボソ
C'MERE A SEC, SHIORI.
WH-WHAT IS IT?

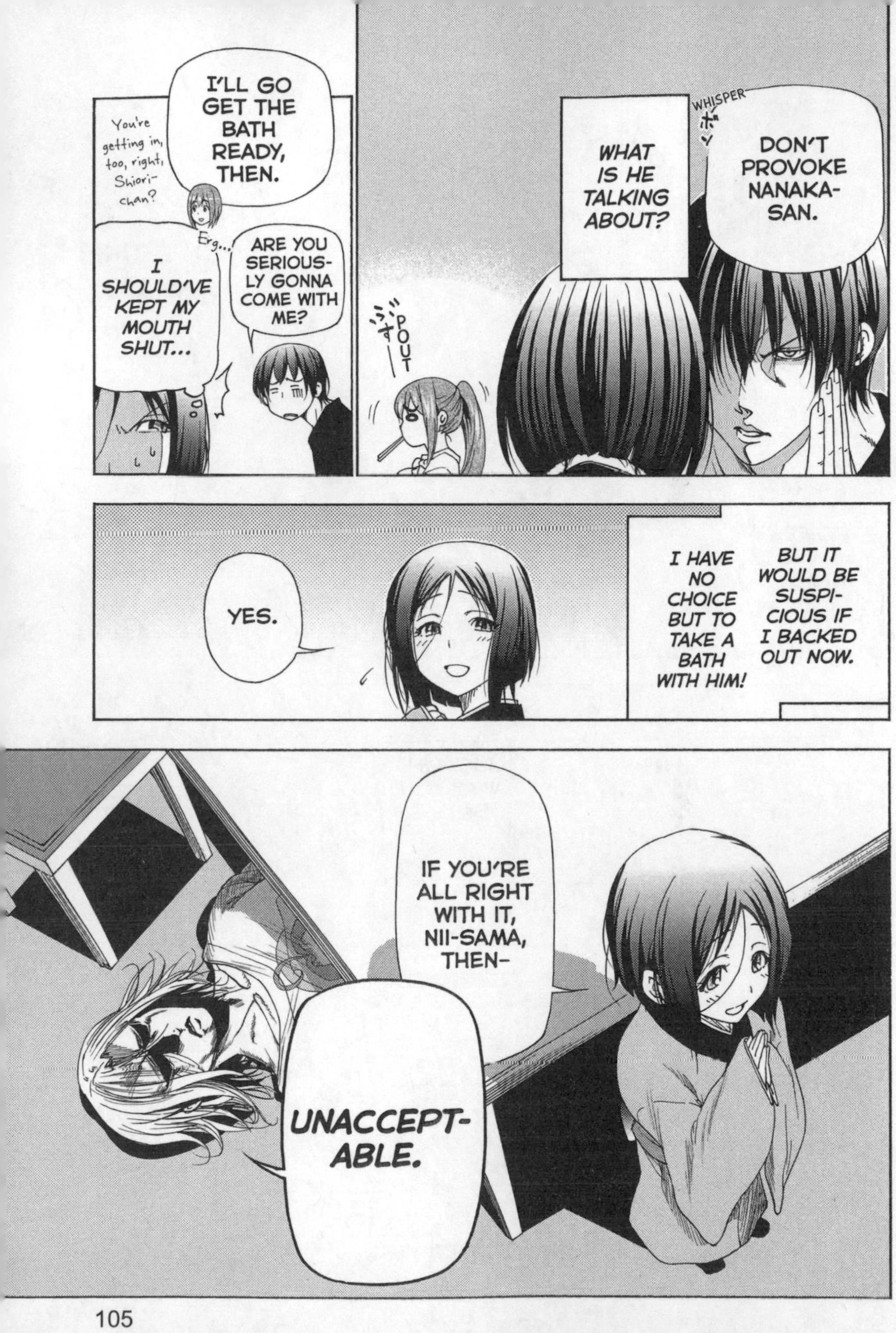
WHISPER
DON'T PROVOKE NANAKA-SAN.
WHAT IS HE TALKING ABOUT?
POUT
I'LL GO GET THE BATH READY, THEN.
You're getting in, too, right, Shiori-chan?
ARE YOU SERIOUSLY GONNA COME WITH ME?
Erg...
I SHOULD'VE KEPT MY MOUTH SHUT...
BUT IT WOULD BE SUSPICIOUS IF I BACKED OUT NOW.
I HAVE NO CHOICE BUT TO TAKE A BATH WITH HIM!
YES.
IF YOU'RE ALL RIGHT WITH IT, NII-SAMA, THEN-
UNACCEPTABLE.

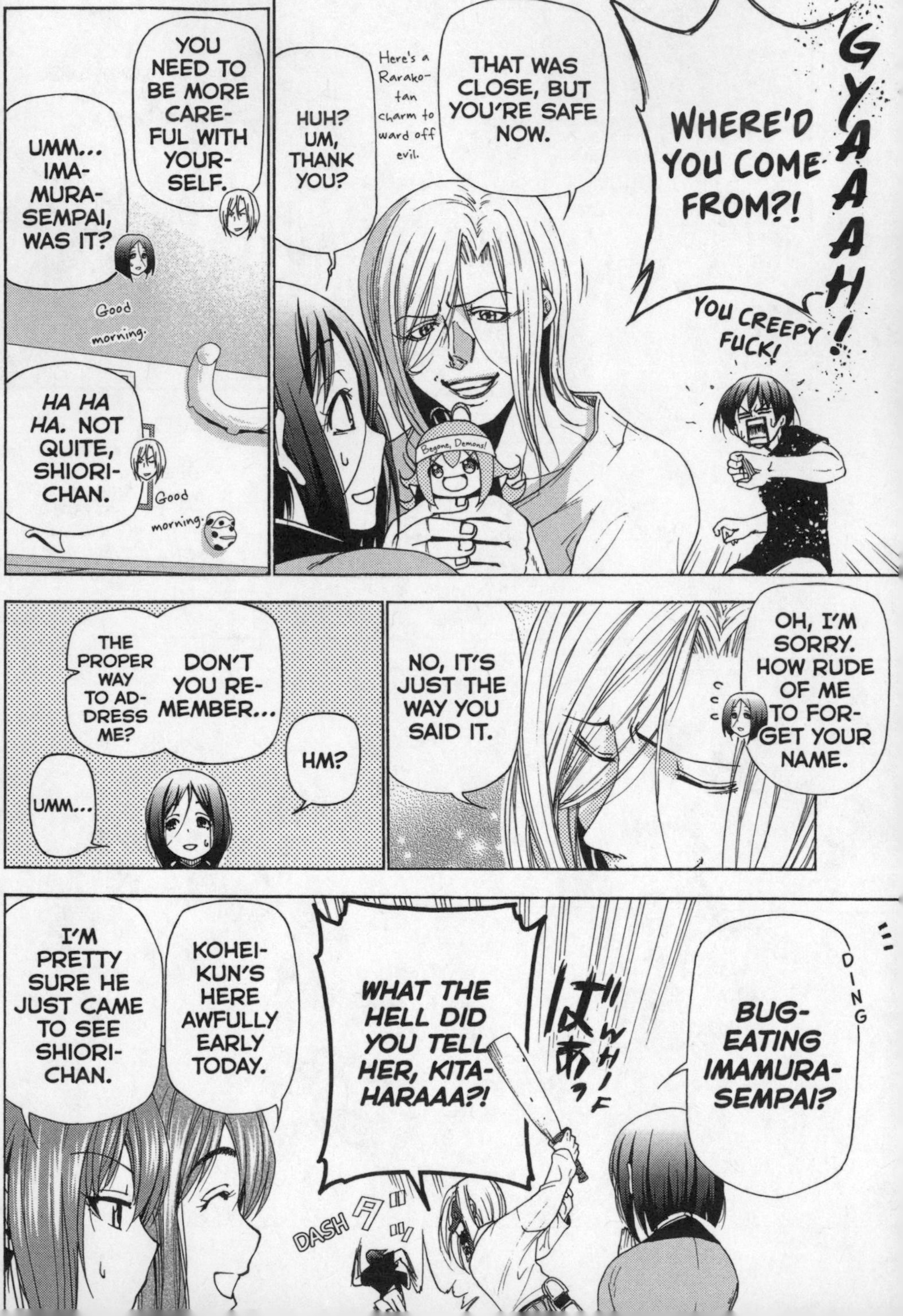
GYAAAAH!
WHERE'D YOU COME FROM?!
YOU CREEPY FUCK!
THAT WAS CLOSE, BUT YOU'RE SAFE NOW.
Here's a Rarako-tan charm to ward off evil.
Begone, Demons!
HUH? UM, THANK YOU?
YOU NEED TO BE MORE CAREFUL WITH YOURSELF.
UMM... IMAMURA-SEMPAI, WAS IT?
Good morning.
HA HA HA. NOT QUITE, SHIORI-CHAN.
Good morning.
OH, I'M SORRY. HOW RUDE OF ME TO FORGET YOUR NAME.
NO, IT'S JUST THE WAY YOU SAID IT.
HM?
DON'T YOU REMEMBER...
THE PROPER WAY TO ADDRESS ME?
UMM...
DING
BUG-EATING IMAMURA-SEMPAI?
WHIFF
WHAT THE HELL DID YOU TELL HER, KITAHARAAA?!
DASH
KOHEI-KUN'S HERE AWFULLY EARLY TODAY.
I'M PRETTY SURE HE JUST CAME TO SEE SHIORI-CHAN.

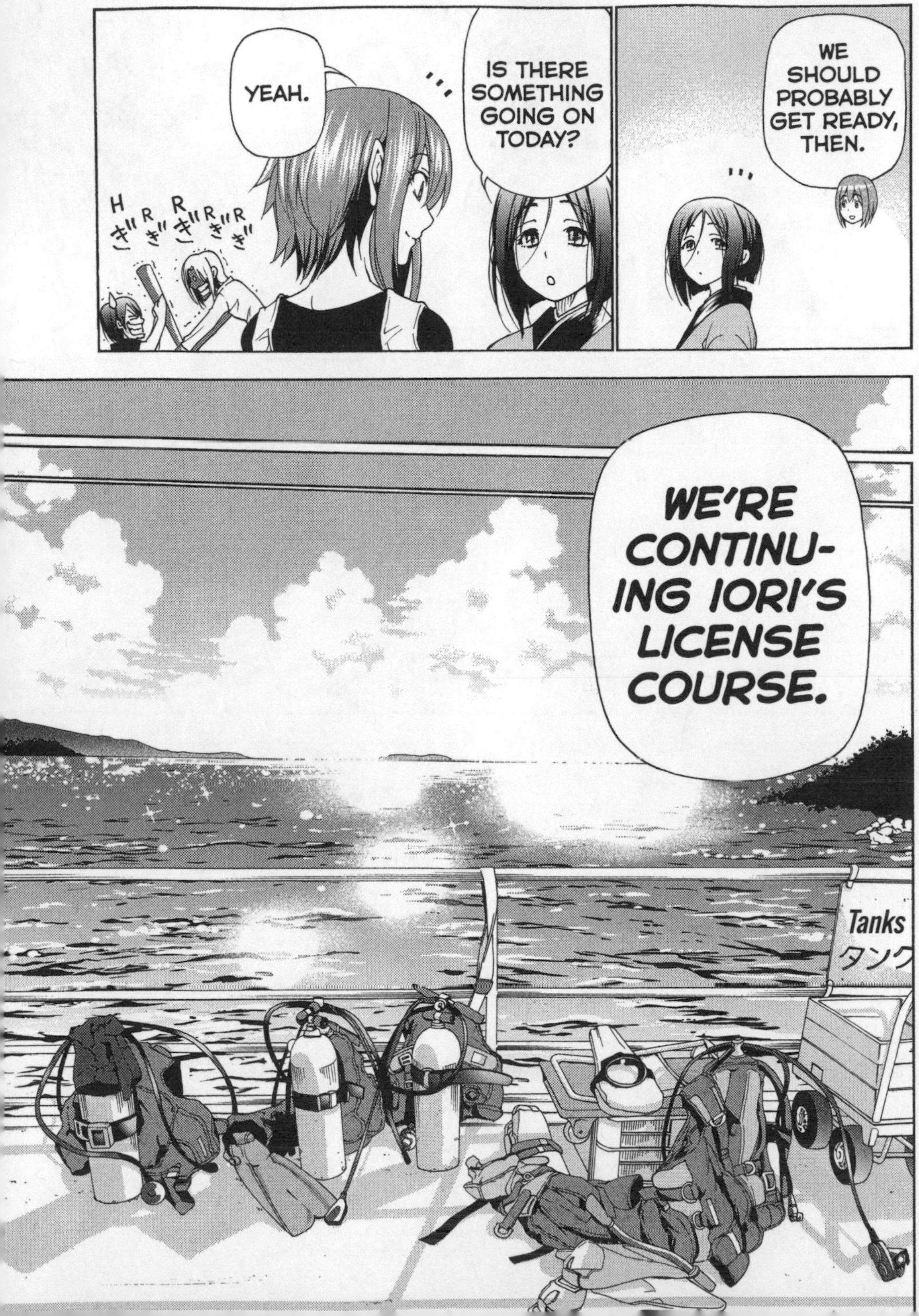
WE SHOULD PROBABLY GET READY, THEN.
...
IS THERE SOMETHING GOING ON TODAY?
...
YEAH.
HRRRR
WE'RE CONTINUING IORI'S LICENSE COURSE.
Tanks
タンク

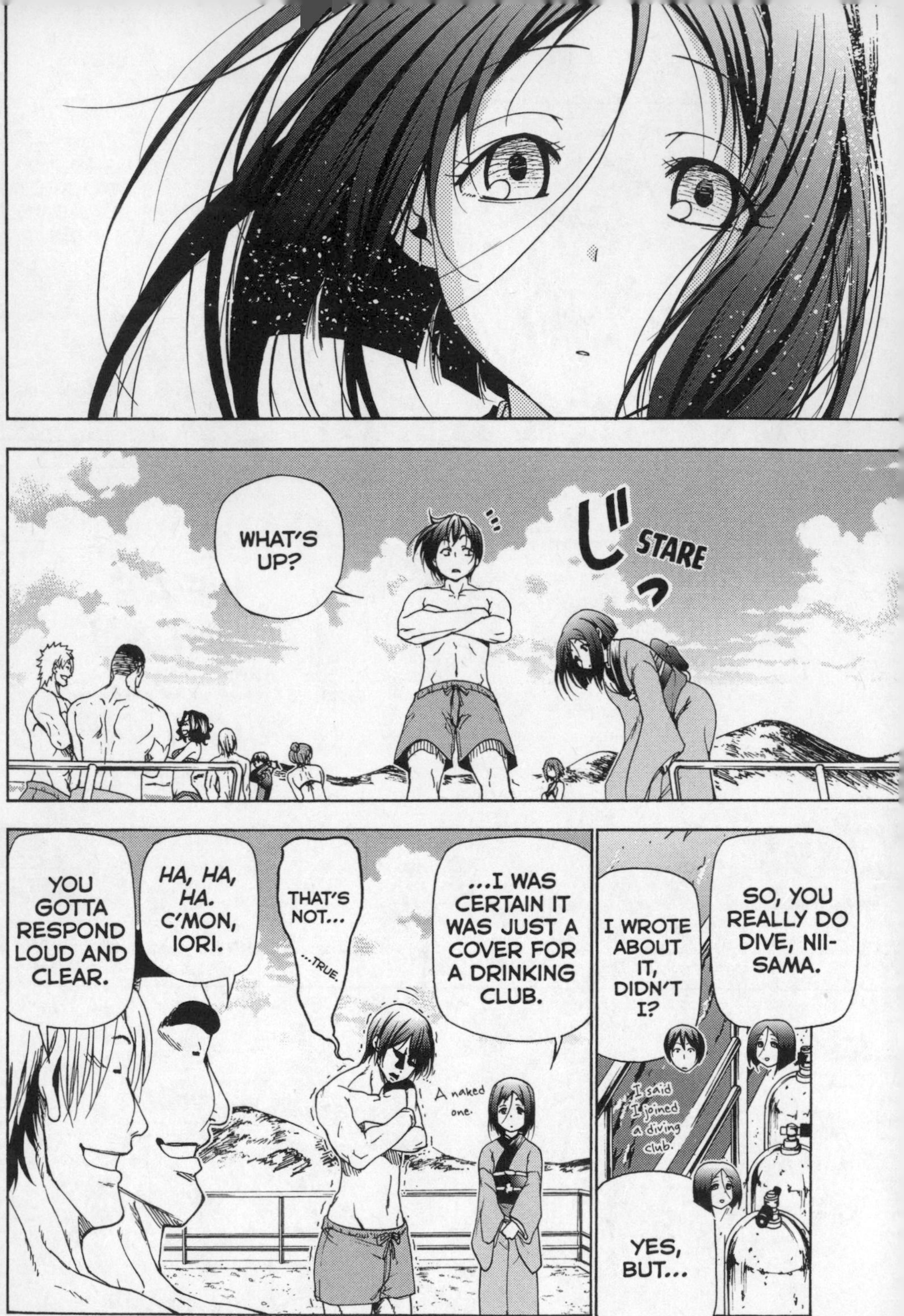
じー
STARE
WHAT'S UP?
SO, YOU REALLY DO DIVE, NII-SAMA.
I WROTE ABOUT IT, DIDN'T I?
I said I joined a diving club.
YES, BUT...
...I WAS CERTAIN IT WAS JUST A COVER FOR A DRINKING CLUB.
THAT'S NOT...
...TRUE.
A naked one.
HA, HA, HA. C'MON, IORI.
YOU GOTTA RESPOND LOUD AND CLEAR.

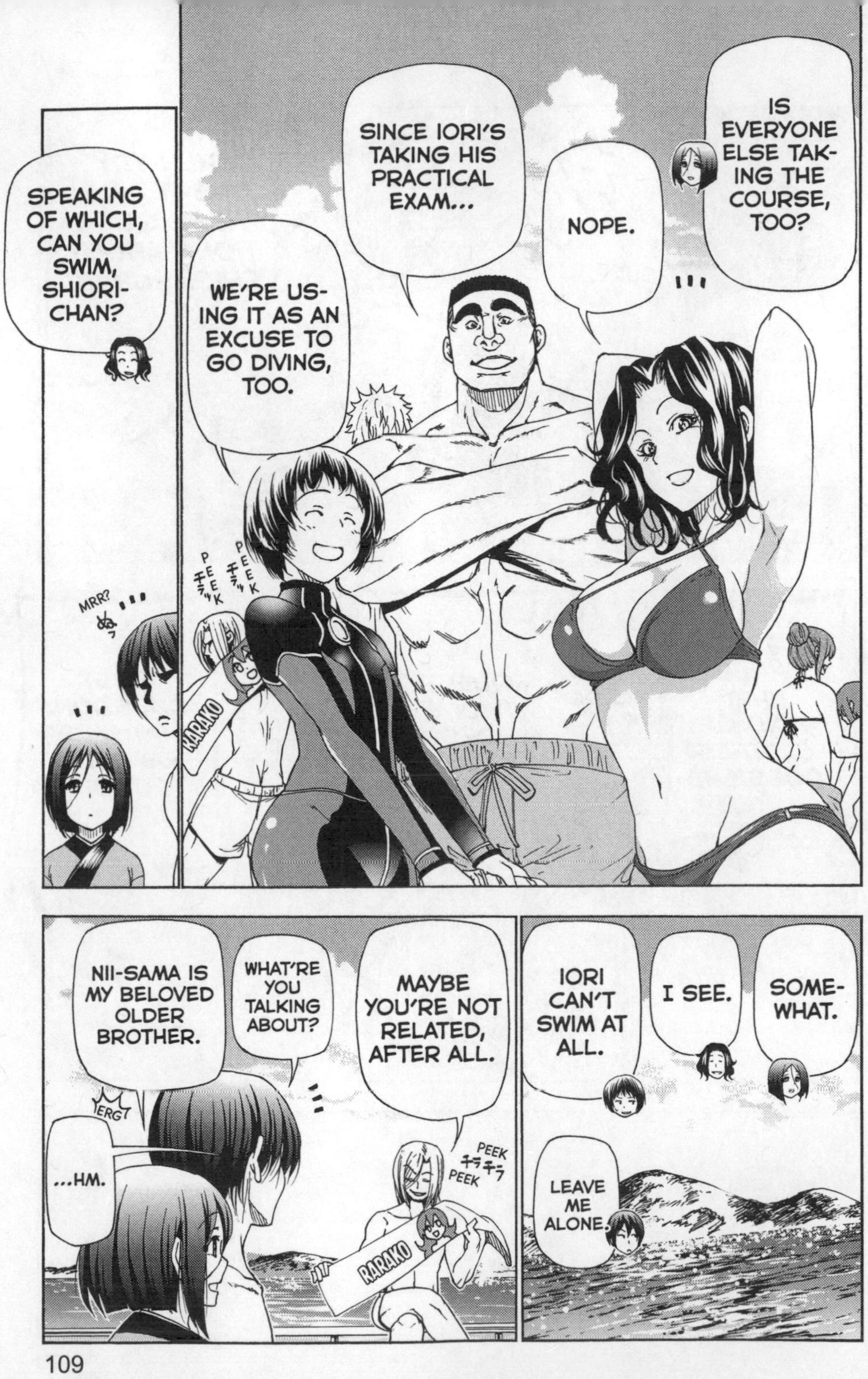
IS EVERYONE ELSE TAK-ING THE COURSE, TOO?
NOPE.
SINCE IORI'S TAKING HIS PRACTICAL EXAM...
WE'RE US-ING IT AS AN EXCUSE TO GO DIVING, TOO.
PEEK
PEEK
MRR?
RARAKO
SPEAKING OF WHICH, CAN YOU SWIM, SHIORI-CHAN?
SOME-WHAT.
I SEE.
IORI CAN'T SWIM AT ALL.
LEAVE ME ALONE.
MAYBE YOU'RE NOT RELATED, AFTER ALL.
PEEK
PEEK
RARAKO
WHAT'RE YOU TALKING ABOUT?
NII-SAMA IS MY BELOVED OLDER BROTHER.
ERG
...HM.

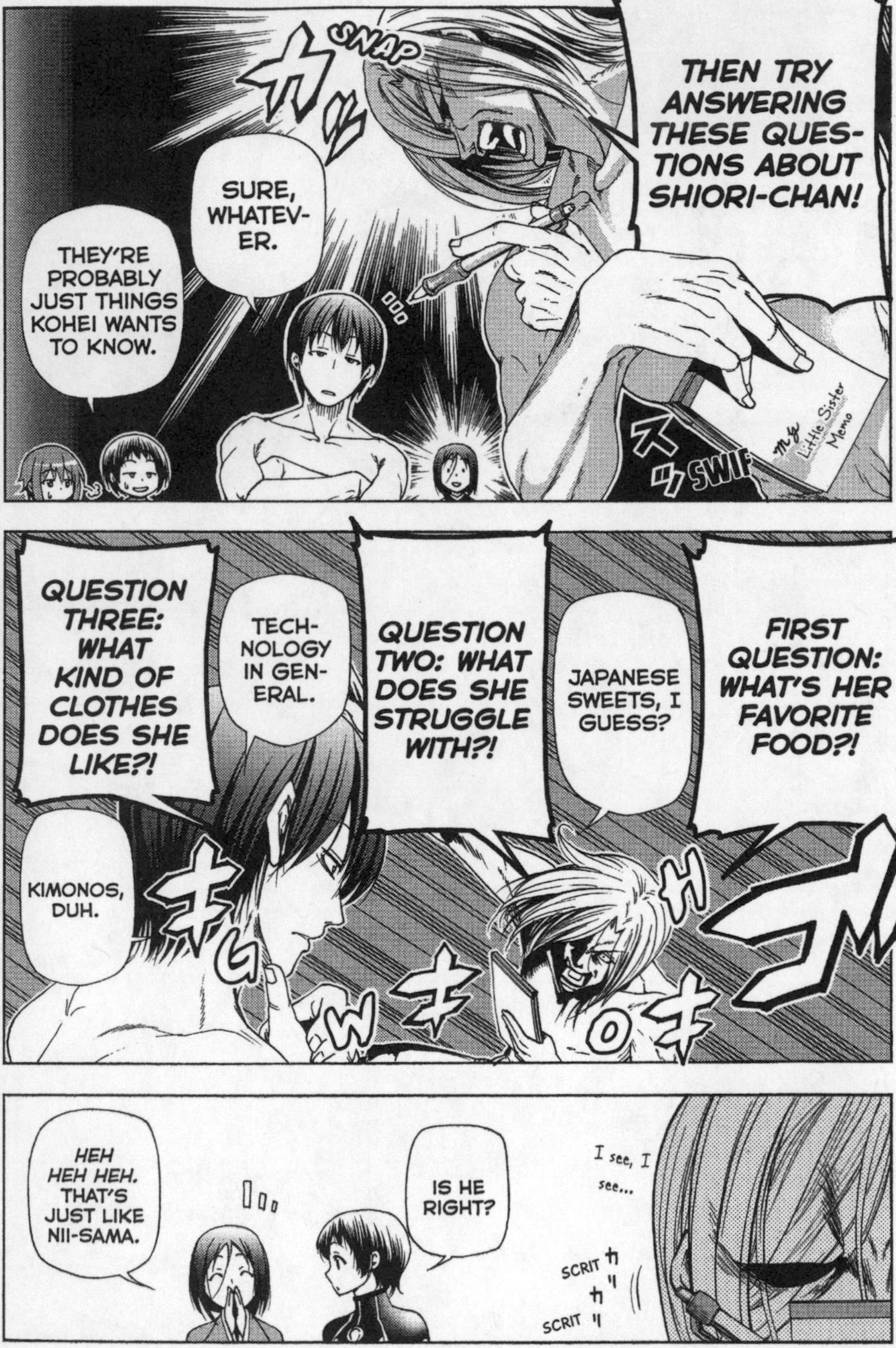
THEN TRY ANSWERING THESE QUES-TIONS ABOUT SHIORI-CHAN!
SNAP
SURE, WHATEV-ER.
THEY'RE PROBABLY JUST THINGS KOHEI WANTS TO KNOW.
SWIF
My Little Sister Memo
FIRST QUESTION: WHAT'S HER FAVORITE FOOD?!
JAPANESE SWEETS, I GUESS?
QUESTION TWO: WHAT DOES SHE STRUGGLE WITH?!
TECH-NOLOGY IN GEN-ERAL.
QUESTION THREE: WHAT KIND OF CLOTHES DOES SHE LIKE?!
KIMONOS, DUH.
H
O
W
I see, I see...
SCRIT
SCRIT
IS HE RIGHT?
HEH HEH HEH. THAT'S JUST LIKE NII-SAMA.

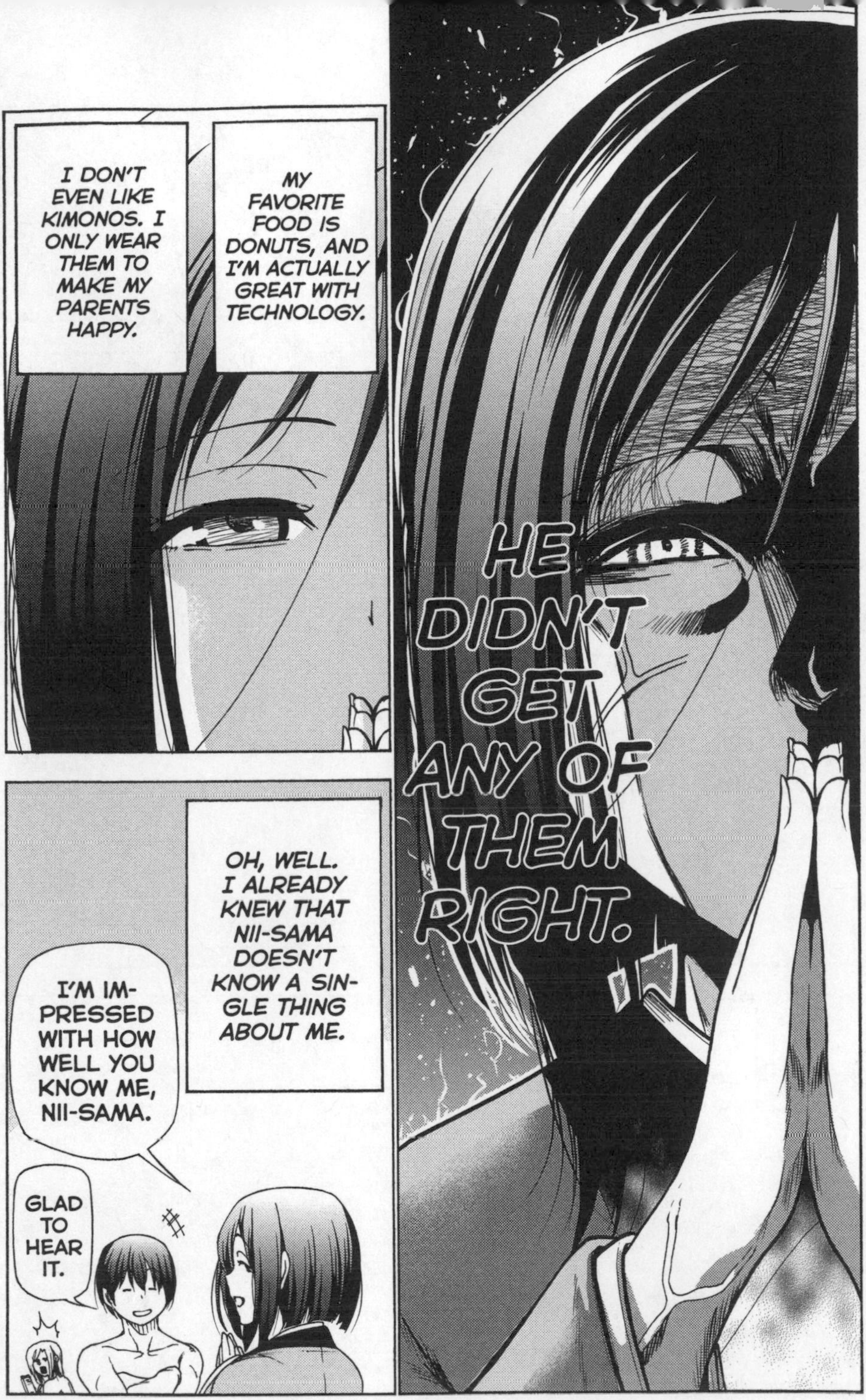
MY FAVORITE FOOD IS DONUTS, AND I'M ACTUALLY GREAT WITH TECHNOLOGY.
I DON'T EVEN LIKE KIMONOS. I ONLY WEAR THEM TO MAKE MY PARENTS HAPPY.
HE DIDN'T GET ANY OF THEM RIGHT.
OH, WELL. I ALREADY KNEW THAT NII-SAMA DOESN'T KNOW A SINGLE THING ABOUT ME.
I'M IMPRESSED WITH HOW WELL YOU KNOW ME, NII-SAMA.
GLAD TO HEAR IT.

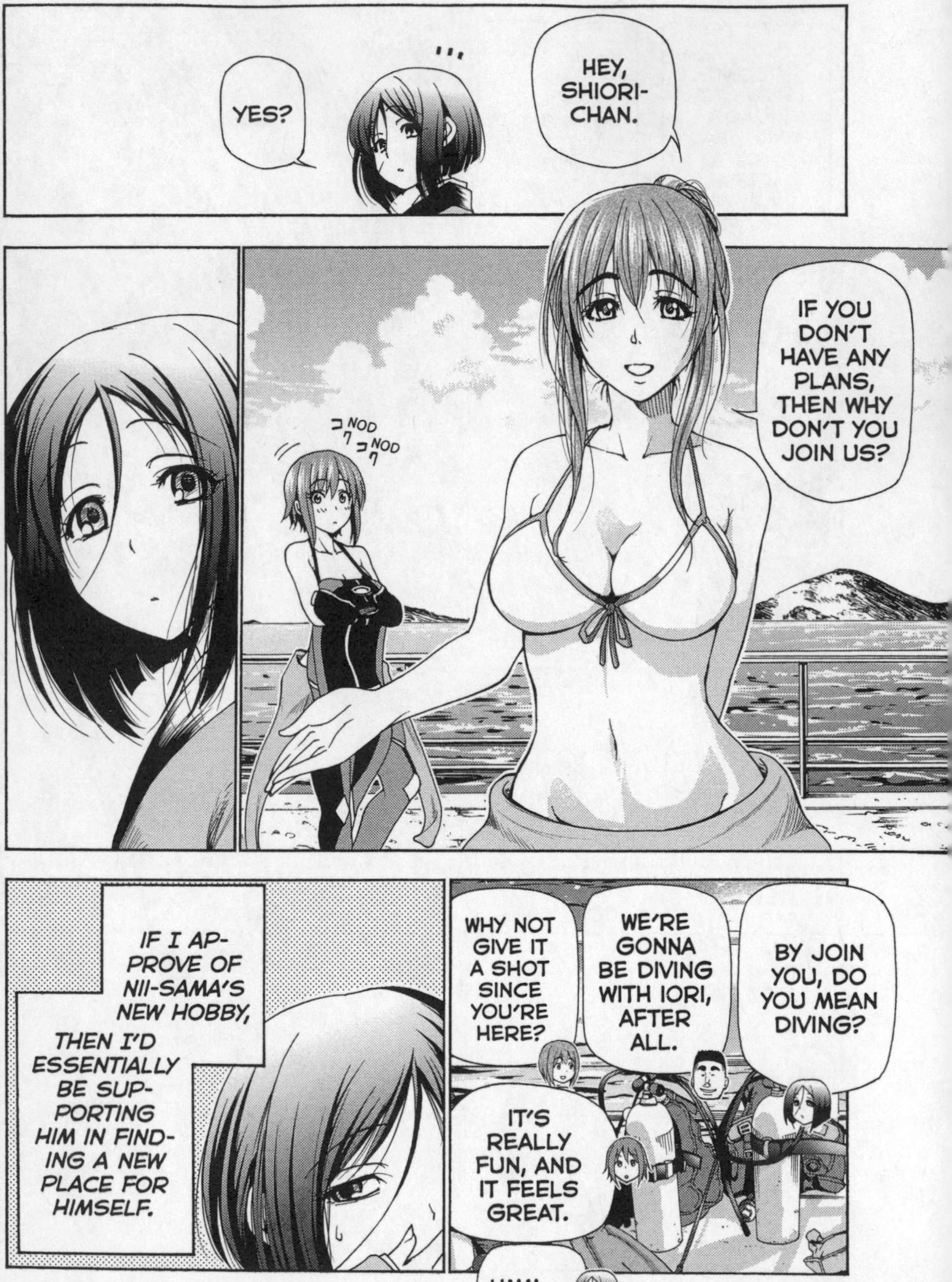
HEY, SHIORI-CHAN.
...
YES?
IF YOU DON'T HAVE ANY PLANS, THEN WHY DON'T YOU JOIN US?
NOD NOD
BY JOIN YOU, DO YOU MEAN DIVING?
WE'RE GONNA BE DIVING WITH IORI, AFTER ALL.
WHY NOT GIVE IT A SHOT SINCE YOU'RE HERE?
IT'S REALLY FUN, AND IT FEELS GREAT.
UMM...
IF I APPROVE OF NII-SAMA'S NEW HOBBY, THEN I'D ESSENTIALLY BE SUPPORTING HIM IN FINDING A NEW PLACE FOR HIMSELF.

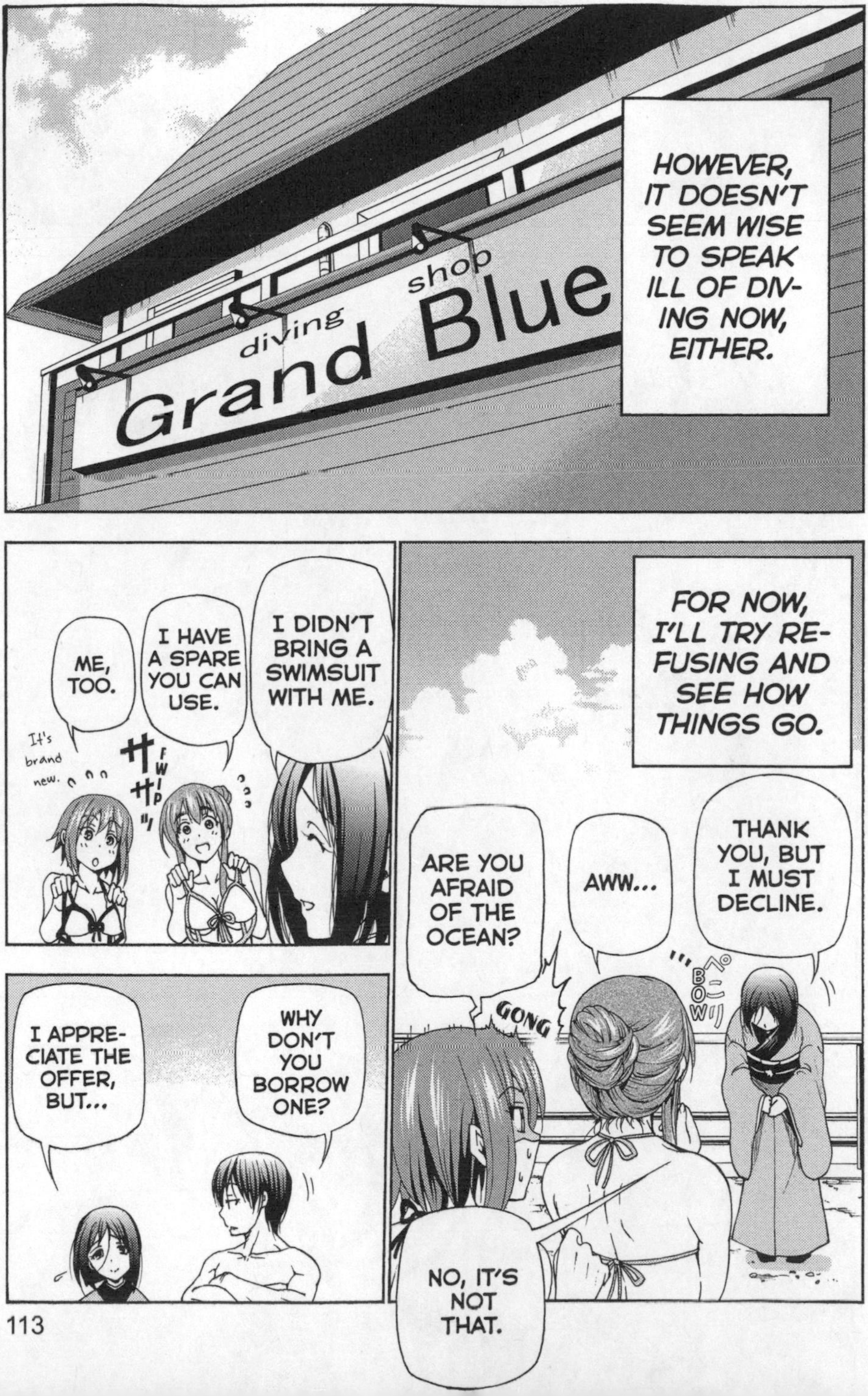
diving shop
Grand Blue
HOWEVER, IT DOESN'T SEEM WISE TO SPEAK ILL OF DIVING NOW, EITHER.
FOR NOW, I'LL TRY REFUSING AND SEE HOW THINGS GO.
THANK YOU, BUT I MUST DECLINE.
BOW
AWW...
ARE YOU AFRAID OF THE OCEAN?
GONG
NO, IT'S NOT THAT.
I DIDN'T BRING A SWIMSUIT WITH ME.
I HAVE A SPARE YOU CAN USE.
FWIP
ME, TOO.
It's brand new.
WHY DON'T YOU BORROW ONE?
I APPRECIATE THE OFFER, BUT...

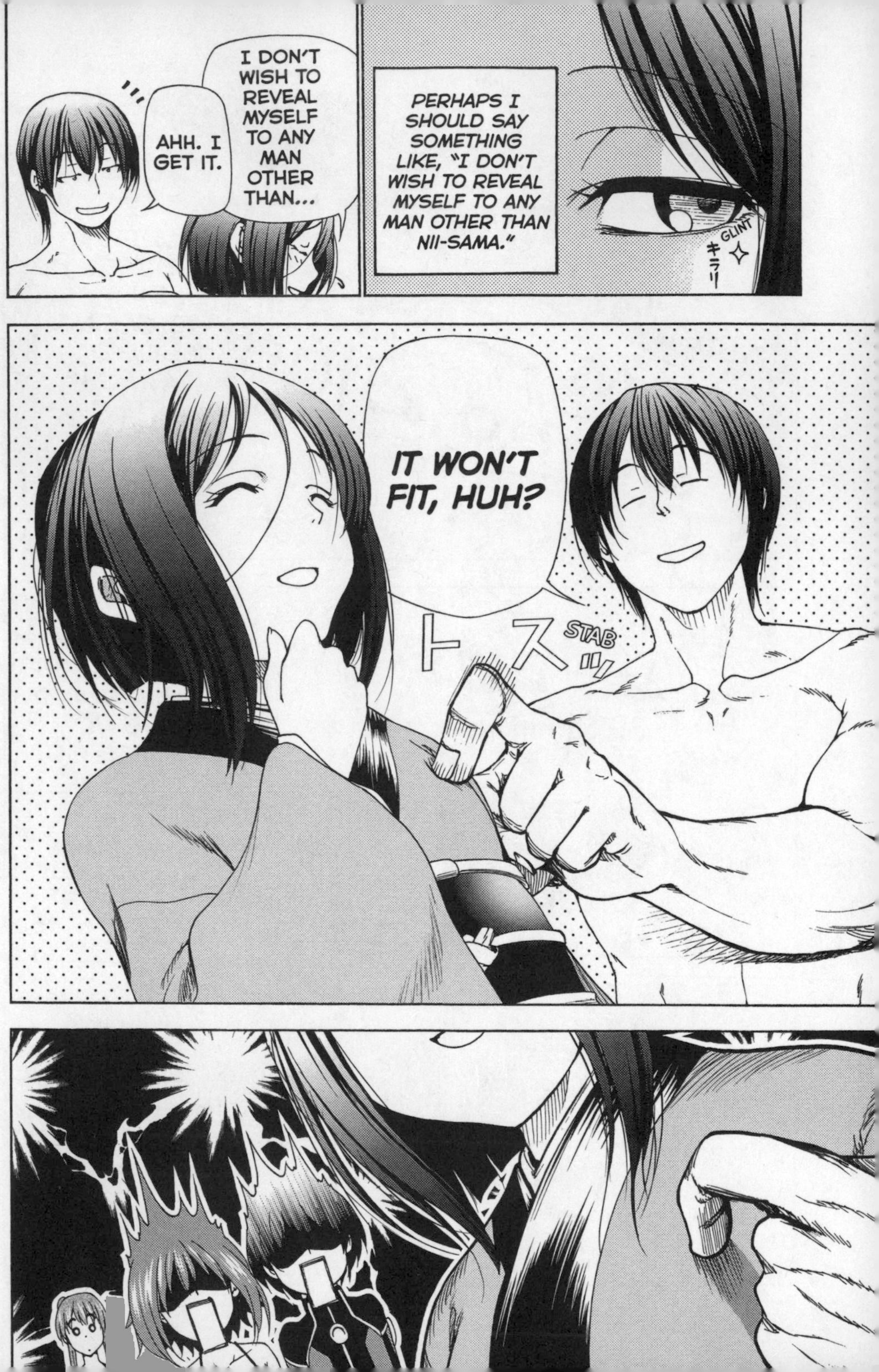
PERHAPS I SHOULD SAY SOMETHING LIKE, "I DON'T WISH TO REVEAL MYSELF TO ANY MAN OTHER THAN NII-SAMA."
GLINT
キラリ
I DON'T WISH TO REVEAL MYSELF TO ANY MAN OTHER THAN...
AHH. I GET IT.
IT WON'T FIT, HUH?
STAB
トスッ

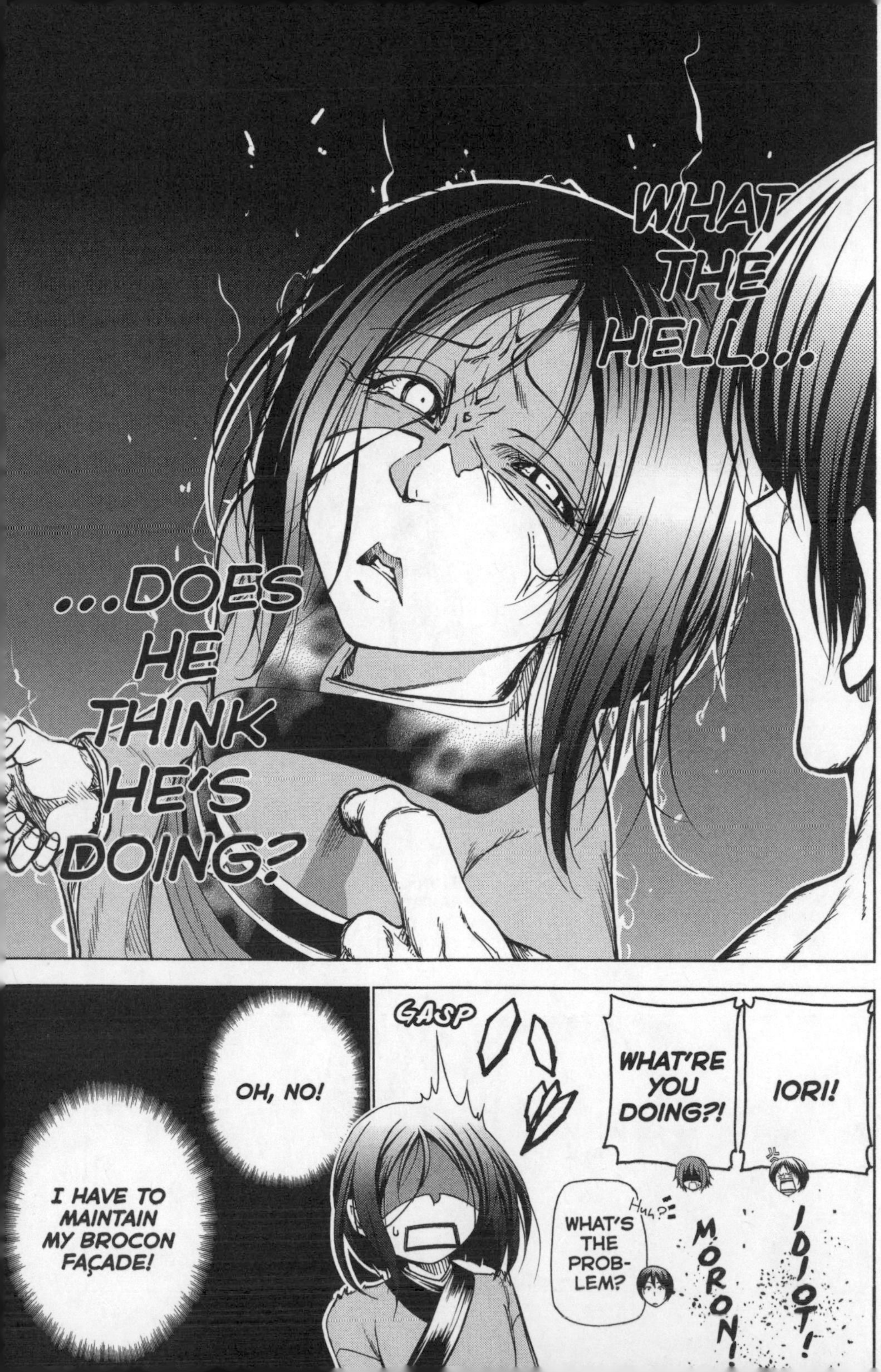
WHAT THE HELL...
...DOES HE THINK HE'S DOING?
IORI!
WHAT'RE YOU DOING?!
GASP
IDIOT!
MORON!
HUH?
WHAT'S THE PROB-LEM?
OH, NO!
I HAVE TO MAINTAIN MY BROCON FAÇADE!

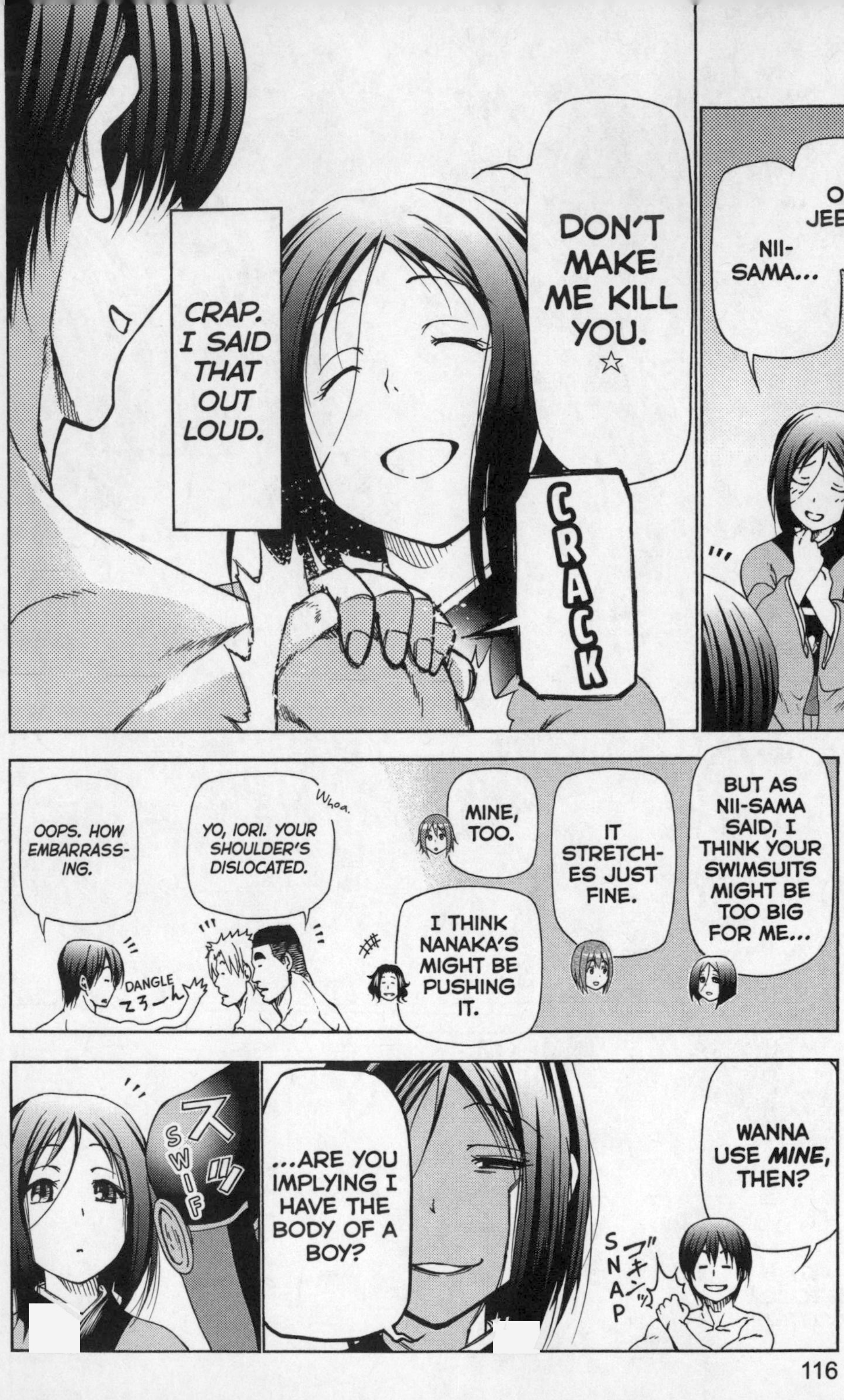

OH, JEEZ... NII-SAMA...
DON'T MAKE ME KILL YOU. ☆
CRACK
CRAP. I SAID THAT OUT LOUD.
BUT AS NII-SAMA SAID, I THINK YOUR SWIMSUITS MIGHT BE TOO BIG FOR ME...
IT STRETCHES JUST FINE.
MINE, TOO.
I THINK NANAKA'S MIGHT BE PUSHING IT.
Whoa.
YO, IORI. YOUR SHOULDER'S DISLOCATED.
DANGLE
OOPS. HOW EMBARRASSING.
WANNA USE *MINE*, THEN?
SNAP
...ARE YOU IMPLYING I HAVE THE BODY OF A BOY?
SWIF

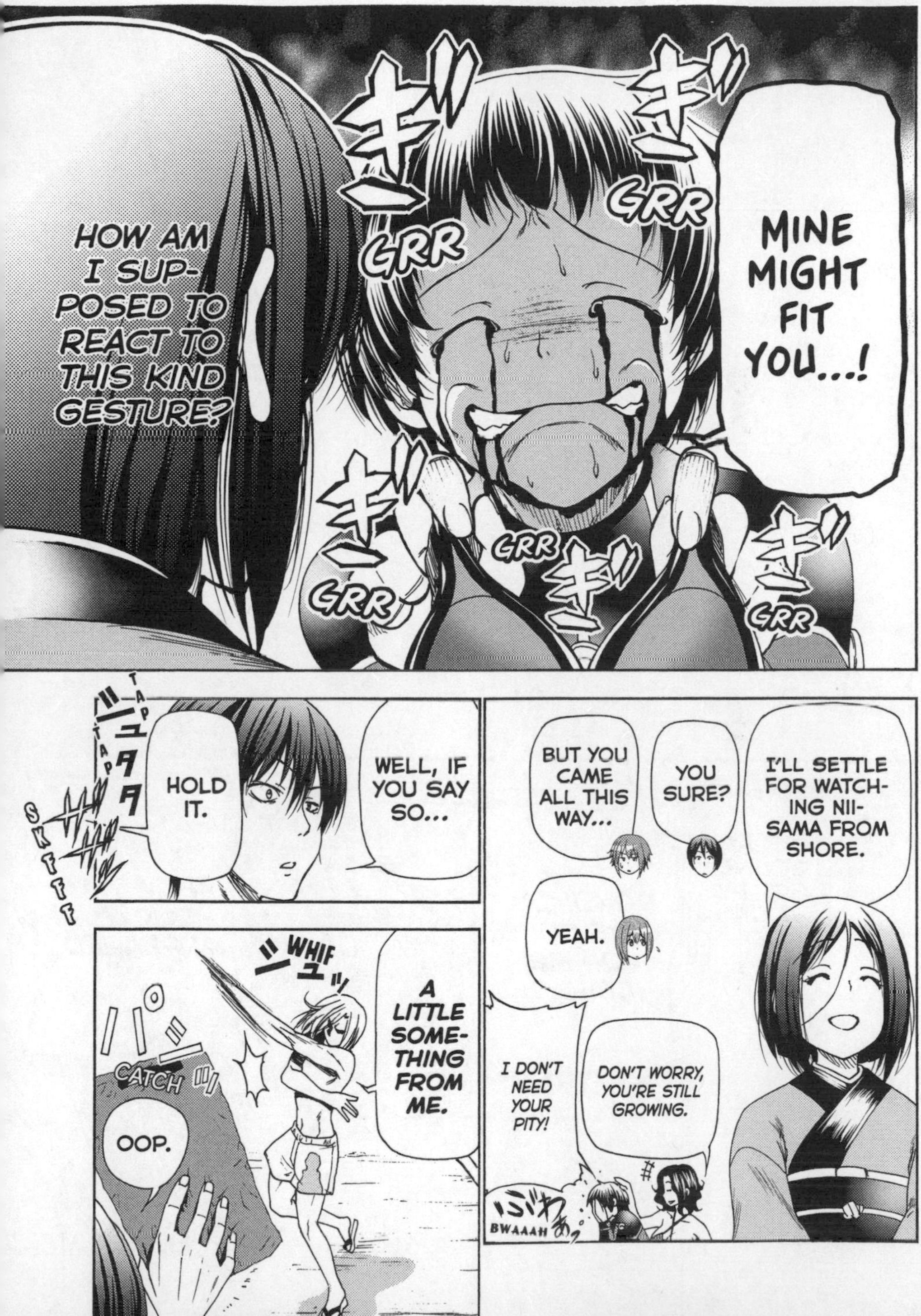
MINE MIGHT FIT YOU...!
GRR
GRR
GRR
GRR
GRR
HOW AM I SUP-POSED TO REACT TO THIS KIND GESTURE?
I'LL SETTLE FOR WATCH-ING NII-SAMA FROM SHORE.
YOU SURE?
BUT YOU CAME ALL THIS WAY...
YEAH.
DON'T WORRY, YOU'RE STILL GROWING.
I DON'T NEED YOUR PITY!
BWAAAH
WELL, IF YOU SAY SO...
HOLD IT.
TAP TAP
SKFFF
A LITTLE SOME-THING FROM ME.
WHIF
CATCH
OOP.

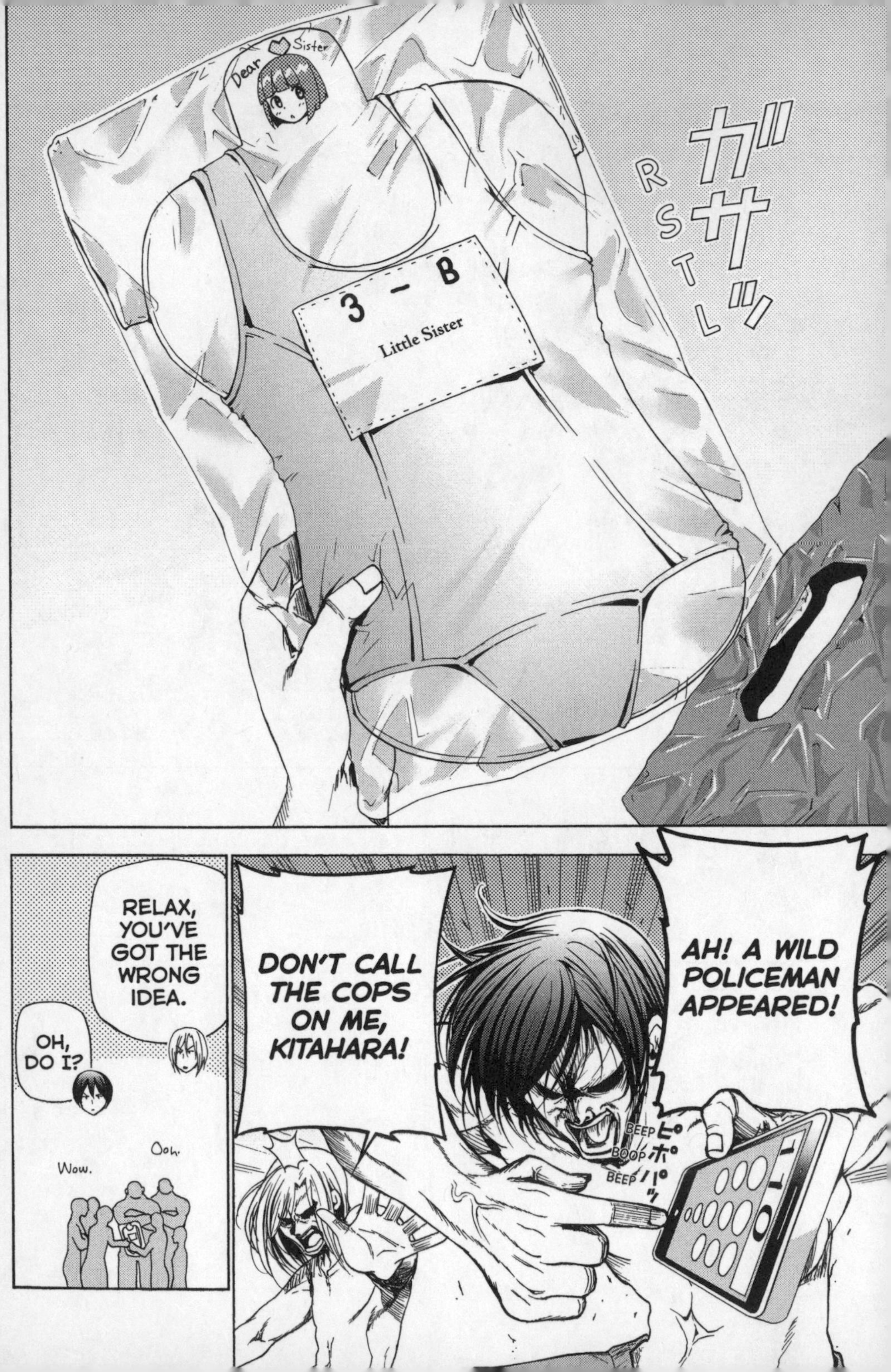
Dear ♡ Sister
3 - B
Little Sister
ガサッ
RSTL
AH! A WILD POLICEMAN APPEARED!
DON'T CALL THE COPS ON ME, KITAHARA!
ピポパッ
BEEP BOOP BEEP
RELAX, YOU'VE GOT THE WRONG IDEA.
OH, DO I?
Ooh.
Wow.

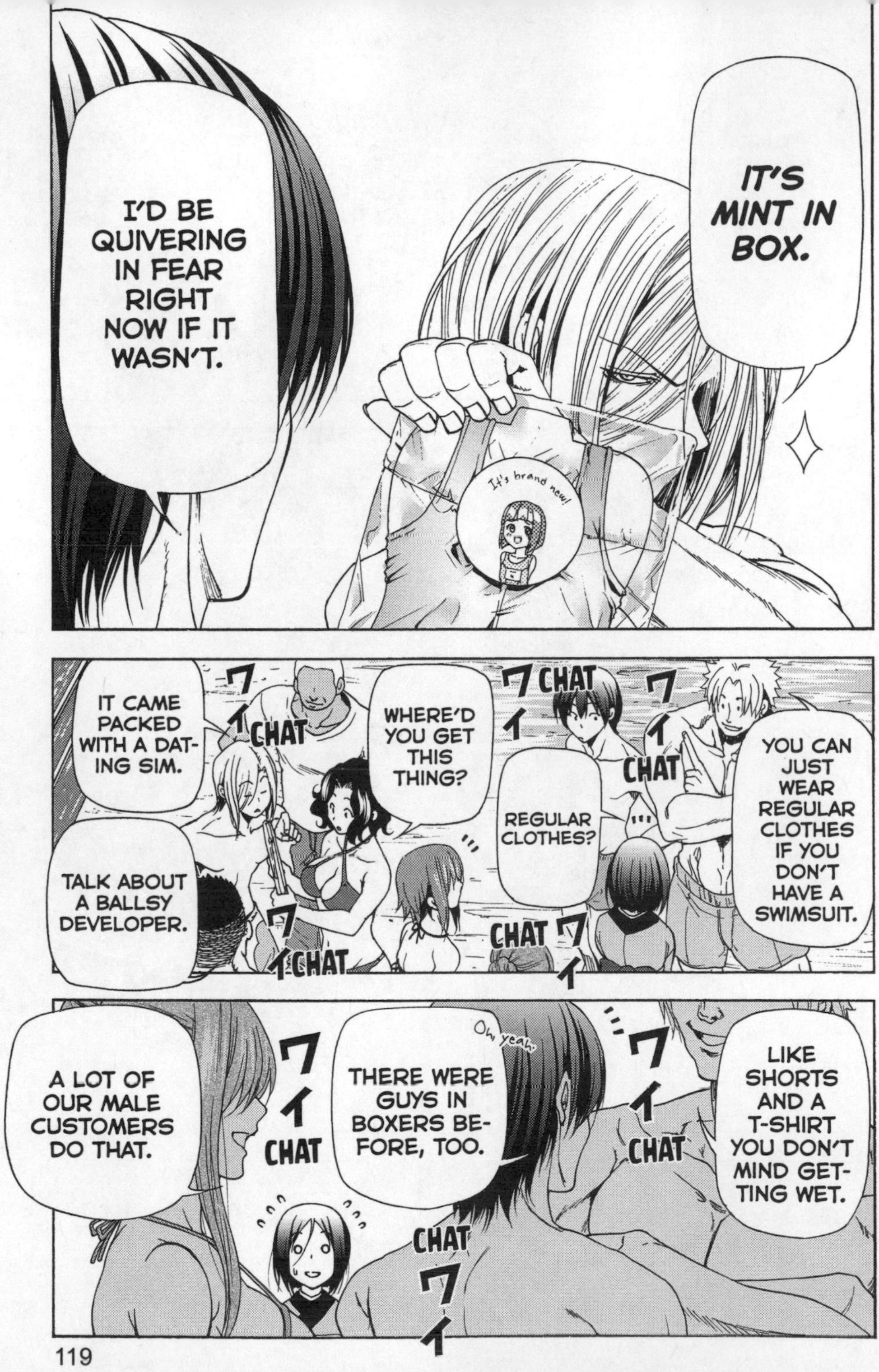
IT'S MINT IN BOX.
It's brand new!
I'D BE QUIVERING IN FEAR RIGHT NOW IF IT WASN'T.
YOU CAN JUST WEAR REGULAR CLOTHES IF YOU DON'T HAVE A SWIMSUIT.
ワイ CHAT
REGULAR CLOTHES?
ワイ CHAT
WHERE'D YOU GET THIS THING?
IT CAME PACKED WITH A DATING SIM.
ワイ CHAT
TALK ABOUT A BALLSY DEVELOPER.
CHAT ワイ
ワイ CHAT
LIKE SHORTS AND A T-SHIRT YOU DON'T MIND GETTING WET.
ワイ CHAT
Oh yeah.
THERE WERE GUYS IN BOXERS BEFORE, TOO.
ワイ CHAT
A LOT OF OUR MALE CUSTOMERS DO THAT.
CHAT ワイ

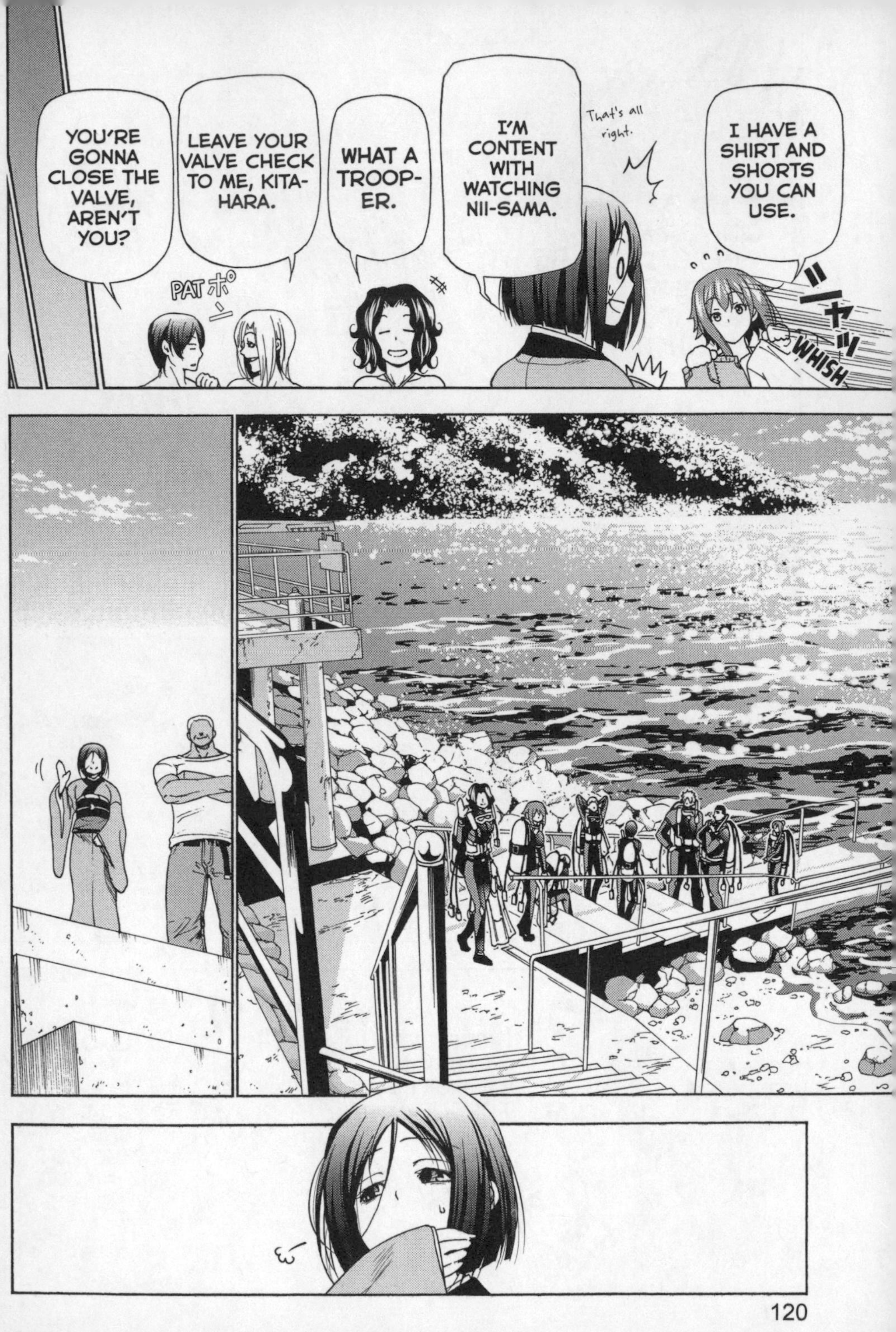
I HAVE A SHIRT AND SHORTS YOU CAN USE.
WHISH
That's all right.
I'M CONTENT WITH WATCHING NII-SAMA.
WHAT A TROOP-ER.
LEAVE YOUR VALVE CHECK TO ME, KITA-HARA.
PAT
YOU'RE GONNA CLOSE THE VALVE, AREN'T YOU?

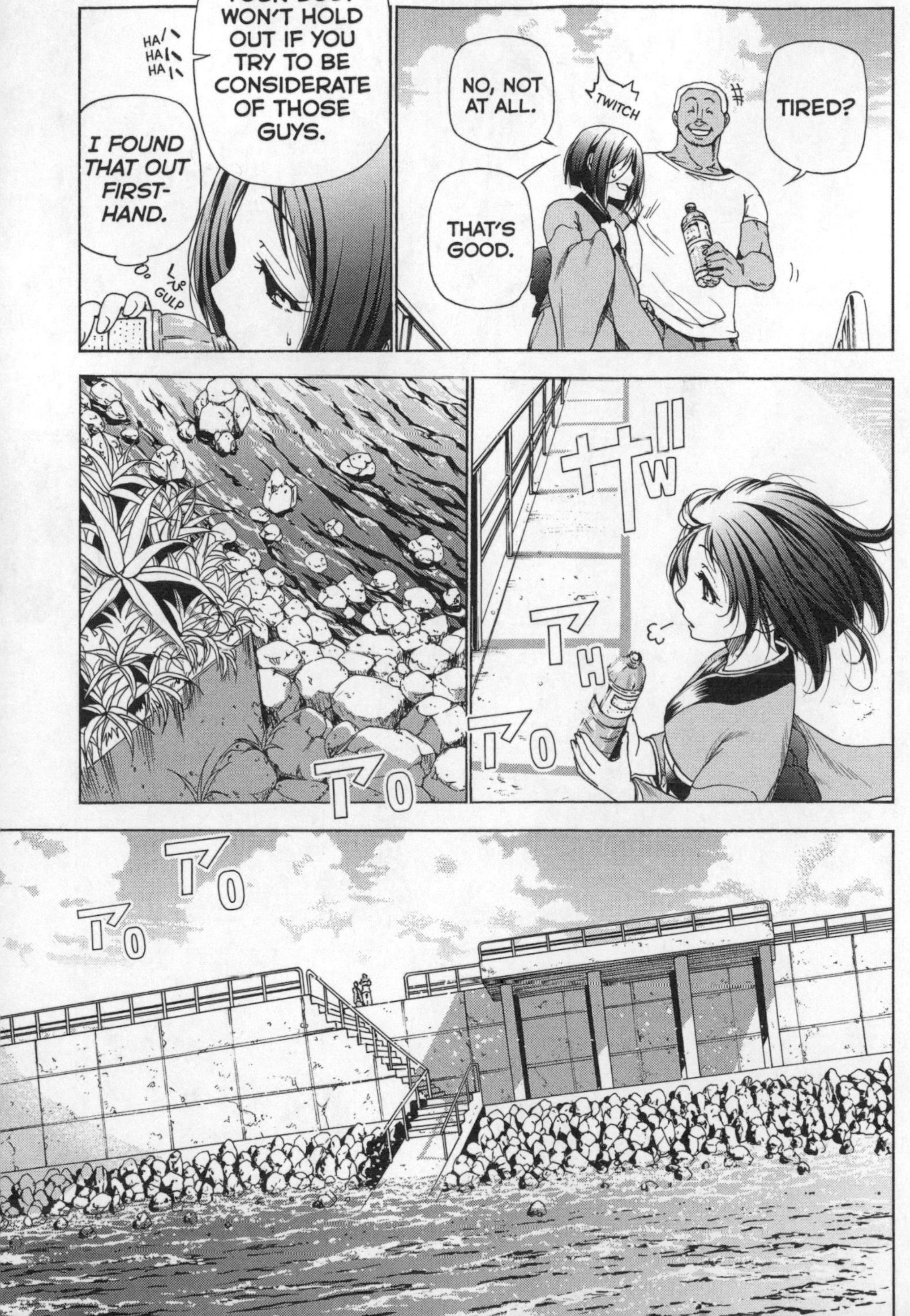
TIRED?
TWITCH
NO, NOT AT ALL.
THAT'S GOOD.
HA HA HA
YOUR BODY WON'T HOLD OUT IF YOU TRY TO BE CONSIDERATE OF THOSE GUYS.
I FOUND THAT OUT FIRST-HAND.
GULP
W
H
O
O
O
O

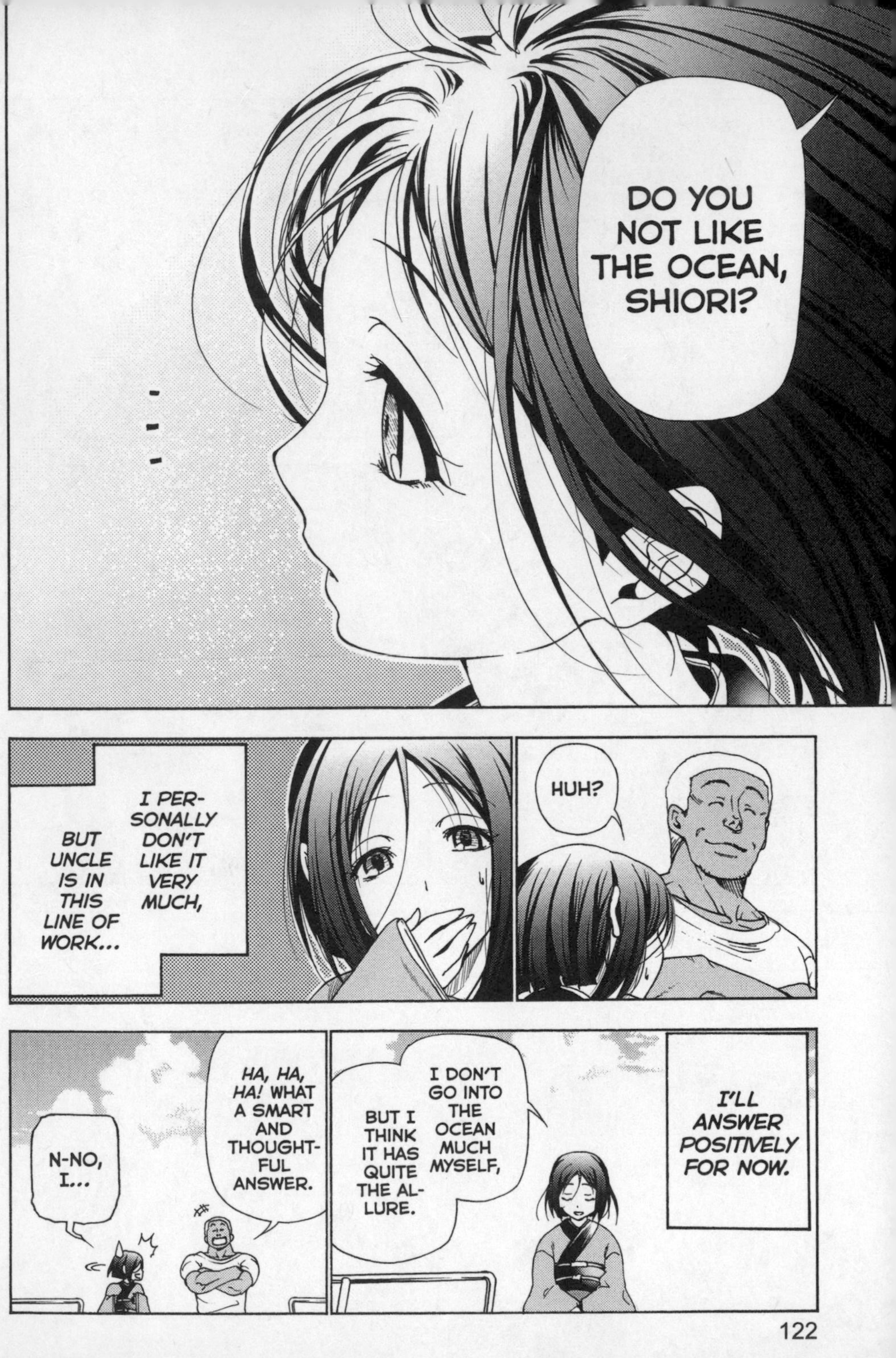
DO YOU NOT LIKE THE OCEAN, SHIORI?
...
HUH?
I PER-SONALLY DON'T LIKE IT VERY MUCH,
BUT UNCLE IS IN THIS LINE OF WORK...
I'LL ANSWER POSITIVELY FOR NOW.
I DON'T GO INTO THE OCEAN MUCH MYSELF,
BUT I THINK IT HAS QUITE THE AL-LURE.
HA, HA, HA! WHAT A SMART AND THOUGHT-FUL ANSWER.
N-NO, I...

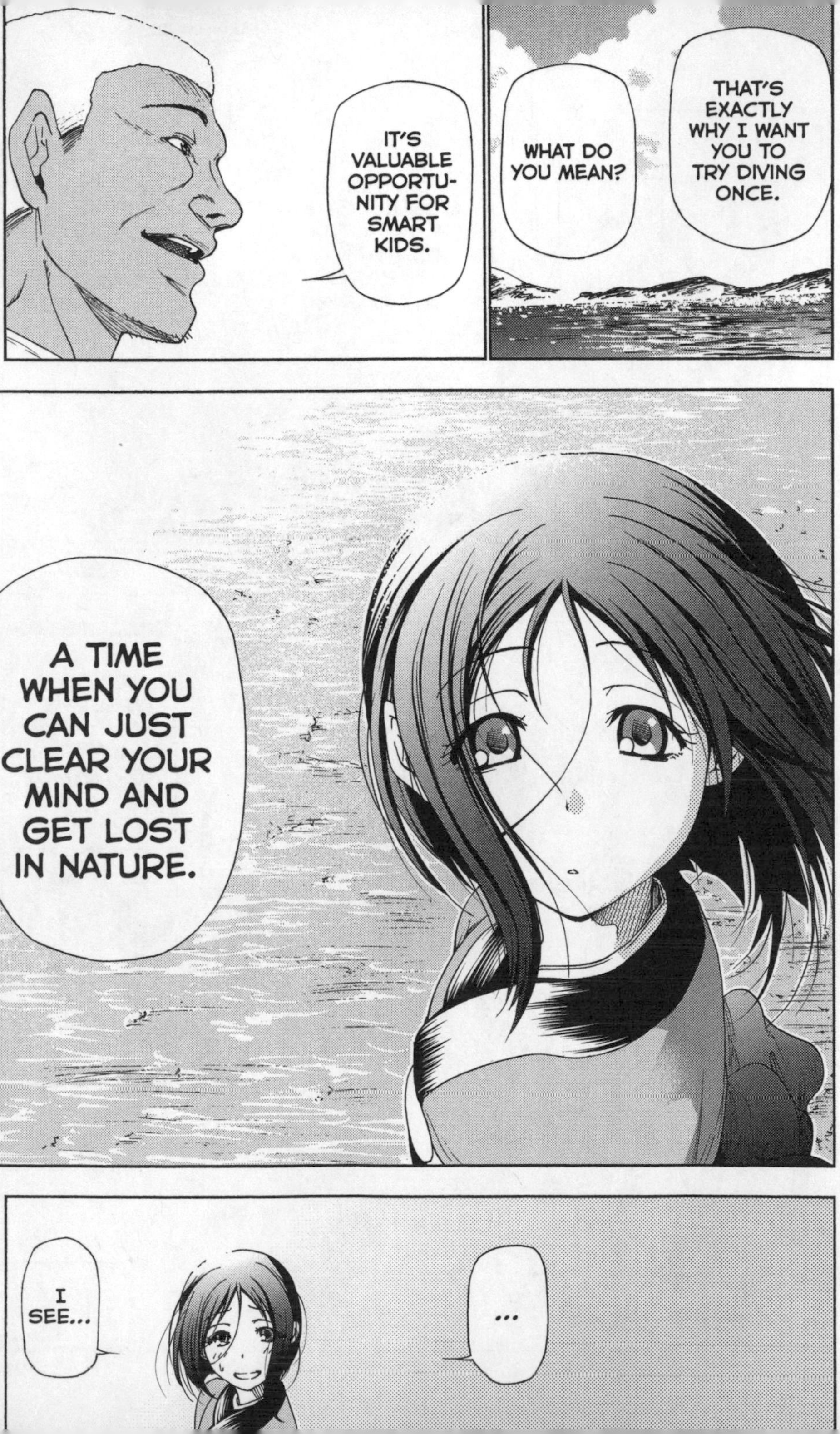
THAT'S EXACTLY WHY I WANT YOU TO TRY DIVING ONCE.
WHAT DO YOU MEAN?
IT'S VALUABLE OPPORTUNITY FOR SMART KIDS.
A TIME WHEN YOU CAN JUST CLEAR YOUR MIND AND GET LOST IN NATURE.
...
I SEE...

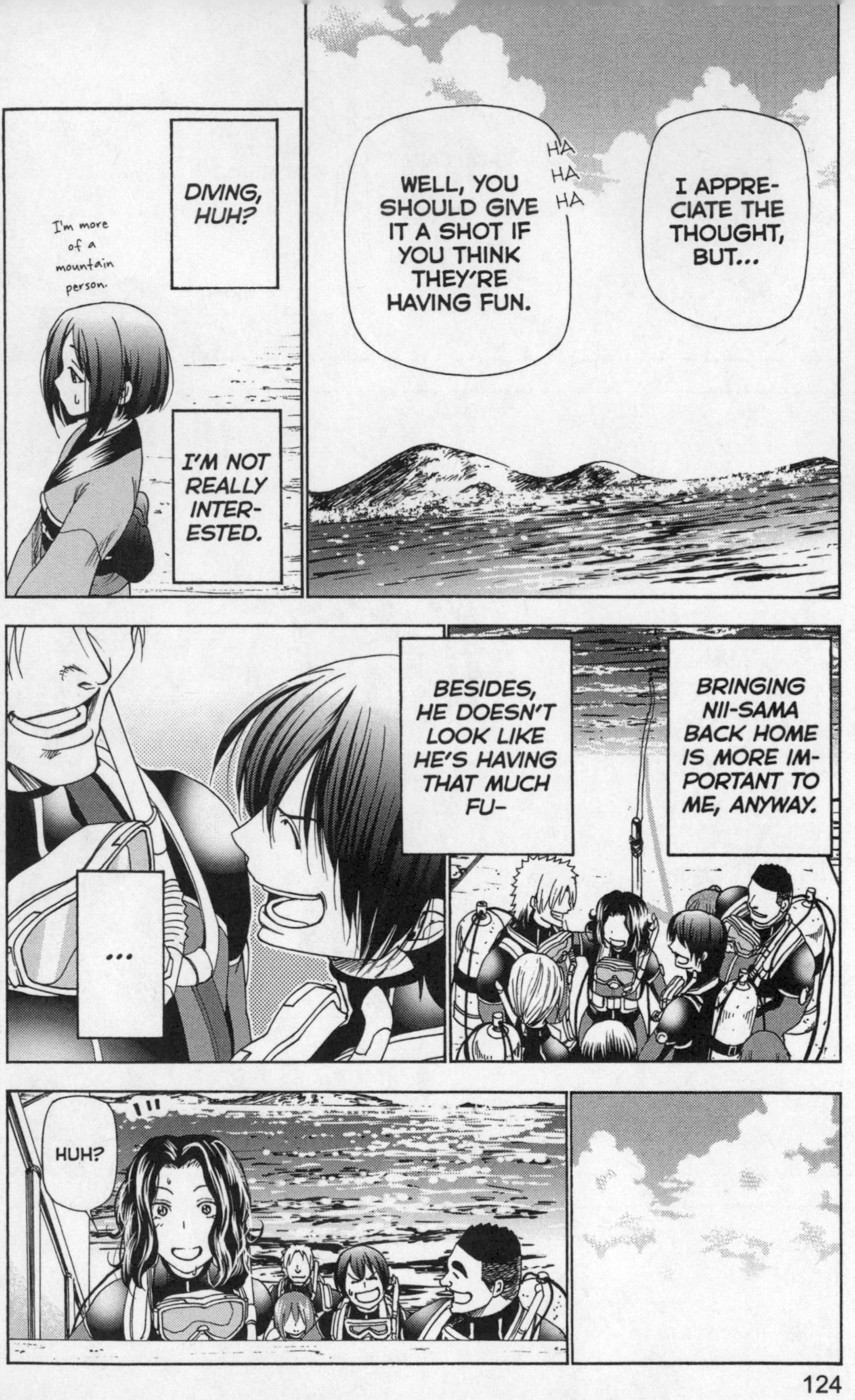
I APPRE-
CIATE THE
THOUGHT,
BUT...
HA HA HA
WELL, YOU SHOULD GIVE IT A SHOT IF YOU THINK THEY'RE HAVING FUN.
DIVING, HUH?
I'm more of a mountain person.
I'M NOT REALLY INTER-
ESTED.
BRINGING NII-SAMA BACK HOME IS MORE IM-
PORTANT TO ME, ANYWAY.
BESIDES, HE DOESN'T LOOK LIKE HE'S HAVING THAT MUCH FU-
...
!!
HUH?

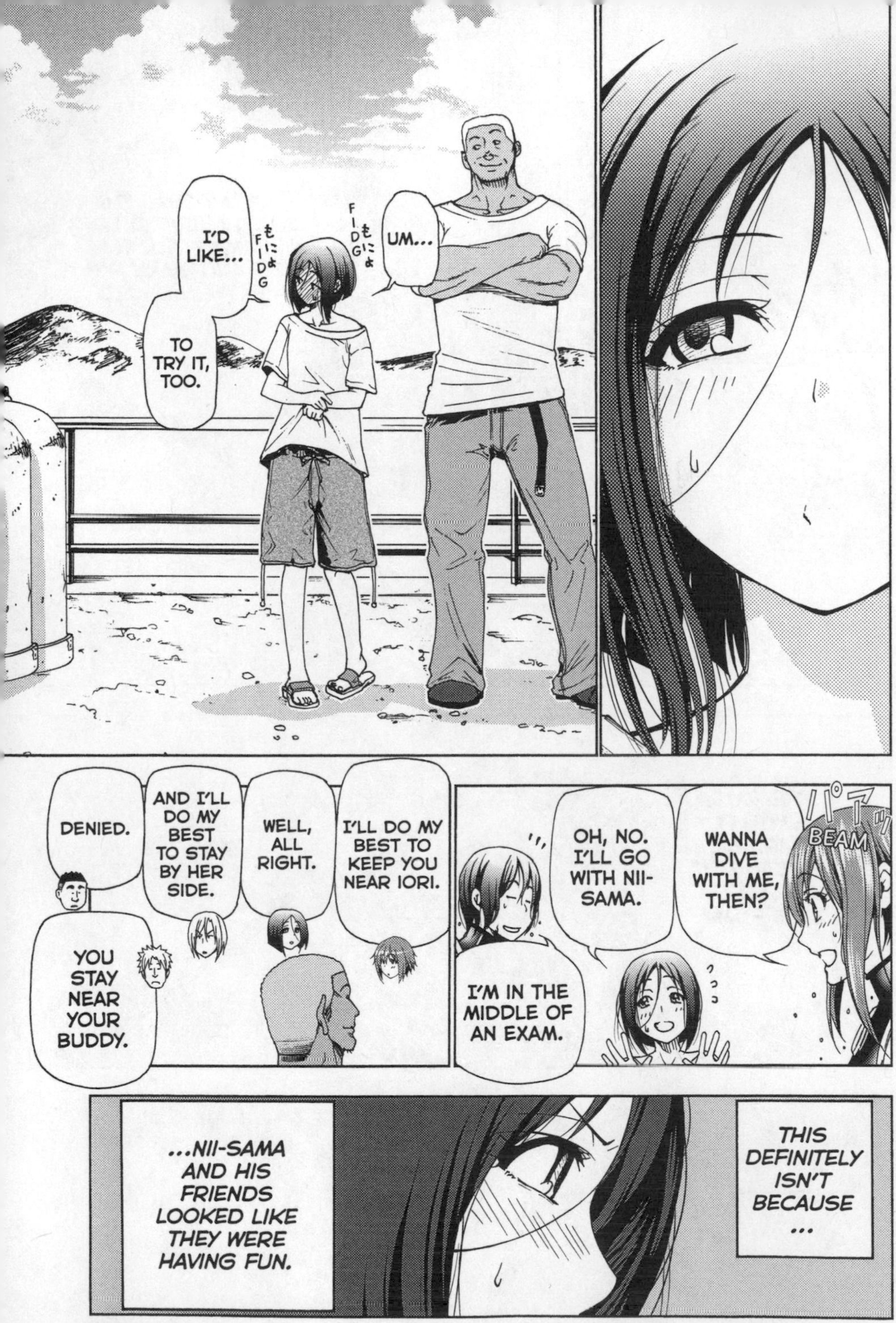
もにょ FIDG
UM...
もにょ FIDG
I'D LIKE...
TO TRY IT, TOO.
パァッ BEAM
WANNA DIVE WITH ME, THEN?
OH, NO. I'LL GO WITH NII-SAMA.
I'M IN THE MIDDLE OF AN EXAM.
I'LL DO MY BEST TO KEEP YOU NEAR IORI.
WELL, ALL RIGHT.
AND I'LL DO MY BEST TO STAY BY HER SIDE.
DENIED.
YOU STAY NEAR YOUR BUDDY.
THIS DEFINITELY ISN'T BECAUSE ...
...NII-SAMA AND HIS FRIENDS LOOKED LIKE THEY WERE HAVING FUN.

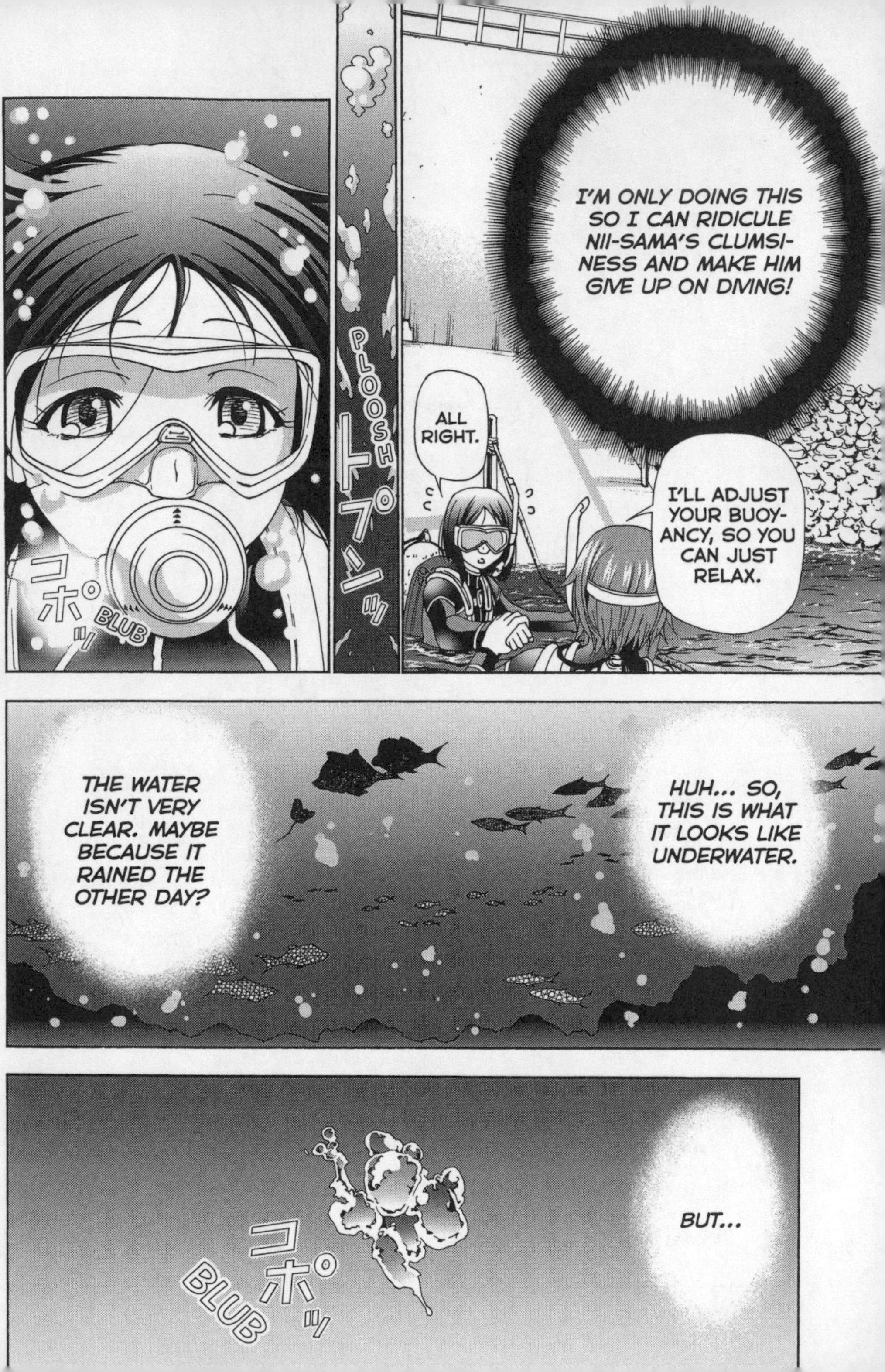
I'M ONLY DOING THIS SO I CAN RIDICULE NII-SAMA'S CLUMSI-NESS AND MAKE HIM GIVE UP ON DIVING!
I'LL ADJUST YOUR BUOY-ANCY, SO YOU CAN JUST RELAX.
ALL RIGHT.
PLOOSH
トプンッ
コポッ
BLUB
HUH... SO, THIS IS WHAT IT LOOKS LIKE UNDERWATER.
THE WATER ISN'T VERY CLEAR. MAYBE BECAUSE IT RAINED THE OTHER DAY?
BUT...
コポッ
BLUB

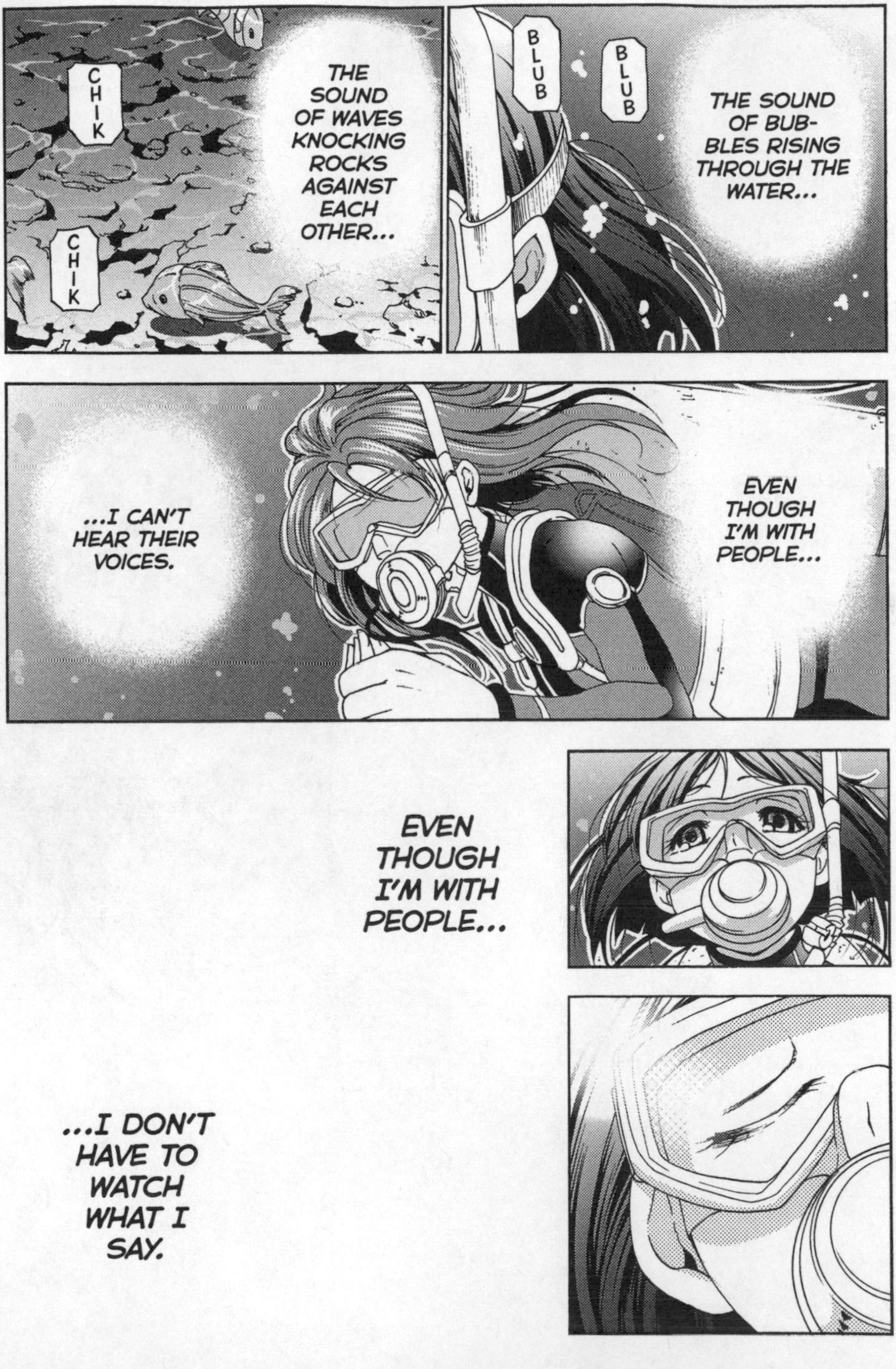
BLUB
BLUB
THE SOUND OF BUB-BLES RISING THROUGH THE WATER...
THE SOUND OF WAVES KNOCKING ROCKS AGAINST EACH OTHER...
CHIK
CHIK
EVEN THOUGH I'M WITH PEOPLE...
...I CAN'T HEAR THEIR VOICES.
EVEN THOUGH I'M WITH PEOPLE...
...I DON'T HAVE TO WATCH WHAT I SAY.

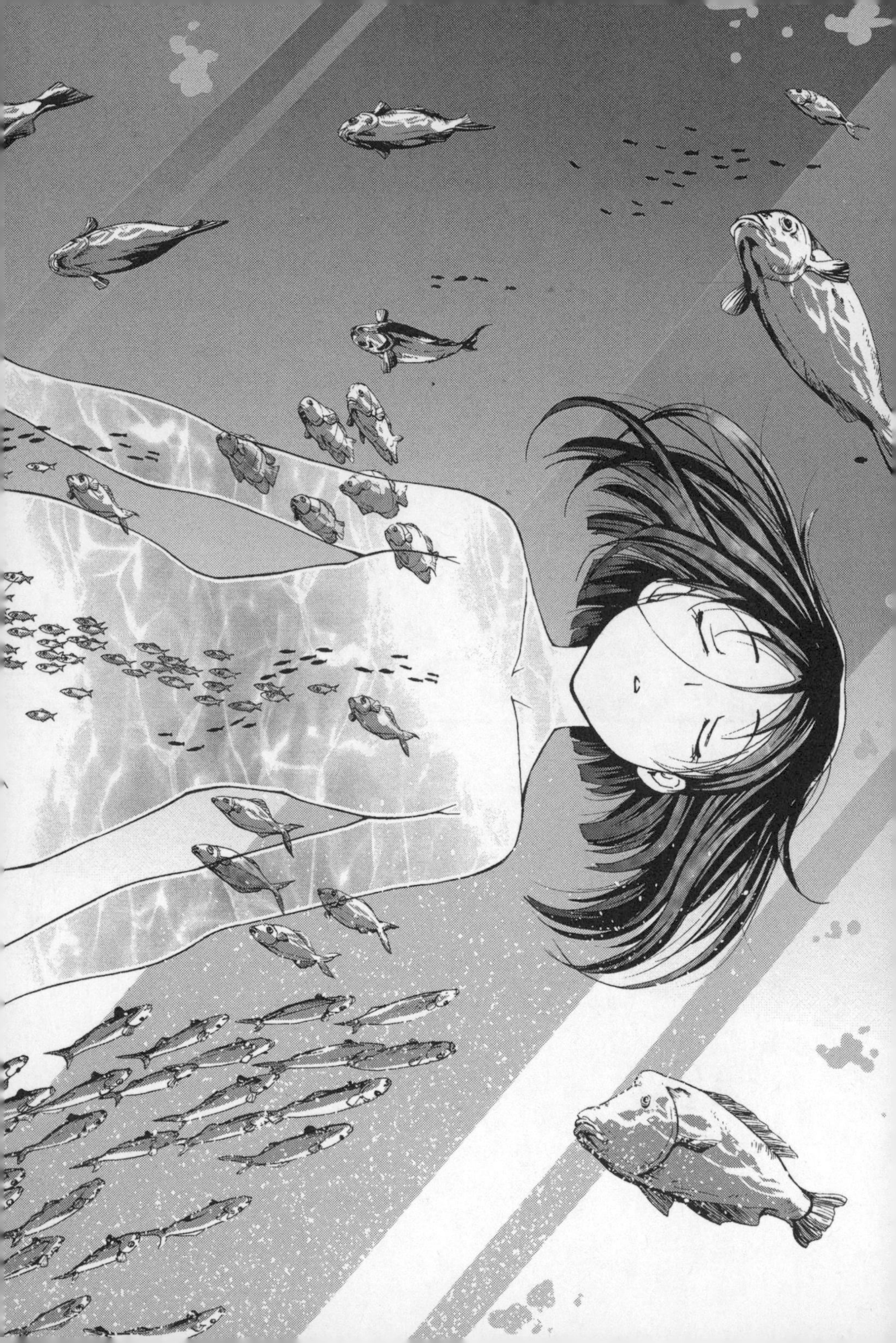

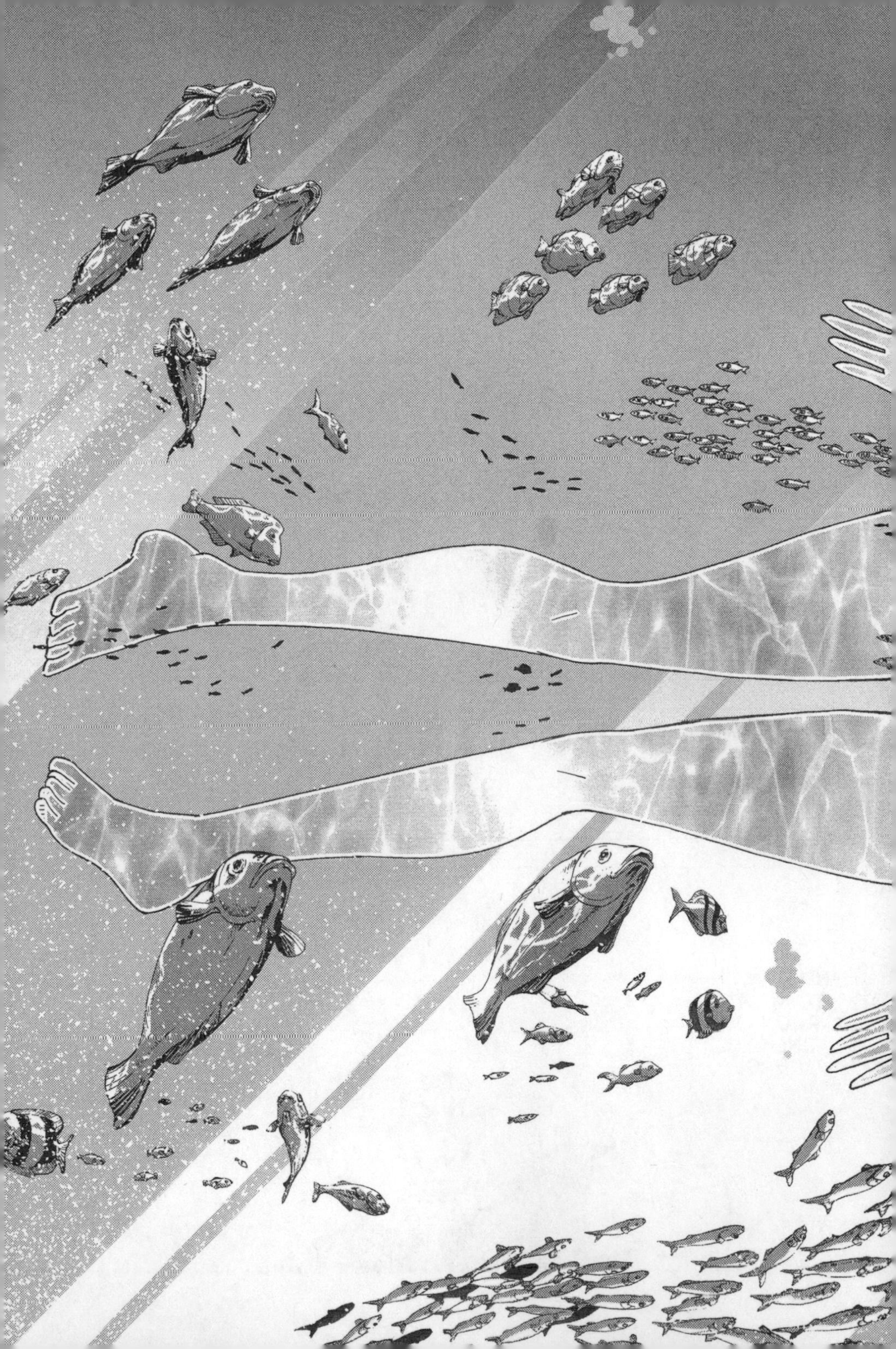

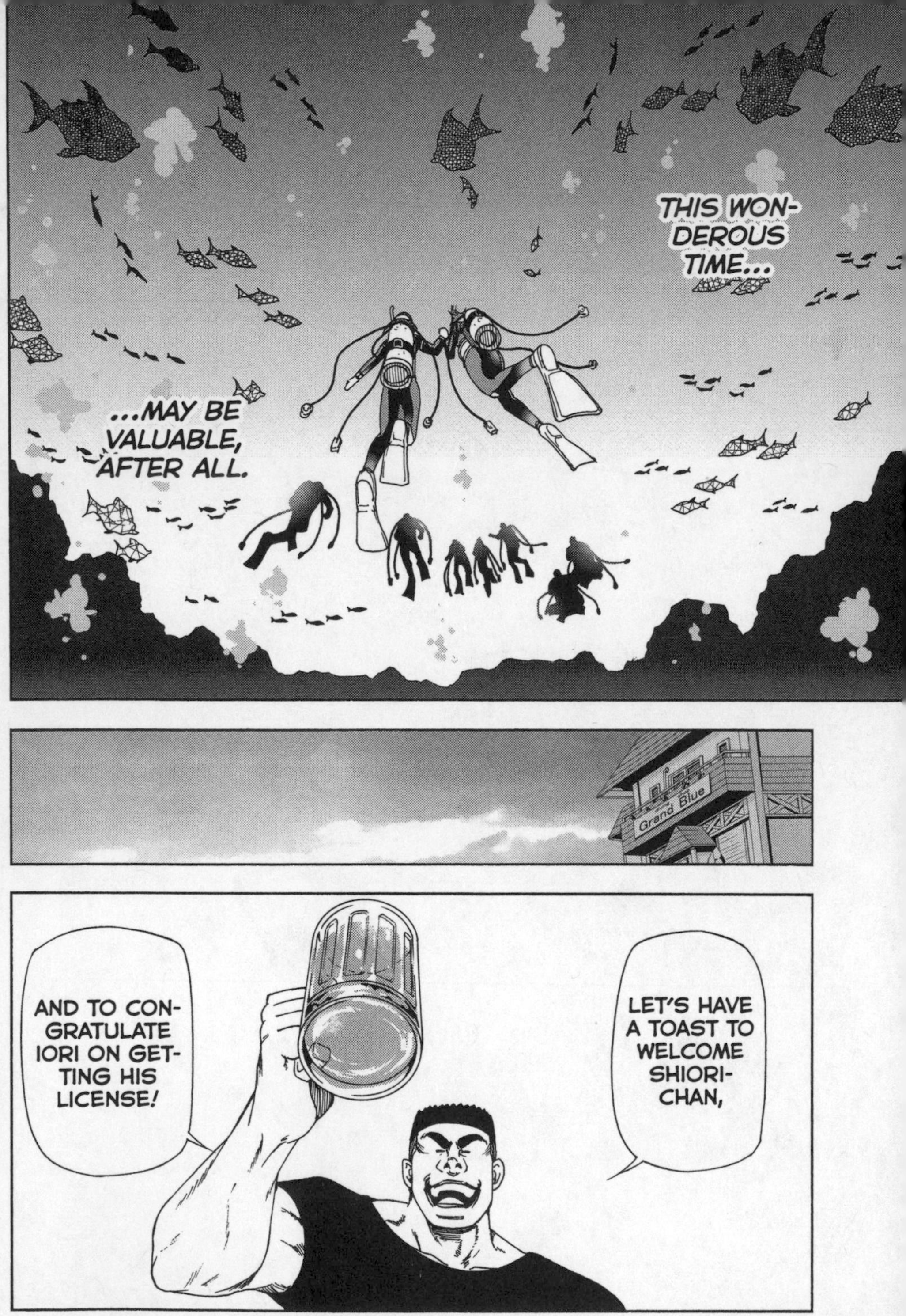
THIS WONDEROUS TIME...
...MAY BE VALUABLE, AFTER ALL.
Grand Blue
LET'S HAVE A TOAST TO WELCOME SHIORI-CHAN,
AND TO CONGRATULATE IORI ON GETTING HIS LICENSE!

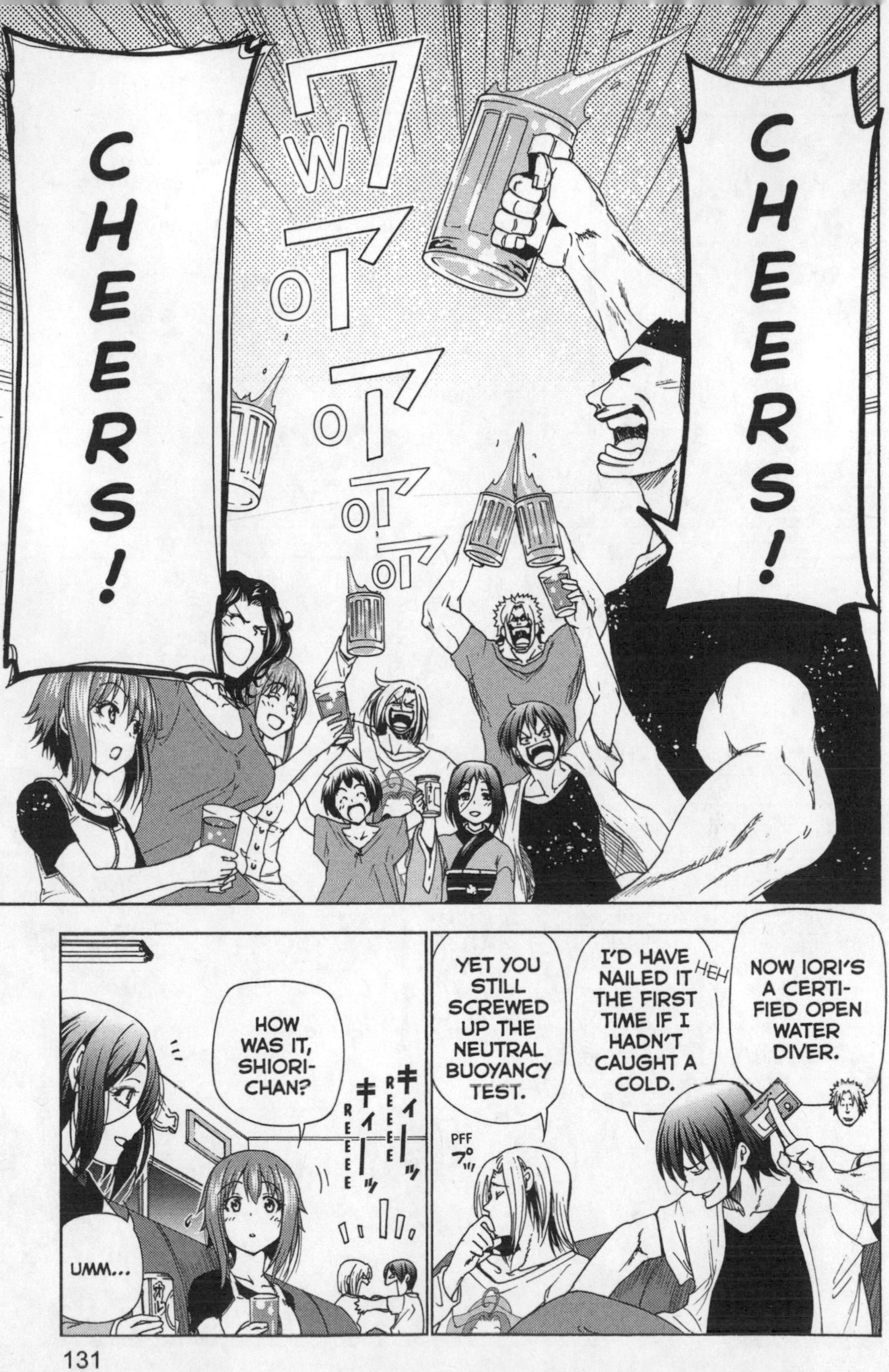
CHEERS!
CHEERS!
WOOO
NOW IORI'S A CERTI-FIED OPEN WATER DIVER.
HEH
I'D HAVE NAILED IT THE FIRST TIME IF I HADN'T CAUGHT A COLD.
YET YOU STILL SCREWED UP THE NEUTRAL BUOYANCY TEST.
PFF
HOW WAS IT, SHIORI-CHAN?
REEEE
REEEE
UMM...

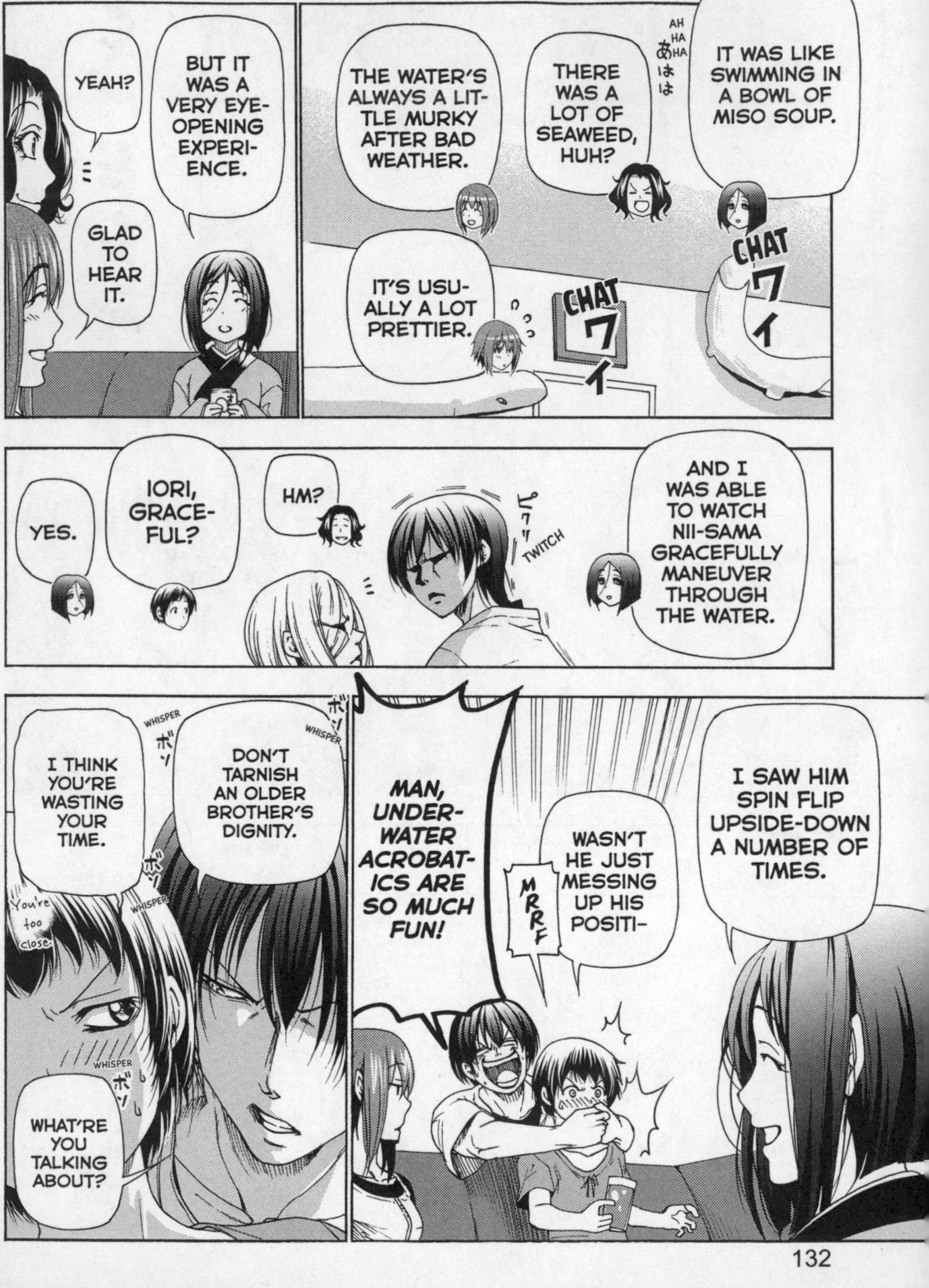
IT WAS LIKE SWIMMING IN A BOWL OF MISO SOUP.
AH HA HA あはは
THERE WAS A LOT OF SEAWEED, HUH?
THE WATER'S ALWAYS A LITTLE MURKY AFTER BAD WEATHER.
CHAT ワイ
IT'S USUALLY A LOT PRETTIER.
CHAT ワイ
BUT IT WAS A VERY EYE-OPENING EXPERIENCE.
YEAH?
GLAD TO HEAR IT.
AND I WAS ABLE TO WATCH NII-SAMA GRACEFULLY MANEUVER THROUGH THE WATER.
ピクッ TWITCH
HM?
IORI, GRACEFUL?
YES.
I SAW HIM SPIN FLIP UPSIDE-DOWN A NUMBER OF TIMES.
WASN'T HE JUST MESSING UP HIS POSITI-
MRRF
MAN, UNDERWATER ACROBATICS ARE SO MUCH FUN!
WHISPER ボソ
DON'T TARNISH AN OLDER BROTHER'S DIGNITY.
WHISPER ボソ
I THINK YOU'RE WASTING YOUR TIME.
WHISPER ボソ
You're too close.
WHISPER ボソ
WHAT'RE YOU TALKING ABOUT?

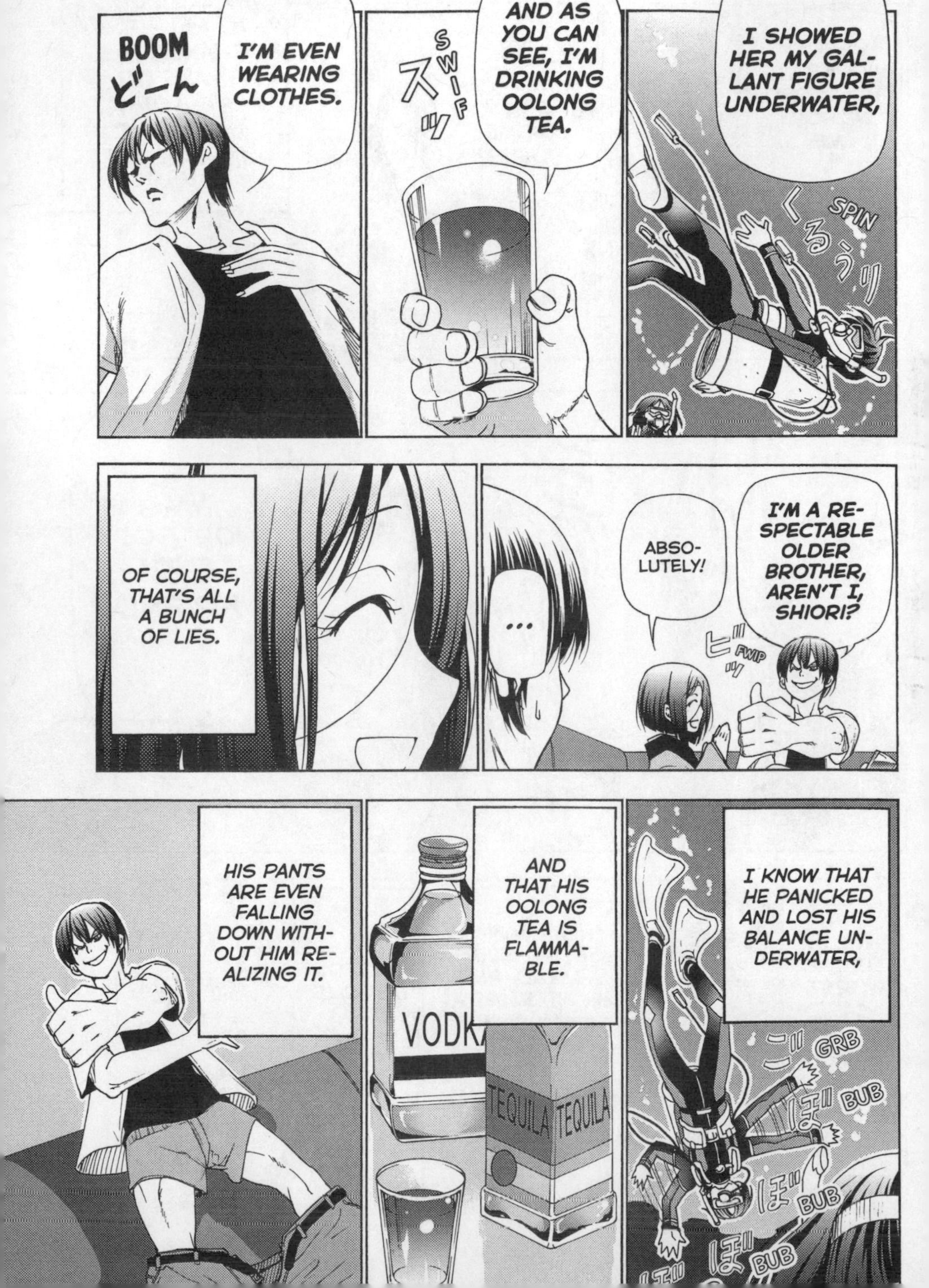
I SHOWED HER MY GALLANT FIGURE UNDERWATER,
くるうり
SPIN
AND AS YOU CAN SEE, I'M DRINKING OOLONG TEA.
スッ
SWIF
BOOM
どーん
I'M EVEN WEARING CLOTHES.
I'M A RESPECTABLE OLDER BROTHER, AREN'T I, SHIORI?
ABSOLUTELY!
ビッ
FWIP
...
OF COURSE, THAT'S ALL A BUNCH OF LIES.
I KNOW THAT HE PANICKED AND LOST HIS BALANCE UNDERWATER,
ご
GRB
ぼ
BUB
ぼ
BUB
ぼ
BUB
AND THAT HIS OOLONG TEA IS FLAMMABLE.
VODKA
TEQUILA
TEQUILA
HIS PANTS ARE EVEN FALLING DOWN WITHOUT HIM REALIZING IT.

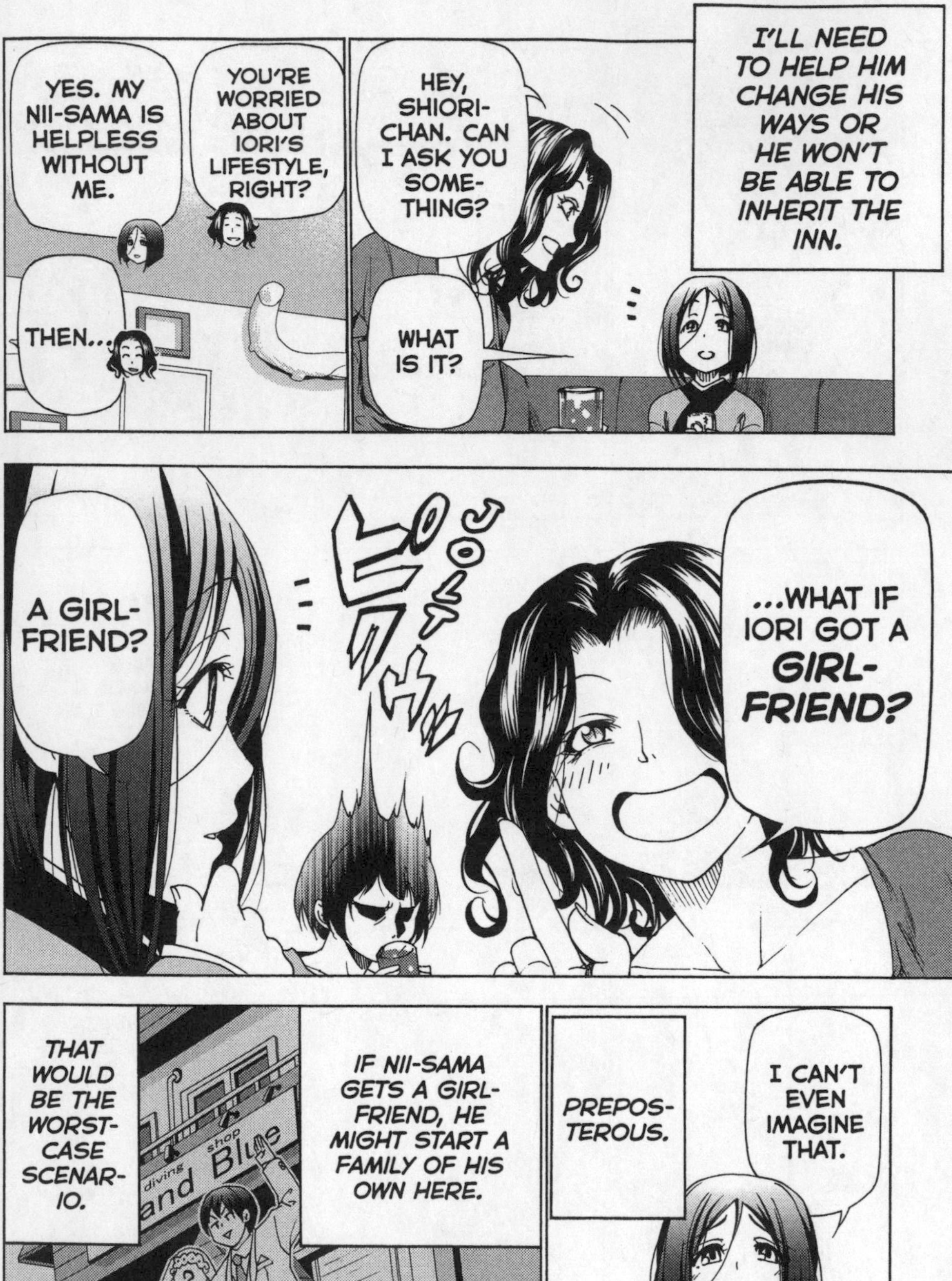

I'LL NEED TO HELP HIM CHANGE HIS WAYS OR HE WON'T BE ABLE TO INHERIT THE INN.
HEY, SHIORI-CHAN. CAN I ASK YOU SOMETHING?
WHAT IS IT?
YOU'RE WORRIED ABOUT IORI'S LIFESTYLE, RIGHT?
YES. MY NII-SAMA IS HELPLESS WITHOUT ME.
THEN...
...WHAT IF IORI GOT A GIRLFRIEND?
JOLT
A GIRLFRIEND?
I CAN'T EVEN IMAGINE THAT.
PREPOSTEROUS.
IF NII-SAMA GETS A GIRLFRIEND, HE MIGHT START A FAMILY OF HIS OWN HERE.
THAT WOULD BE THE WORST-CASE SCENARIO.

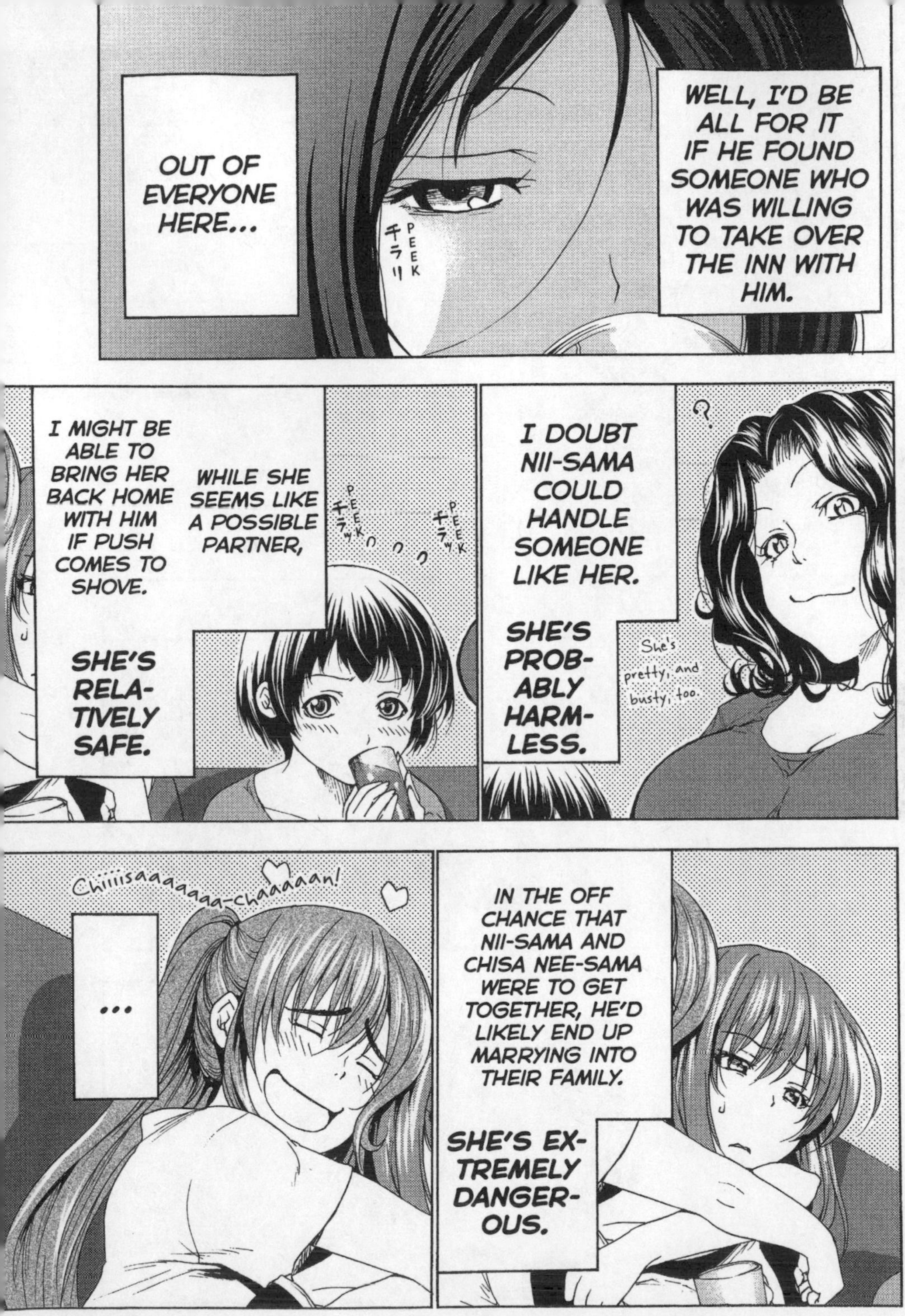
WELL, I'D BE ALL FOR IT IF HE FOUND SOMEONE WHO WAS WILLING TO TAKE OVER THE INN WITH HIM.
チラリ PEEK
OUT OF EVERYONE HERE...
?
I DOUBT NII-SAMA COULD HANDLE SOMEONE LIKE HER.
She's pretty, and busty, too.
SHE'S PROBABLY HARMLESS.
チラッ PEEK
チラッ PEEK
WHILE SHE SEEMS LIKE A POSSIBLE PARTNER,
I MIGHT BE ABLE TO BRING HER BACK HOME WITH HIM IF PUSH COMES TO SHOVE.
SHE'S RELATIVELY SAFE.
IN THE OFF CHANCE THAT NII-SAMA AND CHISA NEE-SAMA WERE TO GET TOGETHER, HE'D LIKELY END UP MARRYING INTO THEIR FAMILY.
SHE'S EXTREMELY DANGEROUS.
Chiiiisaaaaaaa-chaaaaan!
...

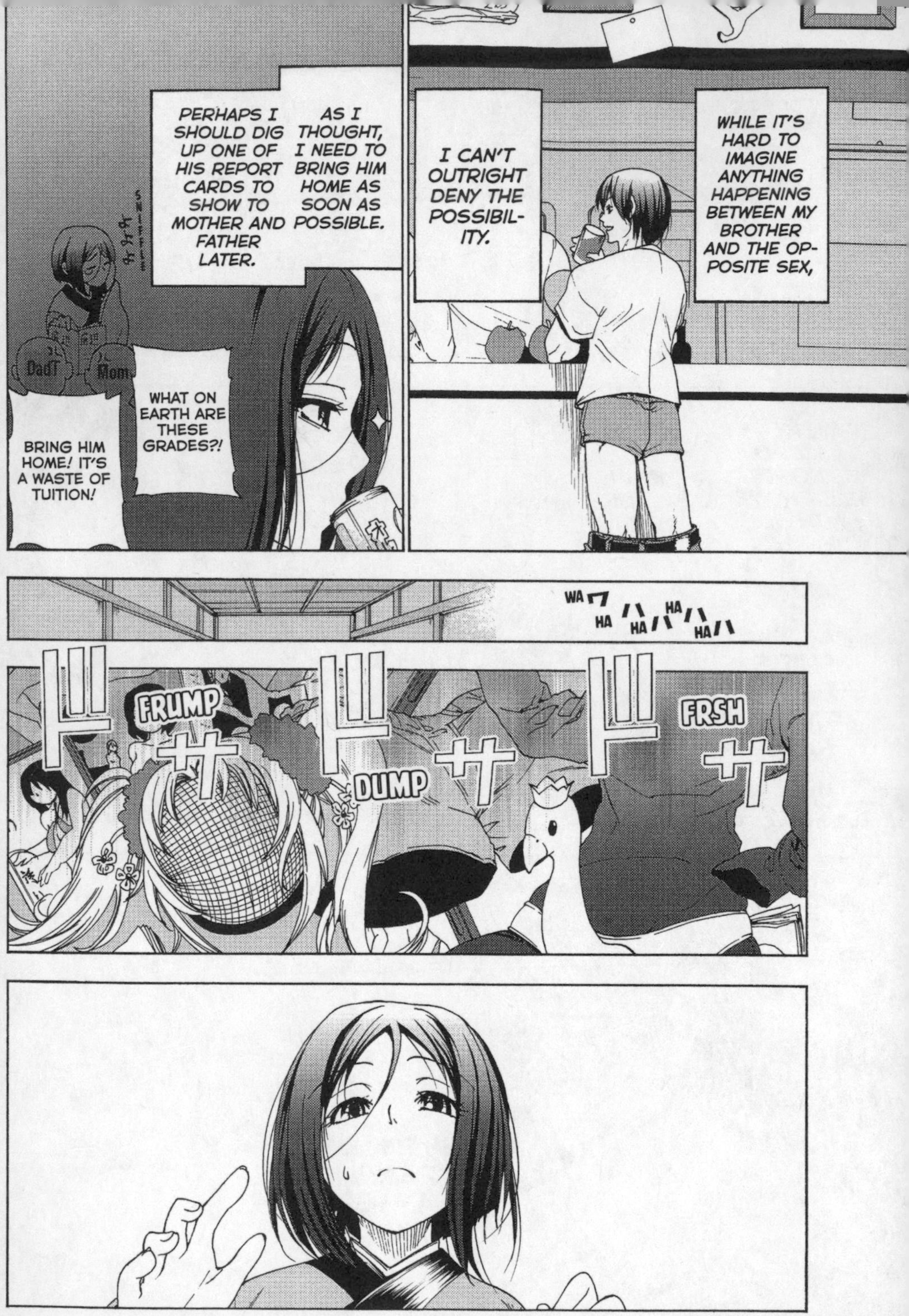
WHILE IT'S HARD TO IMAGINE ANYTHING HAPPENING BETWEEN MY BROTHER AND THE OPPOSITE SEX,
I CAN'T OUTRIGHT DENY THE POSSIBILITY.
AS I THOUGHT, I NEED TO BRING HIM HOME AS SOON AS POSSIBLE.
PERHAPS I SHOULD DIG UP ONE OF HIS REPORT CARDS TO SHOW TO MOTHER AND FATHER LATER.
SNIFF
WHAT ON EARTH ARE THESE GRADES?!
Mom
BRING HIM HOME! IT'S A WASTE OF TUITION!
Dad
WA HA HA HA HA
FRSH
DUMP
FRUMP

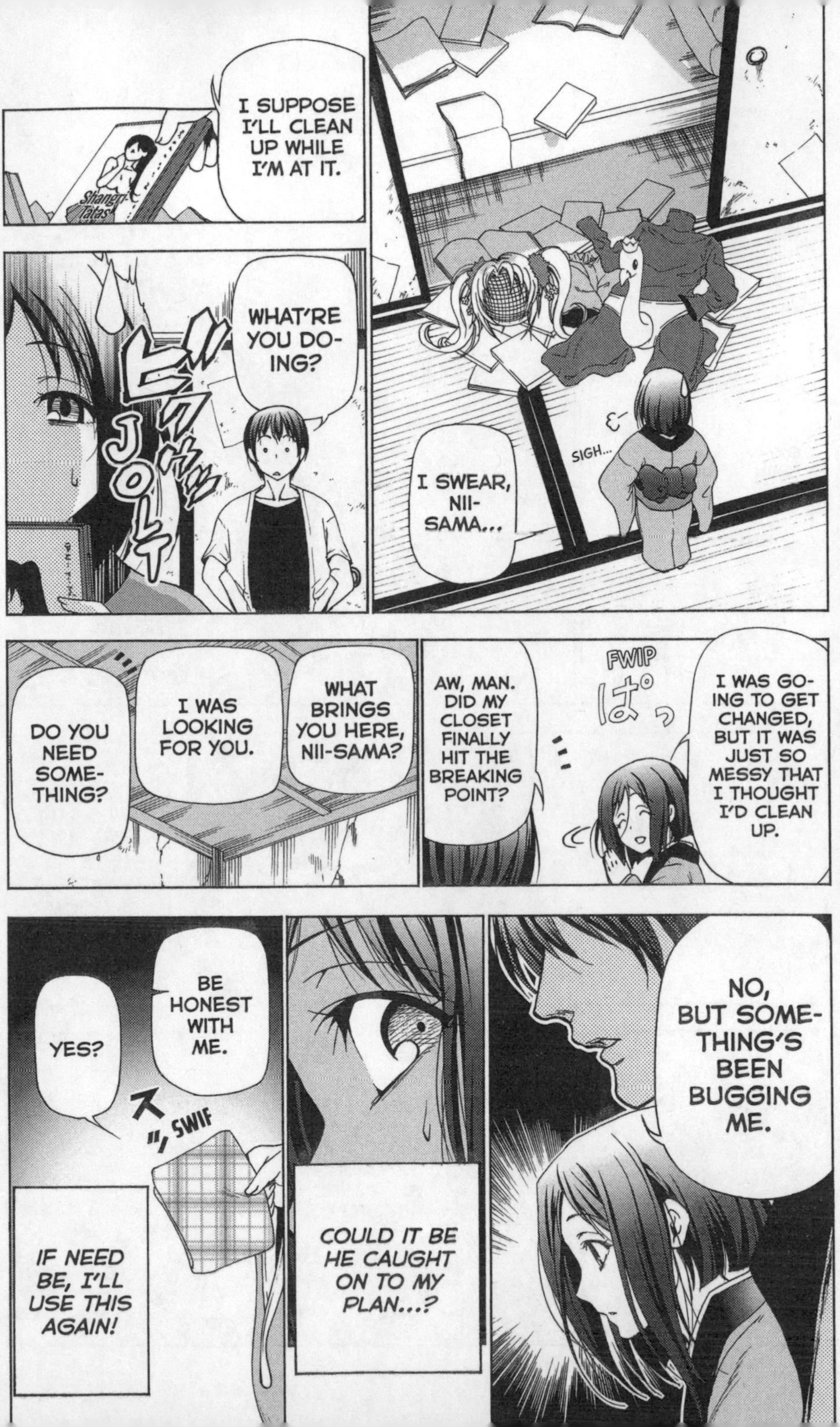
SIGH...
I SWEAR, NII-SAMA...
I SUPPOSE I'LL CLEAN UP WHILE I'M AT IT.
Shangri Tatas
WHAT'RE YOU DOING?
JOLT
I WAS GOING TO GET CHANGED, BUT IT WAS JUST SO MESSY THAT I THOUGHT I'D CLEAN UP.
FWIP
ぱっ
AW, MAN. DID MY CLOSET FINALLY HIT THE BREAKING POINT?
WHAT BRINGS YOU HERE, NII-SAMA?
I WAS LOOKING FOR YOU.
DO YOU NEED SOMETHING?
NO, BUT SOMETHING'S BEEN BUGGING ME.
COULD IT BE HE CAUGHT ON TO MY PLAN...?
BE HONEST WITH ME.
YES?
SWIF
IF NEED BE, I'LL USE THIS AGAIN!

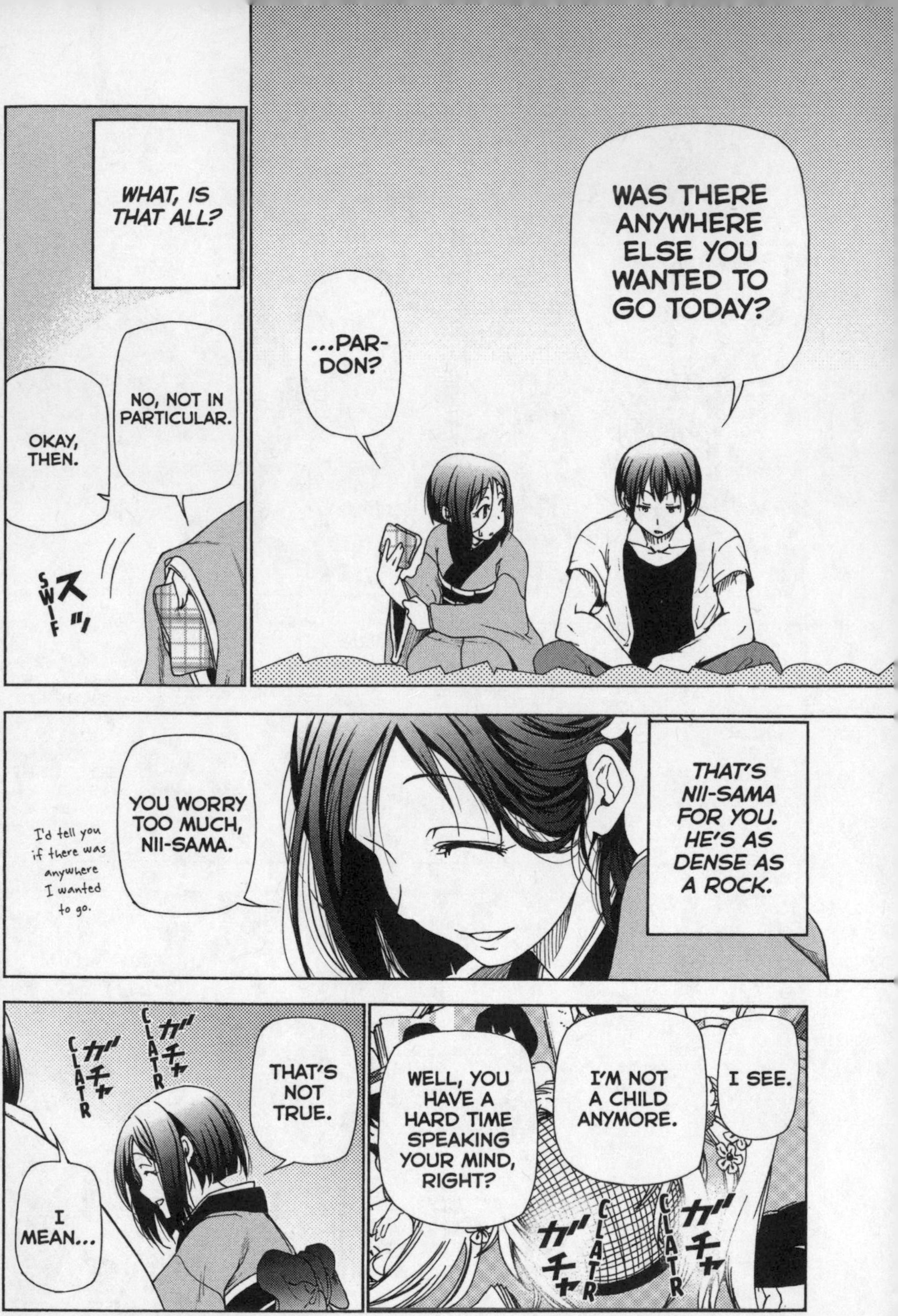
WAS THERE ANYWHERE ELSE YOU WANTED TO GO TODAY?
...PAR-DON?
WHAT, IS THAT ALL?
NO, NOT IN PARTICULAR.
OKAY, THEN.
SWIF スッ
THAT'S NII-SAMA FOR YOU. HE'S AS DENSE AS A ROCK.
YOU WORRY TOO MUCH, NII-SAMA.
I'd tell you if there was anywhere I wanted to go.
I SEE.
I'M NOT A CHILD ANYMORE.
WELL, YOU HAVE A HARD TIME SPEAKING YOUR MIND, RIGHT?
CLATR ガチャ
CLATR ガチャ
THAT'S NOT TRUE.
CLATR ガチャ
CLATR ガチャ
I MEAN...

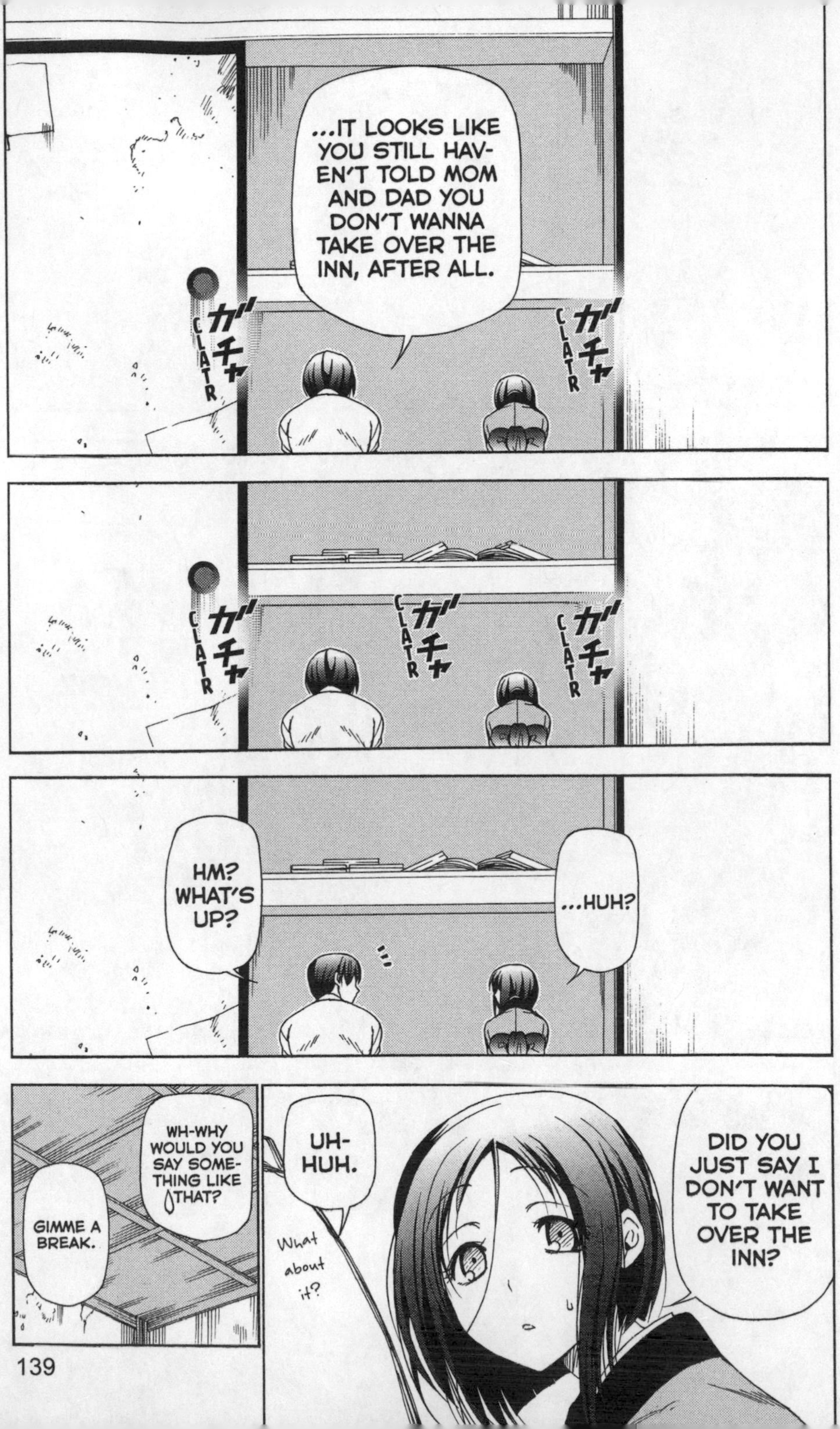
...IT LOOKS LIKE YOU STILL HAVEN'T TOLD MOM AND DAD YOU DON'T WANNA TAKE OVER THE INN, AFTER ALL.
ガチャ CLATR
ガチャ CLATR
ガチャ CLATR
ガチャ CLATR
ガチャ CLATR
...HUH?
HM? WHAT'S UP?
DID YOU JUST SAY I DON'T WANT TO TAKE OVER THE INN?
What about it?
UH-HUH.
WH-WHY WOULD YOU SAY SOMETHING LIKE THAT?
GIMME A BREAK.

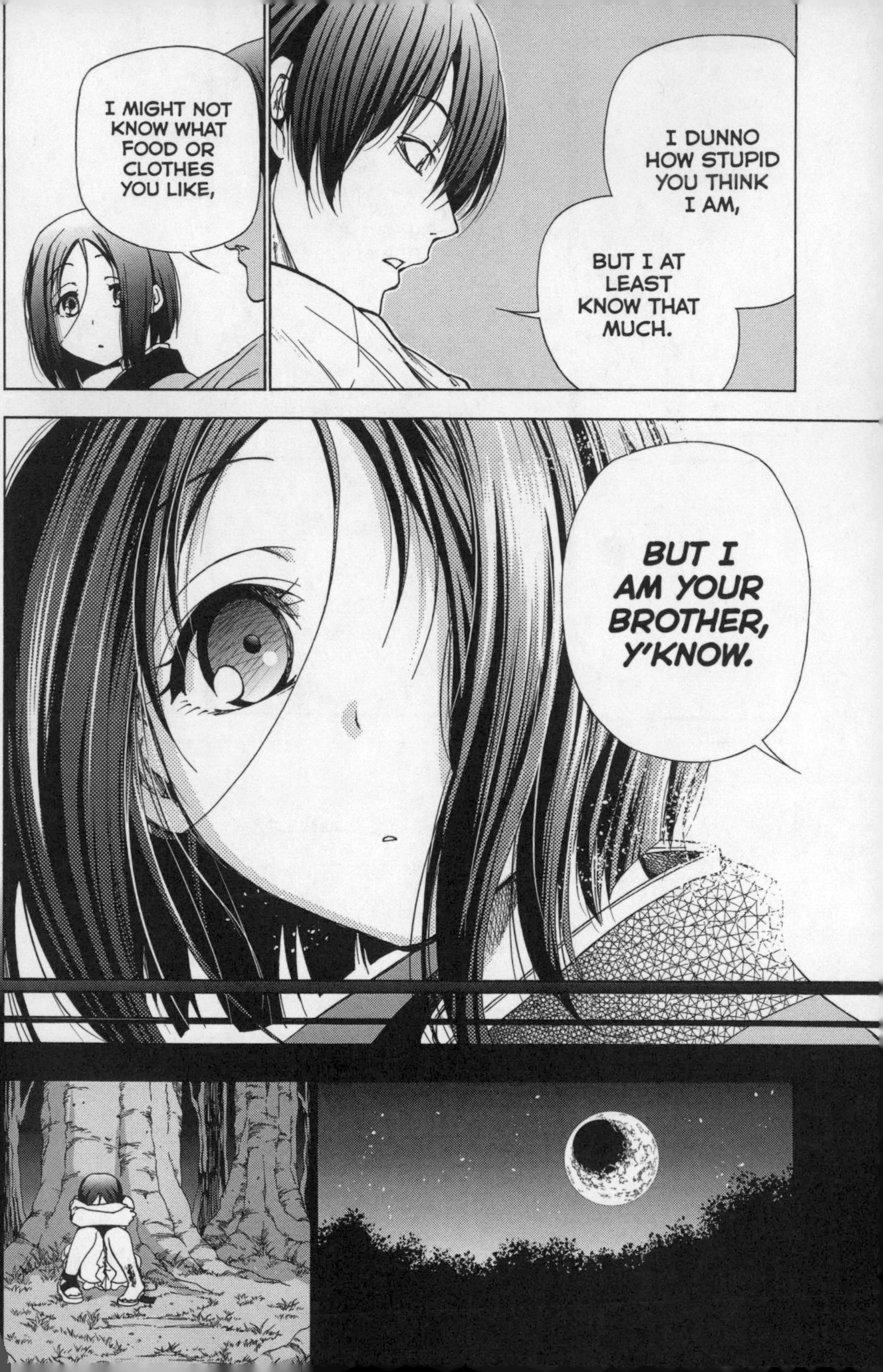
I DUNNO HOW STUPID YOU THINK I AM,
BUT I AT LEAST KNOW THAT MUCH.
I MIGHT NOT KNOW WHAT FOOD OR CLOTHES YOU LIKE,
BUT I AM YOUR BROTHER, Y'KNOW.

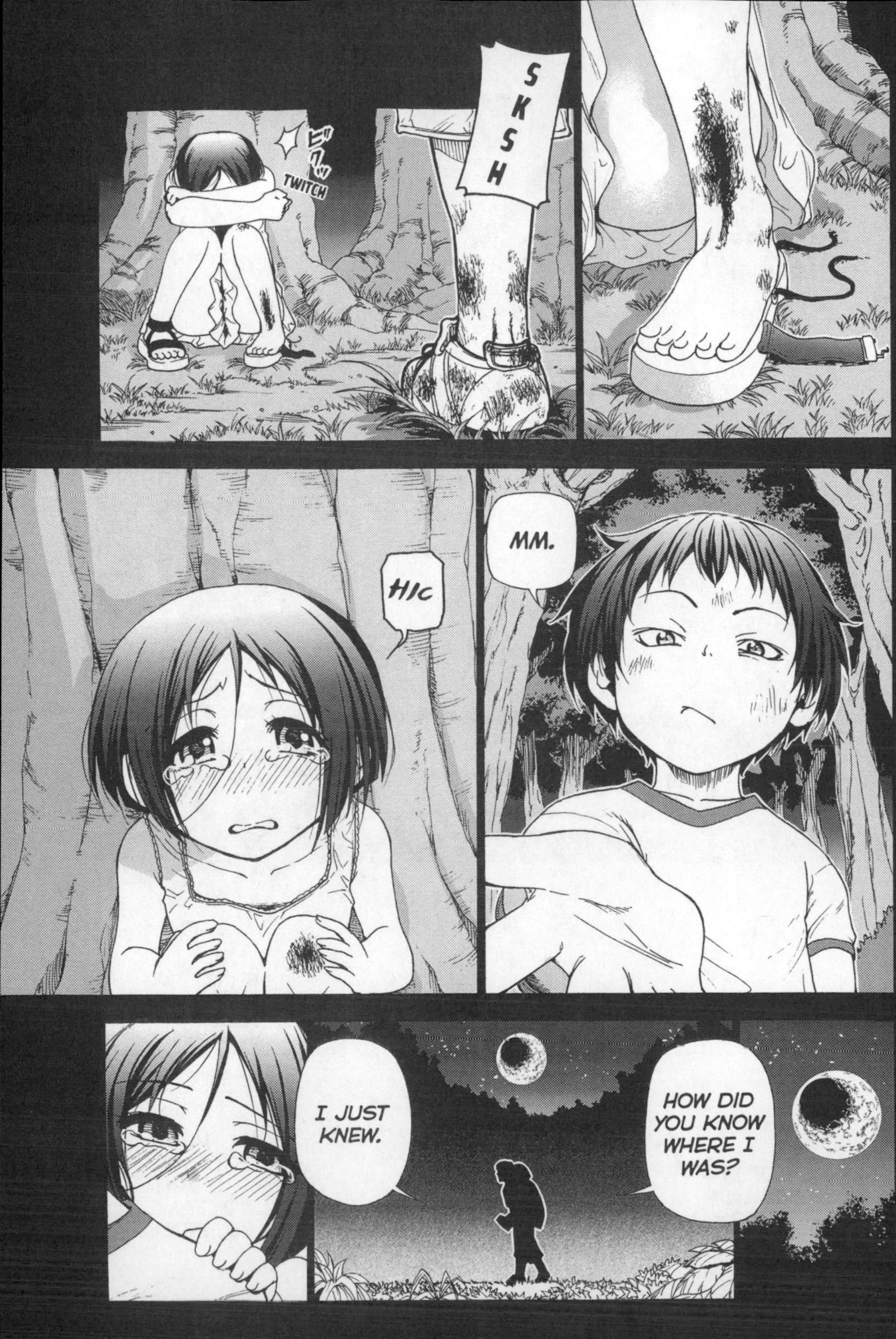
SKSH
ビクッ
TWITCH
MM.
HIC
HOW DID YOU KNOW WHERE I WAS?
I JUST KNEW.

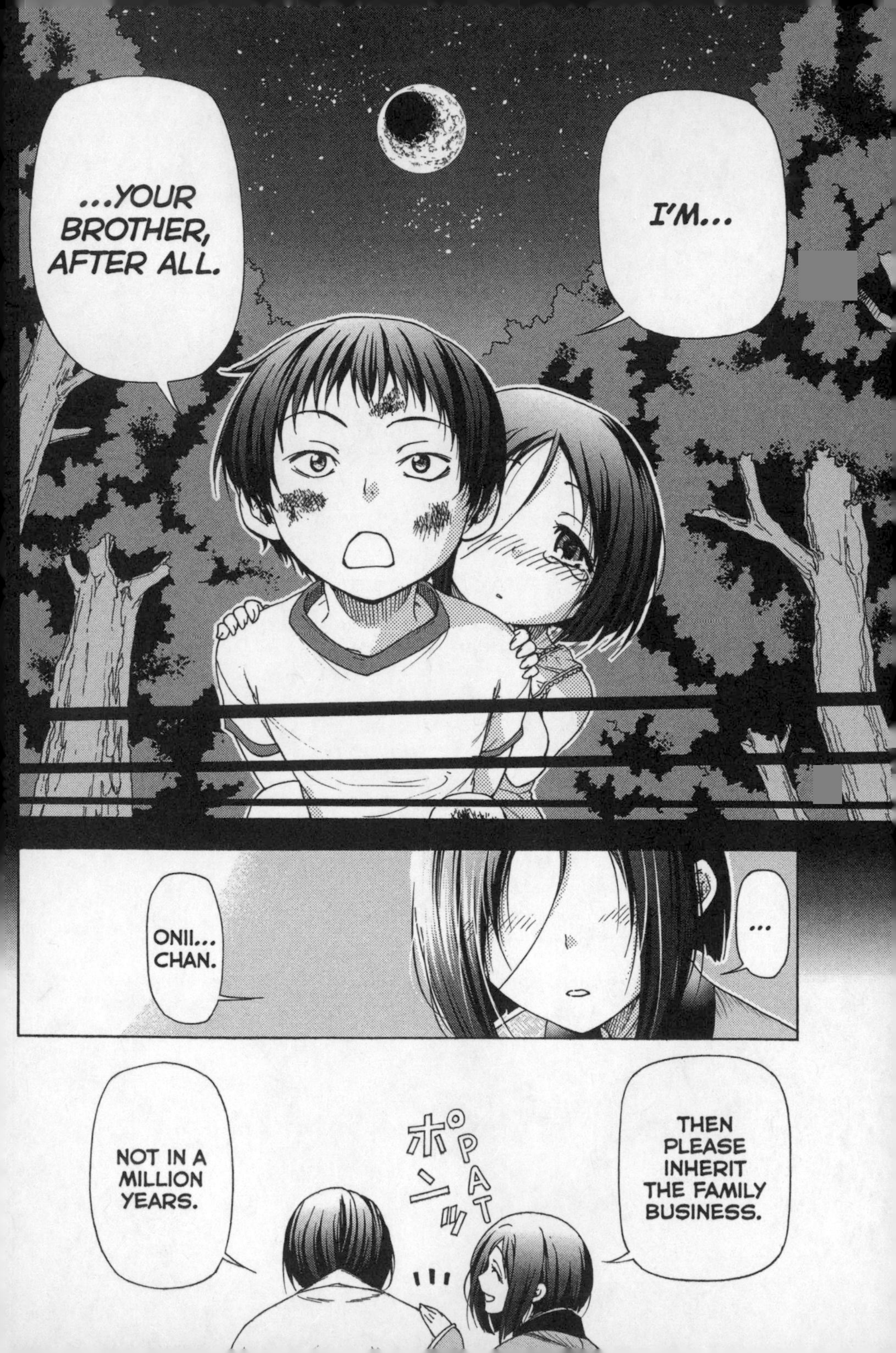
I'M...
...YOUR BROTHER, AFTER ALL.
...
ONII... CHAN.
THEN PLEASE INHERIT THE FAMILY BUSINESS.
ポンッ
PAT
NOT IN A MILLION YEARS.

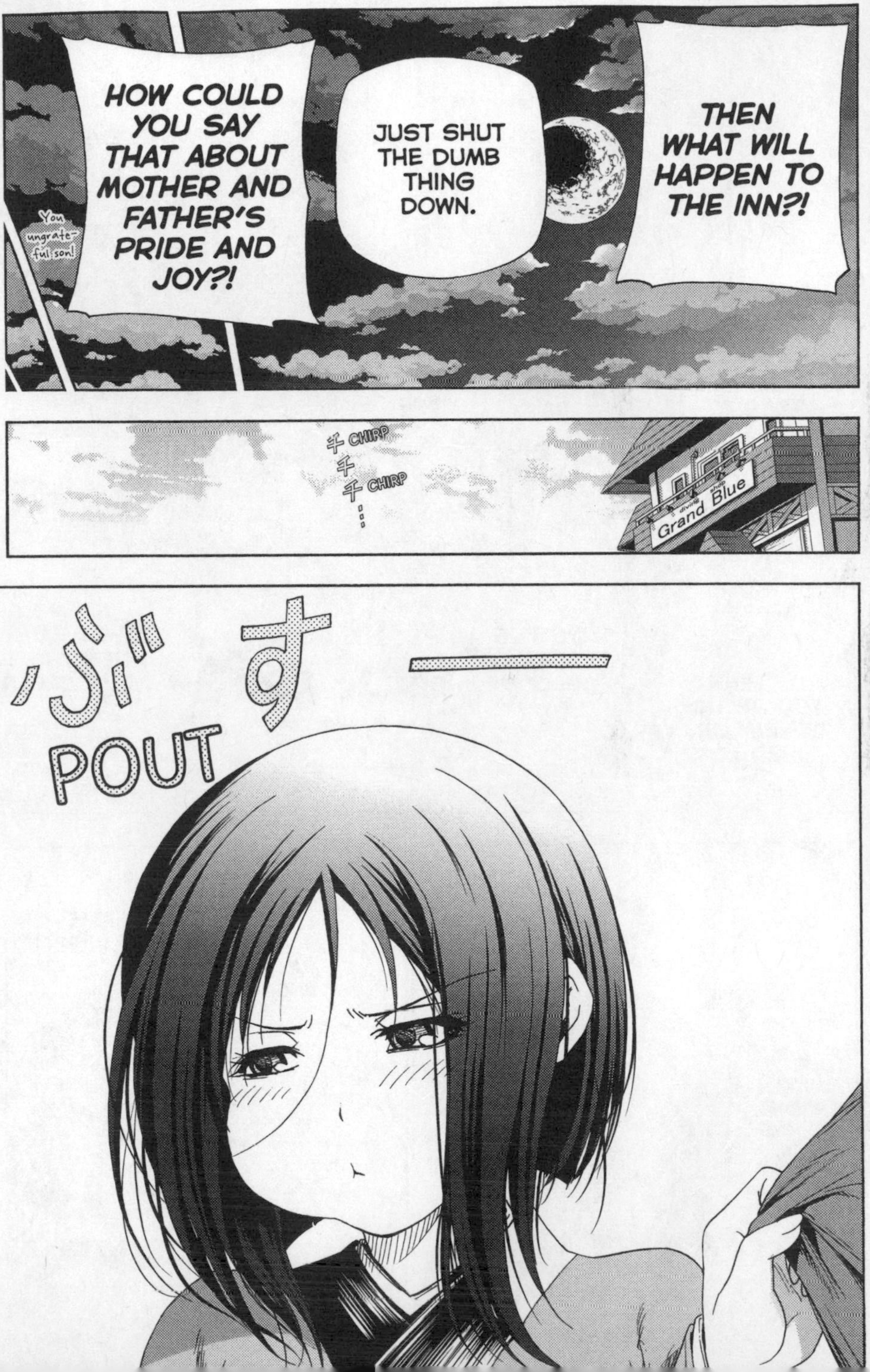
THEN WHAT WILL HAPPEN TO THE INN?!
JUST SHUT THE DUMB THING DOWN.
HOW COULD YOU SAY THAT ABOUT MOTHER AND FATHER'S PRIDE AND JOY?!
You ungrate-ful son!
チ CHIRP
チ
チ CHIRP
diving shop
Grand Blue
ぶすー
POUT

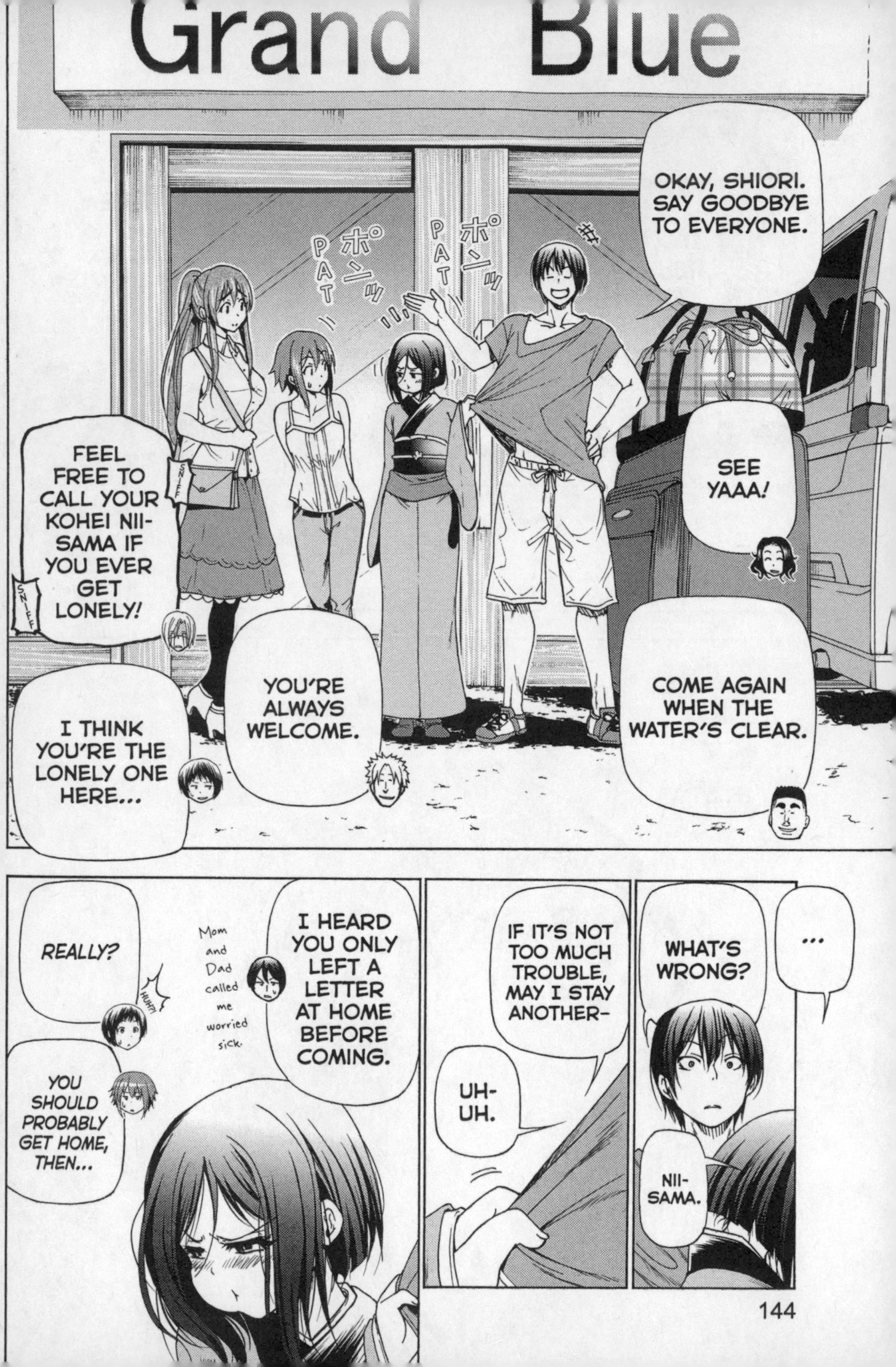
Grand Blue
OKAY, SHIORI. SAY GOODBYE TO EVERYONE.
ポンッ PAT
ポンッ PAT
SEE YAAA!
FEEL FREE TO CALL YOUR KOHEI NII-SAMA IF YOU EVER GET LONELY!
SNIFF
SNIFF
COME AGAIN WHEN THE WATER'S CLEAR.
YOU'RE ALWAYS WELCOME.
I THINK YOU'RE THE LONELY ONE HERE...
...
WHAT'S WRONG?
NII-SAMA.
IF IT'S NOT TOO MUCH TROUBLE, MAY I STAY ANOTHER-
UH-UH.
I HEARD YOU ONLY LEFT A LETTER AT HOME BEFORE COMING.
Mom and Dad called me worried sick.
REALLY?
HUH?!
YOU SHOULD PROBABLY GET HOME, THEN...

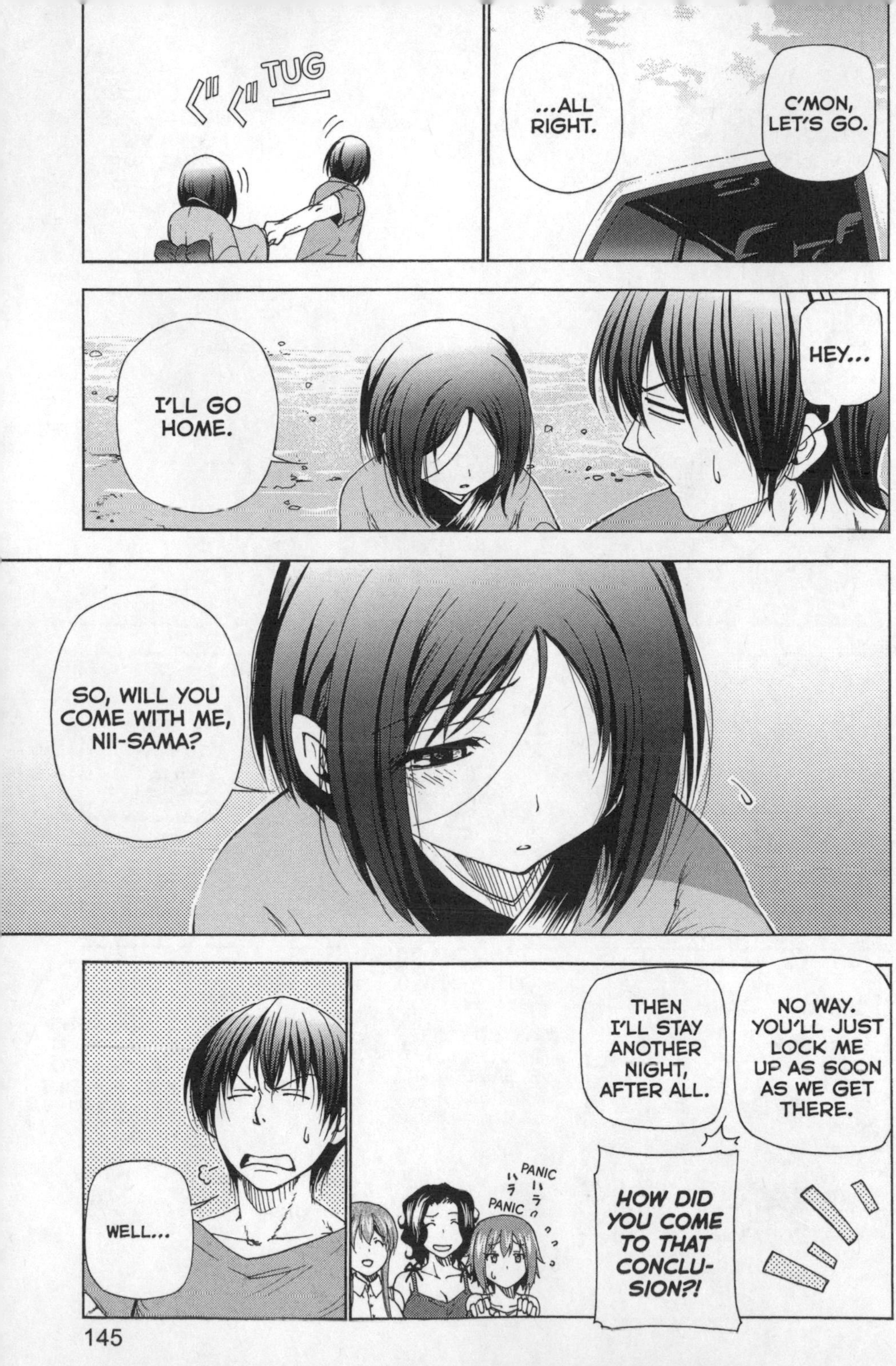
C'MON, LET'S GO.
...ALL RIGHT.
TUG
HEY...
I'LL GO HOME.
SO, WILL YOU COME WITH ME, NII-SAMA?
NO WAY. YOU'LL JUST LOCK ME UP AS SOON AS WE GET THERE.
THEN I'LL STAY ANOTHER NIGHT, AFTER ALL.
HOW DID YOU COME TO THAT CONCLUSION?!
PANIC
PANIC
WELL...

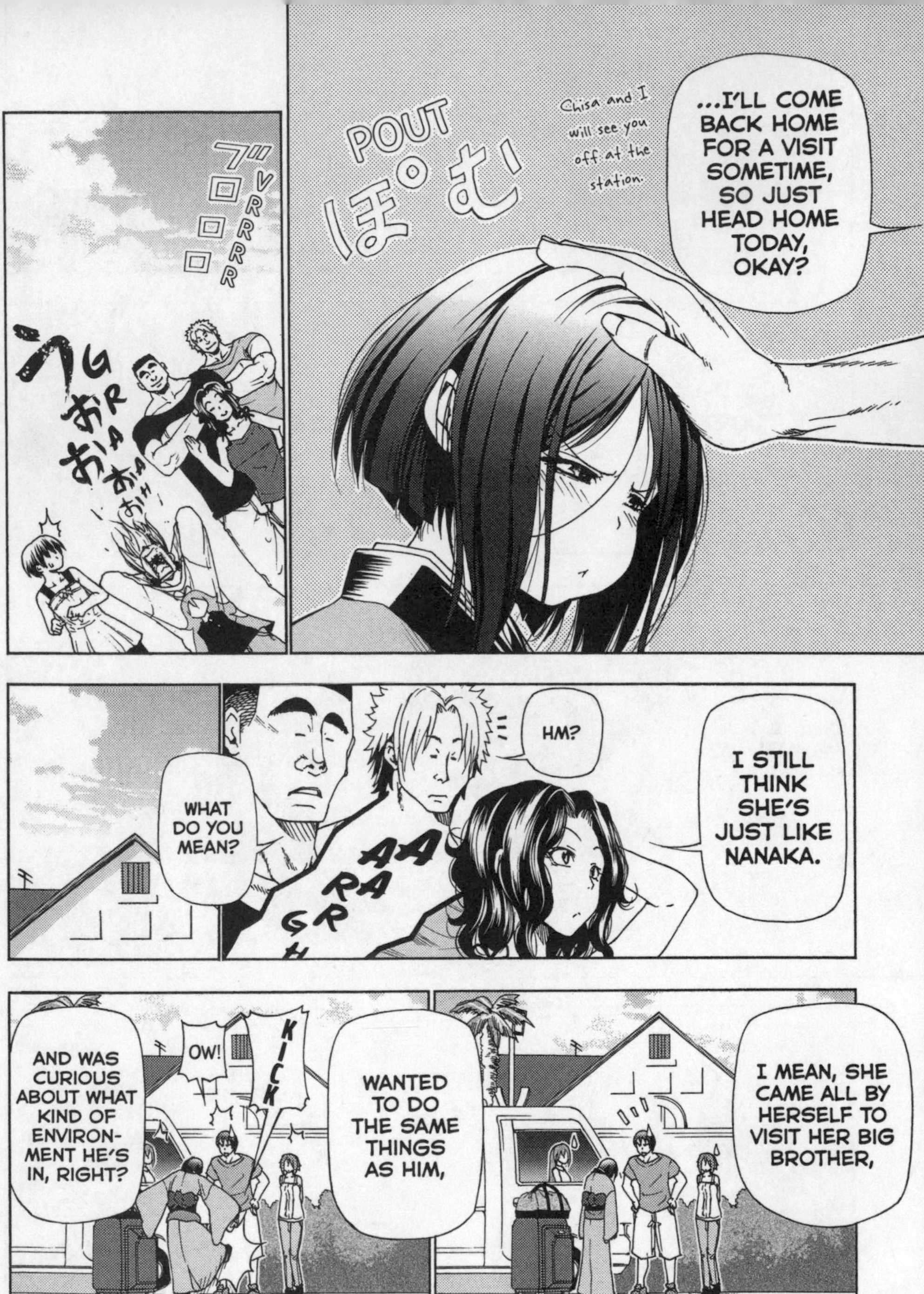
...I'LL COME BACK HOME FOR A VISIT SOMETIME, SO JUST HEAD HOME TODAY, OKAY?
Chisa and I will see you off at the station.
POUT
ほむ
VRRRRR
ブロロロロ
GRAAH
I STILL THINK SHE'S JUST LIKE NANAKA.
HM?
WHAT DO YOU MEAN?
AARAGRH
I MEAN, SHE CAME ALL BY HERSELF TO VISIT HER BIG BROTHER,
WANTED TO DO THE SAME THINGS AS HIM,
KICK
OW!
AND WAS CURIOUS ABOUT WHAT KIND OF ENVIRON-MENT HE'S IN, RIGHT?

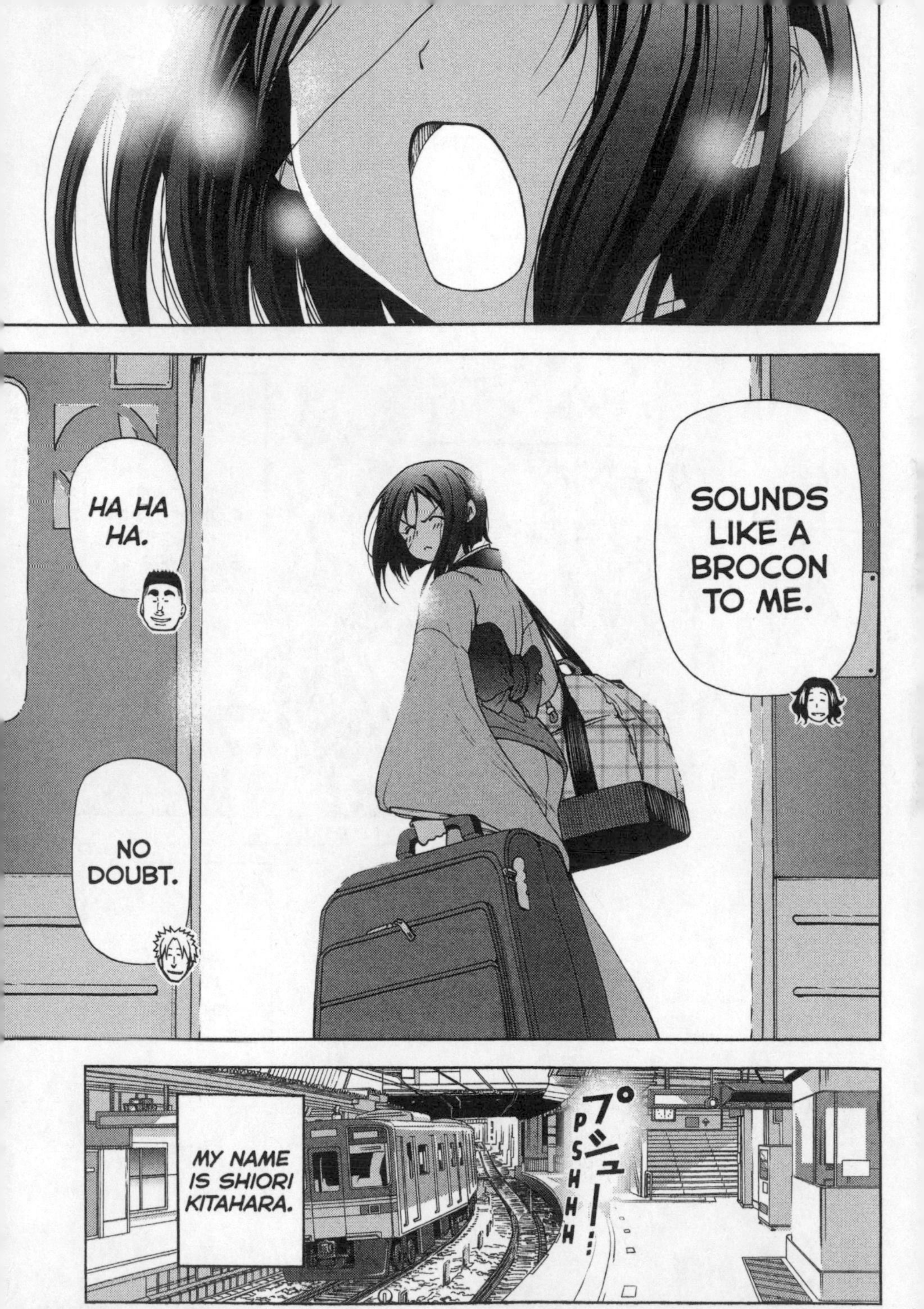
SOUNDS LIKE A BROCON TO ME.
HA HA HA.
NO DOUBT.
プシュー!!
PSHHH
MY NAME IS SHIORI KITAHARA.

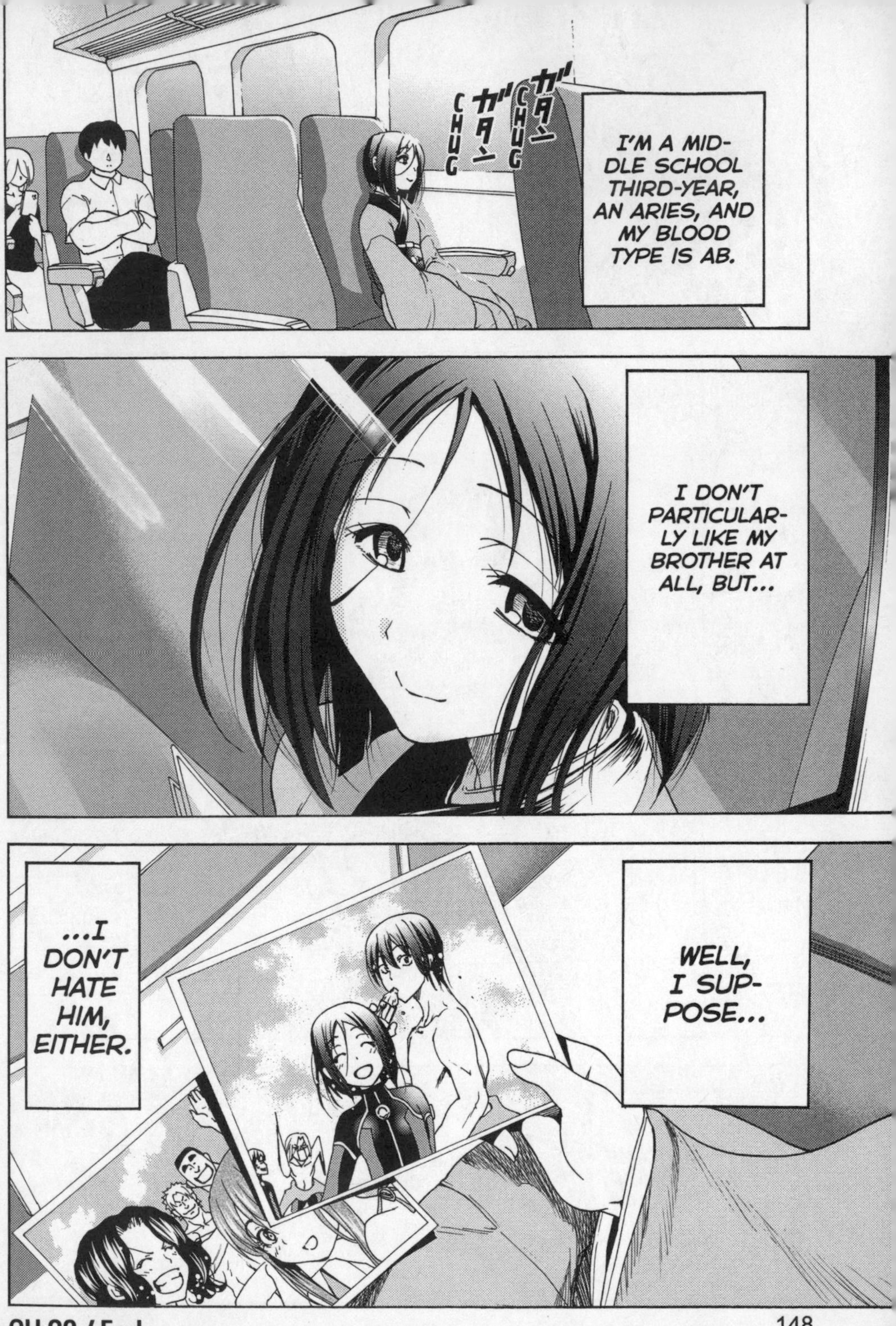

I'M A MIDDLE SCHOOL THIRD-YEAR, AN ARIES, AND MY BLOOD TYPE IS AB.
ガタン CHUG
ガタン CHUG
I DON'T PARTICULARLY LIKE MY BROTHER AT ALL, BUT...
WELL, I SUPPOSE...
...I DON'T HATE HIM, EITHER.

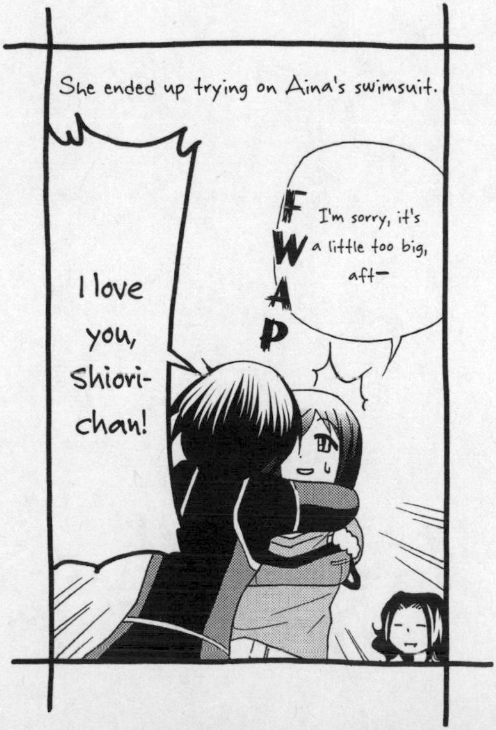
She ended up trying on Aina's swimsuit.
I'm sorry, it's a little too big, aft—
FWAP
I love you, Shiori-chan!

Grand Blue
Dreaming

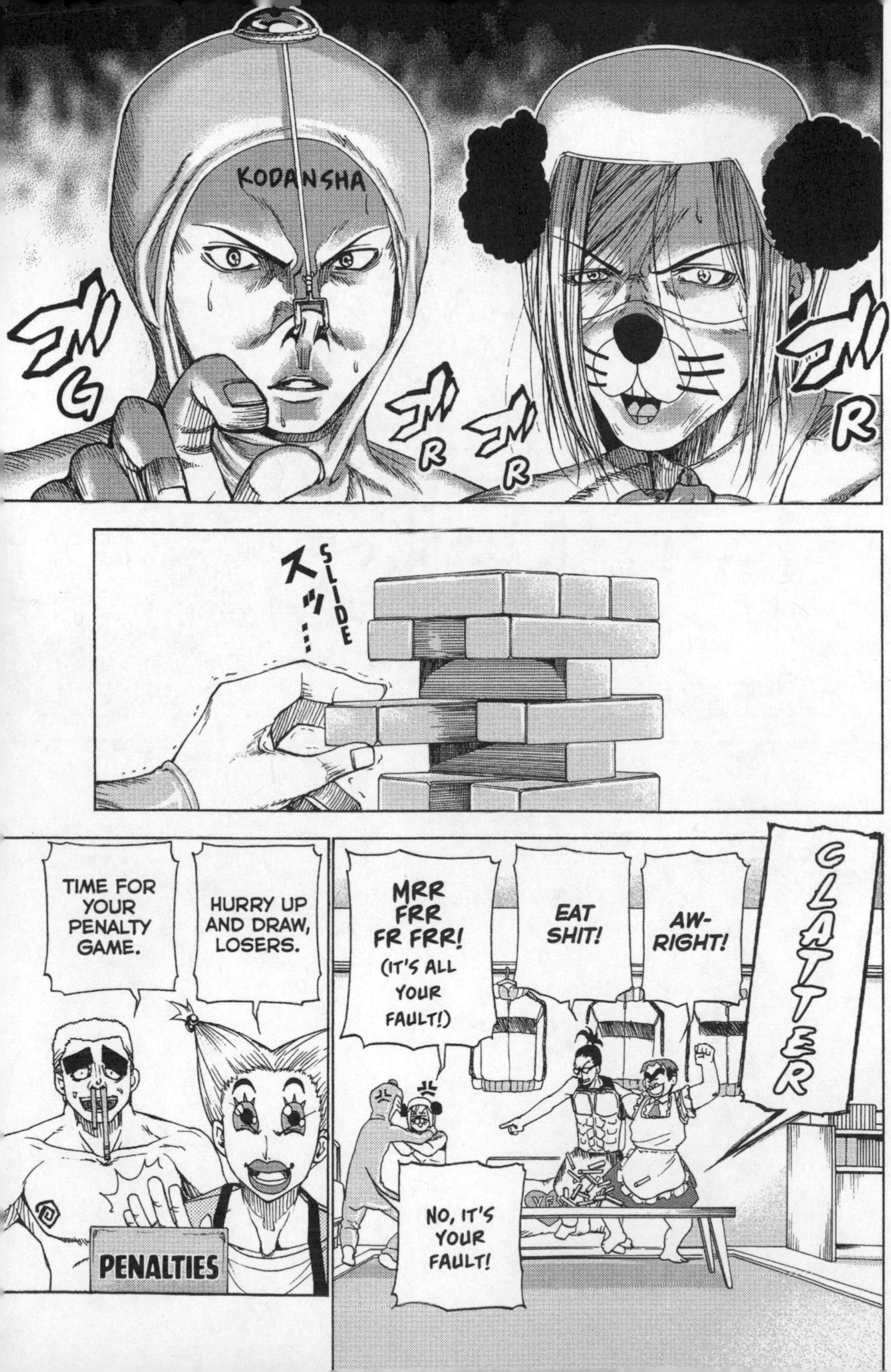
KODANSHA
GRRR
スッ…
SLIDE
CLATTER
AW-RIGHT!
EAT SHIT!
MRR FRR FR FRR! (IT'S ALL YOUR FAULT!)
NO, IT'S YOUR FAULT!
HURRY UP AND DRAW, LOSERS.
TIME FOR YOUR PENALTY GAME.
PENALTIES

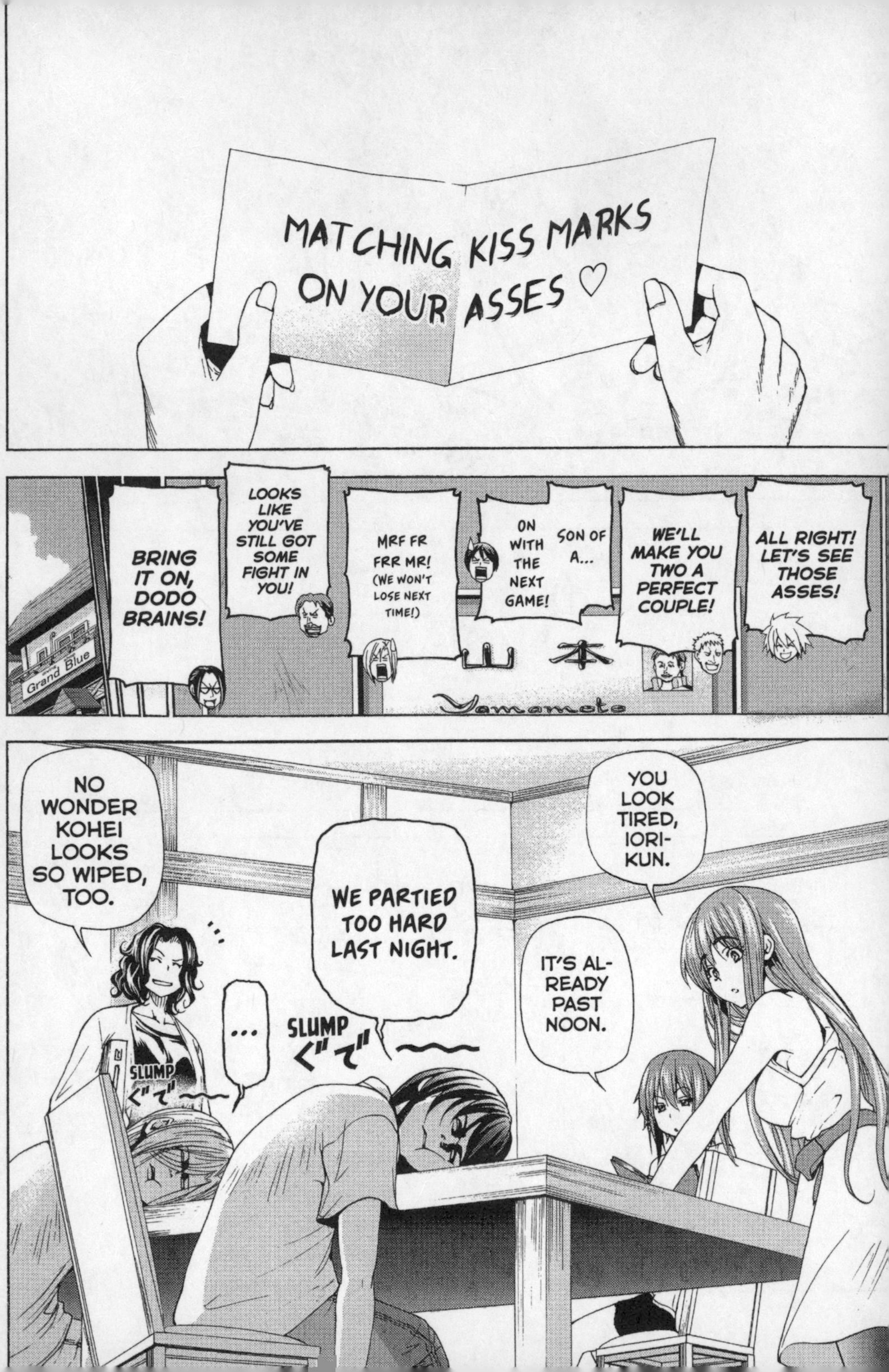
MATCHING KISS MARKS ON YOUR ASSES ♡
ALL RIGHT! LET'S SEE THOSE ASSES!
WE'LL MAKE YOU TWO A PERFECT COUPLE!
SON OF A...
ON WITH THE NEXT GAME!
MRF FR FRR MR! (WE WON'T LOSE NEXT TIME!)
LOOKS LIKE YOU'VE STILL GOT SOME FIGHT IN YOU!
BRING IT ON, DODO BRAINS!
Grand Blue
山 本
Yamamoto
YOU LOOK TIRED, IORI-KUN.
IT'S ALREADY PAST NOON.
WE PARTIED TOO HARD LAST NIGHT.
SLUMP
NO WONDER KOHEI LOOKS SO WIPED, TOO.
...
...
SLUMP

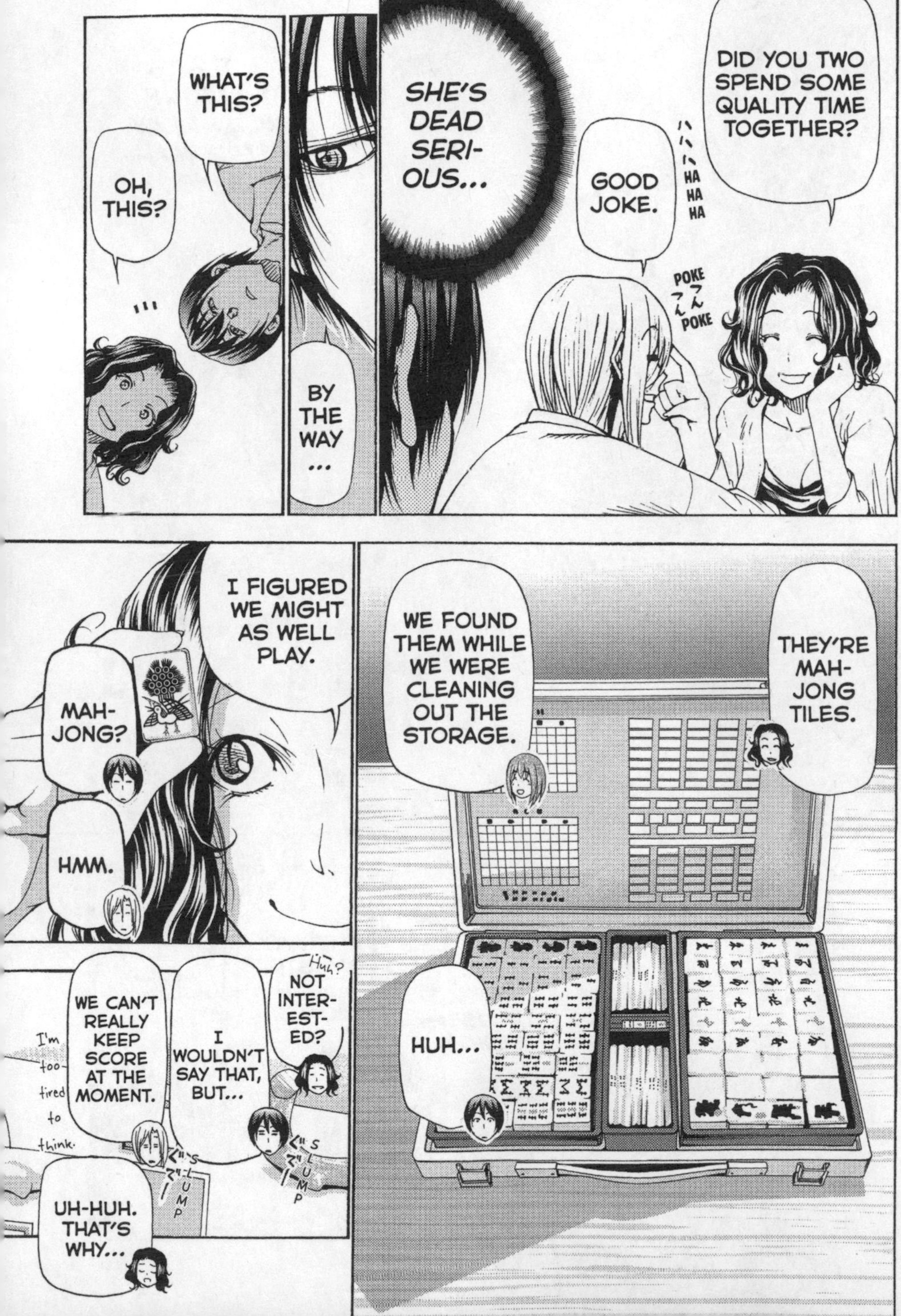
DID YOU TWO SPEND SOME QUALITY TIME TOGETHER?
GOOD JOKE.
ハハハ
HA HA HA
つんつん
POKE POKE
SHE'S DEAD SERI-OUS...
BY THE WAY...
WHAT'S THIS?
OH, THIS?
...
THEY'RE MAH-JONG TILES.
WE FOUND THEM WHILE WE WERE CLEANING OUT THE STORAGE.
HUH...
I FIGURED WE MIGHT AS WELL PLAY.
MAH-JONG?
HMM.
Huh?
NOT INTEREST-ED?
I WOULDN'T SAY THAT, BUT...
SLUMP
WE CAN'T REALLY KEEP SCORE AT THE MOMENT.
I'm too tired to think.
SLUMP
UH-HUH. THAT'S WHY...

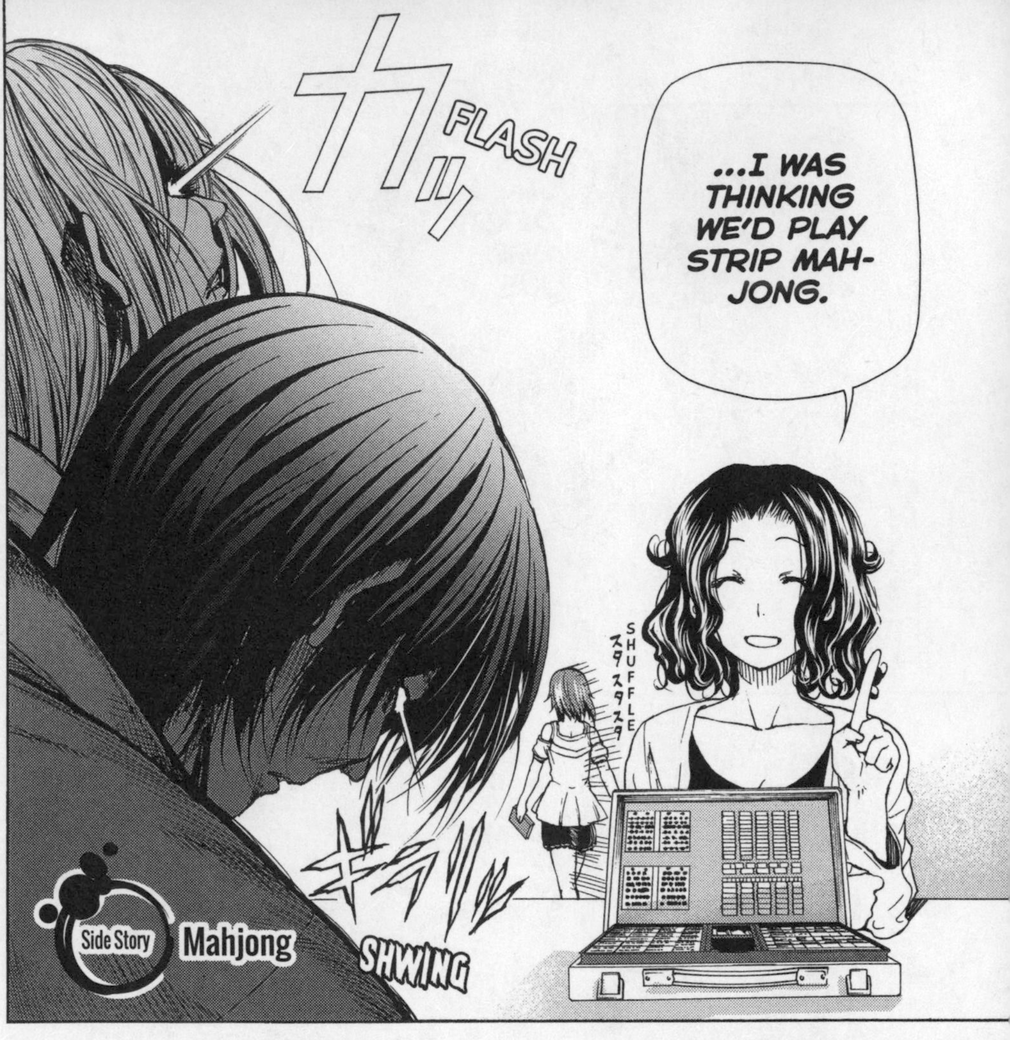
FLASH
...I WAS THINKING WE'D PLAY STRIP MAH-JONG.
SHUFFLE
Side Story Mahjong
SHWING

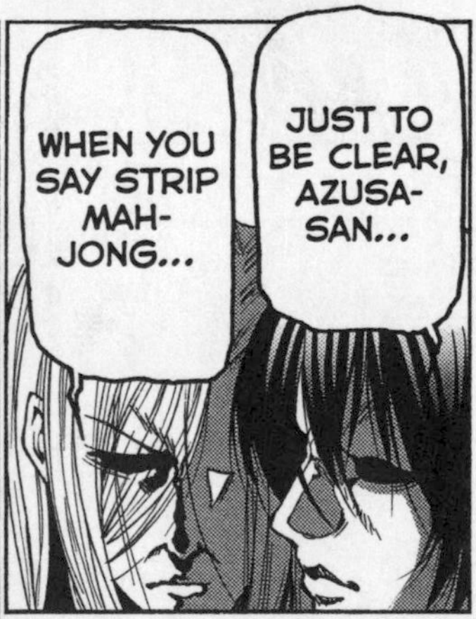
JUST TO BE CLEAR, AZUSA-SAN...
WHEN YOU SAY STRIP MAH-JONG...

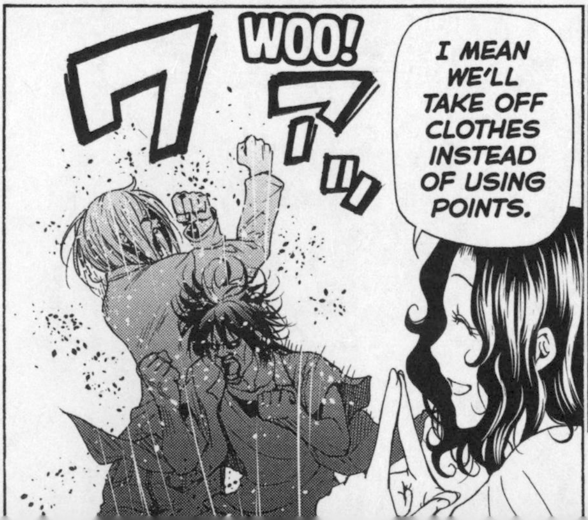
I MEAN WE'LL TAKE OFF CLOTHES INSTEAD OF USING POINTS.
WOO!

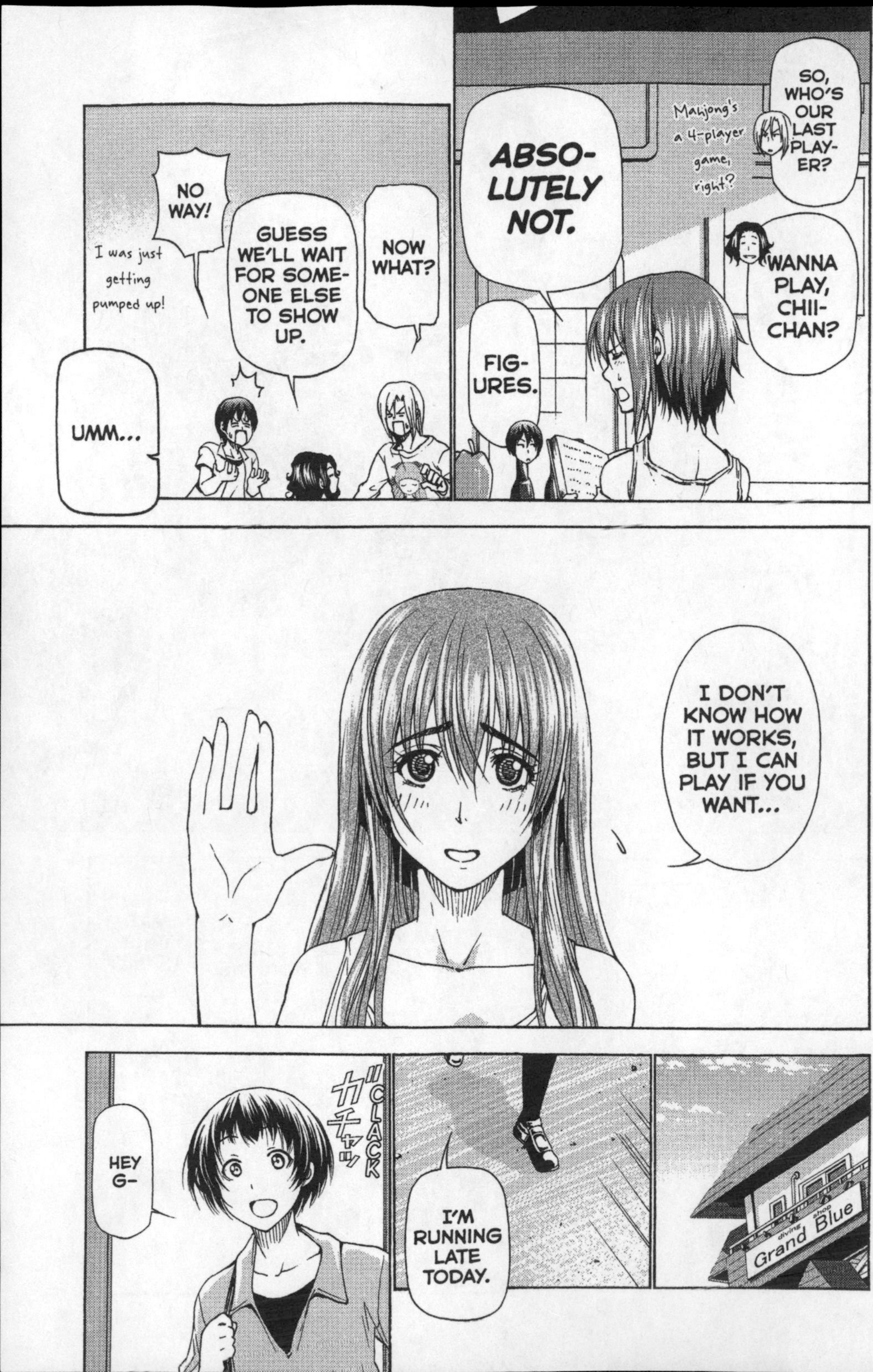
SO, WHO'S OUR LAST PLAYER?
Mahjong's a 4-player game, right?
WANNA PLAY, CHII-CHAN?
ABSO-LUTELY NOT.
FIG-URES.
NOW WHAT?
GUESS WE'LL WAIT FOR SOME-ONE ELSE TO SHOW UP.
NO WAY!
I was just getting pumped up!
UMM...
I DON'T KNOW HOW IT WORKS, BUT I CAN PLAY IF YOU WANT...
diving shop Grand Blue
I'M RUNNING LATE TODAY.
ガチャッ CLACK
HEY G-

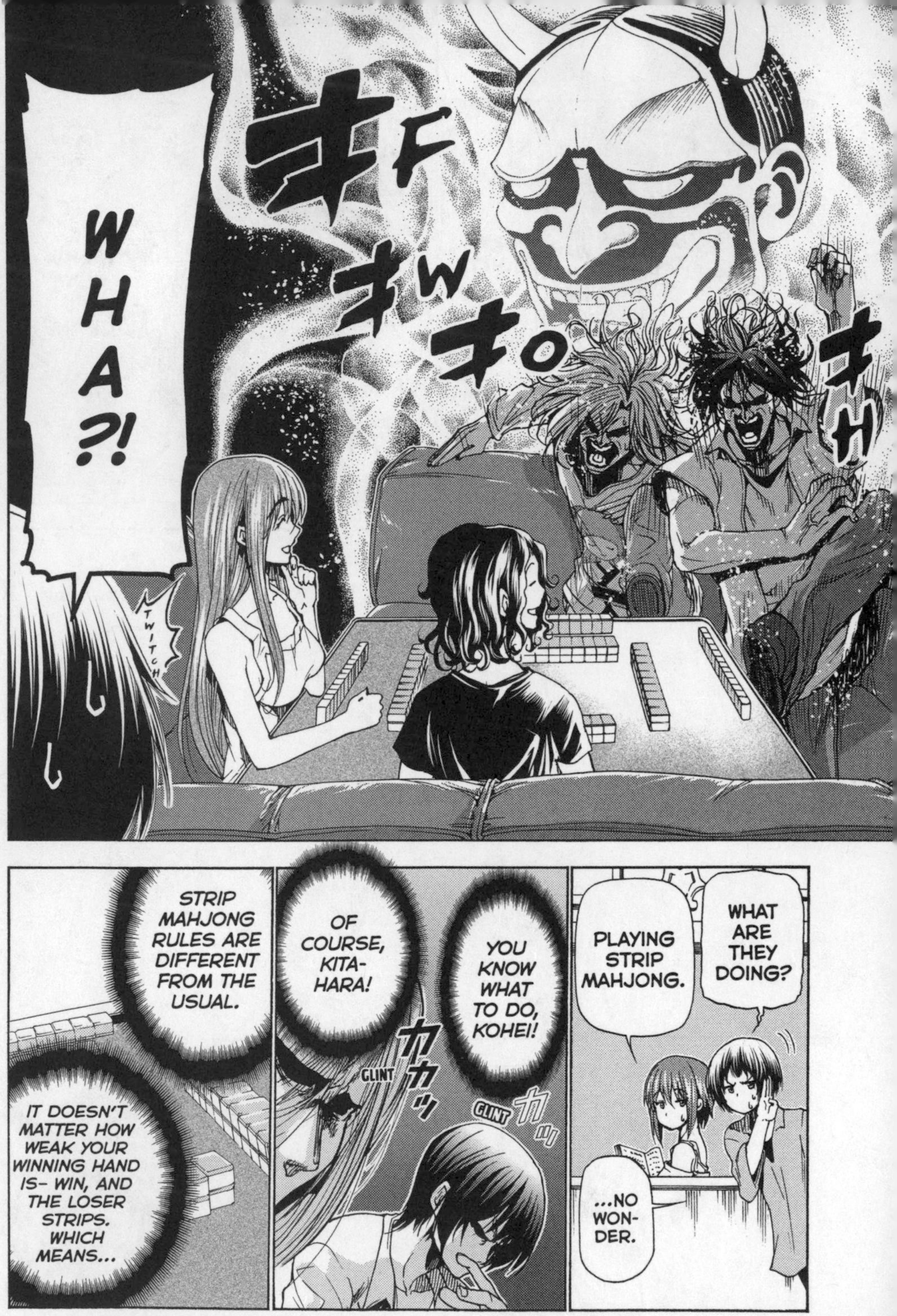
WHA?!
TWITCH
WHAT ARE THEY DOING?
PLAYING STRIP MAHJONG.
...NO WONDER.
YOU KNOW WHAT TO DO, KOHEI!
OF COURSE, KITA-HARA!
GLINT
GLINT
STRIP MAHJONG RULES ARE DIFFERENT FROM THE USUAL.
IT DOESN'T MATTER HOW WEAK YOUR WINNING HAND IS– WIN, AND THE LOSER STRIPS. WHICH MEANS...

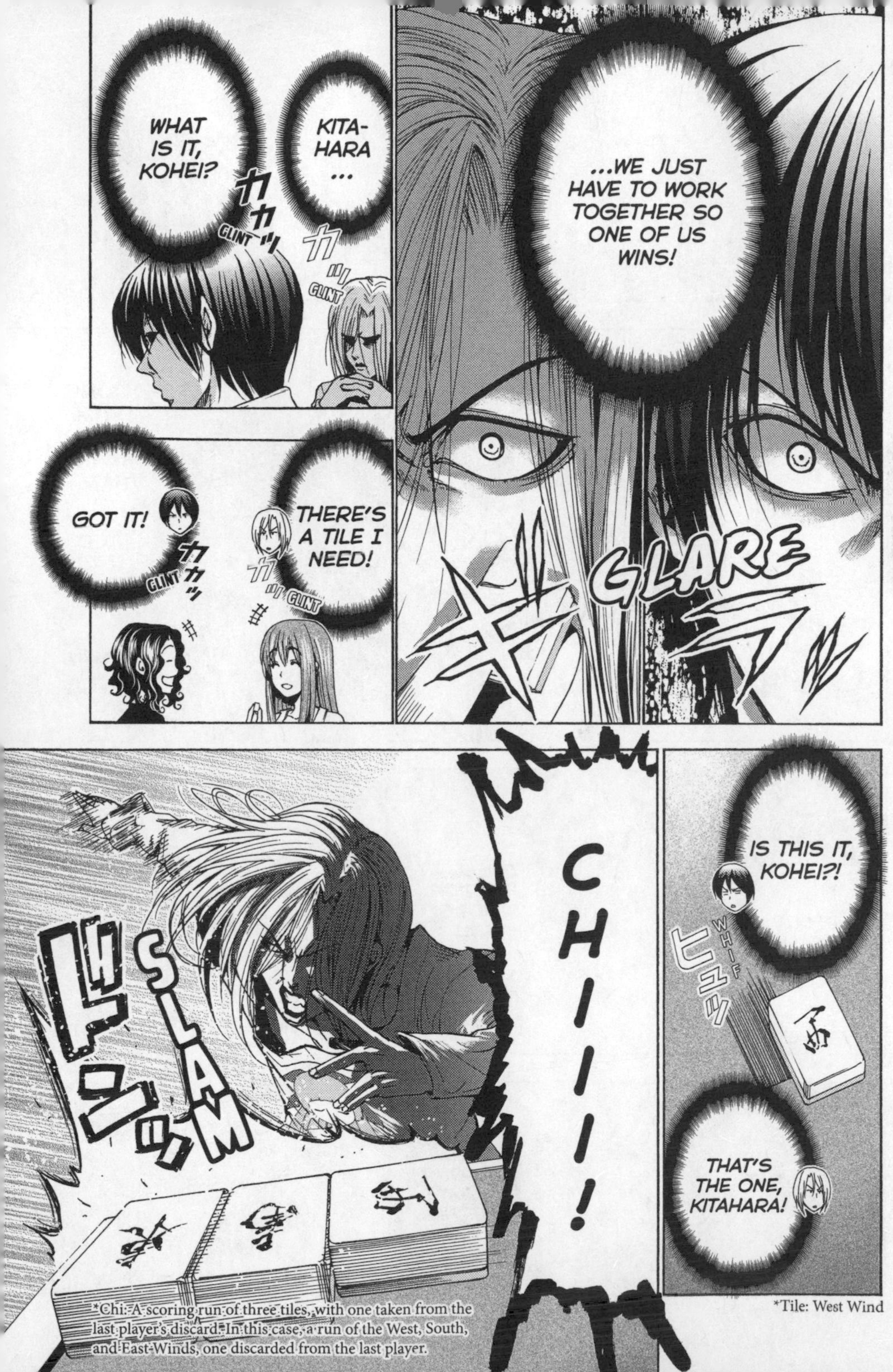
...WE JUST HAVE TO WORK TOGETHER SO ONE OF US WINS!
GLARE
KITA-HARA...
GLINT
WHAT IS IT, KOHEI?
GLINT
THERE'S A TILE I NEED!
GLINT
GOT IT!
GLINT
IS THIS IT, KOHEI?!
WHIF
THAT'S THE ONE, KITAHARA!
CHI!
SLAM

*Tile: West Wind

*Chi: A scoring run of three tiles, with one taken from the last player's discard. In this case, a run of the West, South, and East Winds, one discarded from the last player.

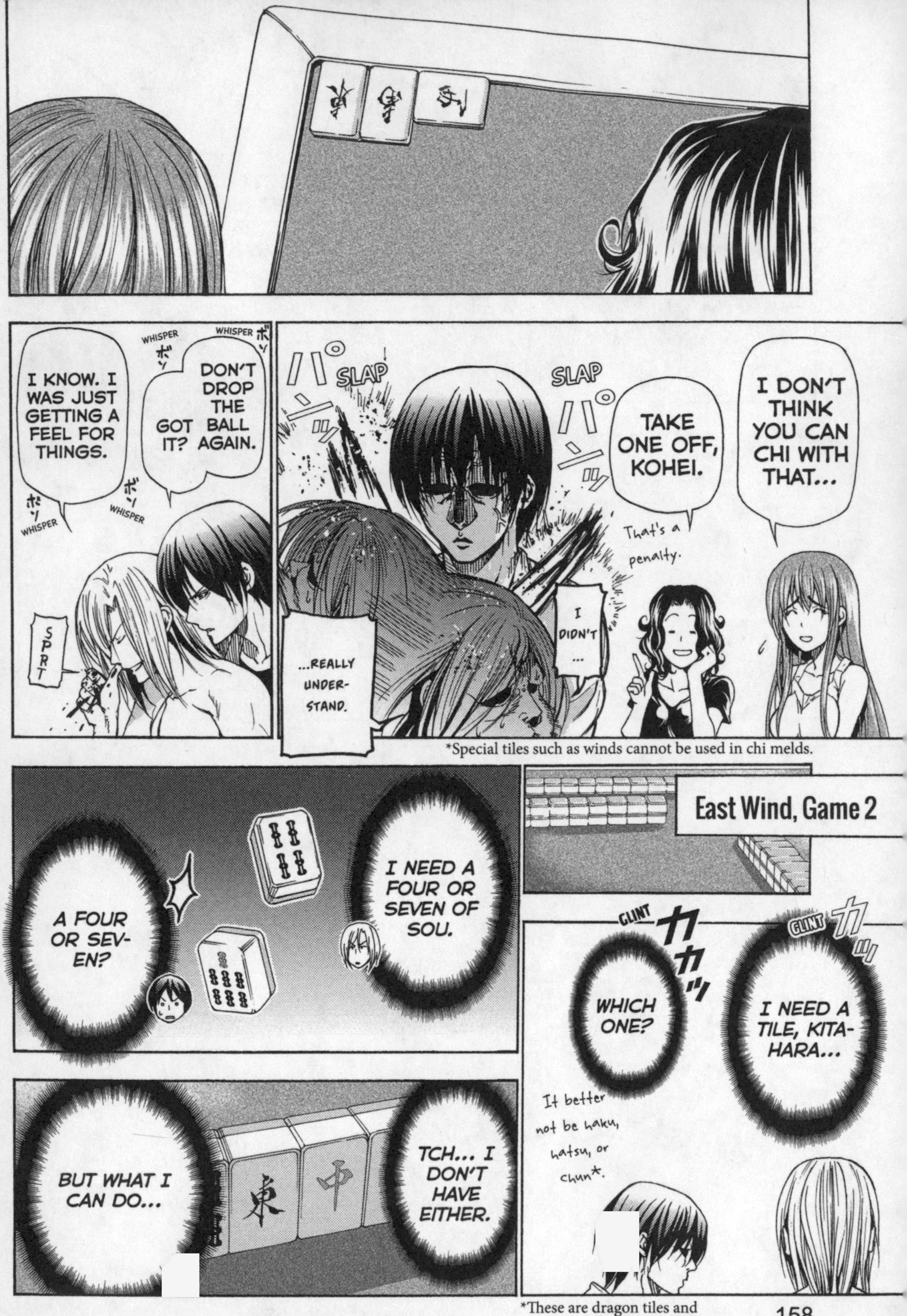
I DON'T THINK YOU CAN CHI WITH THAT...
That's a penalty.
TAKE ONE OFF, KOHEI.
SLAP
SLAP
I DIDN'T ...
...REALLY UNDER-STAND.
WHISPER
WHISPER
DON'T DROP THE BALL AGAIN.
GOT IT?
I KNOW. I WAS JUST GETTING A FEEL FOR THINGS.
WHISPER
WHISPER
SPRT
East Wind, Game 2
GLINT
I NEED A TILE, KITA-HARA...
GLINT
WHICH ONE?
It better not be haku, hatsu, or chun*.
I NEED A FOUR OR SEVEN OF SOU.
A FOUR OR SEV-EN?
TCH... I DON'T HAVE EITHER.
BUT WHAT I CAN DO...

*Special tiles such as winds cannot be used in chi melds.

*These are dragon tiles and also cannot be chi melded.

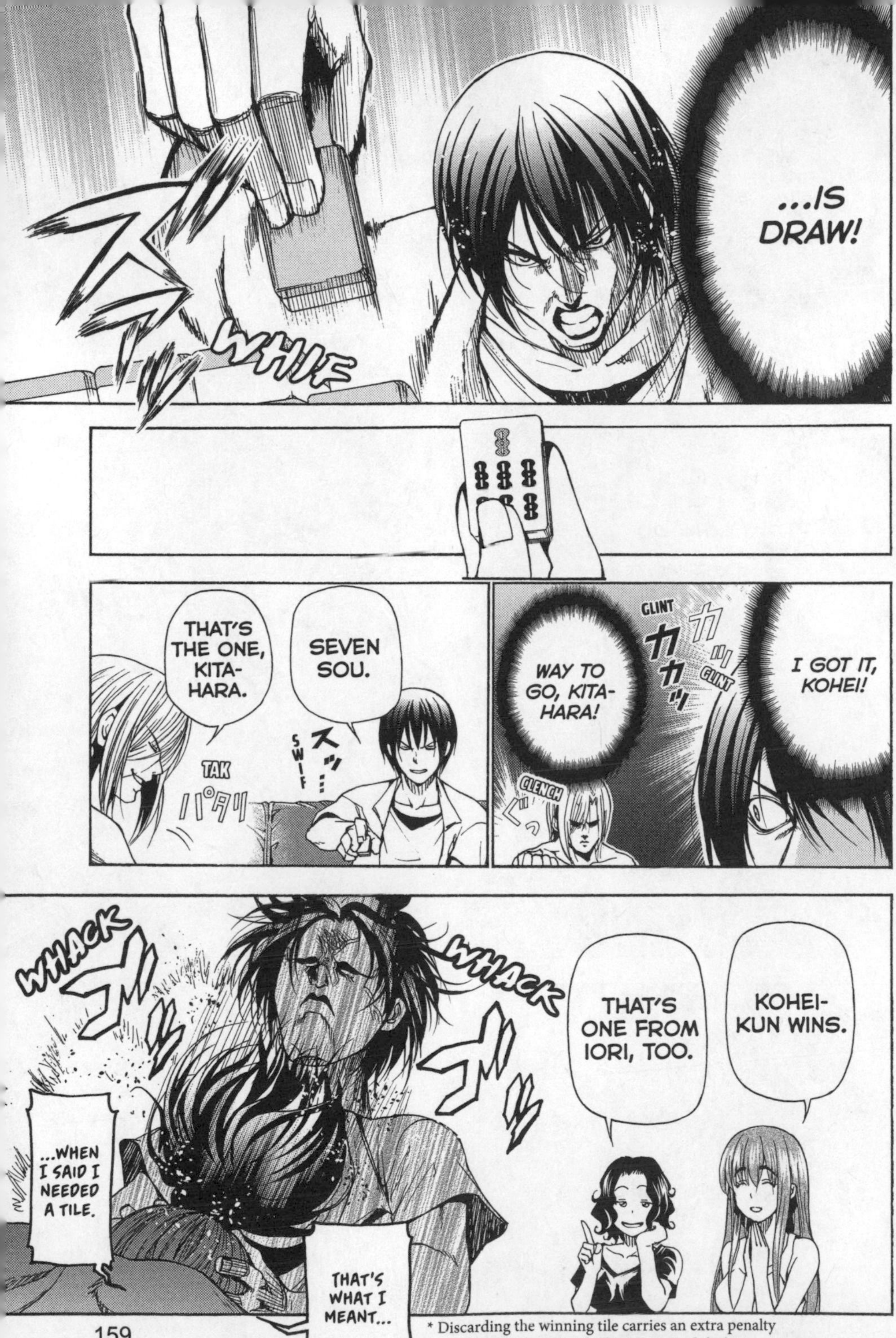
WHIF
...IS DRAW!
I GOT IT, KOHEI!
GLINT
カッ
カカッ
GLINT
WAY TO GO, KITA-HARA!
CLENCH
ぐっ
SEVEN SOU.
SWIF
スッ
THAT'S THE ONE, KITA-HARA.
TAK
パタリ
KOHEI-KUN WINS.
THAT'S ONE FROM IORI, TOO.
WHACK
WHACK
...WHEN I SAID I NEEDED A TILE.
THAT'S WHAT I MEANT...

* Discarding the winning tile carries an extra penalty in mahjong...thus, Iori forfeits a piece of clothing.

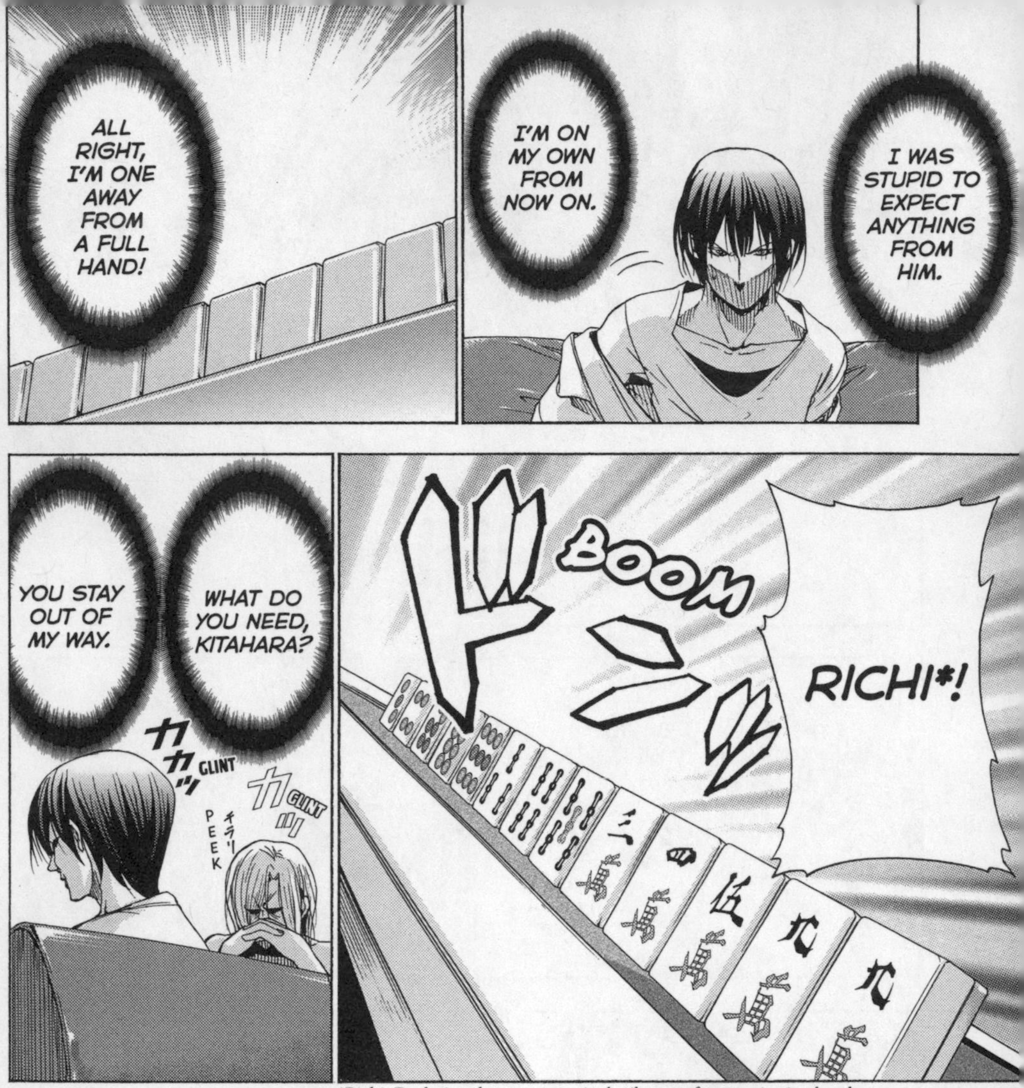
I WAS STUPID TO EXPECT ANYTHING FROM HIM.
I'M ON MY OWN FROM NOW ON.
ALL RIGHT, I'M ONE AWAY FROM A FULL HAND!
RICHI*!
BOOM
WHAT DO YOU NEED, KITAHARA?
YOU STAY OUT OF MY WAY.
GLINT
GLINT
PEEK

*Richi: Declaring that you are a single tile away from a winning hand.

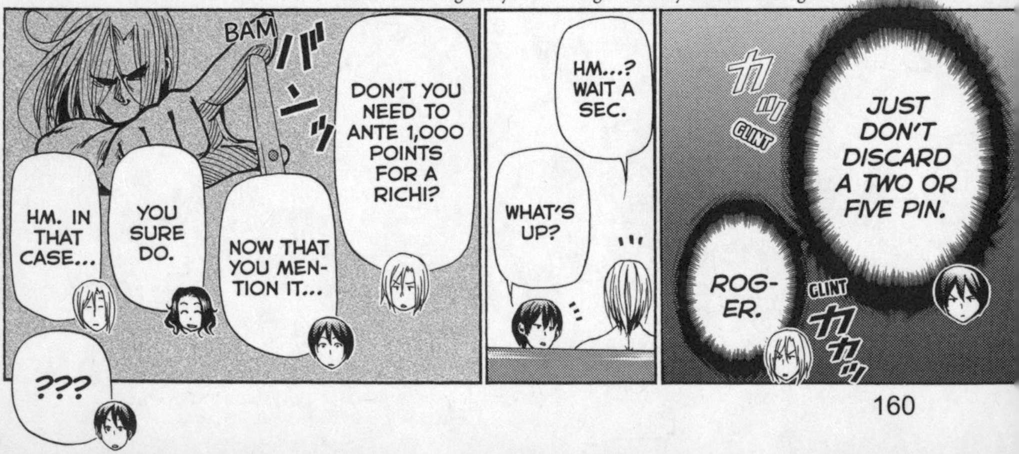
GLINT
JUST DON'T DISCARD A TWO OR FIVE PIN.
ROG-ER.
GLINT
HM...? WAIT A SEC.
WHAT'S UP?
...
DON'T YOU NEED TO ANTE 1,000 POINTS FOR A RICHI?
BAM
NOW THAT YOU MEN-TION IT...
YOU SURE DO.
HM. IN THAT CASE...
???

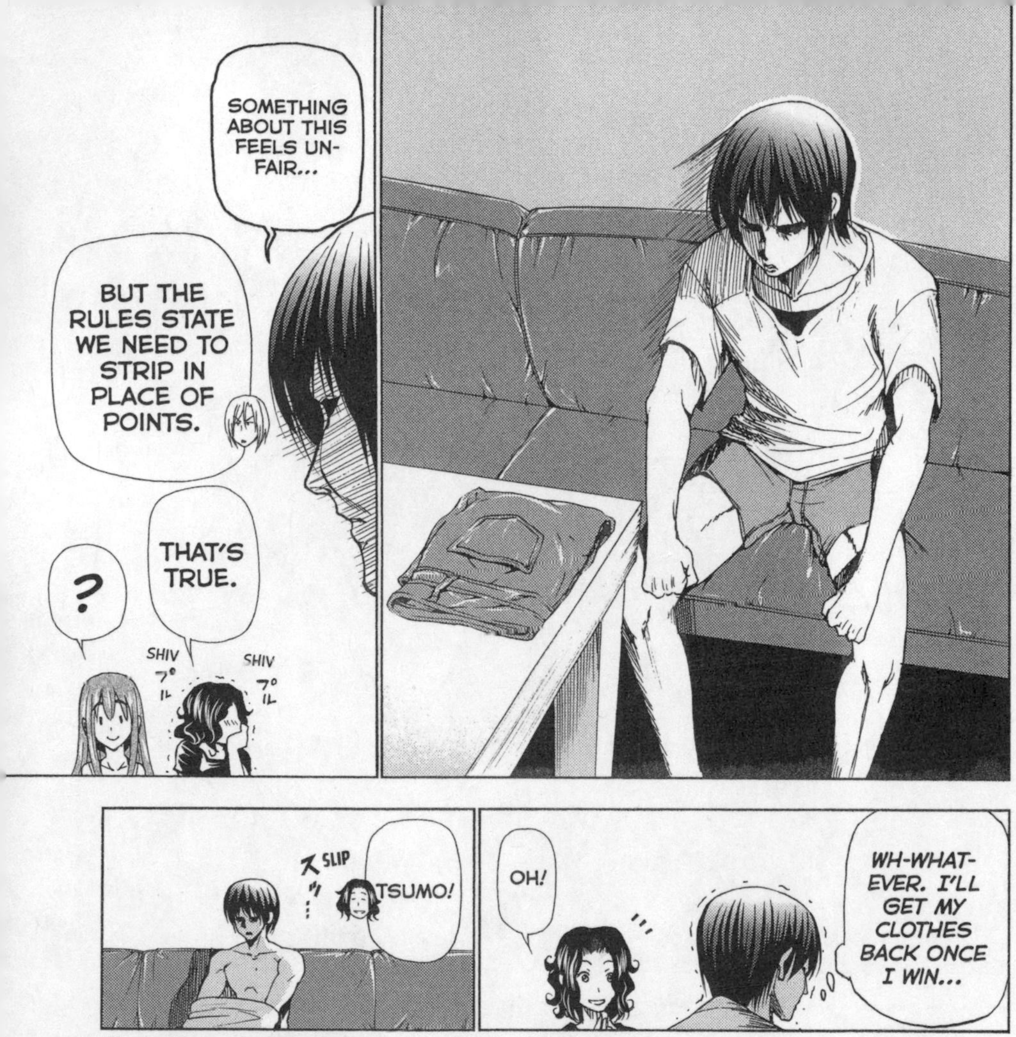
SOMETHING ABOUT THIS FEELS UN-FAIR...
BUT THE RULES STATE WE NEED TO STRIP IN PLACE OF POINTS.
THAT'S TRUE.
?
SHIV
SHIV
WH-WHAT-EVER. I'LL GET MY CLOTHES BACK ONCE I WIN...
OH!
TSUMO!
SLIP

*Tsumo: Winning by drawing a tile from the wall instead of using another player's discarded tile.

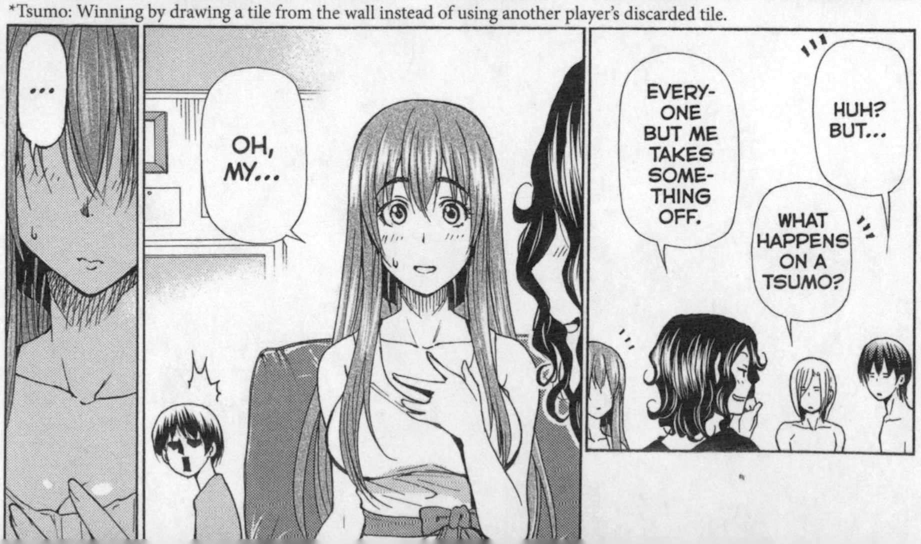
HUH? BUT...
WHAT HAPPENS ON A TSUMO?
EVERY-ONE BUT ME TAKES SOME-THING OFF.
OH, MY...
...

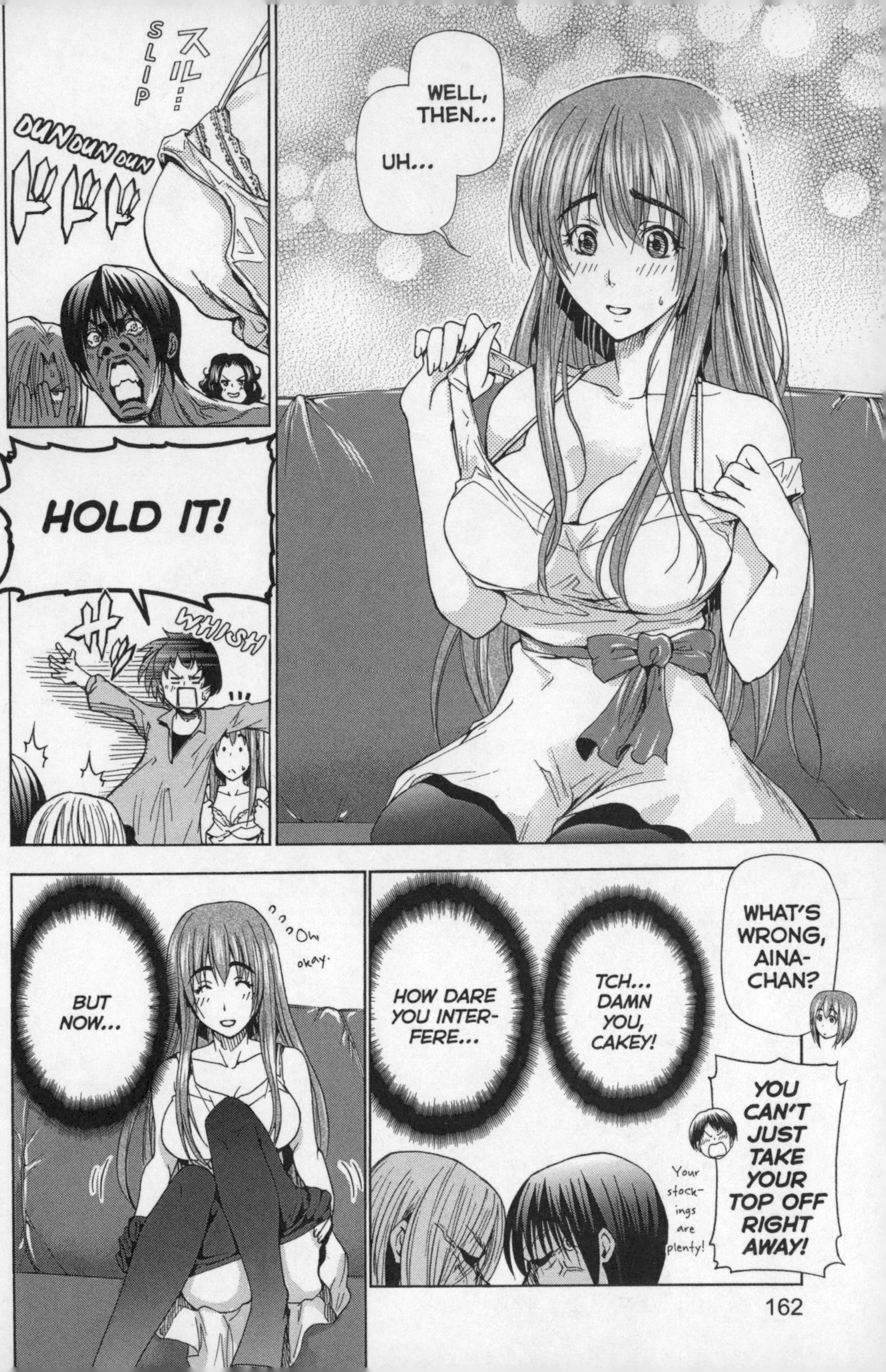
WELL, THEN...
UH...
スル…
SLIP
ドドド
DUN DUN DUN
HOLD IT!
ザ
WHISH
WHAT'S WRONG, AINA-CHAN?
YOU CAN'T JUST TAKE YOUR TOP OFF RIGHT AWAY!
Your stock-ings are plenty!
TCH... DAMN YOU, CAKEY!
HOW DARE YOU INTER-FERE...
Oh okay.
BUT NOW...

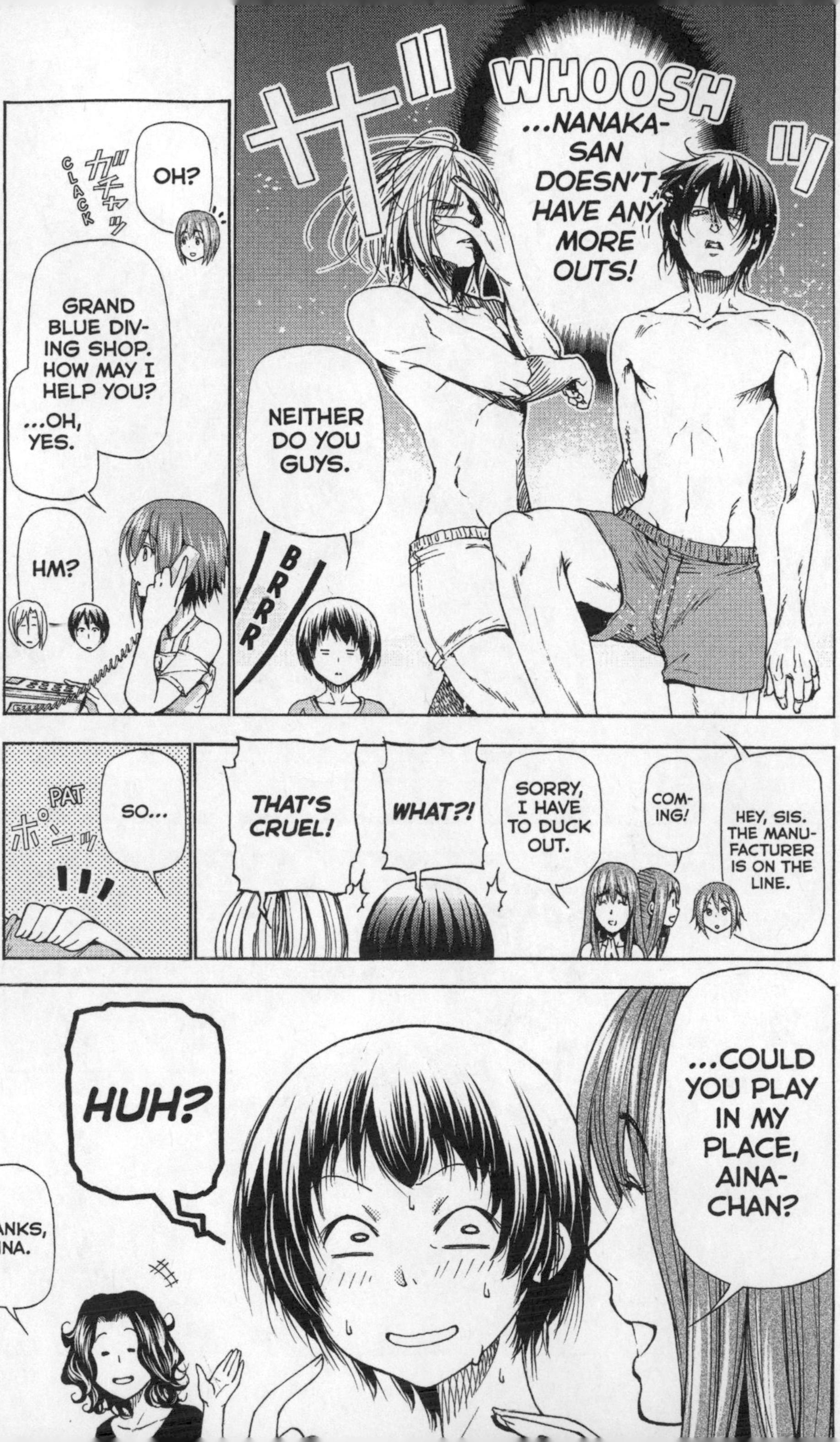

WHOOSH
...NANAKA-SAN DOESN'T HAVE ANY MORE OUTS!
NEITHER DO YOU GUYS.
BRRR
CLACK
OH?
GRAND BLUE DIVING SHOP. HOW MAY I HELP YOU? ...OH, YES.
HM?
HEY, SIS. THE MANUFACTURER IS ON THE LINE.
COMING!
SORRY, I HAVE TO DUCK OUT.
WHAT?!
THAT'S CRUEL!
PAT
SO...
...COULD YOU PLAY IN MY PLACE, AINA-CHAN?
HUH?
THANKS, AINA.

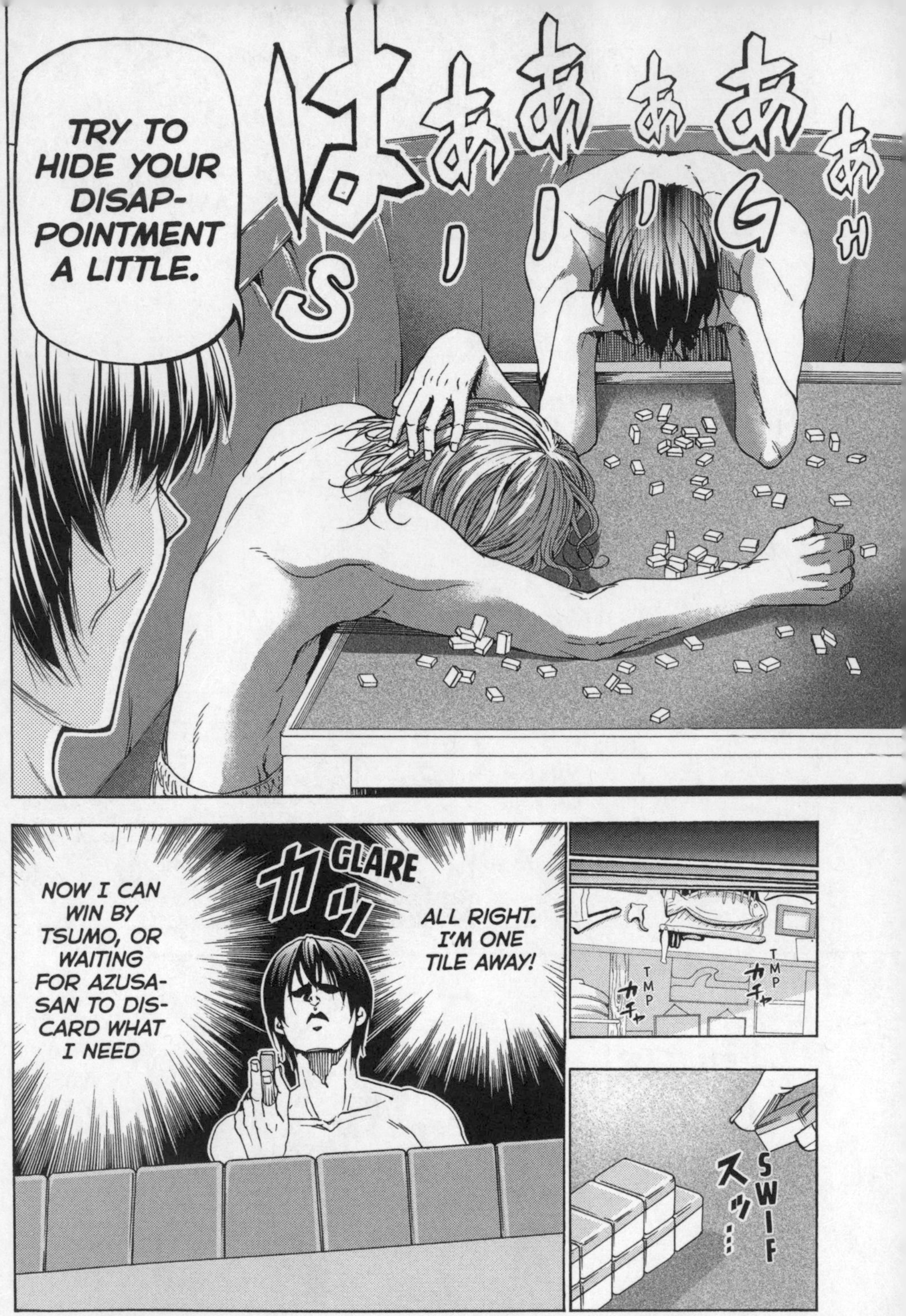

はあぁぁあぁあ
SIIGH
TRY TO HIDE YOUR DISAPPOINTMENT A LITTLE.
カチャ TMP
カチャ TMP
スッ…
SWIF
カッ
GLARE
ALL RIGHT. I'M ONE TILE AWAY!
NOW I CAN WIN BY TSUMO, OR WAITING FOR AZUSA-SAN TO DISCARD WHAT I NEED

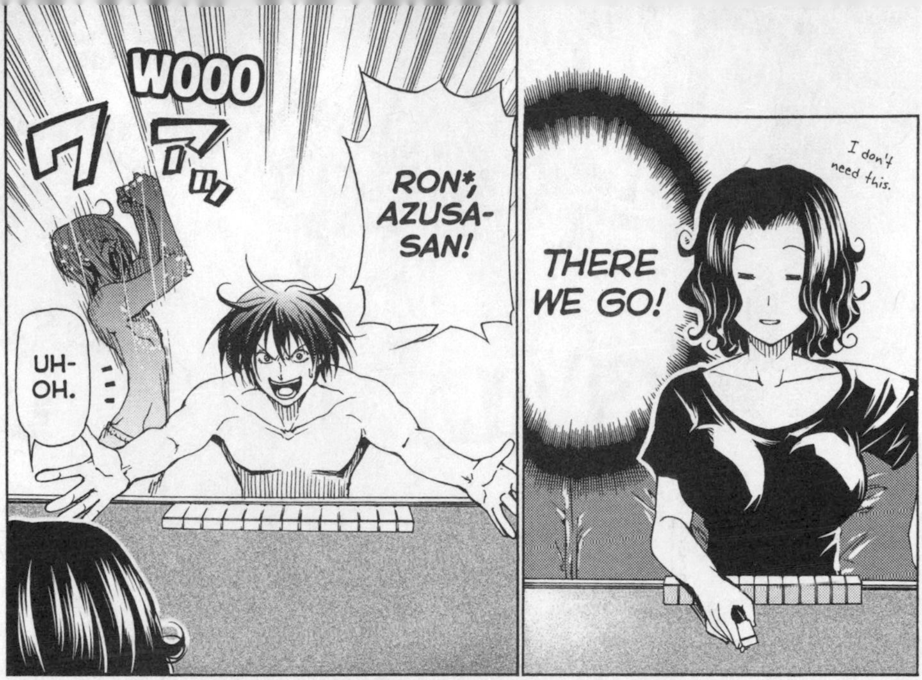
I don't need this.
THERE WE GO!
RON*, AZUSA-SAN!
WOOO
UH-OH...

*Ron: Winning off of another player's discard.

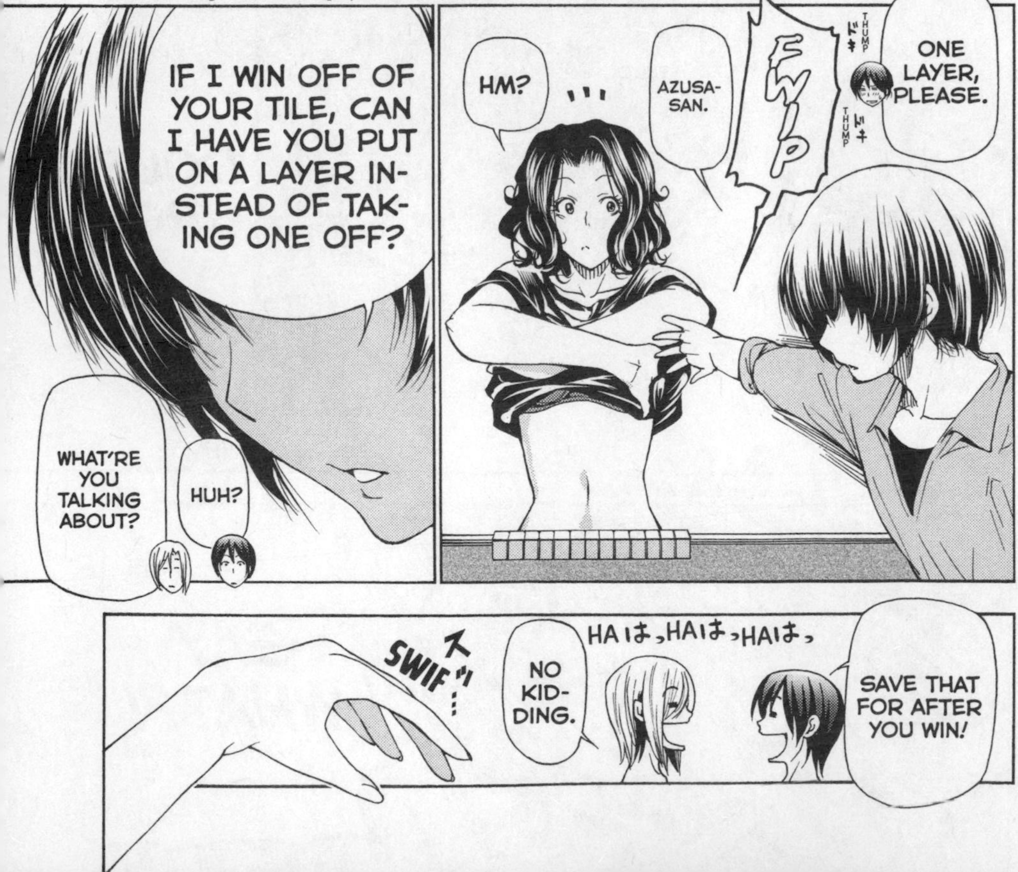
ONE LAYER, PLEASE.
THUMP THUMP
FWIP
AZUSA-SAN.
HM?
IF I WIN OFF OF YOUR TILE, CAN I HAVE YOU PUT ON A LAYER INSTEAD OF TAKING ONE OFF?
HUH?
WHAT'RE YOU TALKING ABOUT?
SAVE THAT FOR AFTER YOU WIN!
HAは,HAは,HAは,
NO KIDDING.
SWIF

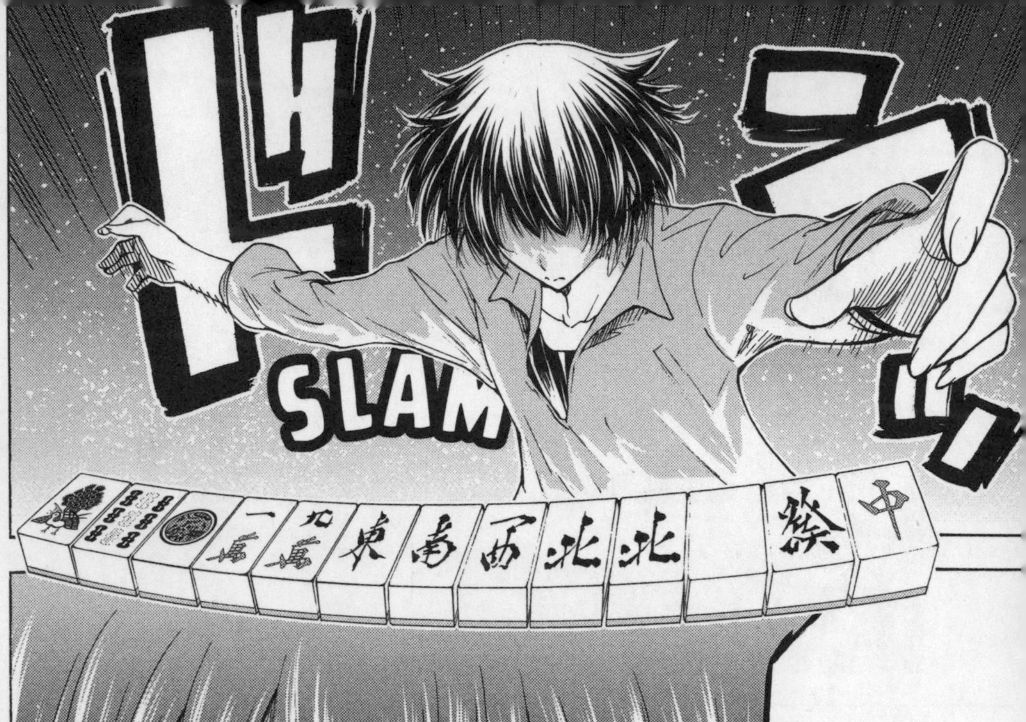
SLAM
DOUBLE RON*

*Double ron: When two players win off of a discarded tile.

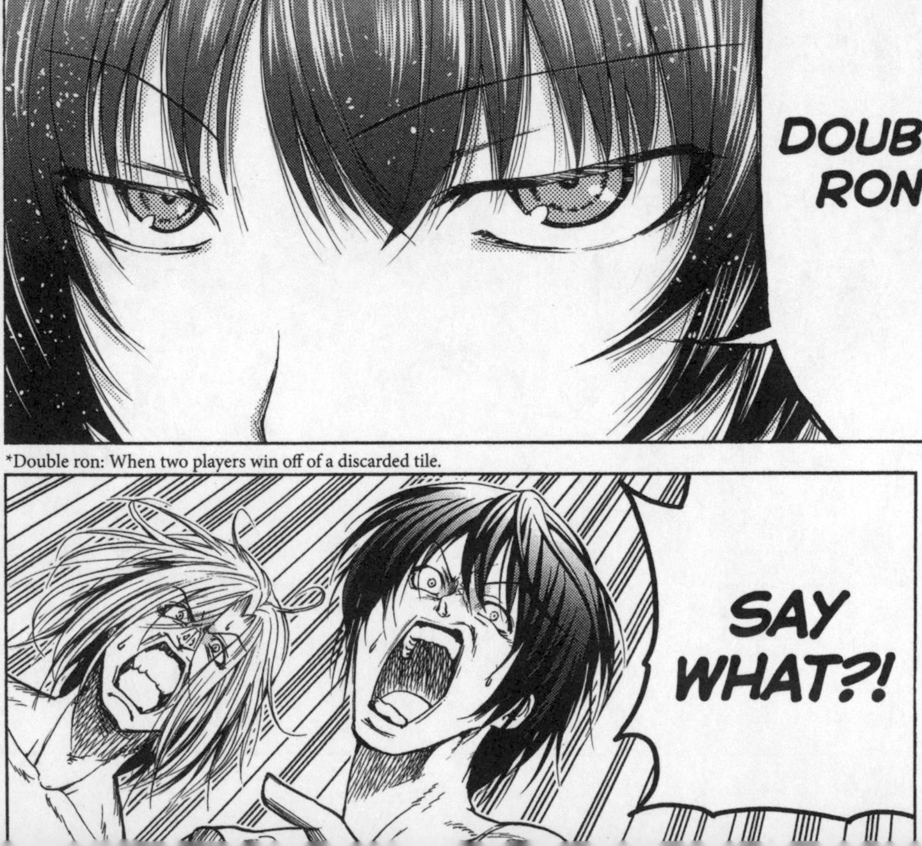
SAY WHAT?!

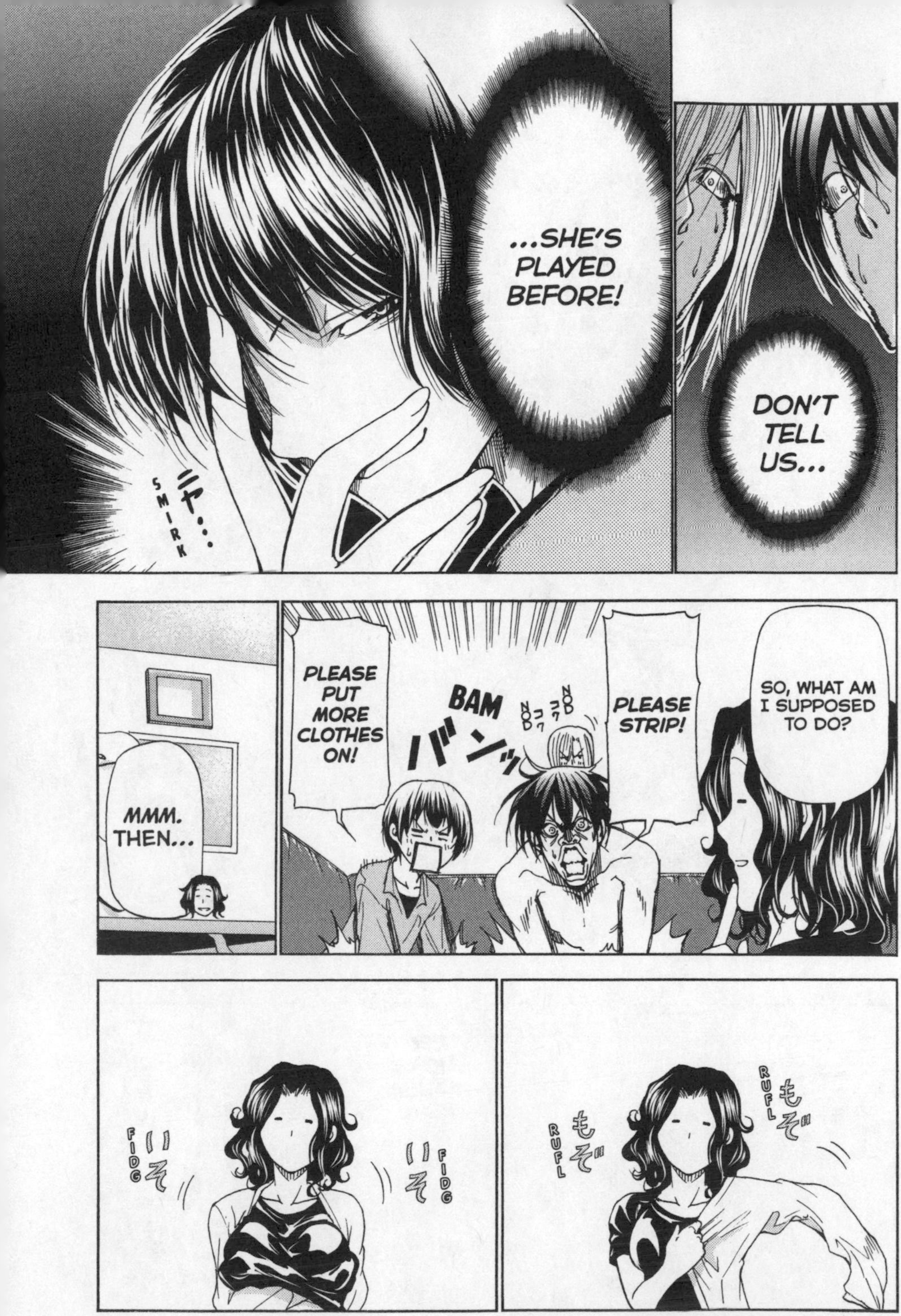
DON'T TELL US...
...SHE'S PLAYED BEFORE!
ニヤ… SMIRK
SO, WHAT AM I SUPPOSED TO DO?
PLEASE STRIP!
コク NOD
コク NOD
BAM バンッ
PLEASE PUT MORE CLOTHES ON!
MMM. THEN...
もぞ RUFL
もぞ RUFL
いそ FIDG
いそ FIDG

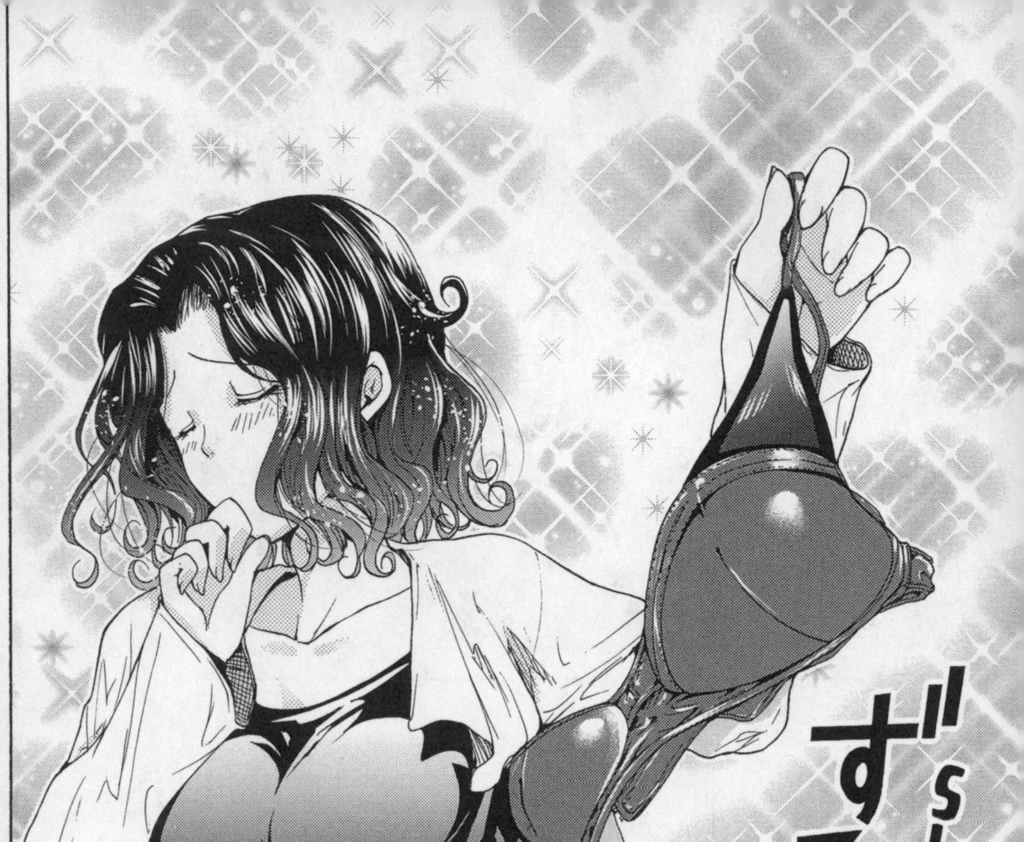
ずるり
SLIP
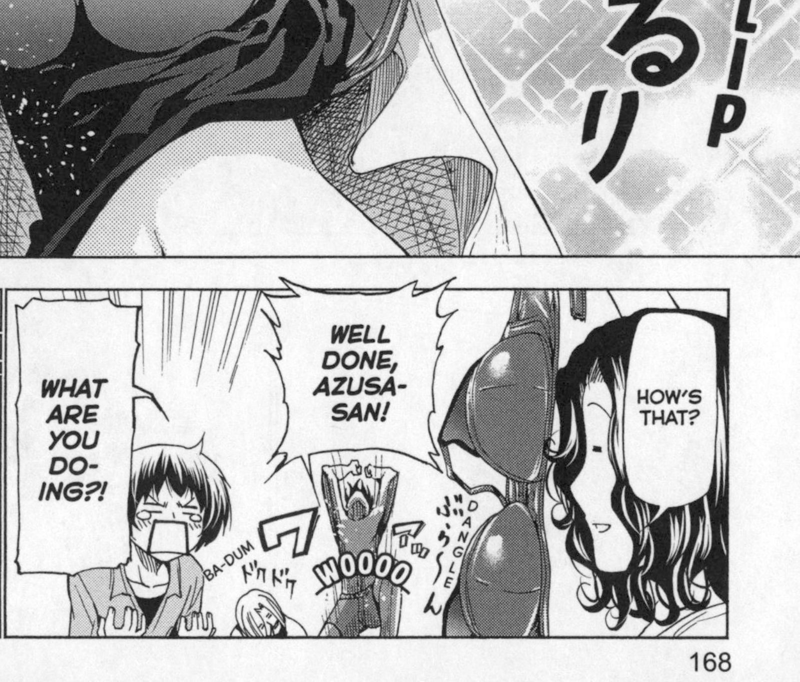
HOW'S THAT?
ぶら～ん
DANGLE
WELL DONE, AZUSA-SAN!
WOOOO
ドクドク
BA-DUM
WHAT ARE YOU DO-ING?!
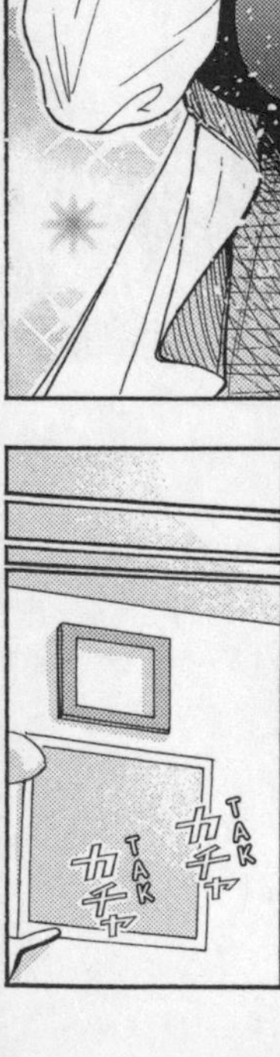
カチャ
TAK
カチャ
TAK

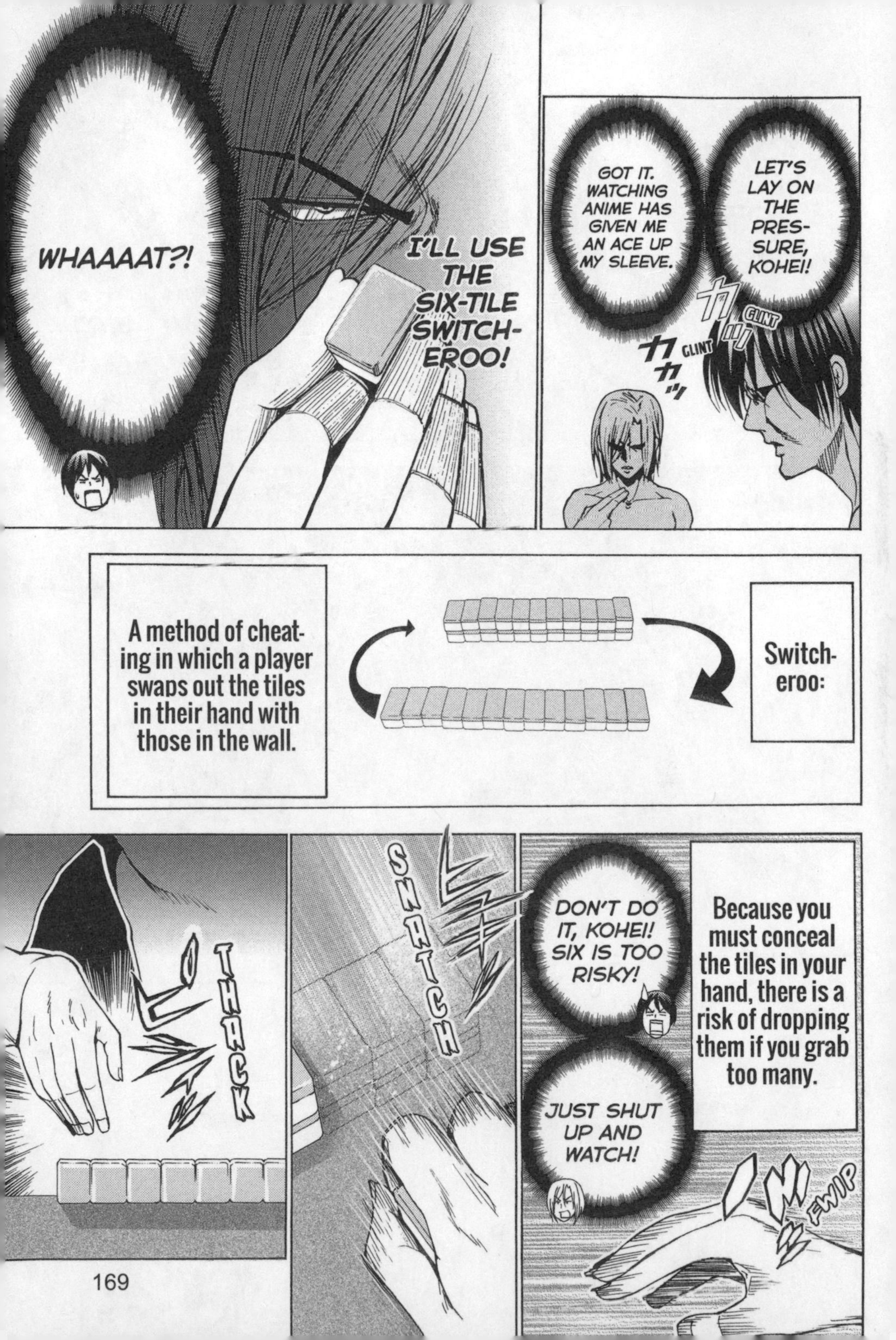
LET'S LAY ON THE PRES-SURE, KOHEI!
GOT IT. WATCHING ANIME HAS GIVEN ME AN ACE UP MY SLEEVE.
GLINT
GLINT
I'LL USE THE SIX-TILE SWITCH-EROO!
WHAAAAT?!
Switch-eroo:
A method of cheat-ing in which a player swaps out the tiles in their hand with those in the wall.
Because you must conceal the tiles in your hand, there is a risk of dropping them if you grab too many.
DON'T DO IT, KOHEI! SIX IS TOO RISKY!
JUST SHUT UP AND WATCH!
FWIP
SNATCH
THACK

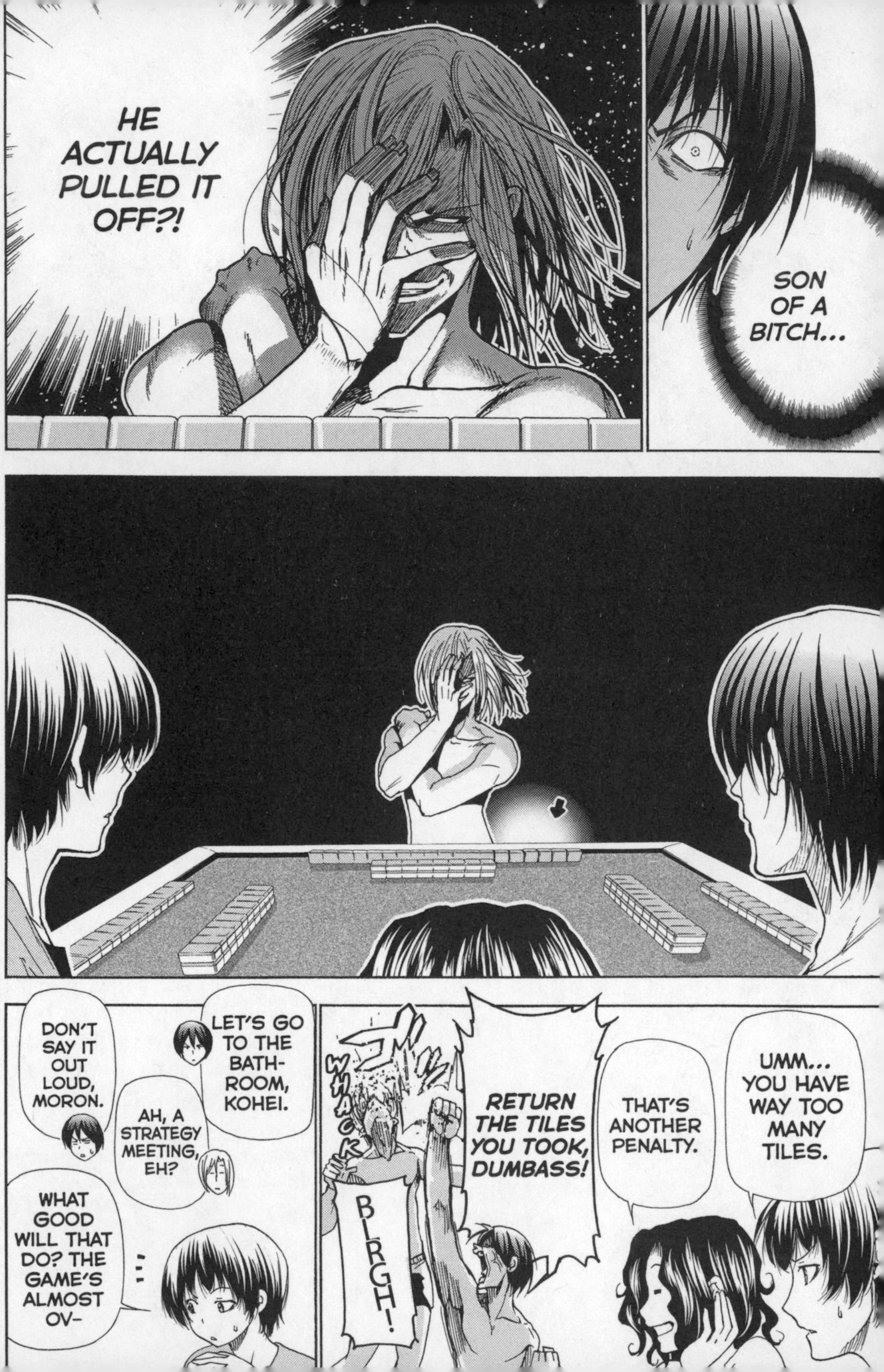
SON OF A BITCH...
HE ACTUALLY PULLED IT OFF?!
UMM... YOU HAVE WAY TOO MANY TILES.
THAT'S ANOTHER PENALTY.
RETURN THE TILES YOU TOOK, DUMBASS!
WHACK
BLRGH!
LET'S GO TO THE BATH-ROOM, KOHEI.
DON'T SAY IT OUT LOUD, MORON.
AH, A STRATEGY MEETING, EH?
WHAT GOOD WILL THAT DO? THE GAME'S ALMOST OV-
...

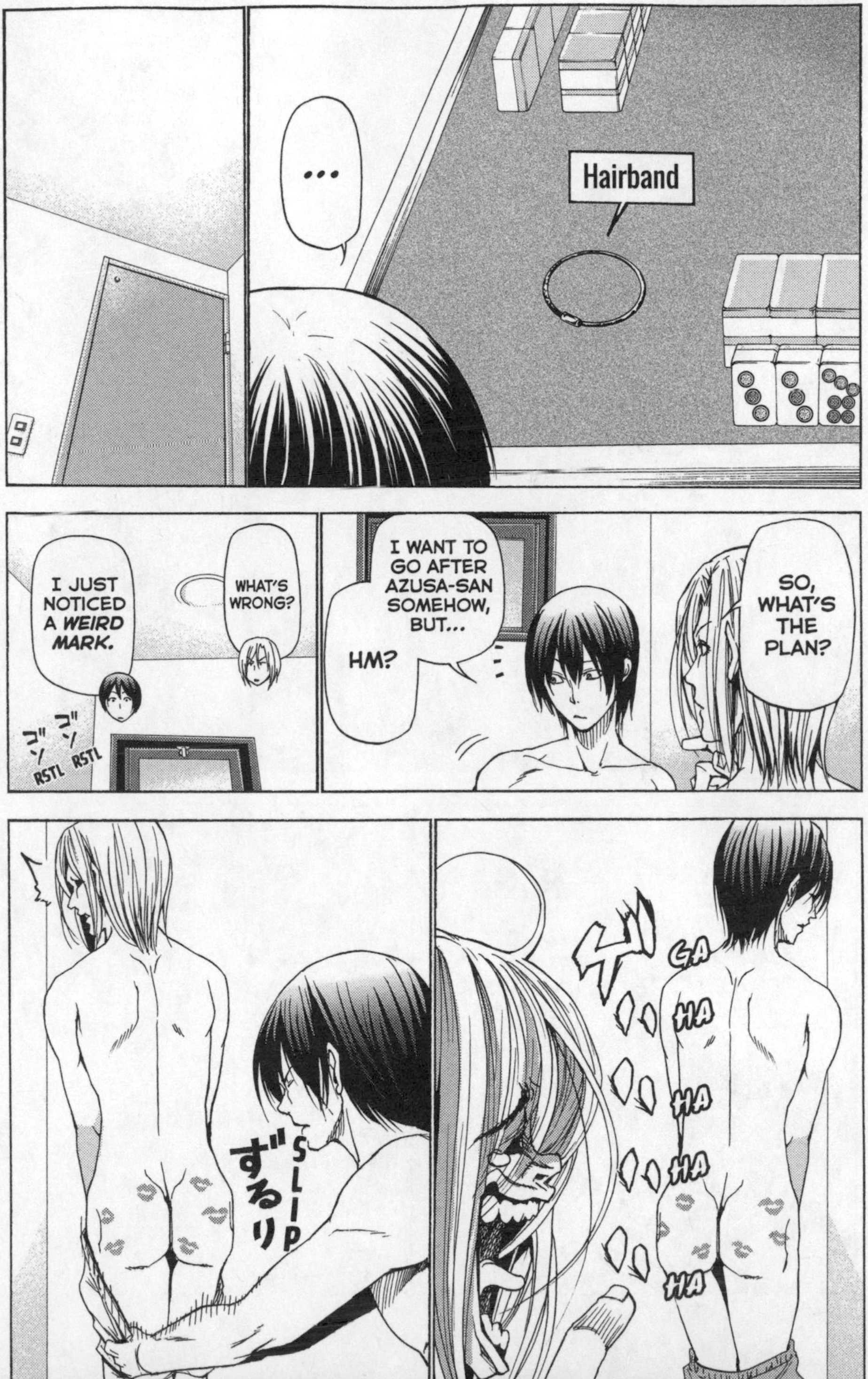
Hairband
...
SO, WHAT'S THE PLAN?
I WANT TO GO AFTER AZUSA-SAN SOMEHOW, BUT...
HM?
WHAT'S WRONG?
I JUST NOTICED A WEIRD MARK.
ゴソ ゴソ
RSTL RSTL
GA HA HA HA HA
ずるり
SLIP

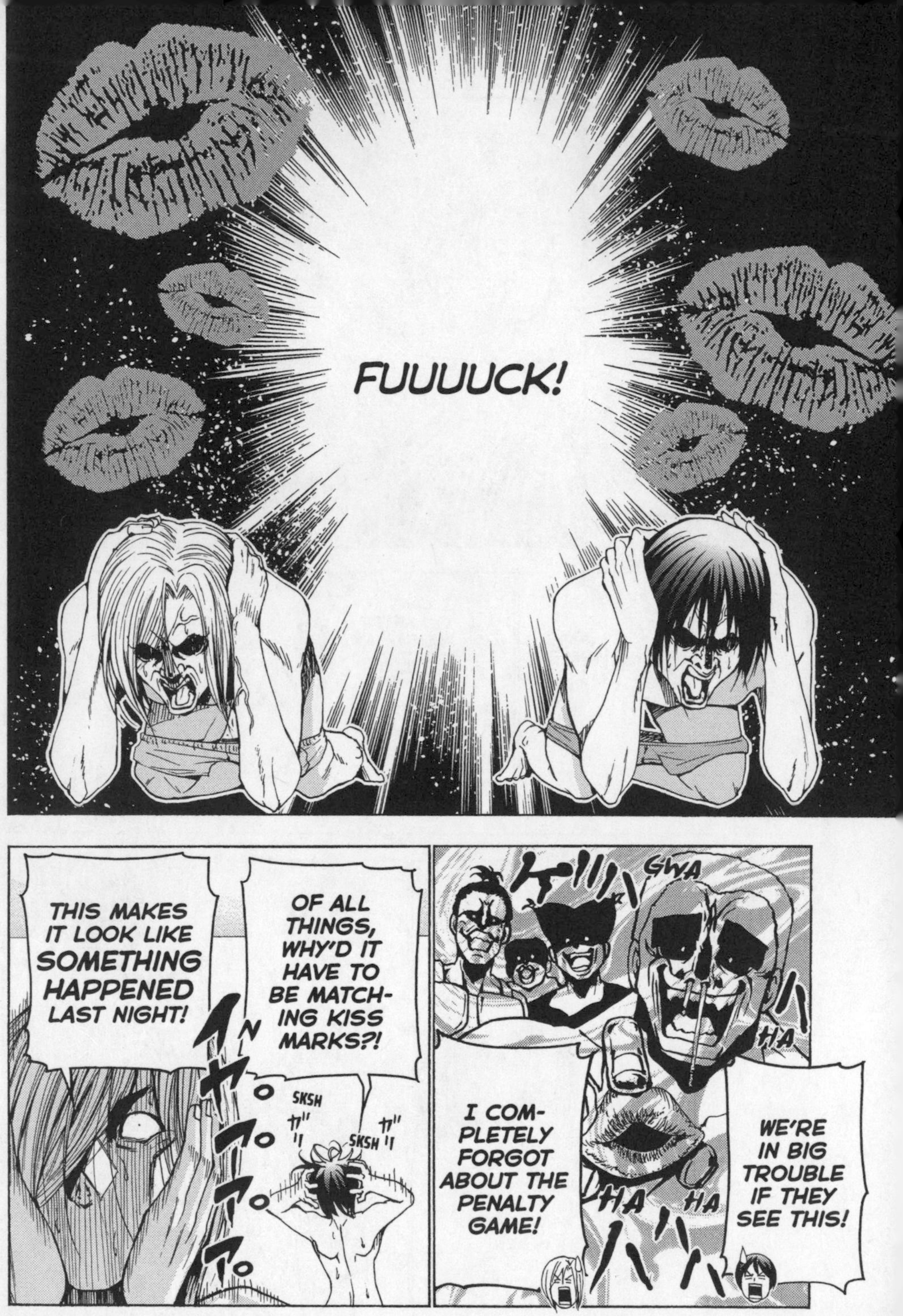
FUUUUCK!
GWA
HA
WE'RE IN BIG TROUBLE IF THEY SEE THIS!
I COMPLETELY FORGOT ABOUT THE PENALTY GAME!
HA
HA
OF ALL THINGS, WHY'D IT HAVE TO BE MATCHING KISS MARKS?!
THIS MAKES IT LOOK LIKE SOMETHING HAPPENED LAST NIGHT!
SKSH
SKSH
N

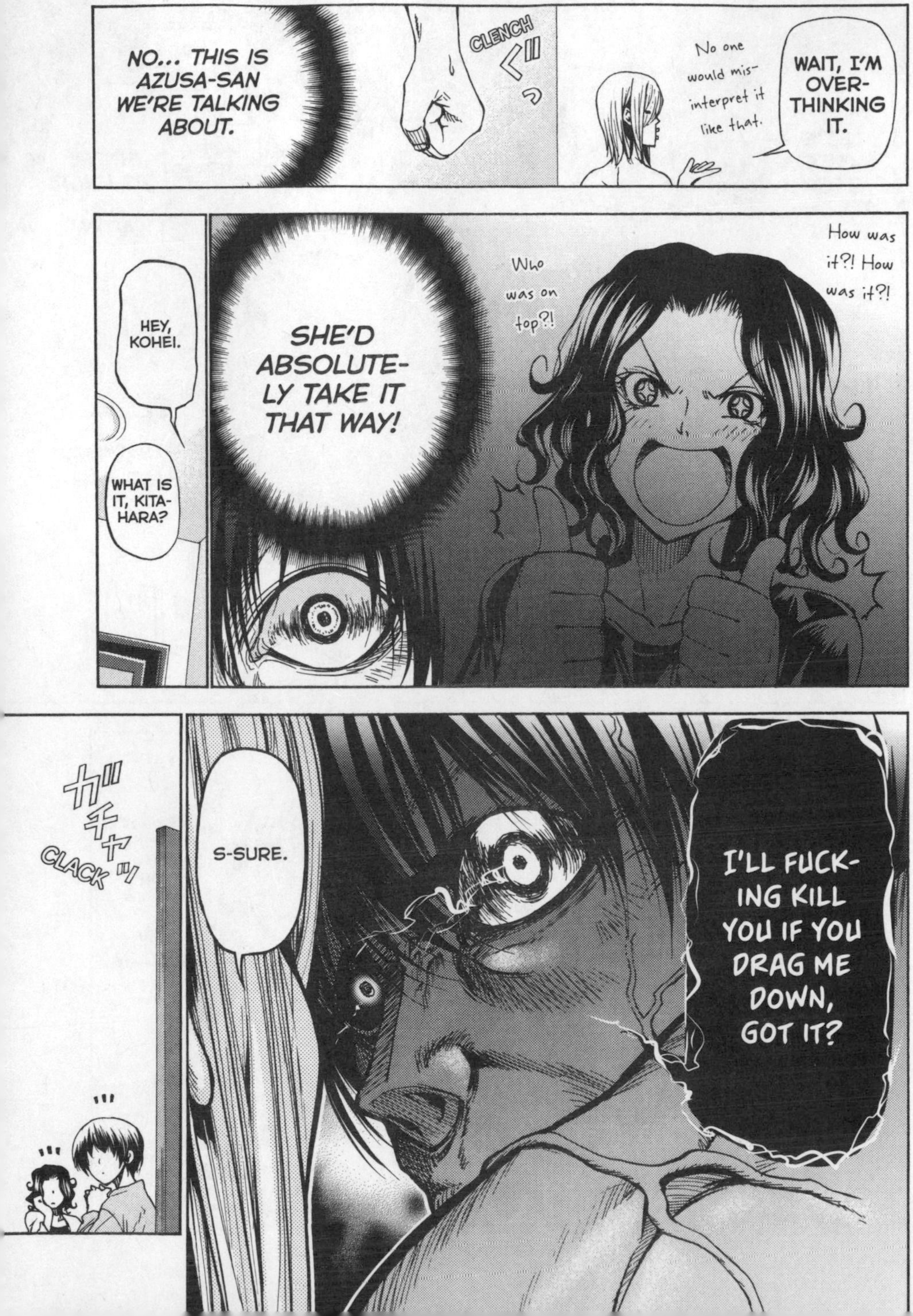
WAIT, I'M OVER-THINKING IT.
No one would mis-interpret it like that.
CLENCH
NO... THIS IS AZUSA-SAN WE'RE TALKING ABOUT.
How was it?! How was it?!
Who was on top?!
SHE'D ABSOLUTE-LY TAKE IT THAT WAY!
HEY, KOHEI.
WHAT IS IT, KITA-HARA?
I'LL FUCK-ING KILL YOU IF YOU DRAG ME DOWN, GOT IT?
S-SURE.
CLACK

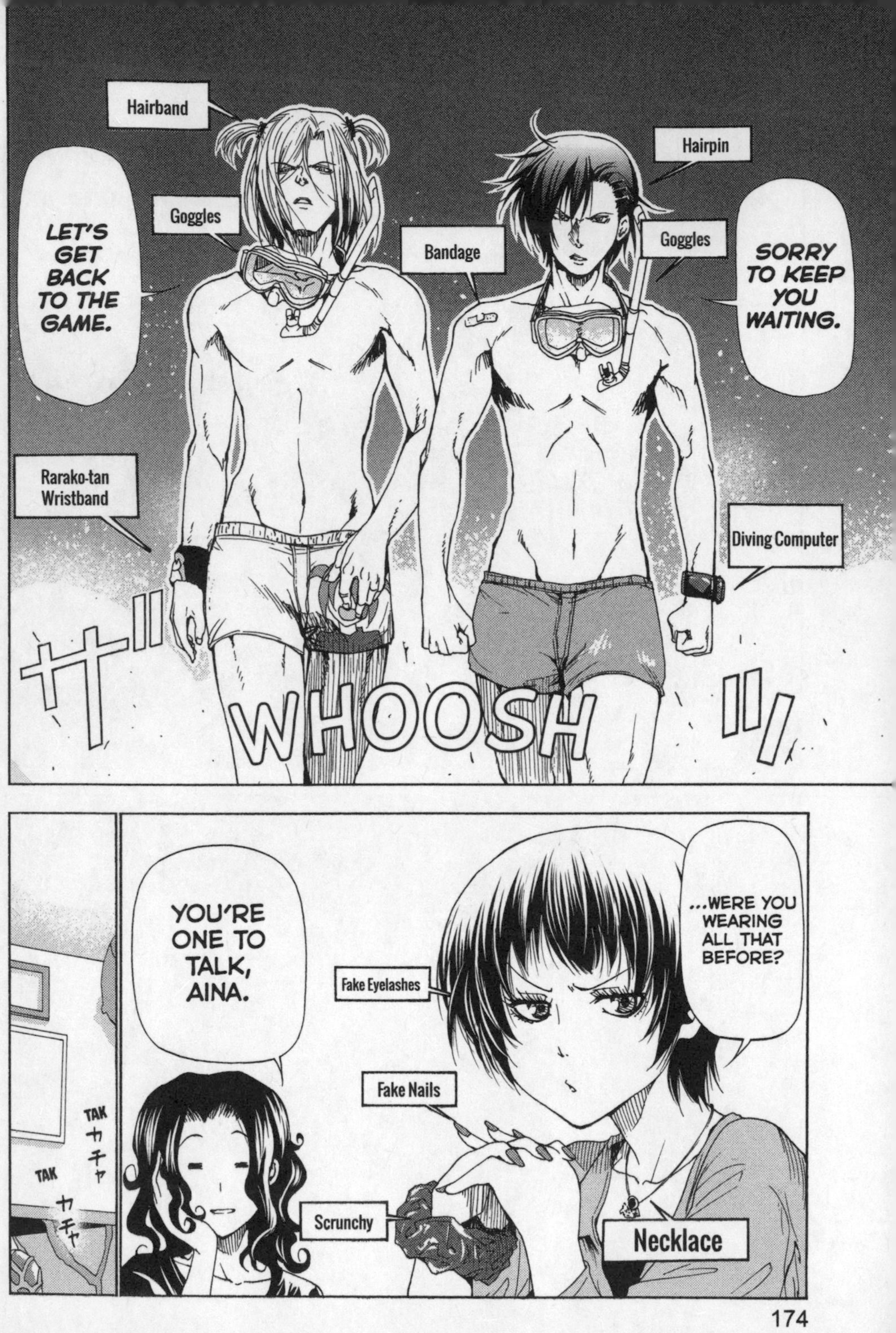
Hairpin
SORRY TO KEEP YOU WAITING.
Goggles
Bandage
Hairband
Goggles
LET'S GET BACK TO THE GAME.
Diving Computer
Rarako-tan Wristband
WHOOSH
...WERE YOU WEARING ALL THAT BEFORE?
YOU'RE ONE TO TALK, AINA.
Fake Eyelashes
Fake Nails
Necklace
Scrunchy
TAK カチャ
TAK カチャ

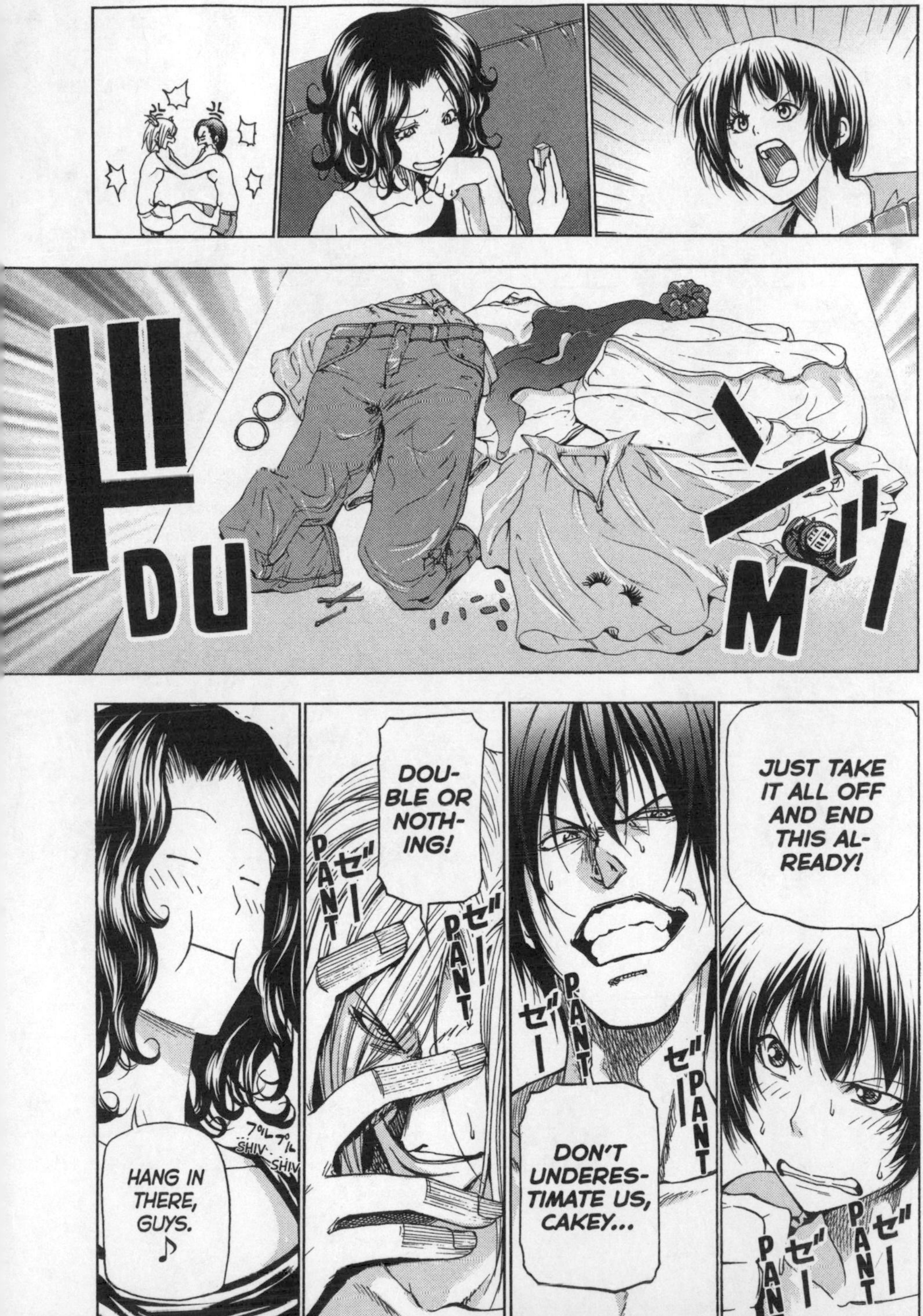
DUM
JUST TAKE IT ALL OFF AND END THIS ALREADY!
PANT PANT
DON'T UNDERESTIMATE US, CAKEY...
PANT PANT
DOUBLE OR NOTHING!
PANT PANT
HANG IN THERE, GUYS. ♪
SHIV SHIV

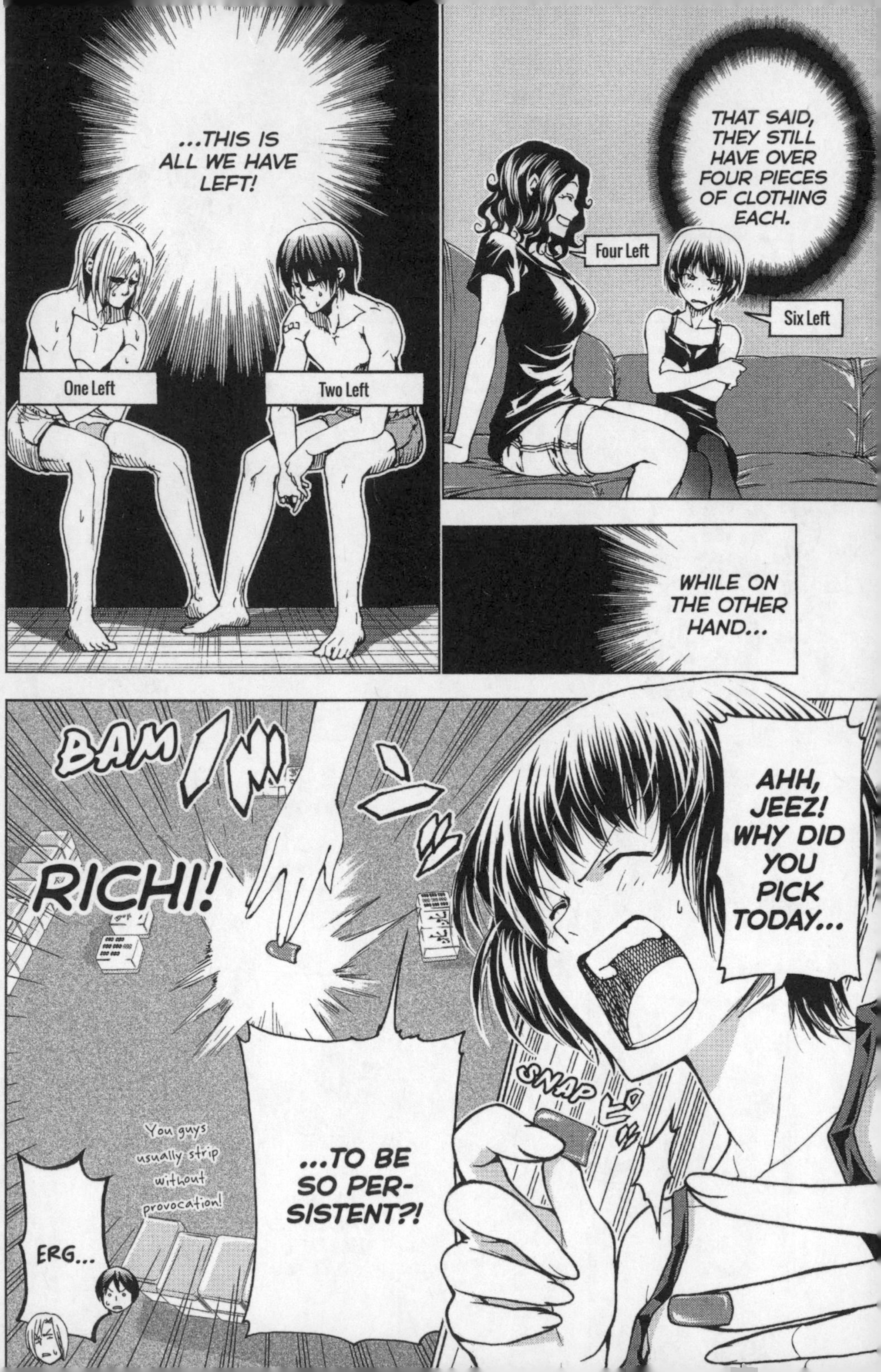
THAT SAID, THEY STILL HAVE OVER FOUR PIECES OF CLOTHING EACH.
Four Left
Six Left
WHILE ON THE OTHER HAND...
...THIS IS ALL WE HAVE LEFT!
Two Left
One Left
AHH, JEEZ! WHY DID YOU PICK TODAY...
BAM
RICHI!
SNAP
...TO BE SO PER-SISTENT?!
You guys usually strip without provocation!
ERG...

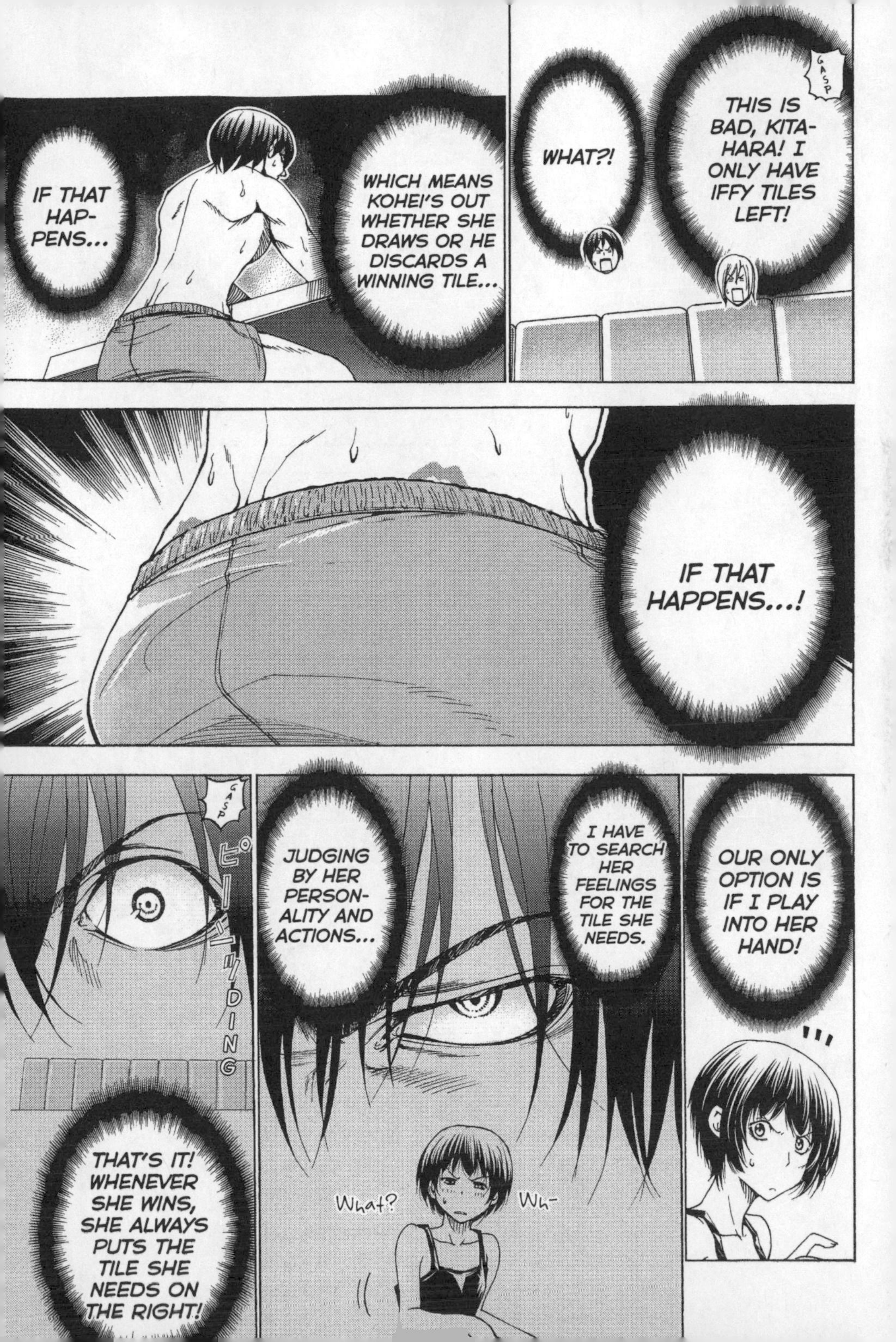
GASP
THIS IS BAD, KITAHARA! I ONLY HAVE IFFY TILES LEFT!
WHAT?!
WHICH MEANS KOHEI'S OUT WHETHER SHE DRAWS OR HE DISCARDS A WINNING TILE...
IF THAT HAPPENS...
IF THAT HAPPENS...!
OUR ONLY OPTION IS IF I PLAY INTO HER HAND!
I HAVE TO SEARCH HER FEELINGS FOR THE TILE SHE NEEDS.
JUDGING BY HER PERSONALITY AND ACTIONS...
Wu-
What?
GASP
DING
THAT'S IT! WHENEVER SHE WINS, SHE ALWAYS PUTS THE TILE SHE NEEDS ON THE RIGHT!

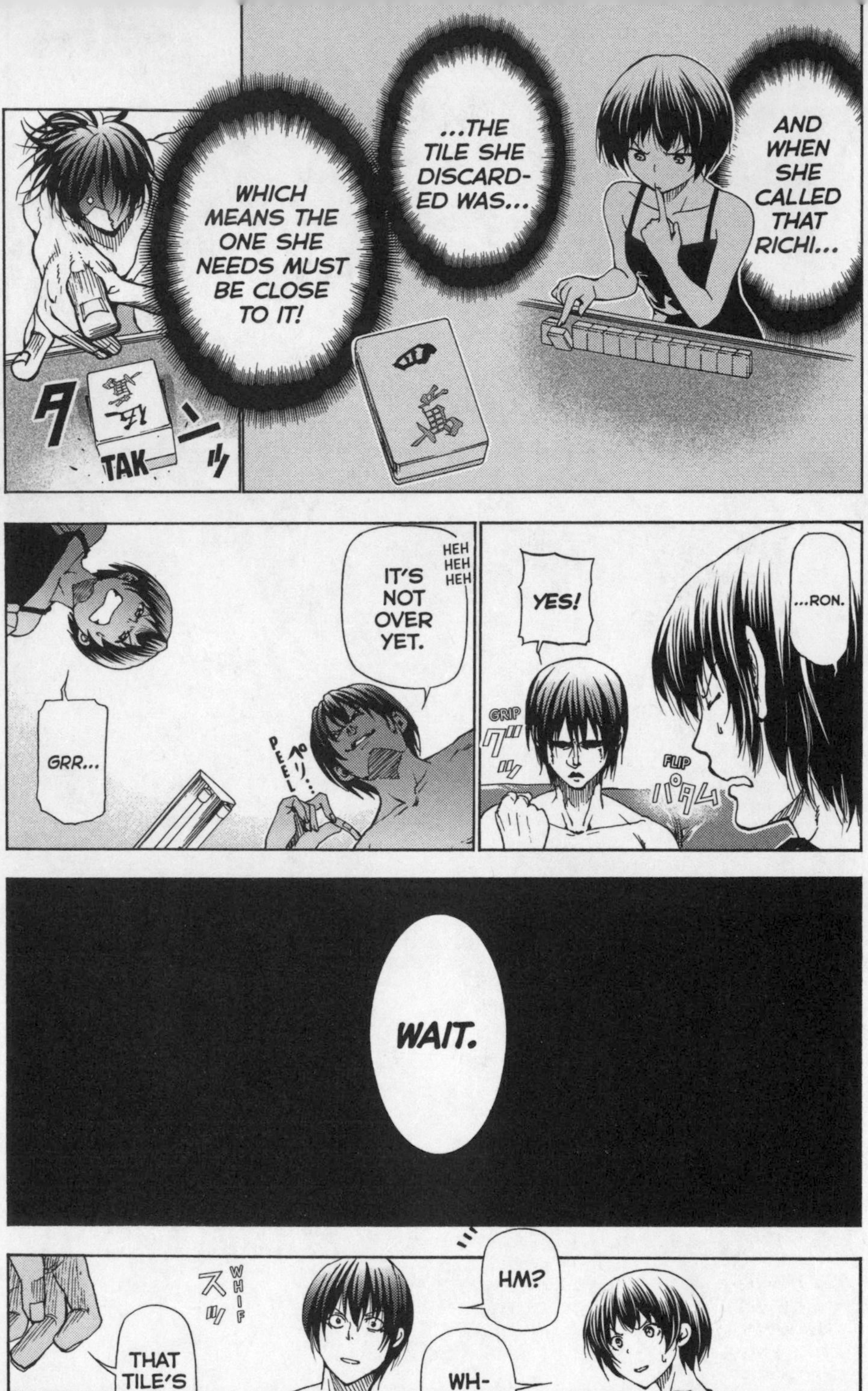
AND WHEN SHE CALLED THAT RICHI...
...THE TILE SHE DISCARDED WAS...
WHICH MEANS THE ONE SHE NEEDS MUST BE CLOSE TO IT!
TAK
...RON.
FLIP
YES!
GRIP
HEH HEH HEH
IT'S NOT OVER YET.
PEEL
GRR...
WAIT.
HM?
WH-WHAT?
WHIF
THAT TILE'S ...

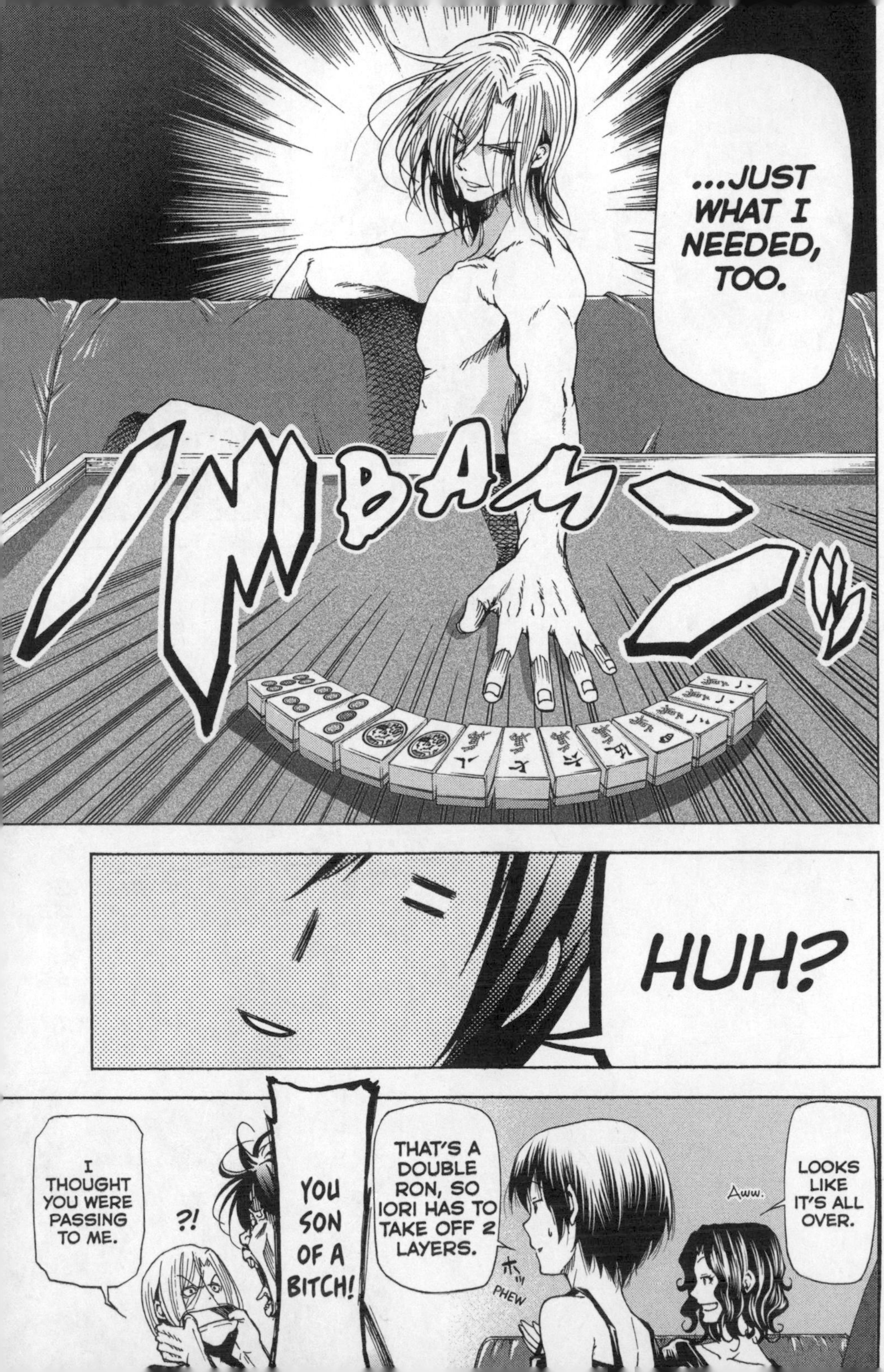
...JUST WHAT I NEEDED, TOO.
BAM
HUH?
LOOKS LIKE IT'S ALL OVER.
Aww.
THAT'S A DOUBLE RON, SO IORI HAS TO TAKE OFF 2 LAYERS.
PHEW
YOU SON OF A BITCH!
I THOUGHT YOU WERE PASSING TO ME.
?!

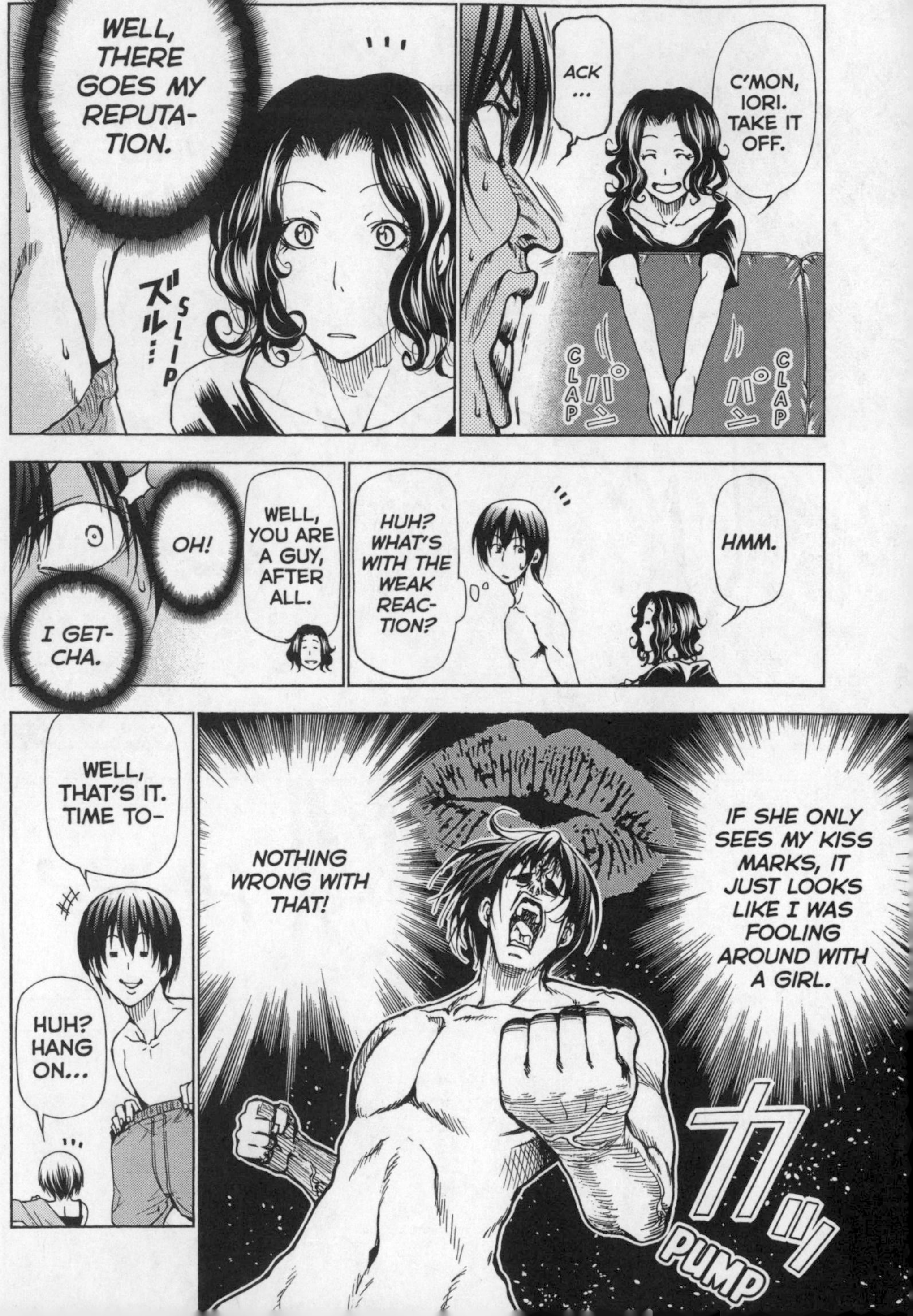
C'MON, IORI. TAKE IT OFF.
ACK ...
パン CLAP
パン CLAP
WELL, THERE GOES MY REPUTATION.
ズル… SLIP
HMM.
HUH? WHAT'S WITH THE WEAK REACTION?
WELL, YOU ARE A GUY, AFTER ALL.
OH!
I GETCHA.
IF SHE ONLY SEES MY KISS MARKS, IT JUST LOOKS LIKE I WAS FOOLING AROUND WITH A GIRL.
NOTHING WRONG WITH THAT!
カッ PUMP
WELL, THAT'S IT. TIME TO-
HUH? HANG ON...

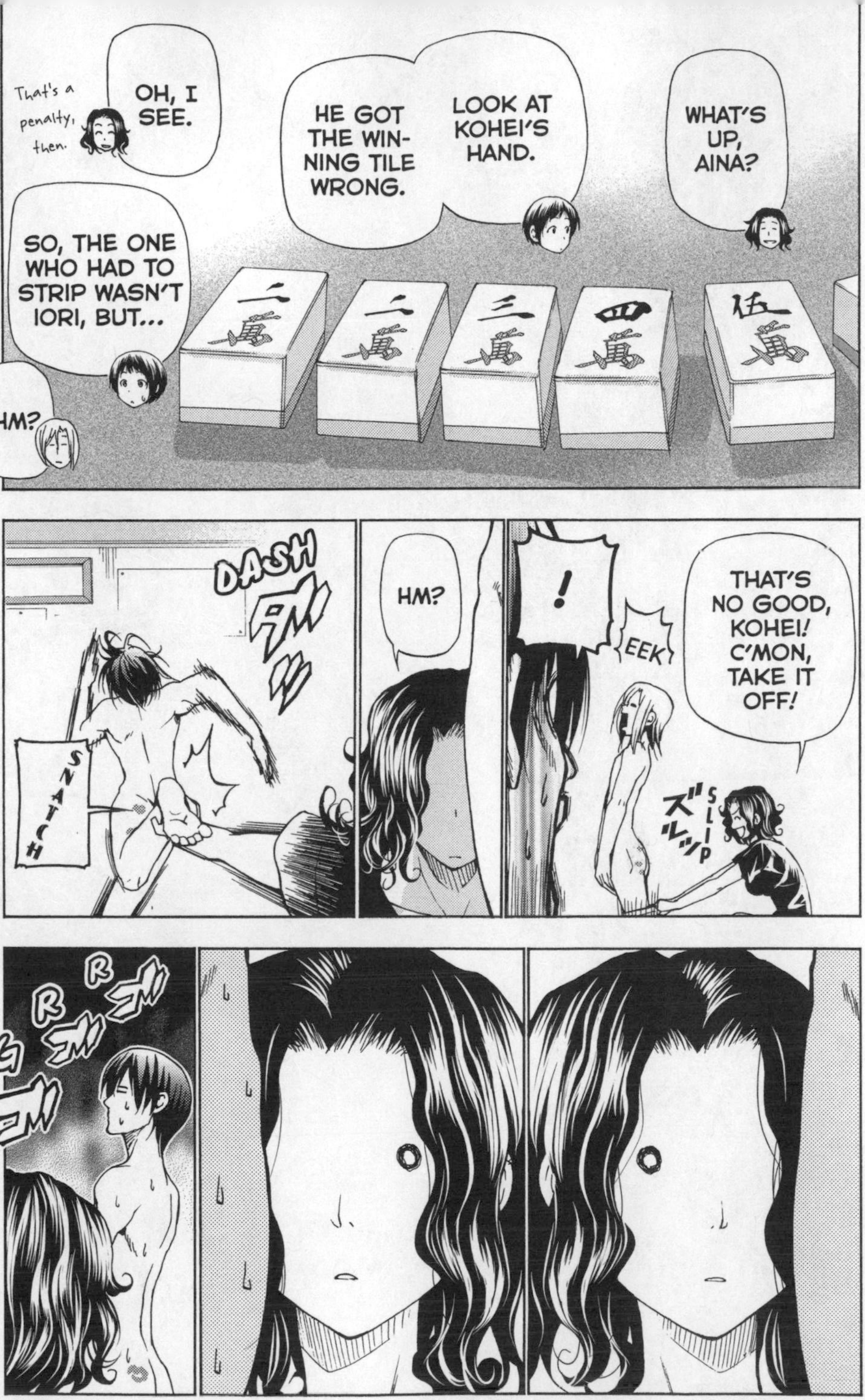
WHAT'S UP, AINA?
LOOK AT KOHEI'S HAND.
HE GOT THE WIN-NING TILE WRONG.
OH, I SEE.
That's a penalty, then.
SO, THE ONE WHO HAD TO STRIP WASN'T IORI, BUT...
HM?
THAT'S NO GOOD, KOHEI! C'MON, TAKE IT OFF!
!
EEK
SLIP
HM?
DASH
SNATCH
GRR

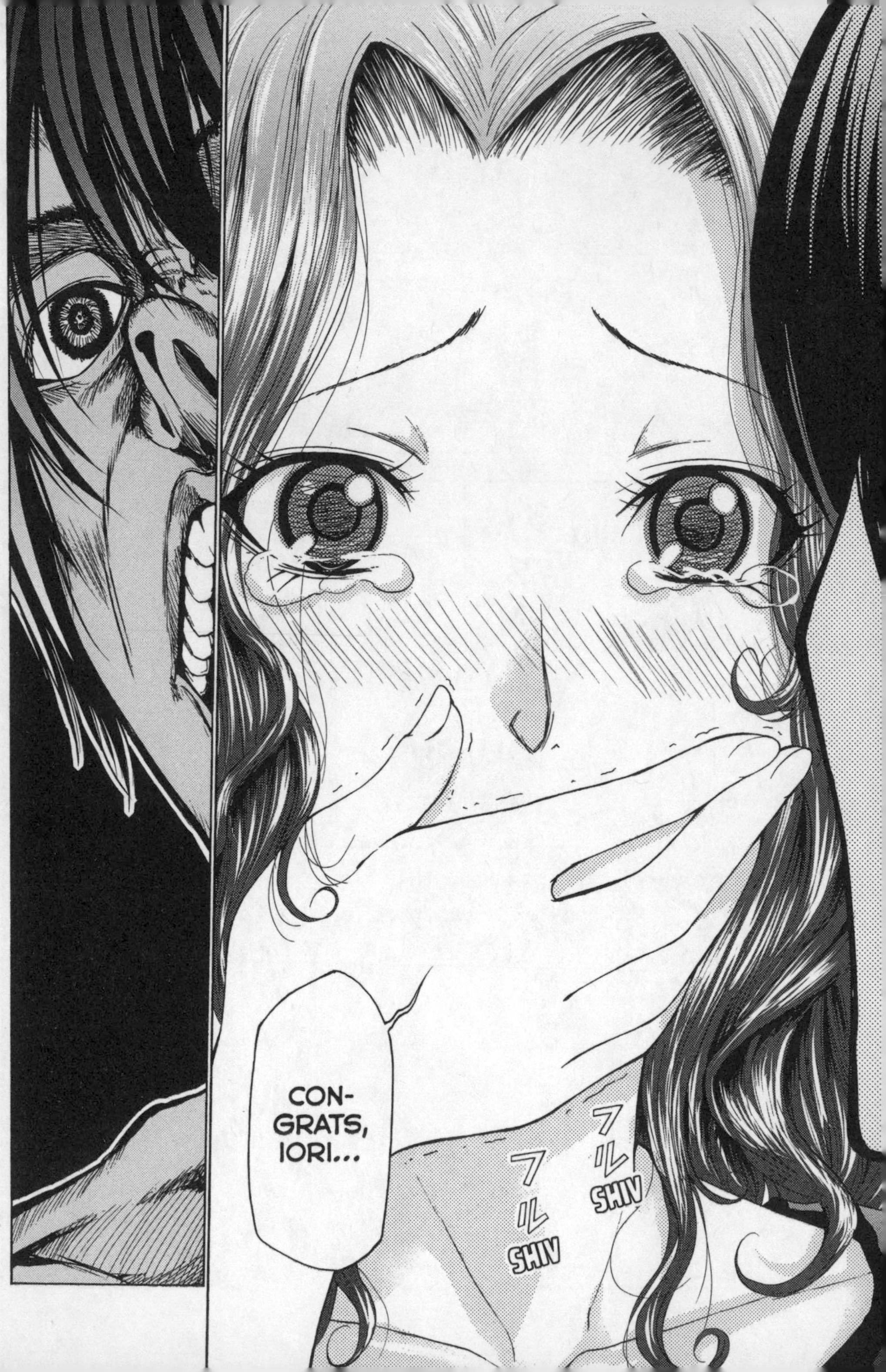
CON-GRATS, IORI...
フル SHIV
フル SHIV

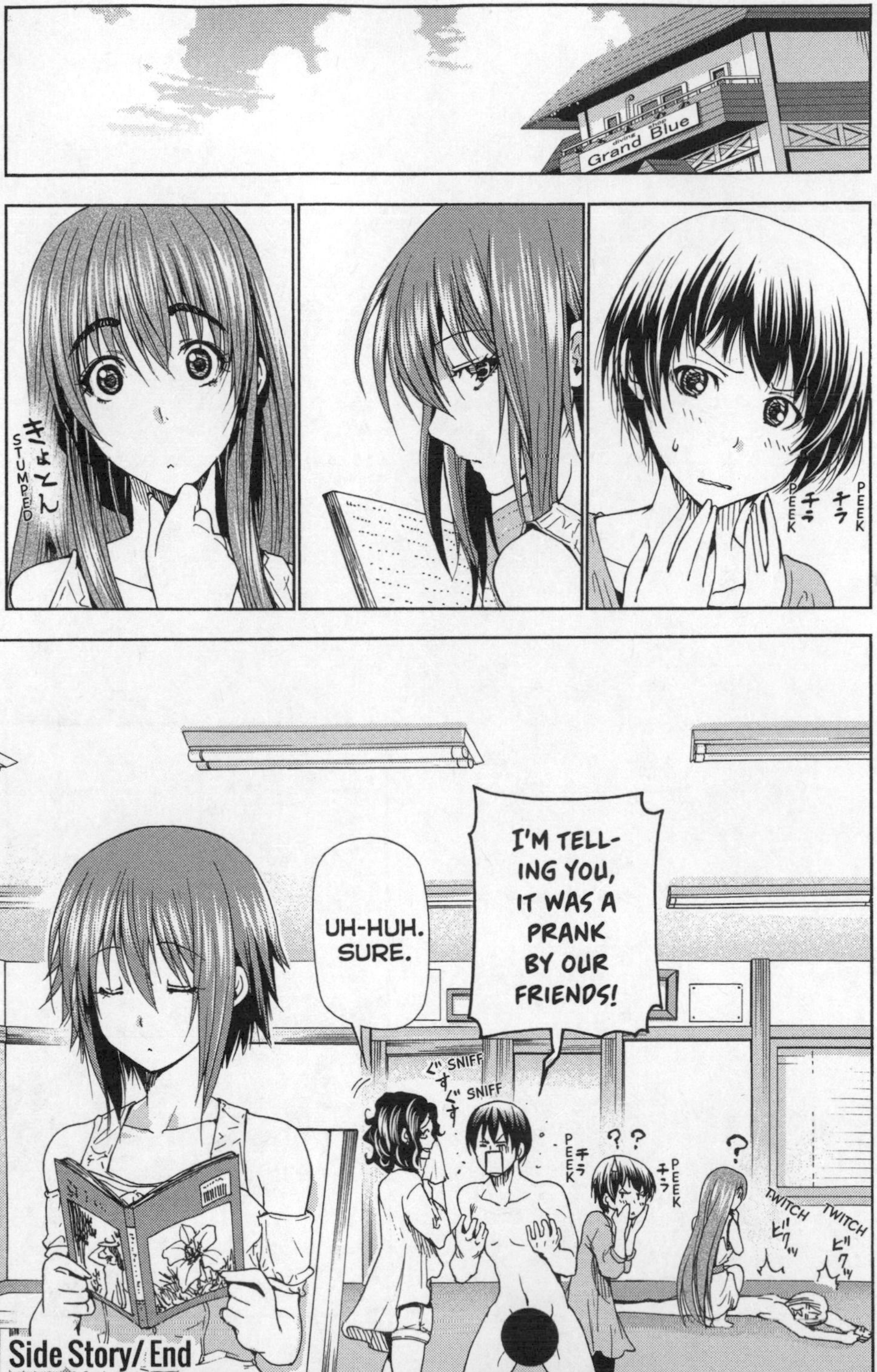
Grand Blue
チラ PEEK
チラ PEEK
きょとん STUMPED
I'M TELL-ING YOU, IT WAS A PRANK BY OUR FRIENDS!
UH-HUH. SURE.
ぐす SNIFF
ぐす SNIFF
チラ PEEK
チラ PEEK
?
??
ビクッ TWITCH
ビクッ TWITCH
Side Story/ End

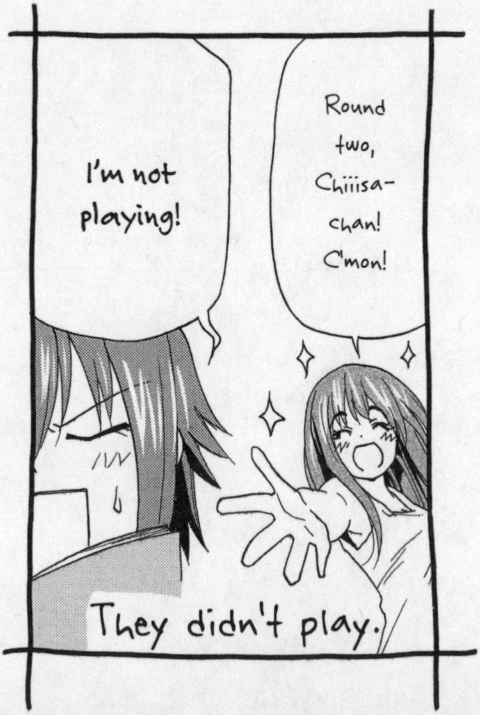
Round two, Chiiisa-chan! C'mon!
I'm not playing!
They didn't play.

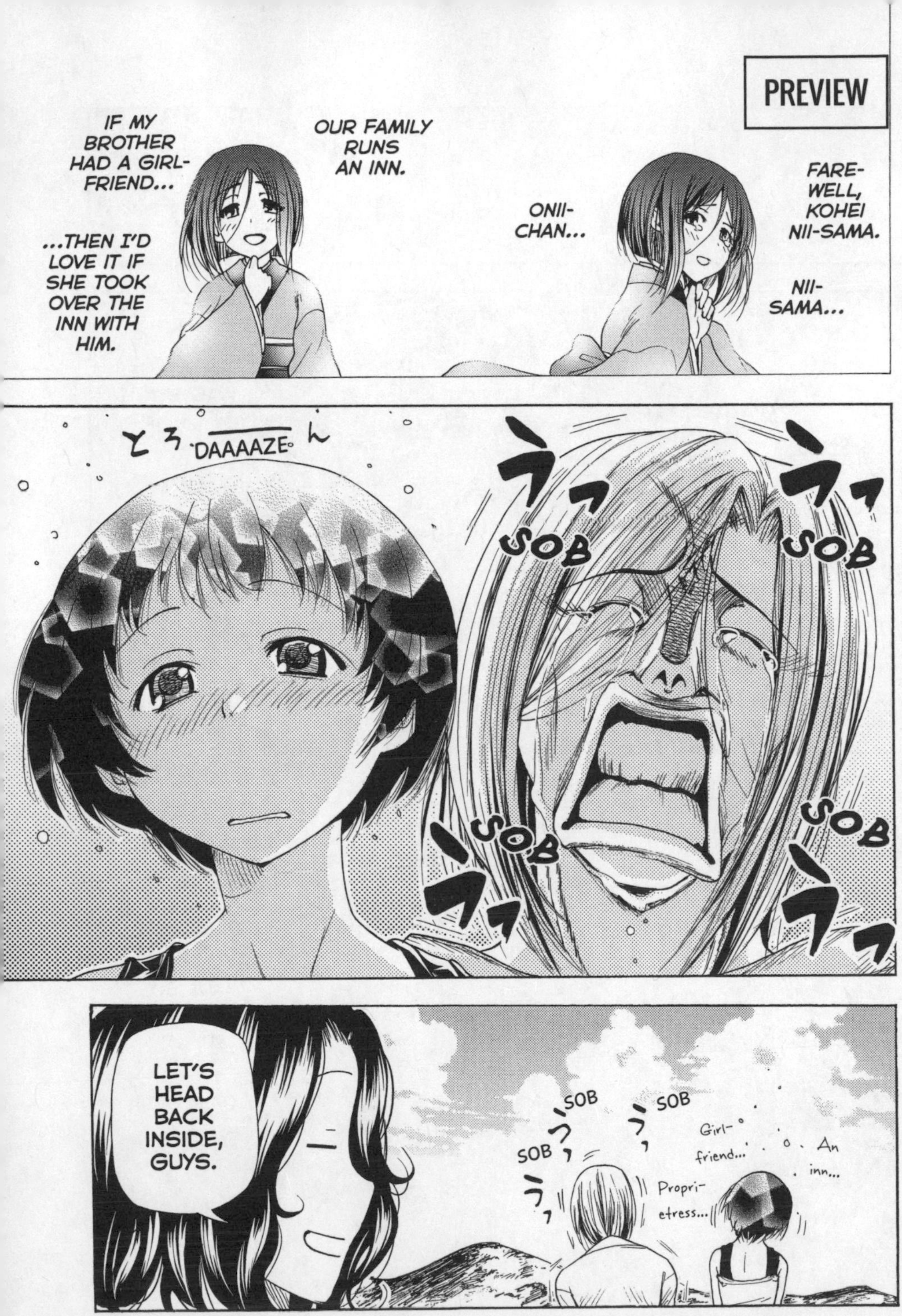
PREVIEW
FARE-WELL, KOHEI NII-SAMA.
NII-SAMA...
ONII-CHAN...
OUR FAMILY RUNS AN INN.
IF MY BROTHER HAD A GIRL-FRIEND...
...THEN I'D LOVE IT IF SHE TOOK OVER THE INN WITH HIM.
SOB
SOB
SOB
SOB
とろ DAAAAZE ん
SOB
SOB
SOB
An inn...
Girl-friend...
Propri-etress...
LET'S HEAD BACK INSIDE, GUYS.

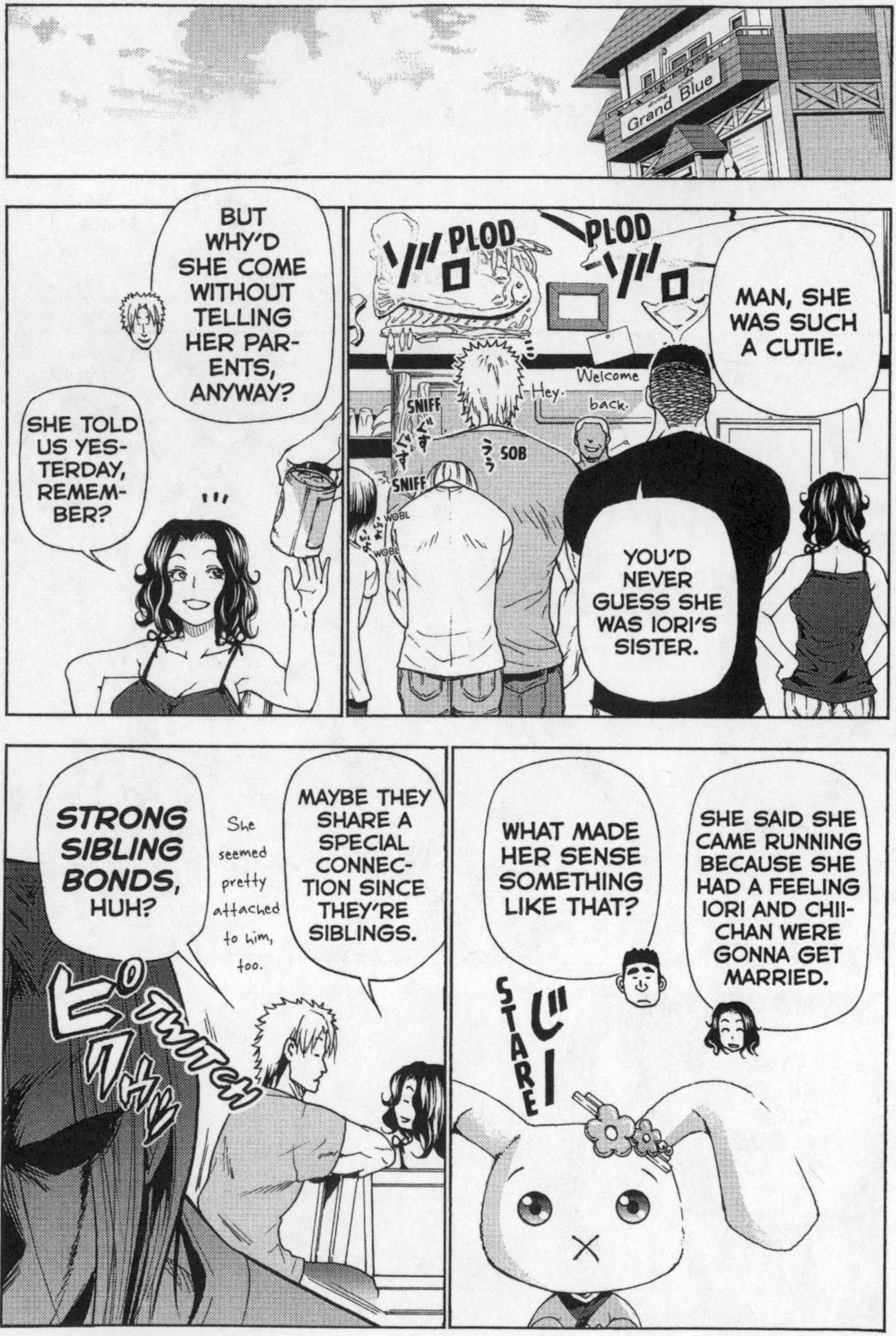
diving shop
Grand Blue
PLOD
PLOD
MAN, SHE WAS SUCH A CUTIE.
Hey.
Welcome back.
SNIFF
SOB
SNIFF
WOBL
WOBL
YOU'D NEVER GUESS SHE WAS IORI'S SISTER.
BUT WHY'D SHE COME WITHOUT TELLING HER PARENTS, ANYWAY?
SHE TOLD US YESTERDAY, REMEMBER?
SHE SAID SHE CAME RUNNING BECAUSE SHE HAD A FEELING IORI AND CHII-CHAN WERE GONNA GET MARRIED.
WHAT MADE HER SENSE SOMETHING LIKE THAT?
STARE
MAYBE THEY SHARE A SPECIAL CONNECTION SINCE THEY'RE SIBLINGS.
She seemed pretty attached to him, too.
STRONG SIBLING BONDS, HUH?
TWITCH

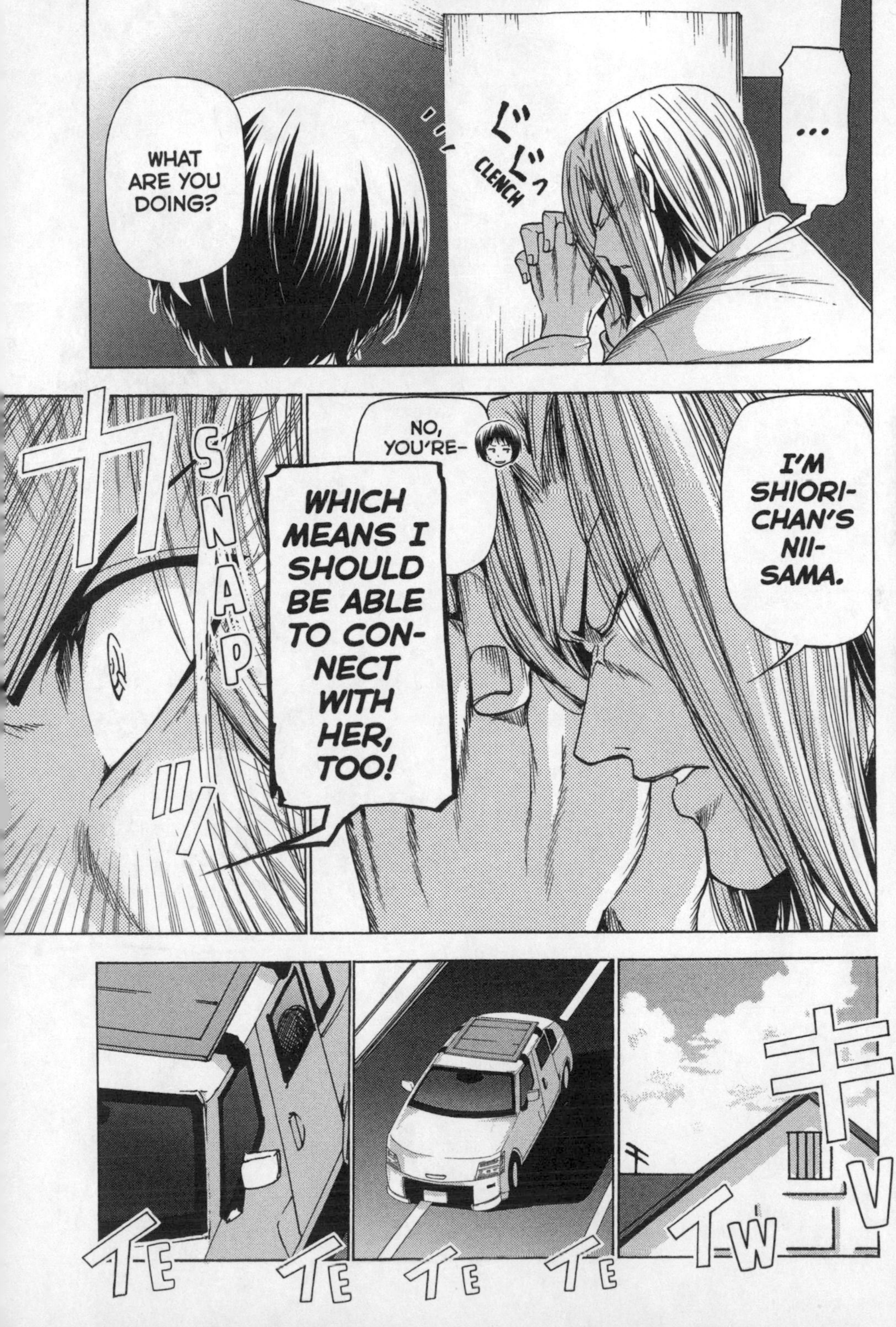
...
CLENCH
WHAT ARE YOU DOING?
I'M SHIORI-CHAN'S NII-SAMA.
NO, YOU'RE-
WHICH MEANS I SHOULD BE ABLE TO CON-NECT WITH HER, TOO!
SNAP
TWV
TE
TE
TE
TE

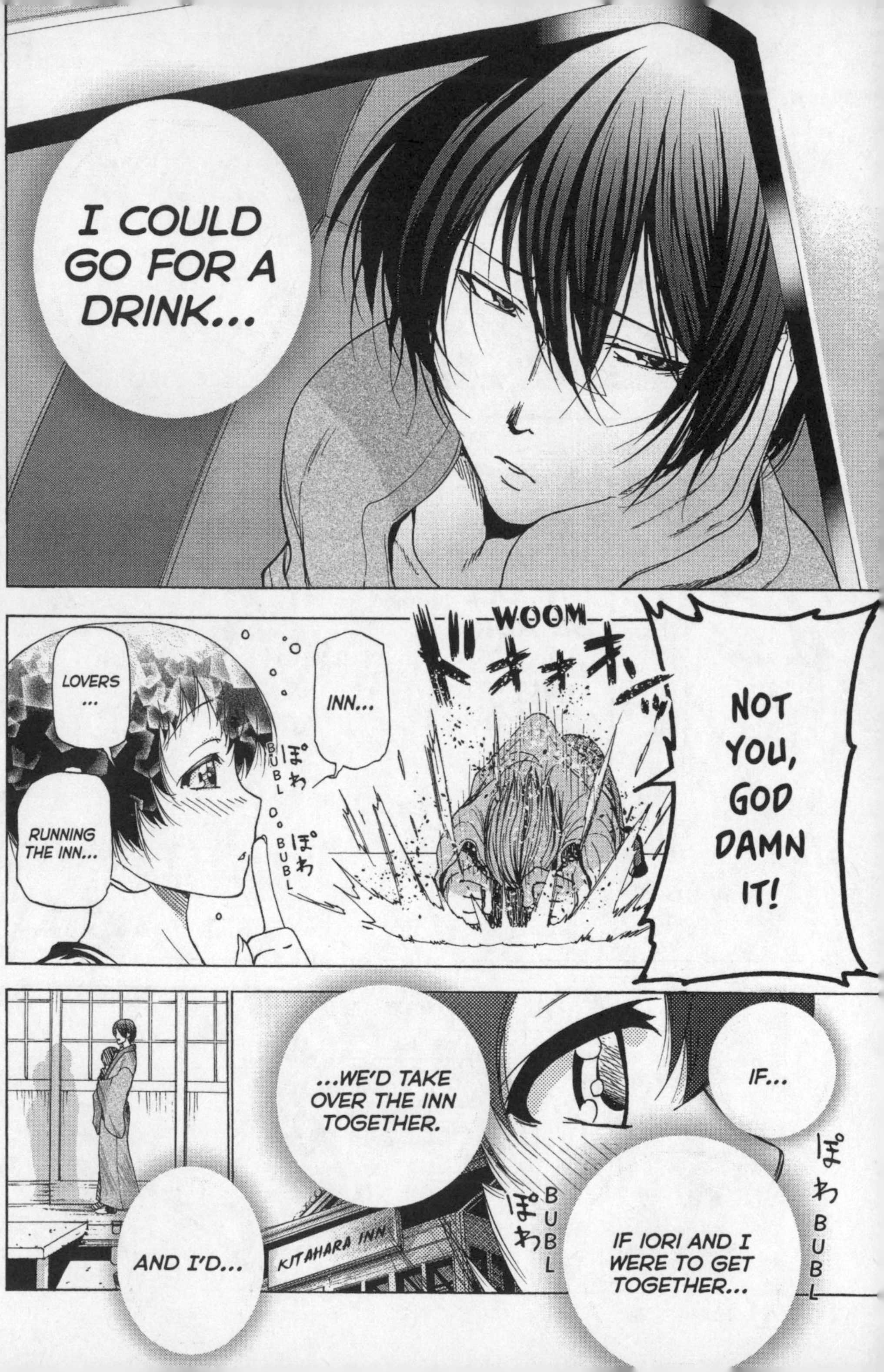
I COULD GO FOR A DRINK...
WOOM
ドォォオッ
NOT YOU, GOD DAMN IT!
INN...
LOVERS ...
ぽわ BUBL
ぽわ BUBL
RUNNING THE INN...
IF...
ぽわ BUBL
IF IORI AND I WERE TO GET TOGETHER...
ぽわ BUBL
...WE'D TAKE OVER THE INN TOGETHER.
AND I'D...
KITAHARA INN

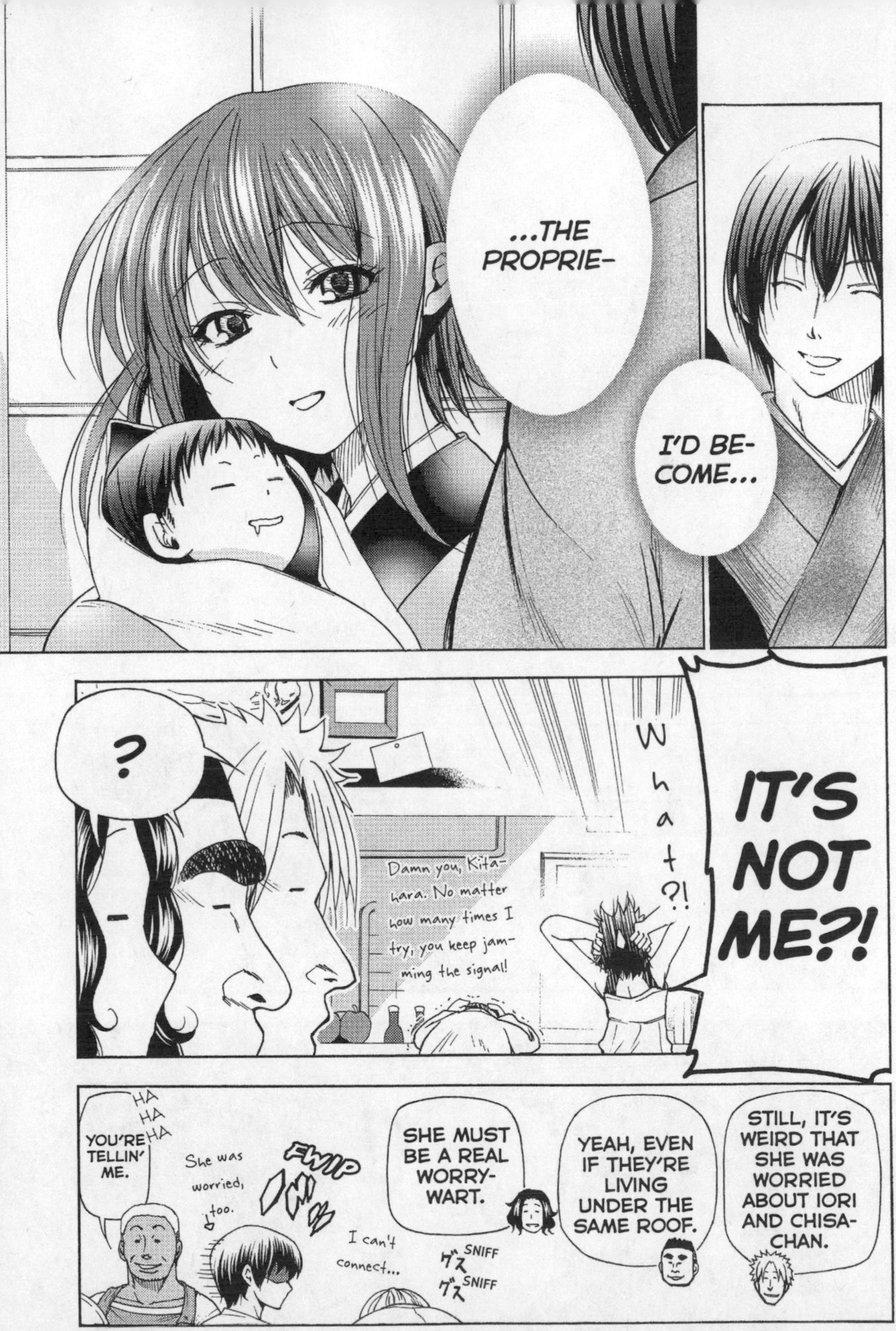
I'D BE-COME...
...THE PROPRIE-
IT'S NOT ME?!
What?!
?
Damn you, Kitahara. No matter how many times I try, you keep jamming the signal!
STILL, IT'S WEIRD THAT SHE WAS WORRIED ABOUT IORI AND CHISA-CHAN.
YEAH, EVEN IF THEY'RE LIVING UNDER THE SAME ROOF.
SHE MUST BE A REAL WORRY-WART.
FWIP
グス SNIFF
グス SNIFF
I can't connect...
She was worried, too.
HA HA HA
YOU'RE TELLIN' ME.

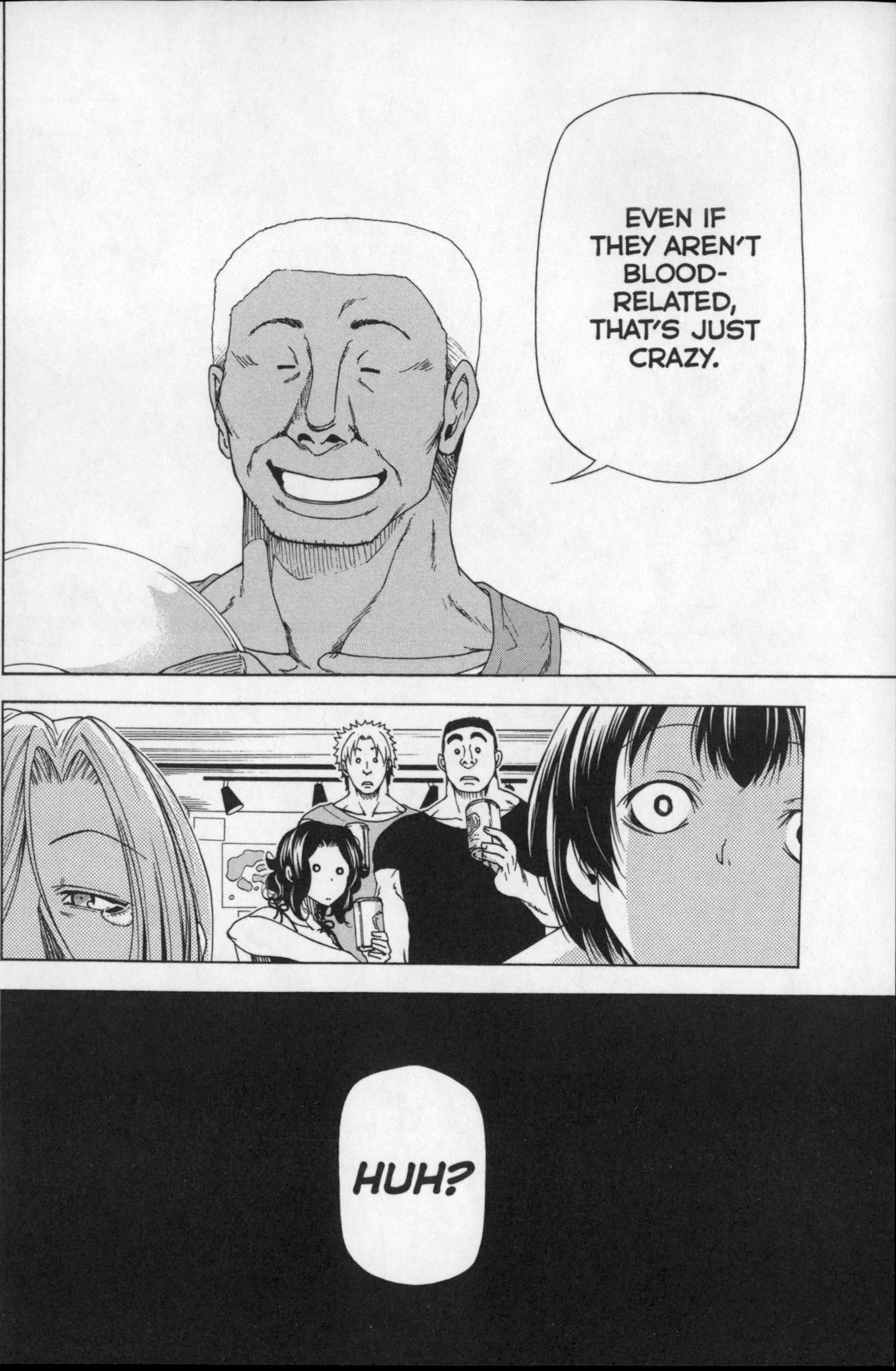
EVEN IF THEY AREN'T BLOOD-RELATED, THAT'S JUST CRAZY.
HUH?

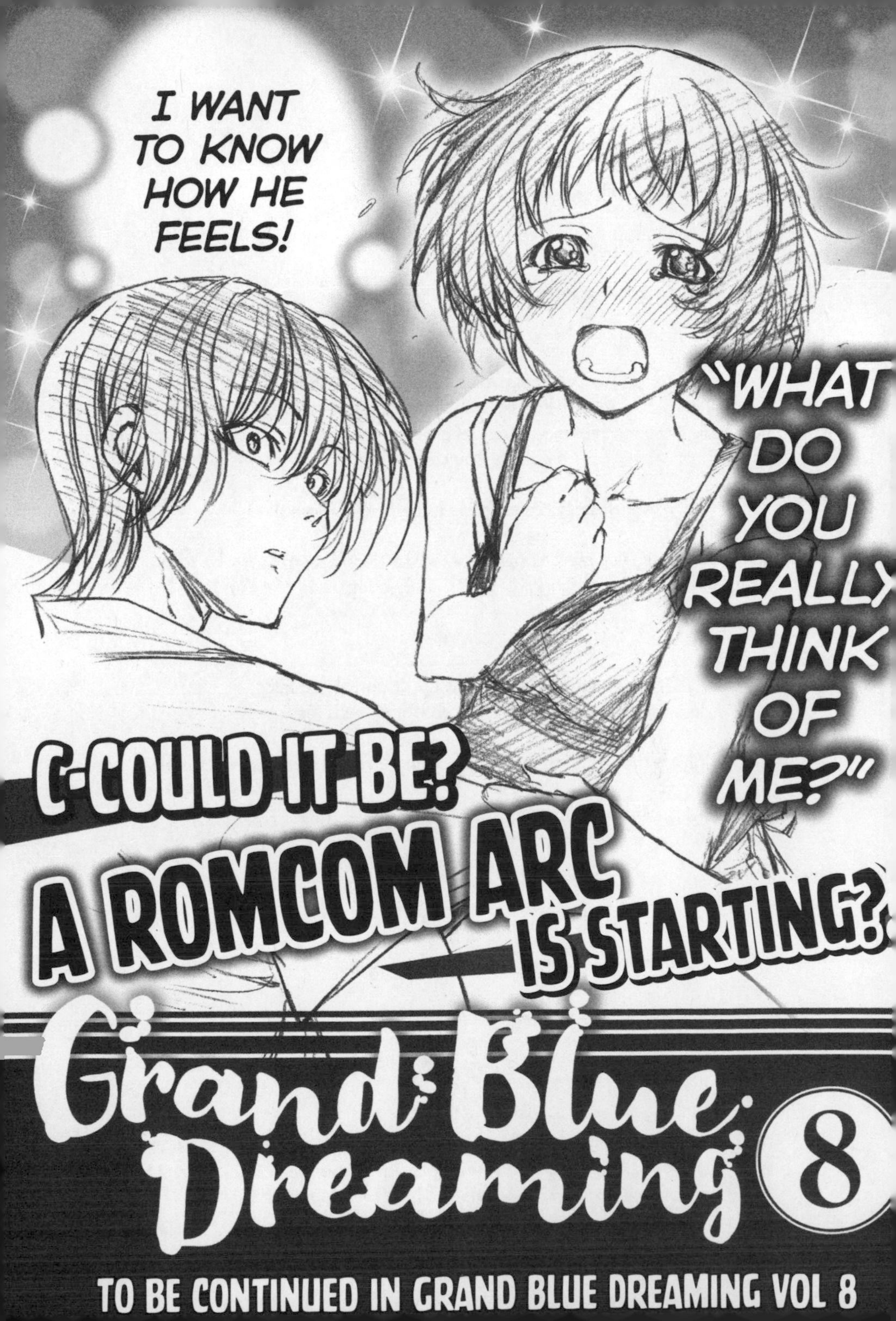
I WANT TO KNOW HOW HE FEELS!
"WHAT DO YOU REALLY THINK OF ME?"
C-COULD IT BE?
A ROMCOM ARC IS STARTING?!
Grand Blue Dreaming 8
TO BE CONTINUED IN GRAND BLUE DREAMING VOL 8

Grand Blue Dreaming volume 7 is a work of fiction.
Names, characters, places, and incidents are the products of the author's imagination or are used fictitiously. Any resemblance to actual events, locales, or persons, living or dead, is entirely coincidental.

A Kodansha Comics Trade Paperback Original.

Published in the United States by Kodansha Comics,
an imprint of Kodansha USA Publishing, LLC, New York.

Publication rights for this English edition arranged through Kodansha Ltd., Tokyo.

First published in Japan in 2016 by Kodansha Ltd., Tokyo.

Cover Design: YUKI YOSHIDA (futaba)

ISBN 978-1-63236-792-1

Printed in the United States of America.

www.kodansha.us

9 8 7 6 5 4 3

Translation: Adam Hirsch
Lettering: Jan Lan Ivan Concepcion
Editing: Sarah Tilson and David Yoo
Editorial Assistance: YKS Services LLC/SKY Japan, INC.
Kodansha Comics Edition Cover Design: Phil Balsman